4.3.74   £3.20

Social Security: Perspectives for Reform

STUDIES IN SOCIAL ECONOMICS

TITLES PUBLISHED

STUDIES IN SOCIAL ECONOMICS

Social Security
PERSPECTIVES FOR REFORM

Joseph A. Pechman
Henry J. Aaron
Michael K. Taussig

THE BROOKINGS INSTITUTION
Washington, D.C.

THE BROOKINGS INSTITUTION is an independent organization devoted to non-partisan research, education, and publication in economics, government, foreign policy, and the social sciences generally. Its principal purposes are to aid in the development of sound public policies and to promote public understanding of issues of national importance.

The Institution was founded on December 8, 1927, to merge the activities of the Institute for Government Research, founded in 1916, the Institute of Economics, founded in 1922, and the Robert Brookings Graduate School of Economics and Government, founded in 1924.

The general administration of the Institution is the responsibility of a self-perpetuating Board of Trustees. The trustees are likewise charged with maintaining the independence of the staff and fostering the most favorable conditions for creative research and education. The immediate direction of the policies, program, and staff of the Institution is vested in the President, assisted by an advisory council chosen from the staff of the Institution.

In publishing a study, the Institution presents it as a competent treatment of a subject worthy of public consideration. The interpretations and conclusions in such publications are those of the author or authors and do not purport to represent the views of the other staff members, officers, or trustees of the Brookings Institution.

Foreword

The social security system is firmly established as a permanent American institution. It is one of the largest and most important of the government's social and economic programs, and the payroll tax that finances it is the third largest federal tax source. Administered with efficiency and integrity, the system has won widespread acceptance.

Yet important questions remain as to the adequacy and equity of its benefits and financing—questions which must be faced as the nation pursues the objectives of reducing poverty and assuring a decent standard of living for all citizens. This study is designed to clarify the issues involved in social security and to examine the need for change. As the first comprehensive analysis of the system in many years, it considers the deficiencies of the present program and alternatives for improvement. On the basis of their analysis, the authors propose an agenda of short-range and long-range reforms to better achieve the goals of social security and to rationalize the place of the system in the broader framework of national policies for economic stability and growth.

The authors wish to express their appreciation to the Social Security Administration for its cooperation in making available data that were essential to the analysis. They are particularly grateful to Robert M. Ball, Commissioner of Social Security, Robert J. Myers, Chief Actuary, and John J. Carroll, Director of the Division of Economic and Long-Range Studies of the Office of Research and Statistics, for carefully reviewing early drafts of the manuscript.

Mollie Orshansky provided information on poverty measures and offered helpful suggestions. William C. Birdsall, Benjamin Bridges, Jr., and Ronald Hoffman also read the manuscript and made useful comments. It should be emphasized that none of these officials bears any responsibility for the views expressed in this volume.

The authors are grateful for the assistance of members of the Brookings staff in completing the project. They owe a major debt of gratitude to Alicia Munnell whose role far exceeded that of a research assistant. She undertook independent research on crucial portions of the text, developed most of the statistical material, and prepared Appendixes B and C. Evelyn Fisher participated in the statistical work, purged the manuscript of numerous errors, and imposed her usual high standards of accuracy on the authors. John A. Brittain, William M. Capron, Samuel B. Chase, Jr., Rashi Fein, and Walter S. Salant read and commented on the manuscript. The Brookings Computer Center, directed by George Sadowsky, provided invaluable aid, as demonstrated by the results reported in Chapters 7 and 8 and Appendixes D, E, and F. Charles R. Backus, Charles J. Hardy, Judith S. Dubester, and Joan L. Allard were responsible for the programming. Dorothy Wescott and Charles B. Saunders, Jr., edited the manuscript; the index was prepared by Helen B. Eisenhart. Marcia Appel acted as secretary for the project and expedited its completion.

Advice and suggestions were received from a large group of experts who read and commented on all parts of the manuscript. The authors gratefully acknowledge the assistance of Jack Besansky, Gerard M. Brannon, James M. Buchanan, Lenore A. Epstein, Margaret S. Gordon, Harold M. Groves, Peter Henle, George J. Leibowitz, Ida C. Merriam, Albert Rees, Bert Seidman, Herman M. Somers, Nancy H. Teeters, Lester C. Thurow, John G. Turnbull, and Melvin I. White.

The views expressed in this volume are the authors' and are not presented as the views of the officers, trustees, and other staff members of the Brookings Institution, or of any of the individuals who commented on the manuscript.

KERMIT GORDON
President

September 1968
Washington, D.C.

Contents

TEXT TABLES

CHAPTER I

Introduction

The social security system is among the most effective and successful institutions ever developed in the United States. Established in 1935 after state and local programs had failed to meet the needs of the millions of older persons impoverished by the Great Depression, it has become one of the economic and social cornerstones of a pluralistic and dynamic society.

Social security is associated primarily with the benefits paid to workers and their wives on retirement, but the Old-Age, Survivors, and Disability Insurance (OASDI) program also provides payments to the disabled, to dependents of retired and disabled workers, and to survivors of deceased participants. Another major provision, health insurance for the aged, took effect in 1966. In early 1968, 24 million persons were receiving monthly OASDI checks, and total monthly payments amounted to $2 billion. As the number of recipients and the average size of benefits have increased, payments have grown in relation to total personal income: they accounted for 0.4 percent of such income in 1950, 2.8 percent in 1960, and 3.4 percent in 1967 (Chart I-1).

Although complex, the program is operated with efficiency as well as integrity. From its beginning through the end of 1967, over $180 billion in benefits had been distributed without a single serious incident of fraud or corruption. The officials of the Social Security Administration are respected by the Executive Branch, the Congress, and the public for their competence, devotion, and honesty.

1

Chart I-1. *OASDI Benefit Payments Compared with Personal Income, 1940–67*

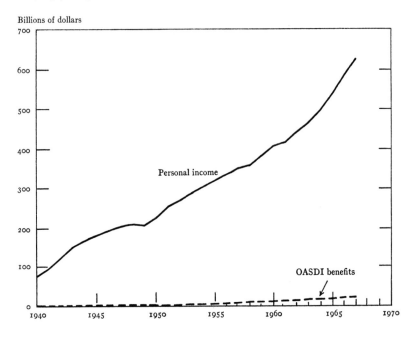

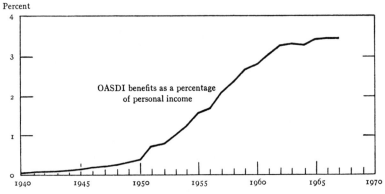

Sources: See Appendix Table G-1.

This is a book about the policy issues related to this major institution and ways in which the institution might be improved in order to achieve the objectives of the program.

Scope and Purpose

This book will concentrate primarily on the old-age and survivors portion of the OASDI program. Little attention will be given to the disability part, which accounted for less than 10 percent of total OASDI benefits in 1967 (Table 1-1). Health insurance is omitted entirely, although it contributes significantly to the welfare of large numbers of the aged. The health and disability programs involve specialized issues that require independent treatment.[1]

Table 1-1. *Distribution of OASDI Benefits, by Program and Class of Beneficiary or Payment, 1967*

Program and Class of Beneficiary or Payment	Benefits (Millions of Dollars)	Percentage of Total Benefits
Old-age	14,361	67.1
Retired workers	12,374	57.8
Dependents	1,677	7.8
Persons with special age-72 benefits	311	1.5
Survivors	5,106	23.9
Monthly benefits	4,854	22.7
Lump-sum payments	252	1.2
Disability	1,939	9.1
Total	21,406	100.0

Source: U.S. Department of Health, Education, and Welfare, Social Security Administration, Office of Research and Statistics, *Monthly Benefit Statistics*, February 20, 1968, Table 1. Figures are rounded and will not necessarily add to totals.

In this study, the term *social security* is used for the most part as a synonym for OASDI. This narrow use of the term is consistent

[1] For an analysis of recent developments in health insurance, see Herman M. Somers and Anne R. Somers, *Medicare and the Hospitals: Issues and Prospects* (Brookings Institution, 1967).

with popular usage. Wherever the reference is to social security in its broader sense, the meaning will be clear from the context.

The intent of the study is to analyze the most significant issues in the social security program, which is a massive item in the federal budget. In common with the other federal expenditure programs, social security is expected to achieve certain objectives. Careful specification of these objectives should be the basis for judging any particular aspect of the benefit structure or its financing. A given change in the program is desirable only if it furthers achievement of the objectives of social security and if, in doing so, it does not obstruct the achievement of other national objectives of comparable or greater importance.

This study, then, will seek to formulate explicit criteria for a social security program in the United States and to apply them to specific features of the present program. As much as possible, the economics of the subject will be stressed rather than institutional details of the vast social security apparatus.

The originators and many current proponents of social security have placed considerable reliance on the "insurance" aspects of the system. Although there are many differences between social security and private insurance, the idea of social security as a form of insurance has widespread acceptance and appeal. The differences are significant, however, and this volume argues that the present program is more appropriately viewed as a system of transfers which, like any other government program, must be financed by taxes. This approach provides the conceptual basis for the analysis and for devising methods to improve the major features of the program.

Organization of the Volume

Chapters II, III, and IV set the stage for the subsequent analysis of specific issues. Chapter II summarizes the income status of the aged. It discusses trends in the labor force status of aged persons and their work-related income, the size and sources of their other income, including social security benefits, and the problem of poverty among the aged. Chapter III traces the development of the

OASDI program and outlines its present major features. This technical material is summarized as briefly as is consistent with accuracy. Chapter IV defines the objectives of social security and establishes the criteria for evaluating the basic features of the system.

Chapters V, VI, VII, and VIII constitute the heart of the book; each discusses in detail the major issues in important areas of the OASDI program. Chapter V is an analysis of the present benefit structure, including the benefits paid to families of different sizes, the minimum benefit, and the relationship of these benefits to those from other public retirement programs and from industrial pension plans. Chapter VI deals with the relationship between social security and retirement and the issues raised by the requirement that beneficiaries should be substantially retired to receive benefits. Chapter VII evaluates the official methods now used to present the costs of the social security program. It also analyzes the question of individual equity in the program, and presents estimates of the relationships between benefits received and taxes paid by past and future retirees under various assumptions. Chapter VIII analyzes the pros and cons of the payroll tax as the major revenue source, suggests alternative methods of financing, and discusses the role of the OASI and DI trust funds.

In conclusion, Chapter IX presents suggestions to improve the benefit structure and the financing of OASDI. It begins with a description of a system that we regard as ideal but which is hardly likely to be enacted in the foreseeable future. This system would provide social security benefits equal to a flat percentage of past earnings. In addition, aged persons whose total money income including social security is below specified levels would be eligible to receive negative income tax payments instead of social security benefits. Pending enactment of a negative income tax, a substantial revamping of the social security system is proposed. This would involve major increases in the minimum benefit and a revision of the benefit formula so that families having the same standards of living before retirement would have roughly equal—though lower—standards after retirement.

CHAPTER II

The Economic Status of the Aged

The aged in the United States on the average have much lower incomes but more assets than have persons in other age groups.[1] Probably the single most important factor determining the income status of the aged today is the long-run trend toward early retirement, a trend that appears to have accelerated in the last generation. The extent to which the aged are willing and able to work is a matter of crucial importance in designing a program for social security. The benefit structure must provide for the needs of the nonworking aged, but it is also a decisive factor in determining the work activity of potential beneficiaries.

For most people, retirement is an economic catastrophe. The cessation of earnings causes a sharp decline in current income, a decline which is moderated slightly in the typical case by income from other sources. Old-age insurance benefits alleviate these circumstances, but are inadequate for people with little or no other income or assets. Although evidence is not available, it is safe to assume that disabled workers and their families, and nonaged dependent survivors, share with the aged the problem of inadequate income.

Economic good fortune among the aged is very unequally distributed. The likelihood of an aged person being desperately poor is greatest among certain identifiable groups—the very old, the sick, those who were poor before retirement, nonwhites, and wid-

[1] Throughout this chapter the word *income* will refer to total money income, including social security benefits and other transfer payments.

ows. To judge by the relative status of those who are between 65 and 72 years of age and those who are 73 or older, prospects become increasingly bleak as physical decline coincides with the steady depletion of lifetime savings.

The foregoing description, like most generalizations, omits important details and qualifications. A fraction of the aged continues to work on a full-time basis after age 65 and earns a satisfactory income. Another fraction, overlapping to a considerable extent with the first, has substantial income from large holdings of assets. For other aged persons, social security benefits are important additions to income, and in certain instances they are even sufficient by themselves to maintain the recipients' income above poverty thresholds.[2] In short, a minority of the aged are economically comfortable, and this minority can confidently be expected to increase over time. Nevertheless, with 30 percent of persons over age 65 officially classified as poor, the major problem of the aged is poverty, not affluence.[3]

A Profile of the Aged Worker

The proportion of aged persons in the labor force has fallen by more than half in the twentieth century. A sharp decline in male participation rates has dominated this trend (Chart II-1). In 1890, more than two-thirds of all men aged 65 and over were either employed or unemployed and looking for work; in the 1960's, the fraction has fallen to approximately one-fourth. The participation rate of women aged 65 and over has remained low and relatively

[2] For a discussion of the poverty levels as officially defined by the Social Security Administration, see Chapter V. In 1966, an aged person was classified as poor if his total money income including social security cash benefits was less than $1,565 a year; the figure for an aged couple was $1,970. For nonaged persons the corresponding incomes were $1,685 and $2,185. All poverty levels are adjusted annually by the Social Security Administration for changes in prices. Mollie Orshansky, *Who Was Poor in 1966*, U.S. Department of Health, Education, and Welfare, Social Security Administration, Office of Research and Statistics, Note No. 23 (December 6, 1967), Table 1.

[3] U.S. Department of Health, Education, and Welfare, Social Security Administration, Office of Research and Statistics, Note No. 5, *The Poor in 1965 and Trends, 1959–65* (February 16, 1967), Table 3.

stable, although it has increased slightly over the same period; even today only about 10 percent of all aged females are in the labor force.

The decline in participation rates of aged men has been uneven. Between 1920 and 1930, for example, about 55 percent of aged men were working or looking for work. After the depression years of the 1930's, however, the rate fell to just over 40 percent; and in the last 15 years, the rate has again fallen sharply. This latest decline coincided with the period in which growing numbers of aged workers became eligible for retirement benefits under the Social Security Act.

Chart II-1. *Labor Force Participation Rates of Persons Aged 65 and Over, by Sex, 1890–1967*

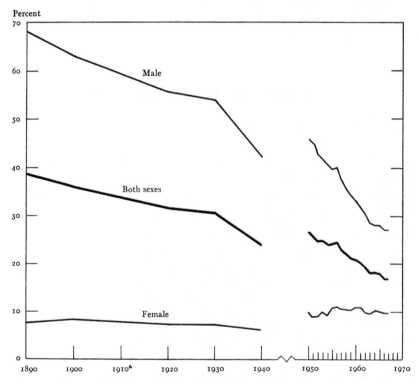

Sources: 1890–1940, U.S. Bureau of the Census, *Historical Statistics of the United States, Colonial Times to 1957* (1960), p. 71; 1950–67, *Manpower Report of the President* (1968), Table A-2, pp. 222–23. Statistics for 1890–1940 are not exactly comparable with those for later years.
a. Interpolated. Data not available.

Table II-1. *Employment Status of the Civilian Population Aged 16–64 and Aged 65 and Over, by Sex, 1967*

Age Group and Employment Status	Number (Millions)[a]			Percentage of Total		
	Total	Male	Female	Total	Male	Female
Aged 16–64						
Not in labor force	37.6	6.2	31.4	33.6	11.7	53.4
In civilian labor force	74.3	46.9	27.4	66.4	88.3	46.6
Employed	71.4	45.4	25.9	63.8	85.5	44.2
Unemployed	2.9	1.4	1.4	2.6[b]	2.7[b]	2.5[b]
Total	111.8	53.1	58.7	100.0	100.0	100.0
Aged 65 and over						
Not in labor force	14.9	5.7	9.2	82.8	72.9	90.4
In civilian labor force	3.1	2.1	1.0	17.2	27.1	9.6
Employed	3.0	2.1	1.0	16.7	26.4	9.3
Unemployed	0.1	0.1	*	0.5[b]	0.8[b]	0.3[b]
Total	18.0	7.8	10.2	100.0	100.0	100.0

Source: *Manpower Report of the President* (1968), Tables A-7, A-8, and A-12, pp. 228, 229, 235. Figures are rounded and will not necessarily add to totals.
* Less than 50,000.
a. Noninstitutional population aged 16 and over.
b. These figures represent the unemployed as a percentage of the civilian noninstitutional population and consequently differ from the familiar concept of the unemployment rate (used in the text), which represents the unemployed as a percentage of the civilian labor force.

CURRENT STATUS

Labor force participation and employment patterns of the aged in 1967 are compared in Table II-1 with those of the nonaged. Of the 18.0 million persons aged 65 and over, only about 3 million, or 16.7 percent, were employed; of the 111.8 million persons aged 16 to 64, 71.4 million, or 63.8 percent, were employed. Unemployment rates for the aged have been relatively low in recent years; for example, the rate of about 3 percent for the aged in 1967 compares with the total unemployment rate of 3.8 percent for all age groups in the same year.[4] One reason for the low unemployment rate for the aged, however, is that many persons become discouraged about their job prospects and retire.

Unemployment lasts longer for the aged than for the nonaged.

[4] *Manpower Report of the President* (1968), Tables A-11 and A-12, pp. 234, 235.

Chart II-2. *Labor Force Participation Rates, by Age and Sex, December 1967*

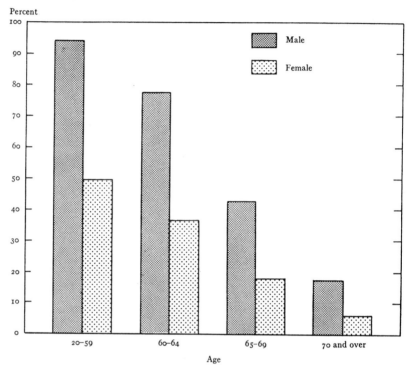

Source: U.S. Department of Labor, Bureau of Labor Statistics, *Employment and Earnings and Monthly Report on the Labor Force,* Vol. 14, No. 7 (January 1968), Table A-3, pp. 36–37.

In 1967, for example, unemployed males aged 65 and over comprised 2.0 percent of all unemployed males, but 7.3 percent of all males unemployed for more than half a year.[5] Long-term unemployment for the aged apparently often merges into withdrawal from the labor force.

Work activity declines sharply after ages 60 and 65 for both males and females (Chart II-2). The participation rate of married men over 65 years of age is approximately double that of single men in the same age group (Table II-2); this is because the former group is younger, on average, than the latter.[6] On the other

[5] *Ibid.,* Table A-18, pp. 241–42.

[6] *Ibid.,* Table B-2, p. 250. However, within every age group, married men have higher participation rates than men who are not married.

Table II-2. *Labor Force Participation Rates of Persons Aged 65 and Over, by Sex and Marital Status, March 1967*

Sex and Marital Status	Percentage in Labor Force
Male	
Single	16.2
Married, wife present	28.8
Widowed, divorced, or separated	15.2
Female	
Single	17.3
Married, husband present	6.6
Widowed, divorced, or separated	9.6

Source: *Manpower Report of the President* (1968), Table B-2, p. 250.

hand, the proportion of aged married women in the labor force is much lower than that of single women. For unmarried women the absence of support and greater past work experience are more important than age in affecting their decisions concerning participation in the labor force.[7]

People do not suddenly become aged when they turn 65; they age gradually over a lifetime. In December 1967, for example, 1.2 million, or 42.6 percent, of the males aged 65 to 69 were in the labor force, while for males aged 70 and over the corresponding figures were 858,000 and 17.4 percent (Chart II-2).[8]

The working aged differ significantly from the nonworking aged. The worker least likely to retire, other things equal, has high earning capacity and, in addition, has substantial other income.[9] Professionals or other highly paid workers comprise a large proportion of the full-time workers aged 65 and over. And the self-employed form a larger fraction of the working aged than

[7] For a discussion of this subject, see Erdman Palmore, "Work Experience and Earnings of the Aged in 1962: Findings of the 1963 Survey of the Aged," *Social Security Bulletin,* Vol. 27, No. 6 (June 1964), p. 9.

[8] U.S. Department of Labor, Bureau of Labor Statistics, *Employment and Earnings and Monthly Report on the Labor Force,* Vol. 14, No. 7 (January 1968), Table A-3, p. 36. Hereafter, this publication will be referred to as *Employment and Earnings.*

[9] Lowell E. Gallaway, *The Retirement Decision: An Exploratory Essay,* U.S. Department of Health, Education, and Welfare, Social Security Administration, Division of Research and Statistics, Research Report No. 9 (1965), pp. 13–17, and Palmore, "Work Experience and Earnings of the Aged in 1962," p. 10.

of the nonaged. In general, the aged person who continues working is a married male, 65 to 68 years of age, in the upper income groups. Although a person with these characteristics is least likely to retire, this does not imply that most people still working after age 65 have above average incomes. Many aged persons, especially old-age insurance beneficiaries, are only part-time workers (Table II-3). They work fewer weeks during the year and fewer hours a week than do those in the nonaged group.[10]

Table II-3. *Average Earnings of Workers Aged 65 and Over, by Sex and Work Experience, 1962*

Work Experience and Age	Males		Females	
	Percentage of aged population	Average earnings (dollars)	Percentage of aged population	Average earnings (dollars)
Usually full-time jobs[a]				
65–72	30.9	3,775	9.9	2,132
73 and over	10.4	3,022	2.8	1,131
Usually part-time jobs				
65–72	15.9	969	9.7	652
73 and over	12.5	765	3.1	525
All workers				
65–72	47.0	2,835	19.6	1,410
73 and over	22.9	1,803	5.8	806

Source: Erdman Palmore, "Work Experience and Earnings of the Aged in 1962: Findings of the 1963 Survey of the Aged," *Social Security Bulletin*, Vol. 27, No. 6 (June 1964), Tables 4 and 5, p. 5. Figures are rounded and will not necessarily add to totals.
a. 35 or more hours a week.

FUTURE TRENDS

Projections for the next two decades indicate relatively little change in the aged as a fraction of the total population.[11] The labor force participation rate of males aged 65 and over is expected to fall—from 26.9 percent in 1965 to 21.8 percent in 1980.

[10] Palmore, "Work Experience and Earnings of the Aged in 1962," pp. 4–11; *Employment and Earnings*, January 1968, Tables A-7, A-18, and A-23, pp. 41, 48, 52.
[11] *Manpower Report of the President* (1968), Tables E-1–E-6, pp. 298–302. Data from these tables are used throughout this paragraph. They are not exactly comparable with data cited previously in this section because they are based on different population estimates.

Table II-4. *Population, Labor Force, and Labor Force Participation Rates of Persons Aged 65 and Over, 1965 (Actual), 1975 and 1980 (Projected)*

Year and Sex	Population (Thousands)	Labor Force (Thousands)	Labor Force Participation Rate (Percent)
1965			
Male	7,932	2,131	26.9
Female	10,225	976	9.5
Total	18,157	3,107	17.1
1975			
Male	8,923	2,087	23.4
Female	12,248	1,205	9.8
Total	21,171	3,292	15.5
1980			
Male	9,606	2,096	21.8
Female	13,481	1,340	9.9
Total	23,087	3,436	14.9

Source: *Manpower Report of the President* (1968), Table E-2, p. 298. Figures are rounded and will not necessarily add to totals.

The rate for aged females is expected to rise slightly—from 9.5 percent in 1965 to 9.9 percent in 1980. The net result of these projected trends—summarized in Table II-4—is that a somewhat smaller percentage of a much larger aged population will be in the labor force in coming years. In 1965, 15.0 million persons out of a population of 18.2 million aged 65 and over were not in the labor force; projections for 1980 indicate that, out of a population of 23.1 million aged persons, 19.7 million will not be in the labor force. If these projections are even approximately correct, earnings will constitute a diminishing portion of total income for the future aged population.

Income and Assets of the Aged

Since wages and salaries comprise about two-thirds of personal income, and the aged work far less than the nonaged, it is not surpris-

Table II-5. *Average Asset Holdings for Families and Unrelated Individuals, by Age and Poverty Status, 1962*

(In dollars)

| Family and Poverty Status[a] | All Ages | Under Age 65 | | | | Aged 65 and Over |
		Total	Under 35	35–44	45–64	
Families						
Poor	5,788	4,155	636	2,776	7,851	12,509
Nonpoor	24,480	20,804	4,458	17,990	32,667	49,536
Unrelated individuals						
Poor	5,723	5,486	n.a.	n.a.	n.a.	5,945
Nonpoor	21,531	18,227	n.a.	n.a.	n.a.	28,943

Sources: Benjamin Bridges, Jr., *Net Worth of the Aged*, U.S. Department of Health, Education, and Welfare, Social Security Administration, Office of Research and Statistics, Note No. 14 (September 28, 1967), Table 6. Detailed data on which this table is based are presented in Dorothy S. Projector and Gertrude S. Weiss, *Survey of Financial Characteristics of Consumers* (Board of Governors of the Federal Reserve System, 1966), Tables A 41, A 42, and A 43, pp. 160–66.
    n.a. Not available.
    a. Mean poverty cutoff is approximately $1,800–1,900.

ing that the income of the aged is considerably below the national average. The median total money income of families headed by a person aged 65 and over in 1966 was $3,645, while the median income of all families was $7,436. The median income for aged unrelated individuals was $1,443, compared with $2,270 for all unrelated individuals.[12]

Among the aged, married couples are much better off than single persons. For aged couples, the 1962 median income from all sources was more than twice that for aged unmarried men and nearly three times that for aged unmarried women. The principal reason for a decline in total income of older persons is, of course, retirement; but also, the older a person is, the more likely it is that his social security and other pension benefits are based on employment at earnings below the current wage level, and the more likely it is that he has reduced or exhausted his assets.[13]

[12] U.S. Bureau of the Census, "Income in 1966 of Families and Persons in the United States," *Current Population Reports,* Series P-60, No. 53 (1967), Table 3, p. 24.
[13] Lenore A. Epstein and Janet H. Murray, *The Aged Population of the United States: The 1963 Social Security Survey of the Aged,* U.S. Department of Health, Education, and Welfare, Social Security Administration, Office of Research and Statistics, Research Report No. 19 (1967), p. 51, and Table 3.3, p. 288.

Since dissaving is considered normal after retirement, the economic status of the aged cannot be accurately gauged without taking assets into account. Assets are more important in the financial position of the aged than of the nonaged, because the aged typically lack wage or salary income and because the life annuity value of any amount of assets is greater for the aged than for the nonaged. (The life annuity value is the annual amount that a person would receive if his assets could be converted into income prorated over his expected life at some interest rate.) Moreover, at each income level, asset holdings of the aged are larger by a substantial margin than those of younger age groups (Table II-5). This circumstance arises quite naturally since retirement reduces incomes but has no immediate impact on asset holdings. Thus, it is clear that, because of the substantially larger asset holdings of the aged, measures of economic status based only on income serve far less well for the aged than for the nonaged.

Table II-6. *Two Estimates of Asset Holdings of the Aged, 1962*

(In dollars)

Type of Asset and Economic Status	Federal Reserve Board Estimates	Social Security Administration Estimates
Average assets		
All aged	30,008	15,109
Liquid assets and marketable securities	4,957	3,783
Poor families[a]	12,509	n.a.
Couples in lowest third of income distribution[b]	n.a.	7,621
Median assets		
All aged	9,860	5,840
Liquid assets and marketable securities	950	570
Poor families[a]	6,580	n.a.
Couples in lowest third of income distribution[b]	n.a.	4,130

Sources: Benjamin Bridges, Jr., *Net Worth of the Aged*, U.S. Department of Health, Education, and Welfare, Social Security Administration, Office of Research and Statistics, Note No. 14 (September 28, 1967), Tables 1, 2, 3, and 4. Details on the Federal Reserve estimates are presented in Dorothy S. Projector and Gertrude S. Weiss, *Survey of Financial Characteristics of Consumers* (Board of Governors of the Federal Reserve System, 1966). For additional information on the Social Security Administration estimates, see Lenore A. Epstein and Janet H. Murray, *The Aged Population of the United States: The 1963 Social Security Survey of the Aged*, U.S. Department of Health, Education, and Welfare, Social Security Administration, Office of Research and Statistics, Research Report No. 19 (1967).

n.a. Not available.

a. Mean poverty cutoff: approximately $1,800–1,900. Mean income: $1,490.

b. Income range: under $2,202. Mean income: $1,521.

When assets are taken into account, the economic prospects which the aged face become somewhat less bleak than when current income alone is considered. Unfortunately, it is impossible to tell precisely how much less bleak, because the two principal sources of information on assets of the aged (surveys by the Board of Governors of the Federal Reserve System and by the Social Security Administration) yield widely divergent estimates of the size

Table II-7. *Actual Median Income and Median Income with Prorated Assets for Units Headed by Persons Aged 65 and Over, 1962*

(In dollars)

Marital Status	Actual Income	Income with Prorated Assets[a]	
		Excluding equity in home	Including equity in home
Married couples	2,875	3,130	3,795
Unmarried men	1,365	1,560	1,845
Unmarried women	1,015	1,130	1,395

Source: Lenore A. Epstein and Janet H. Murray, *The Aged Population of the United States: The 1963 Social Security Survey of the Aged*, U.S. Department of Health, Education, and Welfare, Social Security Administration, Office of Research and Statistics, Research Report No. 19 (1967), Table 5.1, p. 324.

a. Actual income less income from assets plus the portion of asset holdings that would have been available for spending annually if all assets were prorated over the average remaining years of life of the unit, with a 4 percent annual return.

of the asset holdings (Table II-6). Although different methods were employed in the two surveys, methodology alone cannot explain the large observed discrepancies.

The two surveys reinforce each other in certain major respects, however. First, aged couples have larger asset holdings than aged unrelated individuals, thus reinforcing differences in income of the two groups. Second, only a small fraction of total assets was readily convertible into cash and most aged households had very small liquid asset holdings—$950 or less in 1962, according to the Federal Reserve Survey, and $570 or less, according to the Social Security Survey. Third, households with the lowest current income tended to have the fewest assets. Nevertheless, an effort to include the annuity value of assets in income raises the average (Table II-7). When equity in owner-occupied houses is excluded, the increase in income is considerably smaller than when it is included, particularly for couples.[14]

The relative holdings of assets vary in the same way as income, except that the difference in net worth between aged couples and nonmarried aged persons is even more striking; the median for a married couple is about three or four times the asset holdings of the unmarried person (Table II-8).

Table II-8. *Net Worth and Net Worth Excluding Nonfarm Home Equity for Units Headed by Persons Aged 65 and Over, 1962*

(In dollars)

	Median Net Worth	
Marital Status and Sex	Total	Excluding nonfarm home equity
Married couples	10,860	2,740
Unmarried men	2,655	745
Unmarried women	3,090	630

Source: Lenore A. Epstein and Janet H. Murray, *The Aged Population of the United States: The 1963 Social Security Survey of the Aged,* U.S. Department of Health, Education, and Welfare, Social Security Administration, Office of Research and Statistics, Research Report No. 19 (1967), Table 4.1, p. 310.

Poverty among the Aged

Poverty is a more common affliction of the aged than of any other group.[15] Nearly 30 percent of those aged 65 or over, in comparison with 17 percent of the population at large, are officially classified as poor according to the stringent test of the Social Security Administration.[16] The poverty thresholds are based entirely on current money income, however, and take no account of imputed in-

[14] It may be noted that many of the current aged lived their most productive years during the economically depressed 1930's. Future retirees who were not affected by developments in the 1930's will doubtless have relatively larger accumulations of assets.

[15] Social Security Administration, *The Poor in 1965 and Trends, 1959–65,* Table 3.

[16] See footnote 2, p. 7. The poverty thresholds for the aged and for the population as a whole are 7 to 10 percent lower than the corresponding thresholds for nonaged households, because consumption needs of the nonaged exceed those of the aged. See Mollie Orshansky, "Recounting the Poor—A Five-Year Review," *Social Security Bulletin,* Vol. 29, No. 4 (April 1966), p. 23.

Table II-9. *Incidence of Poverty, by Age, Family Status, and Race, 1965*

Age	Total	Families		Unattached Individuals	
		White	Nonwhite	White	Nonwhite
		Number of poor persons (thousands)			
Under 18	14,282	8,652	5,630	a	a
18–24	2,769	1,512	793	389	76
25–54	7,700	4,689	2,189	553	269
55–64	2,640	1,384	404	688	163
65 and over	5,279	2,118	469	2,376	317
All ages[b]	32,669	18,355	9,484	4,007	824
		Incidence of poverty (percent)[c]			
Under 18	20.5	14.5	55.6	a	a
18–24	14.1	9.3	35.8	38.5	52.1
25–54	11.4	8.5	33.6	18.4	34.9
55–64	15.6	10.5	33.6	31.3	50.0
65 and over	29.9	17.7	47.7	55.7	77.1
All ages[b]	17.1	11.6	45.1	38.2	49.8

Source: U.S. Department of Health, Education, and Welfare, Social Security Administration, Office of Research and Statistics, *The Poor in 1965 and Trends, 1959–65*, Note No. 5 (February 16, 1967), Table 3. Figures are rounded and will not necessarily add to totals.
    a. Unmarried persons under 18 years of age are considered members of families.
    b. Since 1965, the total number of poor persons has declined somewhat (29,657,000 in 1966), but the percentage figures shown here have not been altered significantly by the 1966 data. Mollie Orshansky, *Who Was Poor in 1966*, Social SecurityAdministration, Office of Research and Statistics, Note No. 23 (December 6, 1967), Table 2.
    c. Incidence of poverty represents the poor as a percentage of the total number of persons in each category in the noninstitutional population.

come from owner-occupied houses or of dissaving from accumulated assets. While most of the aged poor, like the nonaged poor, have few assets of any kind, and still fewer liquid assets, they do have considerably greater amounts of assets than do younger poor persons, and a considerably larger fraction of these assets is in liquid form. The asset holdings of the aged with incomes under $3,000 in 1962 were more than five times those of poor persons under age 35, and more than twice those of poor persons aged 35 to 54, but about 15 percent smaller than those of persons aged 55 to 64.[17]

    [17] Dorothy S. Projector and Gertrude S. Weiss, *Survey of Financial Characteristics of Consumers* (Board of Governors of the Federal Reserve System, 1966), Table A 8, pp. 110–11.

Chart II-3. *Incidence of Poverty, 1965*

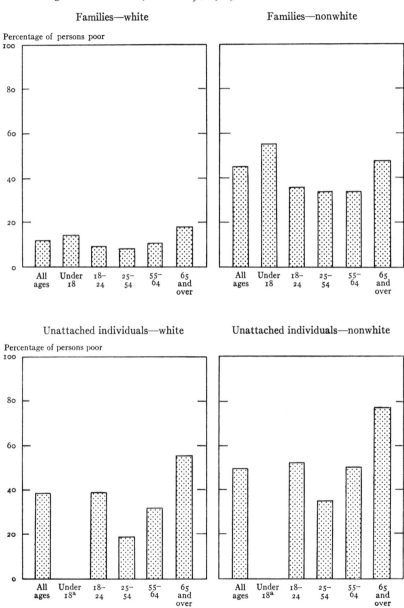

Families—white

Families—nonwhite

Percentage of persons poor

Unattached individuals—white

Unattached individuals—nonwhite

Percentage of persons poor

Source: Table II-9.
a. Unmarried persons under 18 years of age are considered members of families.

Moreover, as noted above, the annuity value of a given amount of assets is greater for the aged than for those who are younger. Consequently, it is clear that the official poverty thresholds overstate the *relative* amount of poverty among the aged. That is, if the annuity value of assets were included in the definition of poverty, the proportion of the aged among the total of poor persons would decline. This observation does not deny, however, the difficult circumstances in which the vast majority of the aged now classified as poor find themselves.

Table II-10. *Living Arrangements of Poor and Nonpoor Persons Aged 65 and Over, 1966*

	Number (Millions)			Percentage		
Family Status	Total	In poor house-holds	In nonpoor house-holds	Total	In poor house-holds	In nonpoor house-holds
Living alone	4.9	2.7	2.2	27.2	50.2	17.4
Living in family units	13.1	2.7	10.4	72.8	49.8	82.6
Head	6.9	1.5	5.4	38.6	28.6	42.9
Wife of head	3.5	0.8	2.7	19.8	15.5	21.6
Other relatives	2.6	0.3	2.3	14.4	5.6	18.1
Total	17.9	5.4	12.6	100.0	100.0	100.0

Source: Mollie Orshansky, *Who Was Poor in 1966*, U.S. Department of Health, Education, and Welfare, Social Security Administration, Office of Research and Statistics, Note No. 23 (December 6, 1967), Table 3. Figures are rounded and will not necessarily add to totals.

Within the poverty definitions now in use, there exists a striking variation in the incidence of poverty on the basis of race and family status. Poverty is most frequent among nonwhite and unattached aged persons. More than three-fourths of all nonwhite, unattached individuals of age 65 or over are poor (Table II-9 and Chart II-3).

The gap between the relative numbers of whites and nonwhites in poverty remains large even after age 65. This occurs although retirement reduces everyone's wage and salary income to zero and most of the aged are retired regardless of race. Furthermore, the social security system is administered in a nondiscriminatory manner, and the benefit formula results in the replacement of a larger fraction of low, than of high, preretirement earnings. Nevertheless, whites enjoy higher incomes from social security, from capital, from private retirement plans, and from other sources.[18]

Mortality rates tend to be inversely related to income;[19] therefore, the lower the income, the higher the probability that one spouse will have died. In addition, incomes of unrelated individuals tend to be lower than are those of families at all ages. After retirement, social security benefits systematically favor couples over unrelated individuals (see Chapter V). In 1966, 2.7 million of the 4.9 million aged persons living alone were poor. Of the aged living in family units, only 2.7 million of the 13.1 million were in households classified as poor (Table II-10).

BENEFICIARY STATUS OF THE AGED

After three decades, social security is only now becoming universal. Ninety percent of all persons aged 65 or over were eligible for benefits in 1967.[20] Many of those not eligible for social security, and some who were eligible, received benefits under other public retirement programs. Coverage under social security and the other public retirement programs will expand until it becomes virtually universal. Since 1966, all persons aged 72 or older have been eligible for special reduced social security benefits either under a transitionally insured status or through payments to noninsured workers who are not receiving public assistance.

Old-age assistance provides benefits to about 12 percent of the aged who are poor as indicated by eligibility for public assistance. These statistics vary greatly from state to state, both because the incidence of poverty is geographically uneven and because the generosity of state assistance programs is extremely unequal.[21] They

[18] For the best discussion of the statistical association between poverty and household characteristics, see Orshansky, "Recounting the Poor," and other articles by the same author in the May and December 1966 issues of the *Social Security Bulletin*.

[19] See, for example, Aaron Antonovsky, "Social Class, Life Expectancy and Overall Mortality," *Milbank Memorial Fund Quarterly*, Vol. 45, No. 2, Pt. 1 (April 1967), pp. 31–73, and sources cited therein.

[20] *Social Security Amendments of 1967*, Hearings before the Senate Committee on Finance on H.R. 12080, 90 Cong. 1 sess. (1967), Pt. 1, p. 224.

[21] U.S. Department of Health, Education, and Welfare, Social Security Administration, Office of Research and Statistics, *Social Security Bulletin, Annual Statistical Supplement, 1965*, Table 16, p. 14.

indicate that approximately two out of five of the aged poor receive old-age assistance.[22] Approximately 5 percent of the aged receive both social security and old-age assistance benefits.[23]

The average old-age retirement benefit in current payment status in December 1967 was $85.37 a month.[24] Couples received more, not only because the couples' benefits are 50 percent larger than those of single persons, but also because the earnings histories of married men tend to be higher than those of nonmarried men and women. The average benefit to a retired worker has been rising steadily; it increased by 15 percent between 1960 and 1967 and by 38 percent between 1955 and 1967 because of both the liberalization of the benefit formula and the higher wage histories of recent retirees.[25]

In general, the higher the retirement benefit, the better is the overall financial position of an aged household. This finding in Palmore's "Work Experience and Earnings of the Aged in 1962" is consistent with normal expectation. The frequency of poverty is greater among nonmarried aged persons than among married couples, but it is less at the upper levels than at the lowest benefit levels (Table II-11).

Whether or not the financial status of recent retirees at each benefit level is the same as the status in 1962 is not clear. Since average benefits to retired workers rose by 13 percent between 1962 and 1968, the number of recipients of relatively high benefits in-

[22] This fraction is considerably higher than the proportion of the nonaged poor who qualify for public assistance. Only one poor child in four lives in a family receiving public assistance, principally because poor households headed by an employed male are generally ineligible for any form of income supplementation. Poor nonaged adults are not paid benefits unless they are blind, permanently and totally disabled, female heads of broken families, or, in some cases, unemployed and the parents of minor children and willing to undergo exhaustive and frequently humiliating application procedures. Approximately one poor, nonaged adult in seven falls in these categories. *Ibid.*, Table 108, p. 103.

[23] *Ibid.*, Table 16, p. 14.

[24] The term *current payment status* is used to designate those benefit payments being made at a given time with no deductions or with deductions amounting to no more than one month's benefit. Essentially, this term refers to the benefits actually being received.

[25] *Social Security Bulletin*, Vol. 31, No. 2 (February 1968), Table M-12, p. 42, and U.S. Department of Health, Education, and Welfare, Social Security Administration, Office of Research and Statistics, *Monthly Benefit Statistics*, February 20, 1968, Table 1.

Table II-11. *Incidence of Poverty among OASDI Beneficiary Groups Aged 65 and Over, by Monthly Benefit Levels, 1962*

(Numbers in thousands)

Monthly Benefit Level (Dollars)	Married Couples		Nonmarried Men and Women	
	Number poor	Percent poor	Number poor	Percent poor
Under 50	—	—	1,000	74
50–59	43	59	420	69
60–69	64	55	442	69
70–79	46	46	329	46
80–99	117	45	383	38
100–119	126	33	102	19
120–139	75	18	3	7
140–159	83	14	—	—
All benefit levels	554	21	2,679	55

Source: U.S. Department of Health, Education, and Welfare, Social Security Administration, 1963 Survey of the Aged (unpublished data). Excludes beneficiaries who received their first benefit in February 1962 or later. The nonmarried group includes widows receiving benefits based on deceased husbands' wage records.

creased. However, because of longer coverage and employment during years of higher average wages, recent retirees at each benefit level are likely to have occupied a lower relative position on the wage ladder and accordingly to be *relatively* less wealthy than were earlier retirees at the same benefit levels. Indeed, since the fraction of income saved at each level of income has probably declined over time, it is conceivable that the total income of the aged at each benefit level may also have declined.

Although coverage is rapidly becoming universal, the social security system will remain immature for many years in another significant respect. The earnings level on which benefits are computed has been raised five times since 1950 (see Appendix Table B-8). Although a worker with average earnings of, say, $7,800 would be entitled to monthly retirement benefits of $218 ($323 if he is married), the years in which the $7,800 wage base (or even the $6,600 wage base, which was effective in 1966–67) was in effect will play only a minor part in most benefit computations for years to come. For some time, the preretirement earnings levels which enter into the benefit computation for most workers will be dominated by years in which no more than $4,800 was counted in the wage base. Average wages will, of course, continue to rise. Benefits will increasingly be based on earnings in years when up to $7,800 in earnings (or more, if the contribution ceiling is again raised) can be counted. As a result, benefits will become more adequate and the effectiveness of social security in combating poverty will be enhanced, even if no further liberalization of benefits is enacted.

POVERTY AND BENEFICIARY STATUS

Poverty is far more frequent among aged recipients of low social security benefits than among recipients of high benefits. According to Table II-11, three-fourths of the nonmarried persons with benefits of less than $50 a month, and three-fifths of the married couples with monthly benefits of less than $60, were poor in 1962. Since social security benefits are a principal source of income for most aged households, this result is not surprising.

Over time, the number of aged with incomes below the current poverty threshold will decline, and the distribution of poverty among beneficiary classes may change. A married worker who is employed with reasonable regularity at the current minimum wage ($1.60 an hour) will be entitled under present law to a basic pension of $2,134.80 a year, which is above the poverty level for 1966 as defined by the Social Security Administration. If he is unmarried, he will not fare as well. His benefits will be $1,423.20, only about 91 percent of the present poverty threshold. And should a married worker die before his wife, the widow would be entitled to benefits equal to only about 75 percent of the poverty threshold.[26] As the proportion of workers with credits at these and higher levels rises, the number of aged poor will decline. Moreover, those who receive low or minimum benefits (for example, housewives, and former federal, state, or local government employees) will tend to have marginal attachment to the social security system and will not necessarily be from poor households.

For some time to come, however, poverty among the aged will continue to be substantial and to be concentrated systematically among recipients of relatively low social security benefits.

[26] Orshansky, *Who Was Poor in 1966*, Table 1.

The early retirement provisions permit workers to retire before age 65 at the cost of receiving reduced benefits. In 1965, 62 percent of all newly awarded benefits for men, and 73 percent for women, were reduced because of early retirement.[27] The extent to which such early retirement can be explained by the early retirement provisions is not clear (see Chapter VI). It is evident, however, that early retirees earned less and experienced more unemployment than did workers who retired at age 65 or later.[28] As a result, benefits of early retirees run 25 to 35 percent below those of persons aged 65 or more who retire in the same year and whose benefits are not reduced.[29] While precise data on the poverty status of early retirees are not available, it seems clear that their economic condition must be inferior to that of persons who were aged 65 or older at the time of retirement. Any one factor—early retirement, illness, or unemployment—is likely to cut into savings and to make the beneficiary and his family even more dependent on social security benefits than are other aged beneficiaries. To make matters worse, their benefits are likely to be very small, because they have low earnings histories and because retirement before age 65 means that they must accept permanently reduced benefits.

Summary

Since the turn of the century, the proportion of the aged who do not work has increased substantially. Today, only about one-fourth of the men and one-tenth of the women aged 65 and over are in the labor force. Many of those who consider themselves in the labor force work only part-time. Even fewer aged persons are expected to work in the future.

Cessation of earnings at retirement is the occasion for a sharp decline in incomes. Although the aged have more assets than the

---

[27] *Social Security Bulletin*, Vol. 29, No. 10 (October 1966), Table 1, p. 28.

[28] Lenore A. Epstein, "Early Retirement and Work-Life Experience," *Social Security Bulletin*, Vol. 29, No. 3 (March 1966), pp. 3–10.

[29] *Social Security Bulletin*, Vol. 30, No. 9 (September 1967), Table Q-6, p. 51.

nonaged, current incomes of the aged are very low relative to the incomes of the nonaged population. Four out of five persons aged 65 and over receive social security benefits, but for most people these benefits by themselves are insufficient to prevent poverty. As a result, the incidence of poverty among the aged is higher than among the nonaged. About 30 percent of all persons aged 65 and over are below the officially defined poverty threshold. The proportion is probably overstated because of the failure to consider the assets of the poor, and it will decline as the social security system matures. Nevertheless, the incidence of poverty among the aged will remain high for a long time to come.

CHAPTER III

Development of the OASDI Program

The social security system—although universally regarded as a permanent institution—is still undergoing change and development. Since the end of World War II, Congress has enacted nine major bills that have broadened coverage, increased the level and improved the structure of benefits, and raised the earnings tax.

The system is financed by a tax on the earnings of wage and salary workers and the self-employed. Employers pay one-half of the tax for the employees. Coverage, at first limited to employees in industry and commerce, other than railroad workers, has been expanded to include virtually all persons not covered by a federal, state, or local government retirement plan. During 1966, almost 85 million workers and self-employed persons paid taxes under the Old-Age, Survivors, and Disability Insurance (OASDI) program.

The relationship between taxes and benefits has never been close, but the contributory element has always been emphasized because of the widely held belief that the individual should be primarily responsible for his own security and that of his family. Despite repeated increases, average benefits are still low relative to minimum subsistence requirements.

The earnings tax is earmarked to go into two special trust funds —one for retirement and survivor benefits and the other for disability benefits. This earmarking of receipts 'has helped to establish the principle that workers receive benefits as a right rather than as a government donation.

Historical Background

Until 1935, the federal government followed a classical laissez faire policy toward the groups now protected by social security.[1] Labor force participation rates declined rapidly, partly because of the decline in self-employment, particularly on farms, and partly because retirement had been less frequent in earlier years.[2] To some extent, the short life expectancy of workers reduced the relevance of planning for retirement, if not the problems of survivors.[3] For workers who did survive to what is currently retirement age, retirement was much less common than it is today. Voluntary leisure on a mass scale is a luxury that only a rich society can afford.[4]

ECONOMIC STATUS OF THE AGED BEFORE 1935

Two factors bearing on the economic status of the aged have been of great importance in the nation's history. First, the family farm—the predominant economic institution in the nineteenth century[5]—permitted the individual to reduce his work effort gradually as he grew older and as younger family members took over

[1] For a detailed history of social security legislation in the United States, see Appendix B.

[2] Labor force participation among males aged 65 and over declined from 68 percent in 1890 to 54 percent in 1930 and 27 percent in 1967. Participation rates since 1890 are shown in Chart II-1. See Chapter VI for a detailed discussion of the relationship between social security and retirement.

[3] The life expectancy of white males at age 20 increased from 42.2 years in 1900 to 50.2 years in 1965; for white females, the rise was from 43.8 years to 56.6. U.S. Bureau of the Census, *Statistical Abstract of the United States, 1967* (1967), Table 63, p. 55 (hereafter referred to as *Statistical Abstract*).

[4] For a discussion of the economic problems of the aged prior to 1935, see *Social Security in America* (published for the Committee on Economic Security by the Social Security Board, 1937), pp. 137–80. Two classic works that brought these problems to light in the United States are Isaac M. Rubinow, *Social Insurance* (Holt, 1916), pp. 301–412, and Abraham Epstein, *Insecurity—a Challenge to America* (2d rev. ed.; Random House, 1938), pp. 491–550.

[5] The rural population amounted to 72 percent of the total population in 1880; in 1960 it was 30 percent. U.S. Bureau of the Census, *Historical Statistics of the United States, Colonial Times to 1957* (1960), p. 9 (hereafter referred to as *Historical Statistics*), and *Statistical Abstract*, Table 23, p. 27.

the major share of the workload. Second, the average family in the primarily rural society of the last century was much larger than it is today.[6] When an individual with many children could no longer work, he could often count on some financial assistance from each grown child. These factors, together with shorter life expectancy, made the problem of economic support of the aged much less severe than it is under conditions now prevailing.

Despite the importance of the family and the farm, the nineteenth century in the United States was hardly a Golden Age in terms of economic security for the average worker, and there did exist a real problem in dealing with the indigent aged. Care for the aged was, however, a less specific and less pressing problem for society than it is today. The extent of poverty was more general, and poverty was accepted more readily as an unavoidable part of life. The aged poor, along with other poor groups in the community, were left to the mercies of local poorhouse relief and private charity. Social policy toward the aged was no more strikingly deficient than social policy with respect to poverty in general.

At the risk of exaggerating economic and demographic trends, it may be said that the general tendencies of development in the United States during the second half of the nineteenth century and the first half of the twentieth century brought about a relative decline in the economic status of the aged. First, medical advances steadily increased life expectancies. The number of aged grew not only absolutely but also as a proportion of the total population.[7] Second, increasing industrialization, while a source of the growing prosperity, was detrimental to the relative status of the aged. The factory was not an environment in which the aged worker could gradually curtail his work effort. An older worker who was unable to maintain a minimum work pace generally had to cease work entirely and found himself cut off completely from any means of subsistence. The industrial city transformed the family

---

[6] The population per household declined from 5.04 in 1880 to 3.38 in 1960. U.S. Bureau of the Census, *Historical Statistics*, p. 16, and *Statistical Abstract*, Table 36, p. 36.

[7] The number of persons aged 65 and over increased from 1.7 million in 1880 to 16.6 million in 1960. In relative terms, the growth was from 3.4 to 9.2 percent of the total population. U.S. Bureau of the Census, *Historical Statistics*, p. 10, and *Statistical Abstract*, Table 22, p. 26.

structure and reduced the availability of family support of the aged. Families in the city found children less advantageous than did families on the farms, and the size of families declined sharply. As a result, aged parents had fewer children to support them and were more of a burden to children than if they had lived on farms. Family ties were also weakened by the shift from a rural to an urban economic and social base. Finally, as technical innovations and capital accumulation increased productivity and general living standards, it became more difficult for the older worker to share fully the fruits of progress. To the extent that he could not adapt to new techniques, his position in the labor market deteriorated, and his subsequent poverty stood out more sharply.[8]

A small minority of individuals provided for their old age by saving during their working life. For most, however, lifetime savings were meager, and few people accumulated sufficient savings to permit retirement. Private pension plans lagged behind the rise of industrialism and, until World War II, covered only a tiny fraction of the labor force. The percentage of individual income devoted to saving for retirement before the advent of social security was probably not substantially greater than it is today, and it may well have been less.[9]

All the trends discussed above worked their effects gradually and unevenly over many decades. As social insurance concepts were successfully implemented in other industrialized countries, and as the problems of economic security were increasingly recognized by scholars and political figures in the United States, agitation for social security grew steadily in the early years of this century. The Great Depression brought the economic need of the

[8] See John G. Turnbull, *The Changing Faces of Economic Insecurity* (University of Minnesota Press, 1966), pp. 43–65.

[9] This is not to say that if there were no compulsory social security system private saving for retirement in the much more affluent society of the 1960's might not be greater than it was in earlier years. However, the available evidence seems to suggest that, over the long run, individuals covered by government and industrial pension plans tend to save more than those who are not covered. See Phillip Cagan, *The Effect of Pension Plans on Aggregate Saving: Evidence from a Sample Survey*, National Bureau of Economic Research, Occasional Paper 95 (Columbia University Press, 1965), and George Katona, *The Mass Consumption Society* (McGraw-Hill, 1964), Chap. 19.

aged—and the problem of economic security in general—to a crisis and precipitated a revolution in social policy, which began in 1935.

THE SOCIAL SECURITY ACT OF 1935

The 1935 legislation grew out of studies and recommendations by the Committee on Economic Security, created in 1934 by President Roosevelt to study the general problem of achieving economic security.[10] The Committee considered various alternatives for meeting the specific problems of the aged. As historical precedents, there were the experiences of old-age assistance laws in some of the states, a few public and private retirement systems, and the various social insurance and assistance programs in industrialized nations in Western Europe and elsewhere. The gradual shift in other countries from reliance on assistance programs to contributory insurance systems strongly influenced the views of the Committee. It finally recommended both old-age insurance and old-age assistance programs for the United States.[11] But it clearly intended that the insurance program should eventually meet the needs of most of the aged, while the assistance program should be limited to a small number of residual aged poor who had unusual need or for some reason were excluded from the social insurance system.[12] In general, the historical development of social security and public assistance has followed the lines of the Committee's original intentions, although the decline of public assistance has not proceeded as rapidly as many had hoped.

[10] The detailed background of the Social Security Act of 1935 is available in a number of sources. See, for example, Edwin E. Witte, *The Development of the Social Security Act* (University of Wisconsin Press, 1962; second printing, 1963); Charles I. Schottland, *The Social Security Program in the United States* (Appleton-Century-Crofts, 1963); and Arthur J. Altmeyer, *The Formative Years of Social Security* (University of Wisconsin Press, 1966).

[11] The Social Security Act of 1935 also provided for the federal-state unemployment insurance program and for aid to the blind and to dependent children. In view of the great popularity that old-age insurance has achieved and the subsequent bitter criticism of public assistance, it is ironic that those closest to the legislative deliberations found Congress more receptive to public assistance than to old-age insurance.

[12] *Social Security in America*, Chap. 10.

As already noted, the social security system in the United States was a child of the Great Depression. With respect to social intervention in the area of economic security, this country was far behind other industrialized countries in the 1930's (it still lags in some respects). The depression, by destroying the savings of many of the provident middle class, mocked the ideology of undiluted self-reliance in a modern economy. It demolished the myth of rugged individualism, perhaps the greatest obstacle to any kind of government intervention. Details aside, congressional opposition to proposals for some kind of social insurance system for the aged in the Social Security Act was mild.[13]

Given the pressures then exerted on the Congress, the old-age insurance and old-age assistance provisions in the 1935 Act may be reasonably regarded as a conservative legislative solution to a difficult and explosive problem. In response to the cumulative trends already discussed and to the shock of depression, proposals to aid the aged had gained tremendous political support during the early 1930's. The most popular was the Townsend Plan—a truly radical break with past policy—which, among other things, called for a flat benefit payment to all the aged which exceeded average earnings of the employed at that time. Thus, the old-age provisions in the Social Security Act were in part a first attempt to solve the long developing crisis of the aged and of economic security in general, in a modern, industrialized economy; in part a reaction to the specific short-run crisis of the depression; and in part a compromise measure to blunt the political appeal of the enormously expensive and essentially unworkable Townsend Plan.[14]

These influences produced features of the original act that would have made the old-age insurance system conform, in some respects, to private insurance principles. Emphasis was placed on the principle of "individual equity"—that workers should get out of the system at least as much as they had contributed to it. A large

[13] Unemployment insurance aroused much more opposition than old-age insurance during the initial congressional discussions. See *Economic Security Act,* Hearings before the House Committee on Ways and Means on H.R. 4120, 74 Cong. 1 sess. (1935); and *Economic Security Act,* Hearings before the Senate Committee on Finance on S. 1130, 74 Cong. 1 sess. (1935).

[14] For a statement of the Townsend Plan, see *Economic Security Act,* Hearings before the House Committee on Ways and Means on H.R. 4120, pp. 678–99.

reserve fund was deemed desirable and was to be accumulated by deferring benefit payments until 1942 and basing them on total lifetime earnings. These similarities to private insurance should not be exaggerated. No attempt was made to fund the entire liability of the system on a private insurance actuarial basis, and the benefit formulas favored the low earner from the beginning. Nonetheless, the system as originally enacted differed fundamentally from the system as it operates today.

LEGISLATIVE DEVELOPMENTS SINCE 1935

The Social Security Act has been amended many times during its relatively short lifetime, but the most fundamental revisions were in the first amendments enacted in 1939.[15] These amendments marked the major turning point in the historical development of social security. The principle of individual equity was severely modified by amendments designed to attain other welfare-oriented goals. First, benefits were provided to certain dependents of aged beneficiaries and to survivors of covered workers. Second, the law was changed so that the payment of benefits would begin in 1940 rather than in 1942. Third, benefits were tied to average earnings over a minimum covered period, thus breaking the link between total lifetime contributions and benefits. The effect of the amendments was to permit payment of benefits immediately to families currently in need. The welfare function of benefits, or the principle of "social adequacy," was stressed as a major appropriate goal of social security.[16]

[15] These amendments were based on the recommendations of the first Advisory Council on Social Security, a group of experts representing employers, employees, and the general public. The *Final Report, December 10, 1938*, S. Doc. 4, 76 Cong. 1 sess. (1939), of the Council contains much valuable background information. For details on the legislative history, see Appendix B, pp. 251–72. See also U.S. Department of Health, Education, and Welfare, Social Security Administration, *Social Security Bulletin, Annual Statistical Supplement, 1965*, pp. 111–19; Robert J. Myers, "Old-Age, Survivors, Disability, and Health Insurance Provisions: Legislative History, 1935–65" (leaflet, U.S. Department of Health, Education, and Welfare, Social Security Administration, July 1965); and Robert J. Myers, *Social Insurance and Allied Government Programs* (R. D. Irwin, 1965), Chap. 4.

[16] Careful definitions of the concepts "individual equity" and "social adequacy" and the problems involved in achieving both objectives simultaneously in a social security program are stated succinctly by Myers: "Whenever a social security system

The 1939 amendments also brought about a fundamental change in financing policy. The explicit intention of creating a large trust fund was abandoned. Instead, current benefits to the aged, their dependents, and survivors were to be financed almost entirely out of the contributions of current workers. Thus the system was moved toward a cash basis (often called a pay-as-you-go system)—a policy that has been followed since the mid-1950's. The Old-Age and Survivors Insurance (OASI) and Disability Insurance (DI) trust funds in 1968 are regarded as contingency reserves rather than trust funds in the customary use of the term. According to recent policy statements, the reserves are intended to be sufficient to maintain the solvency of the funds in the event of a severe recession.[17]

During the 1940's, the nation was preoccupied with the problems of World War II and its aftermath, and no changes of substantial importance were made in that decade. Since 1950, many changes have been made which cumulatively strengthened the basic structure of the social security system.

Coverage. The original Social Security Act, which covered employees in industry and commerce, other than railroad workers, was expanded in 1950 to include new groups, such as farm and domestic workers, the nonfarm self-employed (except professional groups), and federal civilian employees not under the Civil Service Retirement System. The 1954, 1956, 1960, and 1965 amendments further extended coverage to the point where OASDI and other public retirement programs are now practically universal.

Benefits. Benefit payments have been liberalized by the post-

---

involves contributions from the potential beneficiaries, the question of individual equity versus social adequacy arises. Individual equity means that the contributor receives benefit protection directly related to the amount of his contributions—or, in other words, actuarially equivalent thereto. Social adequacy means that the benefits paid will provide for all contributors a certain standard of living. The two concepts are thus generally in direct conflict, and social security systems usually have a benefit basis falling between complete individual equity and complete social adequacy. Usually, the tendency is more toward social adequacy than individual equity." *Social Insurance and Allied Government Programs,* p. 6.

[17] See *The Status of the Social Security Program and Recommendations for Its Improvement,* Report of the Advisory Council on Social Security (1965), pp. 19–20. The need for a reserve fund is discussed in Chapter VIII.

1950 legislation, with proportionately larger increases for wage earners at the bottom of the earnings scale. In addition, dependent and survivor benefits have been raised relative to the level of benefits paid to workers themselves. These changes have further strengthened the welfare or social adequacy objectives of the system.

Aside from increasing the amount of benefits, recent legislation has broadened the types of benefits. The 1956 act added disability insurance for persons aged 50 to 64, and the 1960 legislation removed the lower age limit. In 1956, women were permitted to receive old-age insurance benefits at age 62 instead of age 65, but with permanently reduced benefits in order to hold constant the actuarial costs of the benefits. The same provision was enacted in 1961 for men aged 62, also with provision for actuarially reduced benefits. As a result of these and other modifications, benefits today are much broader in scope than benefits paid in 1940, a factor that must be taken into account in evaluating the adequacy of benefit amounts over the lifetime of a covered worker.[18]

Tax rates and tax base. The social security tax rate, initially 1 percent each on employers and employees for wages and salaries up to $3,000 annually, reached 3.8 percent on each in 1968, and is scheduled to rise to 5.0 percent by 1973.[19] Effective January 1, 1968, the top limit on earnings subject to tax was raised to $7,800. Self-employed persons are taxed at about 1.5 times the rate applying to employees, with a maximum limit of 7 percent.

The earnings test. The 1935 act, which prohibited the payment of benefits to persons with earnings, however small, reflected the philosophy—still maintained by a majority of the Congress and by social security officials—that the social security system is designed to provide income support to individuals who have retired. This requirement has been the subject of considerable controversy since its enactment, and the Congress has retreated step by step from its original position.

Before the earnings test was actually applied to the first benefits

[18] See Chapter VII and Appendix A.

[19] Additional taxes are levied on payrolls to finance hospital insurance. In 1968, the total tax, including hospital insurance, is 4.4 percent on employers and employees and 6.4 percent for the self-employed. The rates are scheduled to rise to 5.9 percent for employers and employees, and 7.9 percent for the self-employed, by 1987.

paid in 1940, the 1939 act modified the original law by permitting earnings up to $15 a month without loss of benefits, but requiring that the entire monthly benefit be withheld as soon as the individual earned $15. This limit was subsequently raised a number of times and, in 1960, the earnings test was modified so that only $1 of benefits was withheld for every $2 of earnings between specified amounts. Under present law, these amounts are between $140 and $240 a month. Above $240, $1 of benefits is withheld for each additional $1 of earnings. Despite these liberalizing amendments, the earnings test remains an unpopular feature.[20]

Beyond the legislative changes made in the original act, perhaps the most important development has been the gradual public acceptance of social security as a permanent institution. Both major political parties have worked to strengthen the basic structure of the program. Clearly, social security meets very real needs in our society. Although important issues remain unresolved, the social security system as it has developed is approved by an overwhelming majority of the nation's citizens in all age groups.

Major Features of Present Programs

The average worker in the United States has no direct contact with the social security system during his working life, except that tax is withheld from his paycheck. The system is complicated, and few have mastered its provisions.[21] Fortunately, the Social Security

[20] Until the 1954 act, earnings referred to wages and salaries in covered employment only; since that act, all wages and salaries have been included in earnings, and, in addition, the beneficiary must not engage in substantial self-employment. In determining whether the beneficiary performs substantial self-employment services, consideration is given to such factors as the amount of time devoted to the business, the nature of the services, the relationship of the services to preretirement activities, the amount of capital the beneficiary has invested in the business, the presence of a full-time manager, and the seasonal nature of the enterprise. Generally, unless the beneficiary can submit evidence to the contrary, more than 45 hours of services in a month is considered substantial and the beneficiary is considered not retired. For further details see U.S. Department of Health, Education, and Welfare, Social Security Administration, *Social Security Handbook* (3d ed.; 1966), Sec. 1816, pp. 299–300.

[21] For a detailed description, see Social Security Administration, *Social Security Handbook.*

Administration keeps all the records and makes all the calculations, so that the worker and his family need not concern themselves with details. The more significant features of the law which must be understood for analysis of the issues are discussed in this section.[22]

COVERAGE

The social security system today covers almost all workers, including those who are self-employed. The only members of the labor force now excluded are federal employees under the Civil Service Retirement System, railroad workers who are covered under the Railroad Retirement Act, state and local government employees not covered by a federal-state agreement for coverage, irregularly employed farm and domestic workers, and employees of certain nonprofit organizations who have elected not to be covered.[23] In three instances, there are minimum earnings requirements to reduce compliance and administrative costs: net earnings of the self-employed must be at least $400 a year; cash wages of a farm worker from a particular employer must be at least $150 a year (or the worker must have worked at least 20 days on a time basis for the employer); and domestic servants and employees of nonprofit organizations must earn at least $50 in a calendar-year quarter. Railroad employees are covered by OASDI if they do not qualify for railroad retirement benefits.[24] Members of the armed forces re-

[22] The statistics given in this section are published regularly by the Social Security Administration. See, in particular, *Social Security Bulletin, Annual Statistical Supplement, 1966,* and Appendix G, this volume.

[23] Government employees come under two different types of programs. The Civil Service Retirement System is a compulsory contributory program for federal civilian workers; it provides pensions after as few as five years of contributions to persons who retire because of age or disability. Benefits depend on the worker's earnings and his length of service, and are adjusted automatically for changes in the consumer price index. The benefits are financed by a 6.5 percent contribution from the employee's salary, supplemented by matching payments from the employing agency and congressional appropriations to finance any deficits. In addition to the federal retirement system, the state and local governments have numerous plans with various levels of contributions and types of benefits.

[24] This is accomplished by transferring wage credits (and the funds applicable to them) from the Railroad Retirement System to OASDI for employees with less than ten years of railroad service.

ceived credit for service during and after World War II,[25] and have been fully covered on a contributory basis since the beginning of 1957.

In 1967, 71.5 million workers, or 93.0 percent of workers in paid employment, were eligible for coverage under social security.[26] Most of those still outside of OASDI are federal and state-local employees, so that coverage under some kind of public retirement program is almost universal at the present time.[27] Moreover, even those workers not covered by the system at some point in time are likely to acquire coverage at some other time through work in covered occupations. During 1966, there were 5 million new entrants into the social security system (that is, persons who had taxable earnings for the first time); almost 85 million workers and self-employed persons had taxable earnings. Total earnings in covered employment amounted to $388 billion, of which $310 billion—or 80 percent—were taxable. The $20 billion of benefit payments were 6.5 percent of taxable earnings.

TRUST FUNDS

Amounts equivalent to the payroll tax collections are deposited in the Federal Old-Age and Survivors Insurance Trust Fund and the Federal Disability Insurance Trust Fund. These funds are administered by a Board of Trustees consisting of the Secretaries of the Treasury, Labor, and Health, Education, and Welfare, with the Social Security Administration Commissioner acting as secretary. The administrative expenses as well as the benefits of the programs are paid from the trust funds.[28]

Congress has repeatedly stated its intention to make the OASDI

[25] They were granted wage credits of $160 for each month of active service between September 16, 1940, and December 31, 1956. The OASDI trust funds are reimbursed for these benefits out of general revenues.

[26] Appendix Table G-4. About 2.6 million eligible persons have not elected coverage or have not had coverage elected for them by their employers.

[27] Only 5.4 million workers were not eligible for OASDI coverage in 1967; these included 0.4 million farmers and agricultural workers, 0.7 million domestic servants, 2.7 million government employees, and 1.6 million others (mainly nonagricultural self-employed and employees of nonprofit organizations). See Appendix Table G-4.

[28] The law also provides for reimbursement from the trust funds for the cost of certain vocational rehabilitation services furnished to those receiving disability benefits.

system self-supporting from the earmarked payroll taxes, despite a few instances in which general revenues were used to finance specific benefits. Accordingly, payroll tax rates and the taxable earnings limit have been raised periodically as the level of benefits has been increased. The trust funds have been allowed to build up to moderate size—in recent years, to a level that would approximately equal one year's benefits.[29]

During the first two decades of the existence of the OASI trust fund, income exceeded benefit payments and administrative expenses in every year. From 1957 to 1965, disbursements slightly exceeded income in most of the years and the trust fund balance declined slightly. From 1965 to 1966, the fund grew from $18.2 billion to $20.6 billion, and a further gain of $3.7 billion during 1967 raised the fund to an all-time peak of $24.2 billion (Appendix Table G-2).

ELIGIBILITY FOR BENEFITS

Benefits are paid only to persons who gain "insured status," which depends on the number of quarters of coverage on their social security earnings record. A quarter is considered covered if the individual receives at least $50 of wages or is credited with $100 of self-employment income in that quarter.[30]

Fully insured status entitles a worker and his family to most types of benefits paid on the basis of his social security earnings record. The status can be achieved by having at least as many quarters of coverage as there are calendar years between ages 21 and 65 for men and 62 for women. For persons who reached age 21 prior to 1950, which includes all of the presently retired, the requirement is as many quarters of coverage as there are years between 1951 and retirement age.[31] A person who has forty quarters of cov-

[29] For the most recent report on the trust funds, see *The 1968 Annual Report of the Board of Trustees of the Federal Old-Age and Survivors Insurance and Disability Insurance Trust Funds*, H. Doc. 288, 90 Cong. 2 sess. (1968).

[30] Self-employed with at least $400 of net earnings from self-employment and wage earners with the maximum taxable wages during a year are always credited with four quarters of coverage in that year. Farm workers are credited with a quarter of coverage for each $100 of wages they receive during the entire year.

[31] Fully insured status requires a minimum of six quarters of coverage. In death and disability cases, the elapsed period ends with the year of death or disability.

erage is fully insured for life, so that a full-time year-round worker entering the labor force at age 21 will achieve fully insured status at about age 30.

Beyond fully insured status, the law provides for three other types of insured status:

1. A *transitionally insured status* set up under the 1965 law provides a special minimum benefit to otherwise ineligible persons who reach the age of 72 prior to 1969. This status requires at least one quarter of coverage for each year after 1950 and up to the year when the person retires, with a minimum of three quarters. In 1966, persons over 72 were made eligible to receive a special minimum benefit even if they are not fully or transitionally insured.[32]

2. A *currently insured status* provides payments to survivors or dependents even if the covered worker at the time of his death or disability was not fully insured. This status is achieved by having at least six quarters of coverage in the thirteen-quarter period before death, disability, or retirement.

3. An *insured for disability status* is a special status required for disability benefits or to establish a period of disability.[33] To be eligible for disability insurance, workers need at least twenty quarters of coverage during the forty-quarter period prior to disability. The 1965 amendments provide that persons who become blind before age 31 are insured for disability if they are covered in at least half the quarters beginning at age 21 and up to the time they are disabled. In 1967, this alternative was extended to all workers disabled before age 31, regardless of the nature of the disability.

The fact that a person has attained the appropriate insured status is not a sufficient condition for eligibility to receive a given type of benefit. Eligibility depends also on the individual's ability to meet certain other conditions formally stated in the laws. For example, a worker must be 65 to qualify for his full old-age benefit (62 for actuarially reduced benefits). Benefit payments are also

---

[32] The requirements are that they must (a) attain age 72 before 1968 or (b) attain 72 after 1967 and have three quarters of coverage for every year after 1966 and before age 72 is reached. In addition, they cannot be receiving public assistance.

[33] The earnings record is "frozen" during the period of disability (that is, the period of disability does not count against the individual in figuring his insured status or his average wage).

subject in general to the "retirement" or "earnings" test, which is in effect a requirement that the individual receiving OASDI benefits is not a full-time worker.[34] However, the earnings test does not apply to persons aged 72 or over.

BENEFITS

Of all the OASDI benefits, the most important are those paid to retired workers and their spouses. There were 23.7 million OASDI beneficiaries at the end of 1967: 12.0 million were retired workers; 3.2 million were wives (and dependent husbands) of retired workers; 5.7 million were survivors of insured workers; 2.1 million were disabled workers and their dependents; and 0.7 million were noninsured persons over age 72 with special benefits. For fiscal year 1967, the proportion of total OASDI benefits going to workers and their spouses was approximately 85 percent; 13 percent went to children and mothers; 1 percent went to noninsured persons over age 72; and the remaining 1 percent consisted of lump-sum death payments (Table III-1).

A summary of the eligibility requirements for various types of benefits under OASDI, and of benefit rates, is given in Table III-2. The major types of benefits are as follows:

1. The basic old-age benefit—called the *primary insurance amount*—is paid to workers retiring at age 65 or over. It varies from a minimum of $55 to a maximum of $218 a month, depending on the individual's average monthly wage.[35] An additional 50 percent is added to the benefit if the retired worker is married and the wife (or dependent husband) is over 65 years of age, or if the worker has a child under 18 years of age.[36] Reduced benefits may be elected beginning at age 62.[37] Individuals reaching age 72 before

[34] For details of the present earnings test, see page 36.

[35] In general, the average monthly wage is computed for the period after 1950 and up to age 65 for men and age 62 for women. The lowest five years of earnings and any years under the "disability freeze" are omitted in the computation.

[36] In 1967, a maximum of $105 was set for the wife's or dependent husband's benefit.

[37] The reduction for a worker is 5/9 percent for each month below age 65 at time of retirement. Thus, a person who retires at 62 accepts a 20 percent lifetime reduction. For a wife (or dependent husband), the reduction is 25/36 percent a month, or a total of 25 percent, if she (or he) elects to receive benefits at 62.

Table III-1. *Distribution of OASDI Benefits, by Type of Beneficiary and Payment, Fiscal Year 1967*

(Amounts in millions of dollars)

Type of Beneficiary or Payment	Total Amount	Percent of total	OASI Amount	Percent of total	DI Amount	Percent of total
Retired and disabled workers	13,564	65	12,108	64	1,456	78
Wives and husbands	1,559	8	1,448	8	111	6
Widows and widowers	2,428	12	2,428	13	—	—
Children	2,298	11	2,005	11	293	16
Mothers^a	417	2	417	2	—	—
Parents	34	*	34	*	—	—
Noninsured persons aged 72 and over	200	1	200	1	—	—
Lump-sum death payments	246	1	246	1	—	—
Total	20,746	100	18,886	100	1,861	100

Source: *The 1968 Annual Report of the Board of Trustees of the Federal Old-Age and Survivors Insurance and Disability Insurance Trust Funds*, H. Doc. 288, 90 Cong. 2 sess. (1968), Tables 5 and 10, pp. 17, 24. Figures are rounded and will not necessarily add to totals.
* Less than 0.5 percent.
a. Widows and dependent divorced wives of deceased workers caring for child beneficiaries.

1968 are granted a pension of $40 a month ($60 if a husband and wife both qualify) even if they were not covered under social security.[38]

2. Disability benefits are paid after a waiting period of six months[39] to workers who are totally disabled. The disability benefit is computed in the same way as the old-age benefit, but disability payments tend to be larger on the average because the stricter qualification requirements eliminate low-paid, irregularly employed workers. Disability payments continue until the recipient

[38] The benefit is reduced by an amount equal to the benefits of any other federal, state, or local retirement program for which the individual is qualified. The cost of this extension of coverage is paid out of the general funds of the Treasury in almost all cases (the exception is when the person has more than three quarters of coverage).

[39] The waiting period is waived for an individual who recovers and again becomes disabled within five years.

Table III-2. *OASDI Eligibility Requirements and Benefit Rates, 1968*

Type of Beneficiary or Payment	Requirement		Benefit Rate[a] or Amount of Payment
	Age	Worker's insured status	
Insured worker			
Retired worker	62 or over[b]	Fully	100%[b]
Disabled worker	None	Fully and insured for disability	100
Special, person aged 72	72 prior to 1968	None	$40[c]
Dependents			
Wife, no child present	62 or over[d]	Fully	50%[de]
Wife, child present	None	Fully	50[e]
Child of worker	Under 18[f]	Fully	50
Dependent husband	62 or over[d]	Fully	50[d]
Survivors			
Widow	60 or over[gh]	Fully	82.5%[g]
Widow, child present	None	Fully or currently	75
Child of worker	Under 18[f]	Fully or currently	75
Dependent widower	62 or over[h]	Fully	82.5
Dependent parent	62 or over	Fully	82.5[i]
Lump sum	None	Fully or currently	300[j]

Source: Social Security Act of 1935 as amended through 1967. Table adapted from Robert J. Myers, *Social Insurance and Allied Government Programs* (R. D. Irwin, 1965), Table 4, p. 37.
  a. Percentage of primary insurance amount before effect of maximum benefit provisions.
  b. Benefit is reduced by 5/9 percent for each month below age 65 at time of retirement.
  c. Or $60 a month for a couple, both of whom are eligible.
  d. Benefit is reduced by 25/36 percent for each month below age 65 at time of retirement.
  e. Wife's benefit limited to a maximum of $105 a month.
  f. No age limitation if disabled before 18; also paid at ages 18–21 if in school.
  g. Benefit is reduced by 5/9 percent a month below age 62.
  h. Benefits can be paid to certain disabled widows and widowers of deceased insured workers between the ages of 50 and 62. If the benefit is first awarded at age 50, it amounts to 50 percent of the primary insurance amount. This percentage increases gradually until it reaches 82.5 percent for those persons first receiving benefits at age 62.
  i. Benefit rate for two parents is 75 percent each.
  j. Maximum of $255.

reaches age 65, when old-age insurance takes over. Benefits are also paid for a disabled child, aged 18 or over, who was disabled before 18 and is dependent on a parent entitled to disability or retirement benefits or was dependent on an insured parent who died. As a result of the 1967 amendments, benefits are now provided for disabled widows and widowers (aged 50 or over) of deceased insured workers.

3. Survivor benefits are paid to aged widows (or dependent widowers), children under 18,[40] and dependent parents of deceased workers who were insured. The benefits are 82.5 percent of the primary insurance amount for widows and parents over 62 (with reduced rates beginning at age 60 for widows) and 75 percent for children. If there are two dependent parents, each receives 75 percent. Widows of all ages with children under 18 (or over 18 and disabled since 18) receive 75 percent of the primary insurance amount (PIA) for themselves and an additional 75 percent for each dependent child up to the family maximum.[41]

4. Lump-sum death benefits are paid on the death of an insured individual. This payment is three times the primary insurance amount, up to a maximum of $255. The full amount is payable to a surviving spouse, but in other cases the payments cannot exceed burial costs.

The formula for computing benefits has been changed a number of times, most recently in 1967. It has always provided a larger benefit in relation to earnings for low-paid than for high-paid workers. At present, the benefit for a retired worker aged 65 or over is 74 percent of his average monthly wage if that average was $74; it declines to 50 percent for those with average wages of $206 a month and 34 percent for workers with the maximum taxable wage of $650 a month. Maximum family benefits range from more than 100 percent of average monthly earnings for families of the lowest paid workers to 67 percent for families of workers with maximum taxable wages (Chart V-1 and Appendix Table G-5).[42]

Though benefits have been increasing continuously since the beginning of the program and almost doubled between 1950 and 1965, they are still very low. Retired workers received an average of $42.20 a month at the end of 1950 and $80.10 at the end of 1965. The combined benefit for an aged couple rose from an aver-

[40] Children in school, at ages 18–21, or disabled before age 18, are also eligible for survivor benefits.

[41] The family maximum is based on the insured worker's PIA. Under the 1967 amendments, the maximum ranged from $82.50 (for a PIA of $55) to $434.40 (for a PIA of $218).

[42] The formula for computing the PIA is 71.16 percent of the first $110 of average monthly wage, 25.88 percent of the next $290, 24.18 percent of the next $150, and 28.43 percent of the last $100. But the actual benefits payable vary slightly, for technical reasons, from the results of using this formula.

Table III-3. *Average Monthly OASDI Benefits in Current Payment Status for Selected Beneficiaries at Five-Year Intervals, 1940–65*

(In dollars)

Year[a]	Retired Worker	Disabled Worker	Retired Couple	Widow	Widow with Three or More Children
1940	22.10	—	36.40	20.30	51.30
1945	23.50	—	38.50	20.20	50.40
1950	42.20	—	71.70	36.50	92.40
1955	59.10	—	103.50	48.70	133.20
1960	69.90	87.90	123.90	57.70	181.70
1965	80.10	95.40	141.50	73.90	218.10

Source: U.S. Department of Health, Education, and Welfare, Social Security Administration, *Social Security Bulletin, Annual Statistical Supplement, 1965*, Table 84, p. 82.
a. End of year.

age of $71.70 to $141.50. The average benefit for a widow rose from $36.50 to $73.90, and for a widowed mother with three or more children, from $92.40 to $218.10 (Table III-3). As already indicated, disabled workers receive higher average benefits than retired workers because the requirements for qualification are stricter; their average benefits rose from $72.80 in 1957, when disability payments began, to $95.80 at the end of 1966.

RAILROAD RETIREMENT

Railroad workers are covered by a separate retirement program, but there is a close relationship between the Railroad Retirement System (RR) and OASDI. Benefits and tax rates are higher for railroad workers, but the two programs are operated on similar principles. They are also directly coordinated in three respects. First, railroad wage credits are combined with OASDI credits for social security purposes if the worker does not have enough railroad service (ten years) to qualify for railroad retirement benefits. In such cases, the benefits are paid by OASDI. Second, OASDI and RR earnings credits are always combined for survivor cases; benefits are paid by RR to survivors of employees with ten or more years of service who had a connection with the railroad industry at the time of death, and by OASDI in all other cases.[43] The benefits are based on the combined earnings of the employee in the railroad industry and in industries covered by OASDI. Third, in recognition of the larger contributions, railroad retirement benefits are guaranteed to be at least 10 percent more than the corresponding OASDI benefits.

An individual receives full retirement and disability benefits under both OASDI and RR if he qualifies for them. A widow may receive her own old-age benefit under OASDI and a widow's annuity under RR. She may also receive a widow's benefit under both systems if she had two husbands, each covered by one system. However, benefits of survivors of railroad workers who have earnings under both systems are not duplicated and are paid on the basis of the combined earnings record—by RR if the worker has a current railroad industry connection (and ten years of railroad service) and by OASDI otherwise.

To finance the interchange of benefits, the law provides for an annual transfer of funds between the trust funds. The purpose of the financial interchange is to place the OASI and DI trust funds in the same financial position that they would have held if there had never been a railroad retirement system. Prior to 1958, funds were transferred under this arrangement from the RR account to the OASI fund; since then the flow has been in the other direction.[44]

PUBLIC ASSISTANCE AND VETERANS' PENSIONS

The discussion thus far has been limited to details of the social insurance programs that constitute the basic subject of this volume. Social security, broadly defined, also includes public assistance payments for income support to the needy aged who are not eligible for OASDI benefits or whose benefits are inadequate. In addition, pensions are paid to needy veterans under certain circumstances.

Prior to the enactment of social security legislation, assistance to

[43] The employee must have twelve months of railroad service in the thirty months preceding death or earlier retirement to qualify for a "current" railroad connection.

[44] As of the end of 1967, the RR account had received $3.7 billion on balance from the OASI and DI trust funds.

needy people of all age groups was provided by local governments (with some financial participation by the states). Because of insufficient financial resources, the coverage of these programs was extremely limited and the benefits they provided were wholly inadequate. To remedy these defects, the Social Security Act of 1935 authorized the federal government to share the costs of public assistance with the states and local governments. Originally, federal help was confined to the aged, the blind, and dependent children. The disabled were added in 1950, and medical assistance to aged not receiving old-age assistance was added in 1960.

To be eligible for federal grants, the public assistance programs must be operated throughout an entire state, financed at least in part by the state government and administered fairly and efficiently under the supervision of a single state agency. The payments must be made in cash (except for medical service payments) and take into account the income and other resources of the recipients. For old-age assistance, the minimum age requirement is 65, although states may make payments from their own funds to younger persons.[45]

The share of public assistance financed by the federal government depends on the size of the payments and the relative income of the states. For old-age assistance, it is $31 of the first $37 of a state's average monthly payment per recipient, plus a proportion of the remainder (depending on the relative income status of the state).[46] In 1966, the federal share of the cost of programs in which the federal government participated averaged 55 percent, varying among the states from a low of 41 percent to a high of 79 percent.[47]

Public assistance is designed to help persons who do not have sufficient financial resources to provide the essentials of living. Need is determined on the basis of minimum standards estab-

[45] Only one state—Colorado—has elected to do so.

[46] This is a variable grant of the portion of the average monthly payment from $35 to $75, ranging from 65 percent for states with the lowest per capita personal income to 50 percent for states with the highest per capita income. See U.S. Department of Health, Education, and Welfare, Social Security Administration, *Social Security Programs in the United States* (1966), p. 95, and Myers, *Social Insurance and Allied Government Programs*, pp. 13–23.

[47] Social Security Administration, *Social Security Bulletin, Annual Statistical Supplement, 1966*, Table 118, p. 116.

lished by the states.[48] Payments made by these programs still supplement federal social security benefits where the latter are inadequate to meet the needs of the recipients. However, as social security has grown and matured, old-age assistance has declined in relative importance. The number of recipients reached a peak of 2.8 million in 1950 and then declined to 2.1 million in 1965. But average payments have continued to increase, rising from $44 a month in 1950 to $80 in 1965.[49]

Veterans' pensions are another major source of financial aid to the needy aged. Payments are made to more than 900,000 veterans over age 65 and to 250,000 veterans and their dependents under age 65, plus one million more survivors of veterans.[50] Total federal payment under the veterans' pension program in fiscal 1967 was $1.9 billion—about the same as the expenditures (including both federal and state shares) under old-age assistance.[51] Since the veterans' pension program fulfills many of the same purposes as public assistance, it too is closely related to social security.

Foreign Experience

When the United States passed its Social Security Act in the mid-1930's, twenty-seven countries already had well-developed national retirement systems. Today, most countries—even those considered less developed—have social insurance programs. The scope of these programs, their institutional structure, the size of benefits, and financing arrangements differ widely.[52]

[48] However, some states make payments that do not meet their own standards. In 1967, the President recommended that the states be required to raise their payments at least to these standards, but the Congress did not follow his recommendation. *President's Proposals for Revision in the Social Security System,* Hearings before the House Committee on Ways and Means on H.R. 5710, 90 Cong. 1 sess. (1967), Pt. 1, p. 6.

[49] Social Security Administration, *Social Security Bulletin, Annual Statistical Supplement, 1965,* Table 108, p. 103, and Table 109, p. 104.

[50] Unpublished data provided by the Veterans Administration. Payments are made to veterans over 65 years of age for nonservice-connected disability, but all needy veterans over 65 are considered disabled.

[51] *The Budget of the United States Government, Fiscal Year 1969* (1968), p. 161, and Appendix Table G-10 in this volume.

[52] The material in this section is based on U.S. Department of Health, Education,

NATURE OF FOREIGN PROGRAMS

Qualifications for benefits under most social security programs are based on past contributions or coverage, and the size of benefits varies to some extent with previous earnings. The programs usually cover employees engaged in industry and commerce; agricultural workers and the self-employed are included in most European systems, but rarely in those of other countries.

While workers ordinarily make a contribution to social security (usually a payroll tax), the trend has been toward a threefold sharing of costs by the government, the employee, and the employer. The employer and employee tax rates are frequently the same; in some countries, the employer rate is double that of the employee rate. Contributions by the self-employed are nearly always larger than those of employees. The majority of the programs place a ceiling on the maximum earnings subject to tax. Special trust fund arrangements to separate social security from other government accounts are the rule, but there are exceptions. Similarly, the payroll taxes are usually earmarked for social security, but a few countries rely on general revenue financing.[53]

A large majority of the programs graduate benefits according to past earnings, usually during the last few years of coverage. In some countries, the practice of averaging earnings over all, or a substantial part, of the period of coverage is followed (as it is in the United States). A few countries pay flat pensions to the beneficiaries; seven pay them to every resident aged person, regardless of earlier contributions or employment.[54] In recent years, there has

---

and Welfare, Social Security Administration, Office of Research and Statistics, *Social Security Programs Throughout the World, 1967* (1967); and Henry J. Aaron, "Social Security: International Comparisons," in Otto Eckstein (ed.), *Studies in the Economics of Income Maintenance* (Brookings Institution, 1967), pp. 13–48. See Appendix C in this volume for further details.

[53] General revenue financing usually prevails in countries with general pension systems or social assistance programs; for example, Australia, Canada, Denmark, Finland, New Zealand, South Africa, and Sweden.

[54] Flat pensions are paid in Cyprus, Ireland, Israel, Jamaica, Malta, the Netherlands, and under the basic British program. Universal pensions are paid in Canada, Denmark, Finland, Iceland, New Zealand, Norway, and Sweden.

been a tendency to add a supplementary graduated pension to the basic flat pension.[55]

Several countries paying wage-related benefits revalue wages earned in earlier years to bring them into line with changes in national average wages or the cost of living index. A substantial group follows the practice of automatically adjusting benefits to changes in the official wage or price index.[56]

Most countries provide retirement benefits at ages between 60 and 65; in a few, the ages are as low as 50, and in others as high as 70. Women receive benefits at the same age as men in about half of the countries; in the others, they receive them at a younger age, usually five years earlier.

A sizable number of countries pay benefits to aged workers even if they continue in full-time employment;[57] others require that workers be fully or partially retired (which is the U.S. requirement until age 72). Practically all countries provide benefits for permanent disability as well as for retirement. Survivor benefits are also included almost everywhere, although a few pay only lump sums.

RELATIVE SIZE AND DETERMINANTS OF PROGRAMS

Among twenty-one countries for which social security payments[58] for the aged as a percentage of their 1960 national incomes were tabulated,[59] only seven—Australia, Canada, Ireland, Japan, Portu-

[55] The United Kingdom took this step in 1958, Sweden in 1959, Finland in 1963, Denmark in 1964, and Norway in 1966. "Social Security Programs of Foreign Countries," *Social Security Bulletin*, Vol. 27, No. 9 (September 1964), p. 20, and unpublished data from the Social Security Administration.

[56] In 1967, revaluation of earlier wages was practiced in Algeria, Austria, Belgium, Canada, France, the Federal Republic of Germany, Norway, Sweden, Switzerland, Turkey, and Yugoslavia. (In Norway and Sweden, the revaluation applies only to the wage-related benefit, not to the flat pensions which are paid under a separate system.) Benefits are adjusted to an official price or wage index in Belgium, Canada, Chile, Denmark, Ecuador, Finland, France, Iceland, Israel, Luxembourg, the Netherlands, Norway, Sweden, Uruguay, and Yugoslavia.

[57] As of 1967, these countries included Algeria, Chile, France, the Federal Republic of Germany, Iceland, Iran, Ireland, Italy, Luxembourg, the Netherlands, Norway, Panama, Paraguay, Sweden, Switzerland, and Venezuela.

[58] For a discussion of the difficulties in determining the boundaries for the term "social security" in various nations, see International Labour Office, *The Cost of Social Security, 1958–1960* (Geneva, 1964), pp. 2–3.

[59] See Appendix D for supporting statistical material on international comparisons.

Table III-4. *Social Security Expenditures for Old-Age Benefits as a Percentage of National Income and of per Capita National Income in Twenty-one Countries, 1960*

Country	Percentage of National Income	Percentage of Per Capita National Income[a]
Germany	11.8	109
Austria	9.6	62
Italy	6.6	41
Belgium	6.3	42
France	5.8	34
Sweden	5.5	54
Netherlands	5.2	60
Denmark	5.2	46
Norway	4.8	70
New Zealand	4.6	53
United Kingdom	4.4	29
Finland	4.3	58
Switzerland	4.2	37
United States	4.1	45
Ireland	3.7	49
Australia	3.3	32
Canada	3.0	61
Portugal	2.8	37
Spain	1.5	18
Japan	1.3	12
South Africa	1.3	26

Sources: International Labour Office, *The Cost of Social Security, 1958–1960* (Geneva, 1964); United Nations, Department of Economic and Social Affairs, Statistical Office, *Yearbook of National Accounts Statistics, 1965* (1966); United Nations, Department of Economic and Social Affairs, Statistical Office, *Demographic Yearbook—1965* (1966), and issues for 1961, 1962, and 1963.
a. Average old-age benefits expressed as a percentage of per capita national income.

gal, South Africa, and Spain—showed percentages that were smaller than that for the United States (Table III-4). The median for the twenty-one countries was 4.4 percent, compared with the U.S. percentage of 4.1.

The U.S. showing is improved somewhat if the comparison is made with per capita national income. As a percentage of that income in 1960, social security payments to the aged in five of the seven countries mentioned above—Australia, Japan, Portugal, South Africa, and Spain—and also Belgium, France, Italy, Switzerland, and the United Kingdom were smaller than the U.S. percentage. The median for the twenty-one countries was the U.S. figure of 45 percent.

The most important factor that explains the relative expenditures on social security among countries is the age of the system. Countries, such as Germany, which began to introduce major programs early spend relatively more than latecomers, such as the United States. Benefits increase as social insurance programs mature. Forces that produce relatively early commitment to welfare expenditures by the government, such as greater public acceptance of government intervention in economic affairs, may also act to raise the level of these benefits.

The type of taxation used to support welfare systems also appears to be significant. Countries that rely on general revenues, rather than payroll taxes, appear to spend relatively less for old-age benefits, but this is offset by relatively higher transfer payments to other groups. In countries where old-age benefits are financed by earmarked payroll taxes, benefits are usually not subject to annual legislative review and do not regularly compete with other government expenditures for approval.

Summary

Social security programs in the United States were developed in response to the growing problem of economic insecurity in a society that had become increasingly industrialized and urbanized. The Social Security Act of 1935, a major landmark in social legislation, was both a response to the immediate crisis of the Great Depression and an attempted solution to the more fundamental long-run problem of achieving economic security in the face of risks to earned income, such as old age, disability, and premature death of the family head.

The program included in the 1935 legislation was heavily influenced by private insurance practices. Subsequent amendments to the original Act, especially the 1939 amendments, have moved the program away from its original orientation and given it its own distinctive characteristics. The trust funds have remained small and now serve largely as contingency reserves. The insurance principle of individual equity has been substantially modified in order to use OASDI as an instrument for attaining broad welfare goals.

Legislation since 1935 has broadened the coverage of OASDI to the point where today it and other government retirement programs protect virtually all workers and their families. Congress has repeatedly revised benefit schedules, tax rates, and other features of the program in an attempt to keep OASDI up to date.

OASDI is financed by an earnings tax which is levied on workers, their employers, and the self-employed. These taxes are earmarked for payment into the OASI and DI trust funds, which in turn are the official sources of benefit payments. Eligibility for OASDI benefits grows out of work in covered employment. With minor exceptions, persons must work in covered employment for specified minimum time periods in order to achieve the insured status that is a prerequisite for various types of benefits. Generally, benefits are paid only to insured persons who have retired or who earn relatively modest amounts.

Benefits are paid under OASDI to retired workers and their dependents, to disabled workers, and to the survivors of insured workers. Benefit amounts are calculated on the basis of the earnings records of insured workers. The benefit formulas are weighted to replace a greater fraction of previous covered earnings for low wage earners than for persons at the upper end of the earnings scale. Average benefit amounts have increased steadily in recent years; nevertheless, the average payment to a retired worker at the end of 1967 was only $85 a month.

Three distinct major programs are closely related to OASDI. First, railroad employees are covered by the Railroad Retirement System, a separate retirement program with close administrative and financial ties to OASDI. Second, benefits are provided to specific categories of needy persons under the public assistance programs administered by the states. The needy aged can receive supplementary benefits under the old-age assistance program in addition to OASDI payments. Third, needy veterans and their survivors are eligible for pensions or survivors benefits. In addition, most federal, state, and local government employees are covered by their own retirement plans. Although these public programs keep the majority of aged persons out of poverty, the residual incidence of poverty among the aged in the United States is still large.

Social security in the United States was predated by social insurance programs in many foreign countries. Foreign social security programs show many similarities to OASDI but also many interesting and suggestive differences. The United States ranks low in the international scale of adequacy of social security expenditures as measured relative to national income and is only about average relative to per capita national income.

CHAPTER IV

The Objectives of Social Security

The social security program aims at two related but conceptually distinct objectives.[1] One is to guarantee minimum income support for the aged, the disabled, and dependent survivors. In recent years, the success of the program in attaining this welfare goal has been judged increasingly by the degree to which it keeps beneficiaries out of poverty. A second objective is to help moderate the decline in living standards when the earnings of the family head cease because of retirement, disability, or death. This earnings replacement objective is independent of the goal of preventing poverty; benefits go to families at all income levels. The distinction between these objectives should be kept in mind, because acceptance of the current social security program and proposals for improving it hinge on an evaluation of their comparative importance.

The case for a social security program intended to attain these objectives depends in part on the observed inability of most people to make adequate financial provision for retirement, disability, or premature death. Mainly, however, it depends on what appear to be widely shared humanitarian values: that (a) the aged, the disabled, and dependent survivors of deceased family heads should not have to live in destitution; and (b) the government should help to protect individuals against catastrophic losses of income.

[1] An early draft of this chapter appeared in *Old Age Income Assurance*, Compendium of Papers on Problems and Policy Issues in the Public and Private Pension System, Pt. III: *Public Programs,* 90 Cong. 1 sess. (1967), pp. 5–20.

55

There is also wide agreement that people should be eligible for benefits without degrading eligibility tests. Explicit acceptance of these values has important implications for social security policy, and these implications are explored in this chapter.

Widespread acceptance of the basic objectives of social security undoubtedly explains its great success, not only in the United States but also in most other economically developed countries. On the other hand, there is sharp disagreement about the proper level and structure of benefits, largely because many people think of social security as a form of insurance. In practice—as well as in principle—social security is a mechanism for transferring financial resources from the working generation to those who cannot work because of age, disability, or dependency status. Evaluation of alternative means of shaping the course of the program requires consideration by policymakers and the public alike of the idea that social security is a tax-transfer system and not an insurance system.

Rationale for Social Security

In an economy where most economic decisions are freely made, why does society choose to override individual choice between private consumption and saving for the risks covered by social security? For simplification, the following discussion of this question is limited to the problem of providing income during retirement, but the analysis can be generalized to the other risks.

NEED FOR A GOVERNMENT PROGRAM

Each person faces daily a multitude of choices about how to spend his income or wealth—how much to spend on food, clothing, entertainment, and other current wants, and how much to set aside for retirement when earned income declines sharply or ceases. In the absence of a compulsory public program, each person makes these decisions on the basis of his own tastes. He invests his savings so as to achieve what he regards as the best mix of yield, liquidity, and safety. In making these decisions, the rational person balances the cost of saving (foregone consumption today) against the benefits of saving (larger income in retirement) and sets aside the amount he considers appropriate. Between his working life and his retirement years, each person should be able to achieve an allocation of consumption that better accords with his tastes than any other allocation.

In this view of the world, social security "distorts" the allocation of consumption over time and, therefore, interferes with individual choice. Many persons may be forced to defer until retirement more of their consumption than they would desire. In the extreme case, an individual with no dependents who is certain he cannot survive to retirement age would "prudently" defer nothing until his retirement. Yet, the government deprives him of the opportunity to dispose currently of the portion of his income claimed by social security taxes. Social security also interferes with the freedom of workers to decide how to invest this portion of their income. If they are skilled investors, they might use these funds to purchase assets with higher yields than the returns which social security implicitly provides. Such individuals would not gain from social security; actually, they may have a lower total income in retirement.[2]

Although the foregoing observations carry considerable weight with anyone who values freedom of individual choice in the making of most economic decisions, there are persuasive reasons why the principle of freedom of individual choice should be modified in the case of provision for retirement. Even the most severe critics of social security will generally concede that voluntary savings cannot yield the poor worker (that is, the worker whose income is close to the amount necessary for subsistence) an income sufficient for retirement.[3] A family which cannot feed and clothe itself adequately from current income cannot be expected to sacrifice present consumption to provide for uncertain consumption needs in retirement.

The problem of poverty does not in itself conclusively negate the argument for individual provision for retirement (even though, as will be observed later, there is reason to presume that

[2] The views described here are expressed forcefully by Milton Friedman in *Capitalism and Freedom* (University of Chicago Press, 1962), pp. 187-89.
[3] *Ibid.*, p. 184.

poor people suffer disadvantages in judging how best to allocate whatever income they may possess).[4] If some are too poor to purchase adequate amounts of any commodity, including savings, a possible solution is to supplement their incomes through transfer payments. When incomes reach whatever level is deemed socially adequate, each person could then determine the amount of retirement protection he wishes to buy. This opens up major issues concerning government policies of income supplementation for all the poor, some of which will be discussed in Chapter VIII. It is sufficient for present purposes to observe that nobody has yet recommended a system of transfer payments that would provide the poor with a sufficient margin for saving, as well as for current consumption.

Furthermore, even individuals who have sufficient earnings during their working lives may have insufficient savings at retirement. Accumulated funds may be used up during prolonged periods of illness or unemployment. People may incorrectly gauge their retirement needs, or personal investments may turn out badly. Alternatively, inflation may erode the purchasing power of savings. Most people would agree that the aged poor should not be left unaided in these circumstances, and that the government bears the ultimate responsibility of providing income support for such unfortunate people. The notion that government should guarantee a minimum level of income support for all the aged on this ground has widespread acceptance.[5] But because "subsistence" is a subjective concept, and because the costs of providing income support for the poor are large, the precise level of support to be guaranteed is a controversial issue.

Once society agrees on a minimum income guarantee, however, a further decision is required on the conditions under which the guarantee will be provided. Take two extreme possibilities: the government either can provide minimum subsistence payments to each eligible person regardless of his other income or can supple-

[4] See pages 62–63.
[5] See, for example, Bert Seidman, "The Case for Higher Social Security Benefits," *AFL-CIO American Federationist*, Vol. 74, No. 1 (January 1967), pp. 1–8; and Chamber of Commerce of the United States, *Poverty: The Sick, Disabled and Aged* (1965), pp. 69–73.

ment his income to the extent that it falls below a stipulated level. The former method—the universal *demogrant*—is followed in Canada and some other countries. The latter method—the *welfare* approach—is exemplified by the public (including old-age) assistance programs in the United States.

Old-age retirement benefits in this country are paid on terms which fall somewhere between these extremes, although they are much closer to those of the universal demogrant than to those of the welfare method. Only persons who have worked long enough to qualify for the required status are eligible to receive benefits. Persons who meet this qualification receive payments without consideration of their income and wealth, unless disqualified by the earnings test. Further, retirement benefits are not intended solely to guarantee a subsistence income to beneficiaries.

The welfare method has one great advantage over the universal demogrant: if the proportion of the aged requiring government help is small and if the administrative costs of determining need are not excessive, the objective of preventing destitution is accomplished at minimum expense by limiting payments to those with demonstrated need.

Nonetheless, one aspect of the welfare method severely limits its acceptability. A welfare program separates people into two groups— those who support themselves and those who require government help.[6] The degree to which this distinction is degrading depends in large measure on the method by which eligibility for benefits is ascertained (that is, the means test). When the method involves detailed probing, and frequently degrading investigations, the number of eligible persons who will even apply for benefits is restricted; this is evident from the history of public assistance. On the other hand, eligibility for veterans' disability pensions is determined on the basis of a simple income affidavit, subject to sample audit, supplied annually by recipients. Neither a sense of alienation nor reticence to apply for benefits has been noted in this program.

The price of rejecting the welfare method of dealing with the

[6] This point is developed fully by Robert M. Ball, "Social Insurance and the Right to Assistance," *Social Service Review*, Vol. 21, No. 3 (September 1947), pp. 331-44.

aged poor is much higher public expenditures to attain similar objectives. This price should be explicitly acknowledged as the cost of avoiding the means test. The historical development of the Old-Age, Survivors, and Disability Insurance (OASDI) program and old-age assistance programs in the United States shows that society has been willing to pay this cost.

Experience with the means test under public assistance has resulted in an unfortunate emotional tendency in the community to reject indiscriminately *any* eligibility test—including the earnings test—for OASDI benefits. It should be kept in mind, however, that the savings to be derived from any device that avoids the problems traditionally associated with the means test, and yet holds down the costs of public assistance, are potentially enormous. The search for such a test, similar perhaps to the test for veterans' disability pensions, continues.

The earnings test, while unpopular, does reduce substantially the cost of social security without raising the problems outlined above. First, since only a minority of persons eligible to receive social security benefits engage in full-time employment and therefore may be subject to the earnings test, benefits are paid to the majority of the aged. Thus, the problem of segregating a minority to be singled out as the needy group does not arise. Second, because the earnings test is by design not an income test, it does not take account of the income from accumulated assets and therefore does not penalize individual savings. For this reason, however, the earnings test results in larger benefit payments to persons with investment income than to those with an equal amount of earned income.

BENEFITS ABOVE POVERTY LEVELS

The argument thus far supports the establishment of a government program that guarantees a minimum of income support for the aged. But this meets only one of the objectives of social security. Many of the characteristic features of social security programs go much further. While minimum benefits under OASDI fall well below the officially defined poverty thresholds (see Chapter V), benefits at the upper end of the scale are above subsistence levels and bear some relationship to the individual's lifetime earnings. A number of arguments have been made in support of such a benefit structure; in combination they add up to an impressive case.

Shortcomings of individual savings decisions. The principle that individuals should bear the responsibility for the decisions that affect their own economic well-being underlies much of the intellectual opposition to social security. Individuals are deemed to be the best judges of their own preferences. That many individuals often make foolish decisions, as recognized after the fact, is not necessarily objectionable; for in learning from their mistakes, they may develop self-reliance and accumulate practical knowledge that will be to their advantage when they make later decisions. The principle of individual responsibility is the basis of the case for free choice about economic matters in general, and there is no strong objection to it in most practical applications.

Decisions about saving for retirement, however, are vastly more difficult than nearly any other economic decision which most people are called upon to make. They depend on anticipation of wants in a much later period—possibly four or five decades. They require an individual to consider his future stream of earnings and other income, and to recognize several possibilities: that he will be married and have a family; that he may be unemployed involuntarily for considerable periods of time; and that he may become disabled or die prematurely. To save intelligently, the individual must also be able to appraise the probable future purchasing power of the income from various assets. Most important of all, the individual may not be aware of his mistakes until he is close to retirement, when the consequences are irremediable.

There is widespread myopia with respect to retirement needs. Empirical evidence shows that most people fail to save enough to prevent catastrophic drops in postretirement income. In 1962, the median amount of investment income of all aged persons was less than $300.[7] Not only do people fail to plan ahead carefully for re-

[7] Lenore A. Epstein and Janet H. Murray, *The Aged Population of the United States: The 1963 Social Security Survey of the Aged*, U.S. Department of Health, Education, and Welfare, Social Security Administration, Office of Research and Statistics, Report No. 19 (1967), Table 3.18, p. 302. As indicated in Chapter II, estimates of the asset holdings of the aged vary greatly and the figure cited above may be understated.

tirement; even in the later years of their working life, many remain unaware of impending retirement needs.[8] Unfortunately, the mistakes of youth are to a large degree irreversible, since it is generally impossible to accumulate in a short period just before retirement sufficient assets to provide adequate retirement income. In an urban, industrial society, government intervention in the saving-consumption decision is needed to help to implement personal preferences over the life cycle. There is nothing inconsistent in the decision to undertake through the political process a course of action which would not be undertaken individually through the market place.[9]

Even if a person plans ahead and gauges accurately his retirement needs under normal conditions, it is questionable that he has sufficient knowledge about other relevant considerations to make the necessary investment decisions. The depression of the 1930's illustrated dramatically the difficulties that even experts encounter in planning their personal investments. The information required for intelligent long-run investment planning is expensive; for small investors, the cost of hiring professional investment counseling is frequently prohibitive. Deficiencies in government economic policy that permit depressions and inflations may sweep away the carefully planned savings of even the most provident and skillful investors. The available evidence suggests that the problem of uncertainty may explain why people do not save enough. Apparently, once a private pension plan has provided a minimum base of retirement income,

[8] According to a field survey taken in 1960, less than half of nonretired persons over 55 years of age were able to estimate the amount of income that they would obtain from their retirement program and from social security. More than two-fifths were unable to estimate their income requirements during retirement. See James N. Morgan, Martin H. David, Wilbur J. Cohen, and Harvey E. Brazer, *Income and Welfare in the United States* (McGraw-Hill, 1962), p. 442. See also the discussion by Derek C. Bok, "Emerging Issues in Social Legislation: Social Security," *Harvard Law Review*, Vol. 80, No. 4 (February 1967), pp. 738–39.

[9] This tendency to make economic decisions politically is reviewed by William J. Baumol, *Welfare Economics and the Theory of the State* (2d ed.; Harvard University Press, 1965). See also Stephen A. Marglin, "The Social Rate of Discount and the Optimal Rate of Investment," *Quarterly Journal of Economics*, Vol. 77, No. 1 (February 1963), pp. 95–111.

most people are willing to save *more* on their own, rather than less.[10]

A person who is saving for retirement generally faces the dilemma of choosing between fixed-yield assets that offer little protection against inflation and other instruments that require financial sophistication or carry considerable risk. Time deposits in commercial banks and other institutions fall into the first category. Yields on such deposits offer small returns after allowance for the steady increase in prices that has occurred since the end of World War II. Common stocks fall into the second category; as the *major* form of savings, they are beyond the sophistication of the majority of the population. Even if such a calamity as the stock-market crash of 1929 is regarded as unlikely to recur, it would be dubious social policy to encourage large-scale investment by individuals in common stocks. Other savings instruments—for example, government savings bonds, cash, annuities—all suffer from one or the other of these shortcomings as vehicles for large amounts of long-term savings.[11]

It has also been pointed out that the decision to provide minimum benefits may weaken individual incentives. A government guarantee of minimum income to the aged may at the same time discourage private saving. Some people may take the opportunity to consume all income in their youth, secure in the knowledge that they can fall back on government support when they retire. In addition, the knowledge that improvident individuals may finance retirement at public expense may discourage saving by people who otherwise would prefer to provide for their own retirement needs rather than depend on government support.[12]

[10] See Phillip Cagan, *The Effect of Pension Plans on Aggregate Saving: Evidence from a Sample Survey,* National Bureau of Economic Research, Occasional Paper 95 (Columbia University Press, 1965); and George Katona, *The Mass Consumption Society* (McGraw-Hill, 1964), Chap. 19.

[11] For a summary of a recent study of this problem, see H. J. Maidenberg, "Personal Finance: Annuities at Age 65," *New York Times,* June 22, 1967, p. 51, col. 5.

[12] This rationale for social insurance is developed by Richard A. Musgrave, "The Role of Social Insurance in an Overall Program for Social Welfare," in William G. Bowen and others (eds.), *The American System of Social Insurance: Its Philosophy, Impact, and Future Development* (McGraw-Hill, 1968).

Private group saving. The foregoing discussion leads to the conclusion that individual saving decisions cannot be relied on to provide a socially acceptable level of income for most of the aged.
This point appears to be widely recognized, and it serves as the
rationale both for a government social security program and for
government subsidies to private *group* saving, principally to the
numerous private pension plans. The United States, for several
reasons, has adopted a mixed approach to the problem of economic
security for the aged; the social security program and private pension plans coexist with surprisingly little friction. The historical
division of responsibilities between the public and private sectors
is not immutable, but in this volume we shall nonetheless assume
that social security will continue to bear the major share of the
total burden. The subject of private pensions—and especially their
relationship to social security—is vast and complex and requires
separate treatment. It may be noted here, however, that, based on
past experience in the United States, the development of private
pension plans in the near future is unlikely to encroach substantially on the present dominant role of social security.[13]

The shortcomings of private pension plans persist despite incentives given by the income tax and other federal statutes for the development of adequate plans by industry. A major incentive is the
provision that allows an employer to deduct from his taxable income the amounts set aside in a pension plan approved by the Internal Revenue Service. The employee is not required to pay income tax until he receives pension benefits.[14]

In 1965, only about 13–14 percent of the total number of persons aged 65 and older received private pension benefits. By 1980,
the proportion will be between one-fourth and one-third.[15] Moreover, the benefits paid are, on the whole, small. Many plans are
not insured, and many are inadequately financed. Vesting is long
delayed, so that workers can change jobs only if they are willing to
surrender pension credits. Given the limited coverage of private

---

[13] See Roger F. Murray, "Economic Aspects of Pensions: A Summary Report," in
Old Age Income Assurance, Pt. V: *Financial Aspects of Pension Plans,* pp. 36–114.

[14] Internal Revenue Code, Secs. 401–04.

[15] Daniel M. Holland, *Private Pension Funds: Projected Growth,* National Bureau
of Economic Research, Occasional Paper 97 (Columbia University Press, 1966), p. 49.

pension plans, the inadequacy of their benefits for many covered workers, and their other shortcomings, they can hardly be expected to provide sufficient earnings protection in old age for more than a minority of the work force for many years to come.[16]

Social costs of inadequate provision for retirement. As pointed out earlier, it becomes difficult to hold to the principle of individual responsibility when the consequences of individual mistakes are extreme. The case for social intervention becomes overwhelming when it is recognized that one individual's mistakes affect not only his own well-being but also that of his family, friends, and local community. Even those believers in individual responsibility who could bear with equanimity the suffering of the individual "responsible" for his own fate find it difficult to justify the suffering of other "innocent" persons.

The social costs that result from inadequate provision for retirement are considerable, even if all the aged are guaranteed a subsistence income. Suppose that a person with an average income during his working years retired without any personal savings. If he were guaranteed only a minimum subsistence income, the fall in his living standard might impose substantial costs on his relatives and friends, and perhaps even his local government. Even under present social security provisions, heavy costs sometimes fall on children or others who feel obligated to support aged persons at living standards close to those which they had enjoyed earlier. To spread such costs, a government program to provide income maintenance related to previous income standards is needed. To guarantee only a minimum, poverty-line level of income is too severe a policy in a society in which maintenance of status depends so critically on the maintenance of previous levels of income.

DETERMINING THE LEVEL OF BENEFITS

To justify the need for some social intervention in providing for retirement is easier than to determine the proper degree of intervention. The case for overriding individual responsibility has less and less force, the higher an individual's income. Take an extreme

[16] See Robert M. Ball, "Policy Issues in Social Security," *Social Security Bulletin*, Vol. 29, No. 6 (June 1966), p. 5.

example: It is not clear why the public should provide retirement benefits based on the full income of a high-level executive whose earnings exceeded $100,000 a year for many years. Some compromise between amounts no greater than those necessary to guarantee subsistence income levels and amounts related to incomes at the upper tail of the distribution is necessary. But the choice within this wide range is a pragmatic decision, on which analytical considerations are of little help. In reaching a decision, the desirability of making public expenditures for other purposes, or of permitting greater private expenditures by nonrecipients, must be weighed against the desirability of pushing up social security benefits for those with relatively high preretirement incomes.

In practice, OASDI benefits above the minimum are determined on the basis of preretirement earnings. The ratio of benefits to such earnings is called the "replacement rate," because benefits are supposed to replace those earnings. The benefit formula is structured so that replacement rates vary inversely with previous earnings; the higher the preretirement earnings, the lower the replacement rate. Thus, while high earners are entitled to larger absolute benefits, their benefits are less relative to previous earnings than are those of low earners.

This structure is roughly consistent with the two objectives discussed earlier. The high replacement rate for the low earner and the minimum benefit can be interpreted as a guarantee of minimum income support for the aged. The larger absolute benefits paid to the high earner can be viewed as an effort to meet the objective of preventing drastic declines in the incomes of the nonindigent aged. This interpretation of the OASDI benefit structure corresponds roughly to the traditional social security concepts of social adequacy and individual equity.

Image of Social Security

Social security is most commonly viewed as a system of mandatory insurance, different in important respects from private insurance, but nonetheless insurance. This analogy shapes the image of social security and thereby influences the prevailing body of beliefs, conceptions, and opinions that govern popular understanding of the system. It has played a major part in developing public support.[17] Many deem it necessary to continue to identify social security as social *insurance* in popular as well as legislative discussions of the system.[18] But this identification impedes progress toward achieving essential modifications of the system, since many of these modifications will move it even further from an insurance system than it is today.[19]

SOURCES OF THE INSURANCE ANALOGY

The nature of individual saving and private insurance is familiar and enjoys considerable respectability and even prestige. The flow of funds between the individual and the ultimate user of these funds is a vital part of a free market economy. Insurance companies are an important intermediary in this process; they channel the savings of many individuals to firms that wish to add to their productive capacity. The rates of return on individual savings reflect in part the productivity of the physical capital they finance. There is, thus, a relationship among the amount an individual saves, the value of his accumulated assets at retirement, the value

[17] See Eveline M. Burns, "Social Insurance in Evolution," *American Economic Review*, Vol. 34, No. 1, Suppl., Pt. 2 (March 1944), pp. 199–211.

[18] See, for example, Ball, "Policy Issues in Social Security," and Robert J. Myers, *Social Insurance and Allied Government Programs* (R. D. Irwin, 1965), p. 8. For the views of a representative of the insurance industry who expresses concern about the analogy between private insurance and social security, see Ray M. Peterson, "Misconceptions and Missing Perceptions of Our Social Security System (Actuarial Anesthesia)," *Transactions of the Society of Actuaries*, Vol. 11 (November 1959), pp. 812–51. Peterson also has collected statements by various public officials which demonstrate the prevalence of the belief in the insurance analogy; see "The Coming Din of Inequity," *Journal of the American Medical Association*, Vol. 176, No. 1 (April 8, 1961), p. 38.

[19] The views in this section have been expressed many times in one form or another by numerous observers. See, for example, Eveline M. Burns, "Private and Social Insurance and the Problem of Social Security," *Analysis of the Social Security System*, Append. II: *Miscellaneous Documents*, Hearings before the House Committee on Ways and Means, 83 Cong. 1 sess. (1954), pp. 1471–79; Barbara Wootton, "The Impact of Income Security upon Individual Freedom," in James E. Russell (ed.), *National Policies for Education, Health and Social Services* (Doubleday, 1955), pp. 386–87; Peterson, "The Coming Din of Inequity"; and Paul A. Samuelson, "Social Security," *Newsweek*, February 13, 1967, p. 88.

of the annuity he can purchase with his previous savings, and the creation of additional physical capital and productive capacity in the economy. If economic resources are fully employed, these relationships are reasonably straightforward.

The analogy between social security and private insurance is suggested in a number of ways. One way is by the very names—social insurance, old-age and survivors insurance, and disability insurance. Payroll taxes are called "contributions" and are paid into trust funds. Benefits to retirees, survivors, and the disabled are based on preretirement earnings and are paid from these trust fund accounts. Since interest is credited on trust fund balances, the trust funds appear to be similar to the reserves of private insurance companies. Each annual report of the trustees of the OASDI provides a computation of "actuarial balance" between prospective benefits and taxes over a period of 75 years.[20] Finally, statements by social security experts often tend to reinforce the parallel to private insurance. The following statement by the present Secretary of Health, Education, and Welfare is representative of many similar writings:

Under Social Security the risk insured against is loss of earnings from work. When earnings stop because of disability, retirement, or death, insurance benefits are paid to partially replace the earned income that has been lost. The loss occasioned by the occurrence of the risks is actuarially evaluated, and contributions sufficient to cover these costs are provided for. Benefits are paid from those contributions on a predetermined basis when and if the risks covered eventuate. The right to these insurance benefits is a legal right enforceable in the courts. These are the characteristics that make Social Security "insurance."[21]

Nevertheless, when the terminology of social security is stripped away and the structure of the system is examined, it becomes clear that the insurance analogy is no longer applicable to the system as it has developed. The following statement by Barbara Wootton expresses this view:

[20] The Committee on Social Insurance Terminology of the American Risk and Insurance Association has suggested a detailed definition of social insurance which lists many of its characteristics. In presenting this definition, the Committee commented that "in addition to possessing some characteristics that it shares with insurance written by private insurers, social insurance possesses many unique characteristics." Bulletin of the Commission on Insurance Terminology of the American Risk and Insurance Association, Vol. 3, No. 1 (January 1968), p. 2.

[21] Wilbur J. Cohen in a letter to the editor, Washington Post, September 1, 1967, p. A 20.

As things are, everybody now recognizes an increasing element of fiction in current insurance schemes. As Americans have cause to realize, the coverage of income-maintenance schemes tends almost irresistibly to expand. But as these schemes become more generalized, their insurance basis becomes more and more illusory; until in cases where, as in Britain, virtually universal coverage has been attained, fiction ousts fact altogether.

At this point, the simple facts of the situation are that benefits on a prescribed scale have been promised, and that funds must be provided to meet them; that is all. In these circumstances, the allocation of precise fractions of contributors' payments to cover particular risks becomes an academic, rather than a genuinely actuarial, exercise. The performance of this exercise in the sacred name of insurance demands, however, elaborate and expensive systems of recording the experience of millions of beneficiaries. These monumental systems are indeed a tribute to the skill and accuracy of the administrators who devise them, and to the ingenuity of the mechanical devices employed in their operation; but are they really necessary, and have they, indeed, any meaning? Is it, in fact, worth maintaining what has become no more than a facade?[22]

SIMPLE ECONOMICS OF SOCIAL SECURITY

In practice, social security is a system of payroll taxes that are levied on current earnings of workers and of benefit payments that are based on past earnings of the insured workers. The relationship between individual contributions (that is, payroll taxes) and benefits received is extremely tenuous. Within any age group, including those persons presently retired and those still working, the values of individual benefits and taxes (appropriately discounted) vary greatly (see Chapter VII and Appendix A). Present beneficiaries as a group receive far larger benefits than those to which the taxes they paid, or that were paid on their behalf, would entitle them. Furthermore, this situation will continue indefinitely—though to a decreasing extent—as long as Congress maintains benefit levels in line with higher wage levels.

Some participants in private group retirement plans also receive far larger benefits than they are entitled to on the basis of their own contributions. This situation is common at the beginning of a system, since full benefits are frequently awarded to workers who

[22] In James E. Russell (ed.), *National Policies for Education, Health and Social Services*, pp. 386–87.

have contributed to the retirement plan for only a fraction of their working lives. This practice gives rise to "past service credits," the liability which future beneficiaries (or the employer) must bear. Past service credits are also generated when a mature retirement system is liberalized, to the extent that those near retirement age partake of liberalized benefits without having had to make commensurate contributions.

The similarities between past service credits in group insurance and OASDI make it tempting to equate the two types of programs. Despite this similarity, the analogy between group insurance and social security is nearly as tenuous as the more general analogy between individual insurance and social security. One obvious difference is that failure of a firm (or an industry) to pay premiums for a group insurance plan terminates the insurance for members of the group, whereas employees covered by OASDI carry with them quarters of coverage even if their original employers go out of business. While some private plans cover workers in one occupation or industry, no practical method has been found to broaden coverage of these plans beyond these limits.[23]

The essential difference between private insurance and social security turns on whether an individual currently in the labor force is paying for the social security benefits of current retired workers and survivors or for his own or his family's future benefits. In individual insurance, each person's premiums are contractually tied to his own and his family's future benefits. No insurance company knows how many new policies it will sell and, therefore, does not know the amount of its future cash inflow from premiums. Consequently, it must charge its present customers enough to create a reserve fund sufficiently large to meet its future financial obligations. The point in question here is the basis for determining *individual* premium levels; for the economy as a whole, of course, pri-

[23] It is sometimes alleged that there is a closer similarity between private disability plans and the disability part of the social security program; nevertheless, the differences are striking. Private disability benefits are usually computed on the same basis as retirement benefits, and rarely allow for the number of dependents —a feature which is basic to the social security program. See Bankers Trust Company, *1965 Study of Industrial Retirement Plans* (Bankers Trust Company, 1965), pp. 17–19, and U.S. Department of Labor, Bureau of Labor Statistics, *Private Pension Plan Benefits*, Bulletin No. 1485 (1966), pp. 33–65.

vate individual insurance is a mechanism for transferring funds from one group of individuals to another.

In social security, the level of payroll taxation is set to defray costs of benefits for the *currently* retired. The social security program (for very good reasons that are discussed in Chapter VIII) has been financed on a virtual cash, or pay-as-you-go, basis in recent years. On balance, the reserves have increased slightly in the last decade. The accumulated reserves are sufficient to cover only approximately one year of benefit payments at present benefit levels. It is true that most social security bills project surpluses in the distant future, but typically these are reduced by later legislation. Each new law contains benefits and taxes that provide a near balance in the trust funds for the first couple of years, with large surpluses projected thereafter. Before the large surpluses are realized, however, benefits are liberalized, new tax rate increases are scheduled for future dates, and the cycle is repeated. In other words, the money which workers currently pay into the funds is not stored up or invested, but is paid out concurrently as benefits to the various categories of current beneficiaries. Workers pay for benefits to eligible nonworkers. The future benefits of present workers, their dependents, or their dependent survivors will be paid in similar fashion out of the contributions of the working population as of some future date.

The differences between private insurance and social security can be further illustrated by comparing the effect of increased premiums in the one system and higher taxes in the other. Typically, private insurance premiums are raised if the insured person wishes to have higher benefits (or improved coverage) in the *future;* payments by the insurer are not affected at the time the premiums are raised. On the other hand, social security taxes are determined by the level of benefits being paid currently and in the years immediately ahead. While future social security beneficiaries are generally assured benefits that are at least as large as those payable today, the current tax level would not be different if Congress decided to pay future beneficiaries larger or smaller benefits than those payable to current retirees so long as the system remains approximately on a pay-as-you-go basis.

The fact that a fund is not accumulated at some explicit interest rate does not imply that people in the OASDI program fail to share in the growth of the economy. Economic and population growth assure to the average individual covered by the program an implicit rate of return in a currently financed social security system, even if tax rates are fixed. If generation 1 pays t percent of its earnings, Y_1, to support retirement benefits under OASDI, its tax burden is tY_1. Generation 2 similarly pays the same t percent of its earnings, Y_2, to support retirement benefits equal to tY_2 for generation 1. If population and the labor force grow at $100i$ percent a year and per capita earnings grow at $100j$ percent a year, then, after a generation of n years, $tY_n = tY_1(1 + i)^n(1 + j)^n$. The implicit interest rate that generation 1 receives on its OASDI taxes under the above assumptions is approximately $100(i + j)$ percent, or the sum of the rates of growth of population and per capita earnings. Generation 2 and all future generations will receive the same implicit return on their taxes as long as population and per capita earnings continue to grow at the same rates.[24]

Unlike a private insurance firm, OASDI does not have to accumulate large reserve funds to meet its future financial commitments. When benefits promised to current workers come due, the funds will be provided out of tax revenues as of that future date. The financial soundness of the social security program depends only on the government's effective power of taxation. The government's ability to collect taxes sufficient to provide adequate social security benefits in the future depends critically on the maintenance of a sound federal tax system in a healthy, growing economy. The faster the rate of economic growth, other things equal,

[24] This point has been made many times, dating back to the basic article by Paul A. Samuelson, "An Exact Consumption-Loan Model of Interest With or Without the Social Contrivance of Money," *Journal of Political Economy*, Vol. 66, No. 6 (December 1958), pp. 467–82. See also Peter A. Diamond, "National Debt in a Neoclassical Growth Model," *American Economic Review*, Vol. 55, No. 5 (December 1965), pp. 1126–50; Henry J. Aaron, "The Social Insurance Paradox," in *Old Age Income Assurance*, Pt. V: *Financial Aspects of Pension Plans*, pp. 15–18 (reprinted from *Canadian Journal of Economics and Political Science*, Vol. 32, No. 3 [August 1966], pp. 371–74); and Earl A. Thompson, "Debt Instruments in Both Macroeconomic Theory and Capital Theory," *American Economic Review*, Vol. 57, No. 5 (December 1967), pp. 1196–1210. See Chapter VII and Appendix A in this volume for calculations that illustrate this point.

the lighter the burden of taxation that will be required to finance any given absolute level of future social security benefits.

If social security taxes were increased enough to result in government budget surpluses that were used to create a reserve fund, the "financial soundness" of the program would hinge on whether the process affected the rate of growth of the economy. If the economy were at, or below, a full employment level of income when social security taxes were increased, and if the government did not take some offsetting action, the result would be a fall in the level of income and a lower rate of growth. If, on the other hand, the government offset the surpluses by expansionary monetary policy or by increased government capital formation, the result would be a higher rate of growth. The point is that the creation of a social security reserve fund is, in the first instance, only a transfer of monetary claims from the private sector to the government. The ultimate effect of this initial monetary transfer depends on many factors; it is certainly incorrect to assume that there is a mechanism that automatically transforms a government reserve fund into an increased stock of productive capital and, therefore, increases the rate of economic growth. These are the relevant considerations to be taken into account in planning and financing a social security program.[25] They raise difficult conceptual and pragmatic problems for overall government economic policy—problems for which the precepts of private insurance are not relevant.

Even the basic issue of whether social security benefits can be regarded as an earned right by recipients can be resolved without appeal to the insurance analogy. If, in return for his own contributions to the social security funds, an individual does not earn a *quid pro quo* in the private insurance sense, he does earn a *quid pro quo* in a sense that is, perhaps, even more fundamental. Since he gives up part of his earnings during his own working life to support the aged during their retirement, he has a strong moral claim to similar support from future working-age generations dur-

---

[25] For a thoughtful discussion of the implications of social security financing see John J. Carroll, *Alternative Methods of Financing Old-Age, Survivors, and Disability Insurance* (University of Michigan, Institute of Public Administration, 1960), Chaps. 1 and 3. See also Chapter VIII, below.

ing his own retirement. Although the benefits are earned rights, and in this sense may be accorded protection under procedural due process, they are not accorded the property protection which funded premium rights would be given.[26] The only assurance that benefits will continue to be paid is congressional unwillingness to repeal the program.

IMPLICATIONS FOR FINANCING

The practical importance of deemphasizing the insurance analogy is not to discredit the concept of social security, but rather to dispel basic misconceptions about certain aspects of the OASDI program. Once the insurance analogy is seen to be inapplicable, the social security "contribution" must be regarded as a tax, not an insurance premium, nor, indeed, as a "contribution" in the generally accepted sense.[27] The financial interchange between generations does not depend on the existence of a particular tax—the payroll tax. It arises because each generation of workers undertakes to support the eligible nonworking population and implicitly expects similar treatment.

Social security payroll taxes are legally earmarked, but they are not *economically* earmarked. Congress and the President jointly have total discretion about which kinds of taxes (including those on payrolls) shall be used to pay for whatever expenditures they jointly conclude are worth making. If Congress should decide to end the earmarking of the payroll tax (but should allocate it to the general fund) and to earmark enough of, say, the corporate income tax to pay for social security benefits, nothing would be changed except some accounting. Or if Congress should decide that all taxes are to be deposited in the general fund and then should appropriate sufficient funds each year to pay for social security, again nothing would be changed. In each case, the taxes paid by individuals and businesses would be unaltered, the amount of

[26] The courts have held that the "noncontractual interest of an employee covered by the Act cannot be soundly analogized to that of the holder of an annuity, whose right to benefits are based on his contractual premium payments." *Flemming* v. *Nestor*, 363 U.S. 603 (1960).

[27] It is regarded as a tax both by the law and the courts. See Sec. 3101 of the Internal Revenue Code and *Flemming* v. *Nestor*, cited in footnote 26.

borrowing by the government from the public would be unaffected, and the expenditures of the federal government would be the same.

Labeling the payroll tax as a contribution is sometimes regarded as a crucial factor in gaining public understanding and acceptance of the program. Presumably, this practice allows individuals to connect the lowering of income now with the promise of benefits later. But much the same effect could be achieved by devices that do not involve a payroll tax. For example, a certain percentage of the individual's income tax, or of his taxable income, could be designated as a tax to support OASDI. The tax could be withheld by the employer and labeled as the "OASDI tax" on the individual's final tax return, very much as is done today with the payroll tax on the employee's W-2 withholding form. The psychological connection between the tax and promised benefits would remain intact under this alternative, without resort to the payroll tax.[28]

The basic point that emerges from the foregoing observations is that payroll tax receipts are part of the total revenues of the federal government, and that the payroll tax should be evaluated on its merits as a source of taxes. This means that the desirability of changes in payroll taxes should be weighed against changes in other taxes and that social security benefits should be financed by the methods which are most equitable and most conducive to economic growth and efficiency.

In place of the insurance analogy, social security should be regarded as an institutionalized compact between the working and nonworking generations, a compact that is continually renewed and strengthened by every amendment to the original Social Security Act.[29] When viewed in this light, a social security program has the eminently desirable function of forcing upon society a decision at each point of time on the appropriate division of income and

[28] See Chapter VIII for a detailed discussion of alternative methods of raising social security revenue.
[29] The outstanding statement of this view of social security is by Paul A. Samuelson in "An Exact Consumption-Loan Model." The best introduction to social security for the serious student is the entire Samuelson article and the later exchange between Samuelson and Abba P. Lerner concerning some points raised by the article, in "Consumption-Loan Interest and Money," "Reply," and "Rejoinder," *Journal of Political Economy*, Vol. 67, No. 5 (October 1959), pp. 512–25.

consumption between workers (the young) and nonworkers (the old, survivors, and disabled). Workers and nonworkers alike participate in the democratic process that shapes this vital distributional decision. The social security system is the mechanism by which society settles the issue of intergenerational (worker-nonworker) income distribution through the political process rather than leaving its resolution to private decisions and the market.

This last point is more general than the narrow issue of preventing poverty among the aged. Consider two workers, A and B, who always earned at least the maximum taxable wage and thus qualify for the maximum benefit; however, A is married to a woman aged 65 or older while B is unmarried. The benefit paid to A (and his wife) is 50 percent greater, while they are both living, than the benefit paid to B; and a widow's benefit is payable after A's death, while only a small lump-sum payment is paid to B's survivors (as it is also to A's), despite the fact that, by assumption, each had equal earnings before retirement and the question of poverty is not at issue. The wife's benefit is an extremely important redistributional device that has no connection with the problem of poverty. In short, the benefit structure under OASDI is, like the system of personal exemptions under the personal income tax, a means by which society can adjust the distribution of income that results from the workings of the private market for nonmarket, welfare considerations, such as family size.[30]

Finally, the foregoing discussion strongly suggests that there is little basis for according autonomy to the social security system in the federal budget. This has been recognized by the changes incorporated in the budget for fiscal year 1969—following recommendations by the President's Commission on Budget Concepts[31]—which combined trust funds and other federal expenditures and revenues in a single budget. Social security today is too intimately linked on both the benefit and tax sides with the total government budget for fiscal autonomy to make sense. The integration of OASDI into government budget planning is a necessary step in rationalizing the processes for attaining the objectives of social security.

[30] Unfortunately, these same considerations have been completely ignored on the tax side of OASDI. See Chapter VIII.

[31] *Report of the President's Commission on Budget Concepts* (October 1967), esp. Chap. 3.

Summary

The case for social security rests on a solid basis. Given widely accepted humanitarian values and a few fundamental facts about economic behavior in our culture, it follows that the government should maintain and continually strengthen the social security system to protect individuals from severe declines in living standards in retirement and against other risks. To serve the purposes which justify its creation, the system should be financed by the best methods available to the government at any given time; it should guarantee minimum benefits sufficient to keep beneficiaries out of poverty; and it should pay benefits above the minimum level determined, at least in part, by the previous income or earnings experiences of beneficiaries.

Two basic features of the social security system which are widely approved and help to explain the public's acceptance of the system as a desirable permanent public institution can be traced to the analogy with private insurance. These features are the belief that benefits are earned rights to which no stigma attaches, and that they depend at least in part on past earnings of participants. The insurance analogy is misleading, however, in fundamental respects. On the assumption that social security will continue to be financed approximately on a current basis, the currently employed will always be taxed enough to pay for the benefits of those who are retired. The practical importance of distinguishing between social security and private insurance is that it forces the major elements of the social security system—taxes and benefits—to be considered in the appropriate perspective. Benefits of the currently retired need not, and should not, depend on their past taxes; they should be based on decisions reached by democratic political processes as to how much of the nation's total income should be allocated for retirement, disability, and survivor benefits. Similarly, the tax should not be regarded as an insurance premium, but rather as a financing mechanism—to be judged on its own merits—for a large, essential government program. Decisions about social security taxes and benefits should be recognized as being closely interdependent with other tax and benefit decisions in the federal budget.

CHAPTER V

The Benefit Structure

The Old-Age, Survivors, and Disability Insurance (OASDI) benefit structure today expresses the dual objectives of social security.
Reflecting the concern about poverty, a minimum benefit is paid
to all fully insured persons regardless of their previous earnings
histories. Reflecting the concern about sharp drops in income for
families at all income levels, wage-related benefits above minimum
benefits are paid to moderate the impact of decreased earnings
after the retirement, death, or disability of the head of the household. As suggested in Chapter IV, families with similar living
standards before such contingencies occur should receive benefits
that assure them roughly equal—though lower—standards after the
contingencies have occurred. Since many factors other than earnings help to determine living standards, benefits should depend
not only on wages and self-employment income but also on whether
the beneficiary is a retired worker or a survivor, whether he is
above or below a certain age, whether he has dependents and, if
so, how many. However, the present benefit structure takes these
factors into account imperfectly. The result is that families enjoy-
ing identical living standards while the head is working may have
very different living standards after his retirement, death, or disability.

The Benefit Formula

Benefits are computed on the basis of a complex formula that de-
termines a basic pension or primary insurance amount (PIA).

The formula has three key features. First, a worker with a low earnings history or with small earnings under the OASDI system, who has achieved fully insured status,[1] receives a minimum benefit of $55 a month if he retires at age 65 ($82.50 if he is married and his wife is over age 65); if he retires before age 65, the benefit is reduced by up to 20 percent. A transitionally insured worker or a noninsured worker who attained age 72 before 1968 receives $40 a month if single; if married and his wife is over age 72 and also eligible, he receives $60. Second, a worker with average monthly earnings (AME) above the minimum—between $74 and $650 a month under the 1967 amendments to the Social Security Act—receives benefits that are graduated with respect to earnings. Third, earnings in excess of the taxable earnings maximum are ignored in computing benefits. In determining a family's benefit the PIA is reduced or increased, depending on age, sex, or family status of the beneficiary. Total family benefits are subject to maxima which are also based on the PIA.

The benefits at various earnings histories for various types of households are shown in Appendix Table G-5. The corresponding replacement rates are given in Chart V-1.

THE BENEFICIARY UNIT

The basic consumption unit in the economy is the household. Although circumstances vary, most income of every household member enters into the determination of the household's standard of living. If there is more than one earner, the family's living standard does not depend solely on the earnings of the head of the household. Further, for a given disposable income, the family's living standard varies inversely with the number of family members. The relationship of economic welfare to family size is widely recognized. The personal income tax, for example, would be less equitable if tax burdens were computed without regard to the number of dependents of the taxpayer.[2] The definition of the benefi-

[1] For descriptions of types of insured status, see Chapter III, pp. 39–40.

[2] In the United States the taxpayer unit is actually an individual unit, but the law encourages the filing of joint returns by married couples through the income-splitting device. For the issues raised by income-splitting, see Joseph A. Pechman, *Federal Tax Policy* (Brookings Institution, 1966), pp. 81–84.

Chart V-1. *Illustrative OASDI Replacement Rates*[a] *under the 1967 Amendments to the Social Security Act*

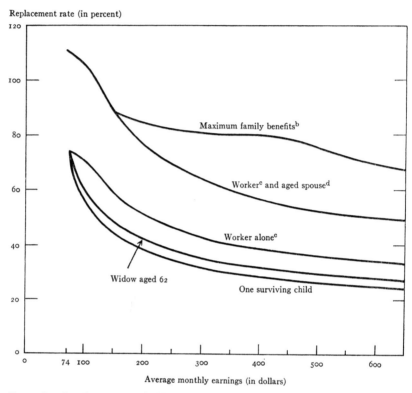

Replacement rate (in percent)

Average monthly earnings (in dollars)

Source: Based on data in Appendix Table G-5.

a. OASDI monthly benefit awards as a percentage of the average monthly earnings of the insured workers.

b. This rate is also applicable to a nonaged widow with two or more children.

c. Retired at age 65 or over, or disabled.

d. Aged 65 or over.

ciary unit is as crucial to the equitable operation of social security as the definition of the tax unit is for income taxation.

Social security has two basic units—one for payroll tax purposes and one for benefit purposes—neither of which is the household. For tax purposes, the basic unit is the worker without regard to his family status or the earnings and tax burdens of other family members. Benefits also depend on the earnings record of the individual retired worker, but there are discounts or increments for widows, dependent children, and wives. Thus the relationship of benefits to *family* earnings histories varies greatly.

Consider the common case of a family unit that includes a working wife. Under the present benefit formula, the benefits based on the wife's earnings record do not add to family retirement income unless they exceed 50 percent of her husband's benefits. For example, a man retiring at age 65 with an AME of $500 has a PIA of $177.50.[3] He is entitled to benefits of $266.25—$177.50 plus $88.75 —if his wife is also aged 65 or older. If his wife also worked and is fully insured, her earnings record adds nothing to the family's benefits unless her AME exceeds $150, the amount above which a single person's benefits exceed $88.75. If her earnings exceed that amount, the family's benefit will be computed as if there were two single workers. Thus, if she earned the same amount as her husband, total family benefits would be $355, only $88.75, or one-third, more than the family's total benefit if she had not worked.

The same problem may be illustrated by comparing the treatment of two married couples with equal total earnings before retirement. If in couple A only the husband worked, while in couple B both spouses worked, A usually receives a larger retirement benefit than B under the present benefit formula. Suppose the husband in A had an AME of $500, while each spouse in B had an AME of $250. If both husband and wife are 65 years of age at retirement, A's monthly benefit is $266.25 while the sum of B's two benefits is only $230.00, a difference of $36.25 a month; thus A's benefit is almost 16 percent more than B's.

Such treatment of the family with a working wife is aggravated by the fact that OASDI regards husbands and wives as separate *taxable* units. If the total earnings of the husband and wife are greater than the taxable maximum, the total tax paid by the couple is greater than that paid by a family with the same earnings for a single worker.[4]

Much the same problem arises in relation to survivor benefits. If family A consists of a father with an AME of $275, a working wife with an AME of $275, and two dependent children, and if both parents are killed in an automobile accident, the survivor

[3] Actually there are no persons in 1968 with AME's of $500 because there has not been time for the increases in maximum taxable earnings under the 1965 and 1967 amendments to be fully reflected in workers' AME's.

[4] See Chapter IX for a discussion of the appropriate tax treatment of married couples under a social security system.

benefits for the children are $181.50. If family B is exactly like A in every respect except that the entire $550 of monthly income was earned by the father, the children receive $284.90 on the death of the parents. Thus, A and B are treated very differently, despite the fact that the family incomes and previous living standards had been roughly equivalent.

Such outcomes are inconsistent with the objectives of social security; they can be eliminated if benefits are based on total family earnings, which provide the best index of a family's preretirement standard of living. Although the use of family earnings, rather than the earnings of one family member, in computing benefits would create some anomalies of its own (as will be noted below), these would be much less serious than those which arise under present procedures.

HOUSEHOLD INCOME, LIVING STANDARDS, AND
REPLACEMENT RATES

While two cannot live as cheaply as one, a married couple can live much more cheaply than two single people. Living alone is relatively inefficient, because many commodities, such as housing, appliances, and automobiles, can be consumed jointly by several household members. Moreover, there is considerable evidence that income needs differ sharply over the life cycle. Five estimates of the relative incomes required to provide families of different size and composition with equivalent living standards are given in Table v-1. Although the results of these estimates differ in detail,[5] they show certain broad patterns:

1) The additional income necessary to sustain standards of living as a family increases in size averages roughly 30 percent of the income of a single person, for each additional member;

2) Income needs of households headed by females are roughly the same as those of households headed by males; and

3) Six-person families need almost three times the income required by a single person to achieve a given living standard.

[5] There are difficult conceptual and statistical problems in making such estimates. For a discussion of these problems, see Mollie Orshansky, "Recounting the Poor—A Five-Year Review," *Social Security Bulletin*, Vol. 29, No. 4 (April 1966), pp. 22–23.

Table v-1. *Indexes of OASDI Benefits and of Income Required To Provide Families of Different Sizes with Equivalent Living Standards*

(Two-person family = 100)

Family Composition	OASDI Benefits (1968)	Bureau of Labor Statistics (1960)	Social Security Administration (1966)		Institute for Defense Analyses (1960)	Bureau of the Census (1950)
			Poverty	Low Income		
One person		76	77	70	n.a.	n.a.
Aged male	67		75	67		
Aged female	55 or 67[c]		74	66		
Nonaged male	—		83	75		
Two persons[b]		100	100	100	100	100
Aged, male head	100		93	94		
Nonaged, male head	—		104	104		
Nonaged, female head	100		100	98		
Three persons[b]		132	123	120	128	137
Female head	100–143[d]		119	117		
Four persons[b]		152	158	152	156	161
Female head	100–143[d]		157	149		
Five persons[b]		182	186	178	181	185
Female head	100–143[d]		184	174		
Six persons[b]		208	209	200	n.a.	n.a.
Female head	100–143[d]		208	196		

Sources: Mollie Orshansky, *Who Was Poor in 1966*, U.S. Department of Health, Education, and Welfare, Social Security Administration, Office of Research and Statistics, Note No. 23 (December 6, 1967), Table 1; Elliot Wetzler, *Determination of Poverty Lines and Equivalent Welfare*, Institute for Defense Analyses, Economic and Political Studies Division (September 1966), p. 8.
n.a. Not available.
a. For nonfarm families.
b. Average for all families of this size.
c. For widows, 55 percent; for single retirees, 67 percent.
d. Range taking into account the family maximum.

The OASDI benefit schedule in 1968 cannot be reconciled with these relationships in a number of respects.

First, widows receive lower benefits than retired workers. The widow's benefit, first introduced in 1939, remained at 75 percent of the PIA until 1961, when it was raised to 82.5 percent. In 1956, it was made payable at age 62, and in 1965, at age 60, with a permanent reduction of 6⅔ percent for each year under age 62. Two factors probably account for the failure to pay widows 100 percent of PIA: (1) the change would impose long-run costs equivalent to a 3 percent across-the-board increase in benefits;[6] and (2) it is considered unfair to working wives to give full benefits to widows who have not themselves paid payroll taxes or have paid very little during their entire lives.

Abolition of the widow's "discount"—one of the major deficiencies in the benefit structure—deserves high priority. None of the five estimates of the income needs of households found that women required significantly less income than men to achieve a given living standard (Table v-1). Widows receive lower incomes, possess fewer assets, and are even less capable of supplementing their benefits with earnings than are other retired persons. As a welfare measure, an increase in the widow's benefit to a full 100 percent of PIA would more effectively aid the poor, per dollar of added cost, than any other change in the system, including a higher minimum benefit. The nonpayment of taxes by the widow is clearly not a determining factor, since she already receives 82.5 percent of the standard benefit on the basis of her husband's earnings. Moreover, conversion of the benefit unit to a family basis would give the working wife added benefits to the extent that she augmented the past family earnings up to the maximum earnings level.

Second, single retirees are treated far less generously than couples. The justification for the couple's "bonus" is the same as the justification for a replacement rate that is higher for workers who had low earnings than it is for those who had high earnings. On a given earnings history, a married couple had lower living standards than a single person. The lower their standard of living before retirement, the less the couple was able to save for its retirement and the more burdensome is any given decline in income. These considerations justify a higher replacement rate for couples than for single retirees, but the present formula is incorrectly com-

[6] Unless otherwise noted, this and other estimates in this volume were prepared by the authors.

puted in principle and provides a benefit for couples that is much too large.

Table v-2 shows the benefits of couples and single persons under the present formula and what they would be if the benefit formula were based on the assumption that couples require 30 to 50 percent more income than do single persons to achieve a given living standard. The table takes as given the replacement rate for couples at an AME 30 percent or 50 percent greater than the AME's shown in the first column. It is clear that single persons today receive lower replacement rates than do couples who had equivalent preretirement income levels.

Table v-2. *Comparison of Single Workers' Benefits under the 1967 Amendments to the Social Security Act and Benefits Based on Alternative Assumptions of Income Needs Relative to Those of Couples*

(In dollars)

Average Monthly Earnings	Benefits under the 1967 Amendments		Equivalent Benefits for Single Workers under Two Assumptions of Single Workers' Income Needs Relative to Those of Couples[a]	
	Couples	Single workers	67 percent[b]	77 percent[b]
150	132.60	88.40	107.70	115.96
250	172.50	115.00	146.40	154.95
350	210.60	140.40	184.20	193.02
450	247.50	165.00	215.32[c]	230.76[c]
550	284.90	189.90	215.32[c]	248.44[c]
650	323.00	218.00	215.32[c]	248.44[c]

a. A couple's average monthly earnings (AME) were calculated by increasing each AME shown by (1) 30 percent and (2) 50 percent, the additional income requirements assumed for a couple over a single worker. Benefits were then determined for each couple's AME from the social security benefit table under the 1967 amendments (Public Law 90-248, 90 Cong., H.R. 12080, January 2, 1968, *An Act* [1968], pp. 4–6), and these were divided by the corresponding couple's AME to obtain the couple's replacement rate. The replacement rates were applied to the corresponding single worker's AME to determine his equivalent benefit.

b. The 67 percent implies that a couple requires 50 percent more income to attain the same standard of living as a single person; 77 percent implies a couple needs 30 percent more income.

c. These figures are not based on the strict social security concept of replacement rate, which is the ratio of a worker's monthly benefits to his average monthly *covered* earnings. For example, an income of $715 for a couple is equivalent to an income of $550 for a single person (assuming that a couple requires 30 percent more income to maintain an equivalent standard of living). The maximum level of earnings for social security benefit calculations is $650, yielding a couple's benefit of $323 for all monthly earnings of $650 or more. Calculating the replacement ratio for the couple earning $715 as the ratio $323/$715 is not in keeping with the social security concept since $715 exceeds maximum *covered* earnings. The single worker's benefit of $248.44 is derived by multiplying his equivalent earnings of $550 by this replacement rate ($323/$715).

For example, with an AME of $350, a single worker today receives $140.40 a month and a couple receives $210.60. If couples required 30 percent more income to achieve the same standard of living as a single person, a couple with an income of $455 would enjoy the same living standard as a single person could with an income of $350. On an AME of $455, the couple would receive a benefit of $250.95, or 55.15 percent of the AME. Applying this factor to the single worker's AME of $350 yields a benefit of $193.02, or $52.62 more than the single retiree actually receives under the 1967 amendments.[7] If an income differential of as much as 50 percent in favor of the couple is deemed necessary, the benefit of the single retiree on the basis of the same replacement rate is too low by $43.80 a month.

Third, on the assumption that each additional person in a household requires an increase of 30 percent of the income of a single person to maintain equivalent living standards, the 75 percent bonus for dependents is too generous and the benefits for large surviving families are inadequate. Large families do not fare as well as small families, because generally the family maximum prevents survivor families of more than three persons from receiving benefits larger than those granted to families of three.[8] The family maximum survivor benefit of $434.40 payable on the 1968 maximum AME of $650 is below the poverty threshold for families of seven or more, while the same amount is twice the poverty threshold for families of three persons. Moreover, in large surviving families, the surviving wife is unlikely to earn income outside of the home, nor are children likely to contribute much to household resources. The limitation on maximum family benefits means that the benefits for large families are less adequate, relative to preretirement living standards, than those for single beneficiaries or for beneficiaries

[7] The same anomaly may be shown in another way. A couple receives a benefit of $210.60 on an AME of $350. This replacement rate is 60.2 percent. A single worker receives a smaller replacement rate if his earnings exceed $147, an income level at which the single worker would have had a far lower standard of living than would the couple with an income of $350.

[8] The family maximum rises from 150 percent of the basic retirement benefit for earnings up to $178 a month to 216 percent for earnings of $432–$436 and then declines to 199 percent at the highest taxable earnings levels. Relative to earnings, the family maximum varies from 107 percent at $100 a month to 67 percent at $650 a month (see Appendix Table G-5).

with only one or two children who may be able to accept employment outside the home. Clearly, the family maximum should not lower the living standards of large families relatively more than it lowers the standards of small families.[9]

SUGGESTED MODIFICATIONS OF THE TREATMENT OF FAMILIES AND SINGLE PERSONS

Many of the foregoing problems could be corrected by making the following relatively modest changes in the treatment of families and single persons.

First, benefits could be based on the earnings of the basic economic unit, the family. This means that earnings of both husband and wife would be added together for benefit computation purposes. (As a practical matter, the earnings of children and other dependent relatives may be disregarded.) Total earnings of the couple, below the taxable maximum, would then be the base for computing benefits. The administrative problems involved in carrying out this change are well within the present capabilities of the Social Security Administration.

Second, the same increment payable to the wife of a retired worker should also be payable for each additional dependent person in a household receiving survivor benefits. The findings of budget studies would justify larger benefits to survivors to reflect the greater cost of living for younger persons. The case for such differentiation is reinforced by the fact that medical expenses for aged persons are now subsidized under Medicare, which removes from their budgets the only major expenditure likely to be larger than the corresponding expenditure in the younger persons' budgets.

Third, the benefits of single workers should be raised substantially, relative to those of married couples. A smaller increment than 50 percent is justified because, at any given earnings level, single persons now receive smaller benefits relative to their previous standard of living than do married couples. As indicated in

[9] This problem cannot be solved, however, apart from the question of the proper size of dependents' benefits relative to benefits of single retirees in general, which is considered on pages 89–91.

the next section, family benefits should be larger than single persons' benefits by about $30 a month for each dependent of the head of household.

The approach suggested here would be straightforward if family status did not change before and after people became eligible for benefits. But family status does change in certain predictable patterns. Children mature and leave home, often during those years of earnings that are used in benefit computations. Death of one spouse may occur just before retirement of the other. In such cases, previous income or earnings may not be an adequate index of living standards for the calculation of benefits. Use of family earnings in determining benefits would give rise to some problems not encountered under the present system, but these could be solved with relative ease. Most of the problems derive from changes in the size of the family unit shortly before beneficiary status is obtained.

For example, consider (a) two childless couples, both with only one worker and identical wage histories, one couple having married at age 21, the other at age 65, or (b) two single aged retirees with identical wage histories, but one of whom was a bachelor while the other became a widower on his 65th birthday. In each case, the family units would be of the same size at time of eligibility, but of differing sizes during the years in which the wage histories were acquired and customary living standards experienced. For the sake of simplicity these complications could well be ignored without serious violence to the principle that benefits should be related to preretirement living standards. If complete consistency were sought, benefits in case (a) could be based on an average of each of the spouses' preretirement incomes, if marriage took place within, say, five years before eligibility; in case (b), the widower might be paid a smaller benefit so that the parallel between benefits and preretirement living standards would be retained.

Such anomalies can occur under the present benefit formula. They cause no difficulty because the whole question of the relationship between benefits and *family* living standards before retirement is largely ignored, with one exception. A divorced widow who had been married more than 20 years is eligible for a widow's benefit based on her former husband's earnings upon reaching retirement age. Additional rules of this kind would be needed if the basic unit under social security were changed from the individual to the family. The changes proposed above would greatly improve the equity of the benefit structure. They merit adoption even if it is necessary to resolve in a pragmatic way the problems for the minority of cases in which a change in family status warrants modification of the basic rules.

CALCULATING BENEFIT INCREMENTS FOR FAMILY MEMBERS

There would be no place for extra benefits for spouses or other dependents in a purely wage-related social security system. The extra payments that are being made on behalf of family members reflect the fact that needs increase with family size. However, the 50 percent increment for spouses and the 75 percent increment for dependent children bear no relationship to the differences in need.

To derive the benefit structures suggested by Table v-2, the increments for each family member should be about 30 percent of the income of a single person. Assume that the monthly social security benefit of a single person consists of a minimum amount, $90, plus 30 percent of his average monthly earnings, E. Then, the benefits of the single person, B_1, and of the married couple, B_2, would be as follows:

$$B_1 = \$90 + 0.3E$$
$$B_2 = \$90 + 0.3E + \$27$$

and each additional family member would add another $27 to the monthly benefit.[10] To assure adequate benefits for persons with

---

[10] Let M be the minimum amount and the wage-related portion of the benefit be $100p$ percent of E. The benefit level for a single worker would be

$$(1) \qquad B_1 = M + pE.$$

If a couple requires $100c$ percent more income than a single person to attain an equal living standard, the benefit required for couples is

$$(2) \qquad B_2 = \left[M + p\left(\frac{E}{1+c}\right)\right](1+c) = M(1+c) + pE.$$

The difference between the couple's and the single person's benefits on a given wage history is low wage histories, it might be assumed that everyone had earnings of at least $100. On this assumption the minimum monthly benefit for a single person would be $120 ($90 + 0.3 × $100), the minimum benefit for a couple would be $147, and so on.

While benefits for nonaged survivors should also be related to standards of living before eligibility, there is no reason to presume that the relationship should be the same as for the aged.[11] Since the aged typically require somewhat less income than the young, apart from medical expenses now partially covered by Medicare, it is arguable that a different and higher minimum and perhaps a higher replacement rate should be used in computing benefits for nonaged survivors.

More complicated benefit formulas than the ones presented above would, of course, yield more complicated relationships among benefits. If the fraction used to compute the wage related portion of benefits should *rise* with the amount of earnings, the increment

$$(3) \qquad B_2 - B_1 = [M(1 + c) + pE] - (M + pE) = cM.$$

Thus, if $M = \$90$, and $c = 0.3$, $cM = \$27$.

For a family of $n + 1$ persons, that is, the family head plus n dependents,

$$(4) \qquad B_{n+1} = \left[M + p \left(\frac{E}{1 + cn} \right) \right] (1 + cn) = M(1 + cn) + pE$$

and

$$(5) \qquad B_{n+1} - B_1 = [M(1 + cn) + pE] - (M + pE) = ncM.$$

Thus the difference between the single person's benefit and the family benefit is n times $27.

[11] Whatever minimum and replacement rate might be used, equation (4) in footnote 10 would need to be modified to compute *survivor* benefits. If a nonaged worker dies, his earnings base should be reduced for purposes of the benefit computation in order to maintain the appropriate relationship between living standards for the survivors before and after the death of the worker. Thus, if a worker had average earnings, E^*, the earnings level for the survivor benefit computation, E, should be

$$(6) \qquad E = \left[\frac{1 + n(c)}{1 + (n + 1)(c)} \right] E^*$$

where n is the number of *survivors*. Thus, if the head of a family of four died with average earnings (E^*) of $400 a month and $c = 0.3$, the earnings used in benefit computation, E, should be

$$E = \frac{1 + 3(0.3)}{1 + 4(0.3)} \times \$400 = \frac{1.9}{2.2} \times \$400 = \$345.45.$$

for couples would *decline* in absolute amount as earnings rose. Conversely, if the fraction used to compute the wage-related portion of benefits should *fall* as earnings rose (as under the present law), the dollar increment for couples would *rise* with increasing earnings.[12]

Under the 1967 amendments, the 50 percent bonus for couples results in differentials between the single person's and couple's benefits ranging from $27.50 at the lowest earnings level to $105 at the highest.[13] Such differentials cannot be rationalized in terms of the standard of living objective which we have been emphasizing.

The Minimum Benefit

The minimum benefit, which is paid to all fully insured workers and their dependents, is justified on the humanitarian ground that benefits should not fall below certain levels. Nevertheless, the minimum benefit is 42 percent of the poverty threshold as officially defined by the Social Security Administration for a single retired worker (50 percent for a married couple). At this level, the minimum is inadequate for any aged person or surviving family lacking other sources of support (Chart v-2).

[12] This may be shown by assuming that $p = f(E)$ and $E' = E/(1+c)$. Then,

(1a) $$B_1 = M + f(E)E$$

(2a) $$B_2 = \left[M + f(E') \frac{E}{1+c} \right] (1 + c)$$

(3a) $$B_2 - B_1 = cM + E[f(E') - f(E)].$$

Since the expression in brackets on the right hand side of (3a) is positive if p declines with earnings, the dollar increment for couples rises as earnings rise.

[13] An example of a benefit formula which reproduces this result is as follows:

(1b) $$B_1 = M + pE$$

(2b) $$B_2 = \left[M + \frac{E}{1+c} (p + 0.1) \right] (1 + c)$$

(3b) $$B_2 - B_1 = cM + 0.1E.$$

With $M = \$90$ and $c = 0.3$, the differential would begin at $37 a month if $E = \$100$ a month and rise to $92 at the maximum of $E = \$650$. Thus, even on this basis the bonus of 50 percent for a couple is somewhat too liberal for high-earnings levels and not liberal enough at the lowest levels.

Chart V-2. *Minimum Social Security Benefits under the 1967 Amendments to the Social Security Act Compared with Poverty-Level Incomes*

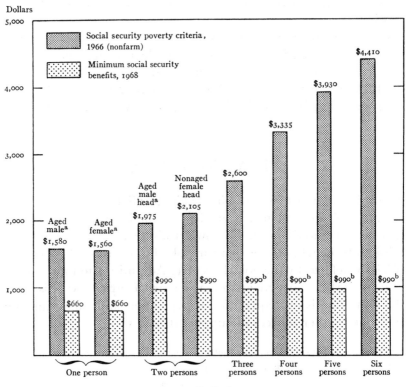

Dollars

Sources: Poverty criteria: Mollie Orshansky, *Who Was Poor in 1966*, U.S. Department of Health, Education, and Welfare, Social Security Administration, Office of Research and Statistics, Note No. 23 (December 6, 1967), Table 1. Minimum benefits: based on data in Appendix Table G-5.
a. Aged 65 or over.
b. No benefits for additional dependents are paid because of the family maximum.

If minimum and low benefits were paid exclusively to aged households with little or no other money income, the case for sharply increasing the minimum would be overwhelming. In the absence of an income test, however, many beneficiaries receive minimum or low benefits because they have had limited attachment to occupations covered by social security, not because they have had low lifetime earnings. Former employees of federal, state, and local governments can enter covered employment late in life and acquire insured status sufficient to entitle them to low or minimum benefits.[14] Nevertheless, it remains true that poverty and low incomes are more frequent among recipients of low or minimum benefits than among recipients of larger benefits.[15] Furthermore, the "leakage" of minimum benefits to groups who have other pension protection (for example, retired government employees) arises largely because of the existence of more than one major *public* retirement system. This problem would diminish with a consolidation of various public pension programs, which is discussed later in this chapter.

The current cost of an increase in the minimum benefit will diminish over time even without any changes in the law, since future retirees will have longer and higher wage histories than did past retirees. Simultaneously, the proportion of those receiving low or minimum benefits who are retired government employees, or others not likely to be poor, will tend to rise. But at least for the near future, the bulk of the cost of an increase in the minimum would be incurred to pay increased benefits for those who have little outside income. Furthermore, consolidation of other public programs with OASDI would prevent much of the leakage.

The need for any minimum benefit would be greatly reduced, or would be eliminated, if there were some method outside the social security system by which the aged poor (and, for that matter, the nonaged poor) could be assured adequate income without the imposition of degrading application procedures. The old-age assistance program is today the only major alternative for providing aid to the aged poor, but payments under it are far from adequate. Moreover, the stringent eligibility requirements in many states exclude a majority of the aged poor. If the old-age assistance program were substantially revised and liberalized, or if a negative income tax were enacted, the objective of reducing poverty among the aged could be achieved at one-half, or less, of the cost of accomplishing this objective through social security. But until enactment of a comprehensive reform of public assistance or of a nega-

[14] Some persons from other countries also gain entitlement to the minimum benefits after brief working experience in the United States.

[15] The characteristics of persons entitled to minimum benefits are discussed by Lenore A. Epstein, "Workers Entitled to Minimum Retirement Benefits Under OASDHI," *Social Security Bulletin*, Vol. 30, No. 3 (March 1967), pp. 3–13.

tive income tax, social security planning will have to proceed on the assumption that old-age assistance will continue to be inadequate.[16]

In these circumstances, increases in minimum social security benefits—and abolition of the widow's discount—should be given high priority.[17] The poverty threshold for 1966, as defined by the Social Security Administration, is $1,580 a year for an aged man and $1,975 for two people. Poverty thus defined would be eliminated among social security beneficiaries if the minimum benefit were $132 a month for all single persons and $165 a month for aged couples. Such minimum incomes should be regarded as a long-run goal for all groups in the population; the means of achieving this goal for the aged involve considerations—to be discussed below, particularly in the section "Social Security and Other Transfer Payment Programs" in this chapter—other than the minimum benefit under social security alone.

Maximum Covered Earnings in Benefit Computation

When benefits under OASDI are computed, earnings in excess of $7,800 a year are ignored for years after 1967. While virtually everyone would agree that payment of benefits on the basis of very high earnings would serve no valid social purpose, there is considerable disagreement about the maximum income level on which benefits should be based.

The view has been expressed that the cutoff point should be increased to $15,000 and then raised at the rate by which the average money wage level increases.[18] This position is advocated on the ground that in 1939 the $3,000 maximum then in effect covered

[16] See Chapter VIII for a discussion of the implications of a negative income tax for social security.

[17] Roughly one-half to three-fifths of the added outlays resulting from increases of up to $30 a month in the minimum benefit would go to the poor; a smaller fraction of larger increases would go to them.

[18] This position has been taken by a number of congressmen and by officials of the labor movement. See, for example, S. 1009 (90 Cong. 1 sess., 1967) introduced by Robert F. Kennedy and ten other senators; and a letter to the editor by Melvin A. Glasser, Director, Social Security Department, United Auto Workers, "Social Security Tax a Burden on Poor," in *New York Times*, January 11, 1968, p. 36C.

92.3 percent of all wages, while in recent years only 75 to 80 percent of all wages have been taxable.[19] From this it is inferred that recent maximum taxable earnings have been too low. This argument is valid only if it can be shown that the relative level of the wage base in 1939 should set the standard for all time.

In fact, there is no objective basis for deciding how high the maximum earnings should go, whether or not there is a linkage between benefits and taxes for purposes of social security. As indicated in Chapter IV, the decision is a matter of judgment on which honest men are likely to differ. However, a number of factors should be taken into account.

First, society's interest in moderating the impact of reductions in earnings grows weaker, once basic needs are met. At relatively high income levels, there is no reason why individual responsibility should not prevail. Those who need or wish greater survivor or retirement protection than is provided by social security can buy it if they desire; and even if they act unwisely, society has no major concern with their imprudence.

Second, increases in the amount of earnings included in the benefit computation involve major prospective commitments of public funds. Under present practices, both OASDI taxes and benefits are based on covered earnings under the taxable maximum. Increases in the maximum would produce immediate increases in revenues but only deferred increases in benefit commitments. The political attractiveness of a procedure that provides funds for liberalizing other features of the system is obvious. What is less obvious is that, since the system is financed essentially on a pay-as-you-go basis, and since "actuarial balance" must be maintained,[20] the use of these surplus tax proceeds at the present time means that tax *rate* increases must be legislated now to take effect later when the higher wage base begins to affect benefit levels. As a practical matter, therefore, every increase in the wage base involves subsequent, unspecified expansion of the system in some direction that may or

---

[19] U.S. Department of Health, Education, and Welfare, Social Security Administration, *Social Security Bulletin, Annual Statistical Supplement, 1965,* Table 22, p. 27, and *Social Security Bulletin,* Vol. 30, No. 12 (December 1967), Table Q-3, p. 60. In 1966, the most recent year for which estimates are available, 80.1 percent of all wages were below the $6,600 maximum that was taxable in that year.

[20] For a discussion of the concept of actuarial balance, see Chapter VII.

may not be so urgent. If the earnings level used for benefit purposes were divorced from the method of financing benefits, the
question of the proper range of earnings for the benefit computation could be settled without the distortion created by the linkage
between the two in the present system.

In view of the competing uses for public funds, including other
changes in the social security system, increases in the taxable maximum earnings base should be modest in the immediate future.
We propose as a rule of thumb that social security benefits be computed on the basis of total family earnings up to about the level of
median family income. The maximum taxable earnings level
might then be adjusted annually by the average growth of median
family income;[21] between 1956 and 1966, this was roughly 4.5 percent a year. In 1968, the median family income will probably be
in the neighborhood of $7,800 a year,[22] which is the maximum
earnings level for tax and benefit purposes under the 1967 amendments. A replacement rate of 40 to 50 percent on total family earnings up to this level is a reasonable goal for OASDI.[23]

Adjustment of Benefits to Changing Economic Conditions

Price inflation and productivity growth are typical of most con-
temporary economies; they raise major problems in designing the
benefit structure in a social security program.

THE EARNINGS BASE FOR DETERMINING
INITIAL BENEFIT LEVELS

If prices and wages did not change over time, benefits could be
based on a worker's history of money earnings without raising any

[21] For a discussion of how this adjustment might be implemented, see Robert
J. Myers, "A Method of Automatically Adjusting the Maximum Earnings Base
Under OASDI," *Journal of Risk and Insurance*, Vol. 31, No. 3 (September 1964),
pp. 329–40.

[22] According to the latest figures, median family income was $6,957 in 1965. The
growth in income and prices between 1965 and 1968 will almost certainly be sufficient to raise the median close to $7,800. For the 1965 data, see U.S. Bureau of the
Census, "Income in 1966 of Families and Persons in the United States," *Current
Population Reports*, Series P-60, No. 53 (1967), p. 19.

[23] See Chapter IX for a proposed benefit schedule.

major equity problems. But since real wages grow, the inclusion in benefit computations of earnings received early in life ties benefits to obsolete levels of earnings. Inflation aggravates this problem, since the difference between the money wage level in the early years of the working life and that in later years is even greater than the difference in real wages. The problem is complicated by the fact that profiles of lifetime earnings differ among occupations. Earnings of workers in white collar jobs, particularly those requiring long training, are generally at or near their peak in the years just before retirement. Earnings of workers in unskilled or semiskilled occupations or in declining industries often fall relatively, and sometimes absolutely, in later working life.

There are a number of possible solutions to this problem. The simplest is to base retirement benefits on a relatively brief period of highest earnings, ignoring earnings in all other years.[24] But this approach has serious drawbacks. With the passage of time the formula, unless amended, will include earnings from years long before retirement. Consequently, benefits will be based on average earnings that are much lower than the worker is currently receiving. This problem has already arisen in OASDI, and it will become more serious until Congress reduces the weight attached to early earnings.

An alternative approach would take into account the relative, rather than the absolute, level of a worker's earnings. Thus, if a worker has received, say, two-thirds of the national average of earnings throughout his working life, his retirement benefit would be computed on the basis of two-thirds of the average earnings level at the time he retires. The fact that this amount would, in general, be considerably greater than actual earnings is not relevant, since the worker's *relative* position on the wage scale should be controlling. The worker's retirement benefit, in practice, might be based on a weighted average of his relative position in a num-

[24] This method has been used up to this time in the United States. Retirees are permitted to exclude from the benefit computation earnings prior to 1951 and, in recent years, nearly all retirees have found it advantageous to do so. In addition, the benefit computation excludes the five years of lowest earnings. Currently, benefits for a man retiring at age 65 in 1968 would be based on earnings in the best 12 years after 1950, and for a woman on earnings in the best 9 years. For persons retiring in 1968 at older ages and for those on the roll who retired in the past, the period is shorter. For further details, see Appendix B.

ber of years. This method, which is employed in the Federal Republic of Germany, takes into account increases in productivity
during a worker's life. The same result would be obtained if the
earnings record for each worker were revalued in benefit computations by the amounts by which prices and real wages have increased, a method adopted in Canada in 1965.

An intermediate approach would be to adjust the earnings record of each worker for changes in prices (as measured, say, by the
consumer price index), but not for changes in real wages. This
would protect benefits against the inroads of inflation, but would
not guarantee to workers a share of the nation's productivity
growth during their working careers.

A choice among these approaches should be consistent with the
objectives of social security. Since one major purpose of old-age retirement benefits is to reduce the financial shock of retirement, the
initial benefit should be related to the living standard to which
retirees were accustomed immediately before retirement. Earnings
received long before retirement generally play a smaller role than
recent earnings in shaping the consumption patterns and style of
life of retirees. It would therefore be desirable to exclude such
early earnings in determining the initial benefit amount. Adjustment of a worker's earnings record for price changes only is not
sufficient for this purpose. An effective, pragmatic solution to this
problem would be to base the initial benefit on earnings in, say,
the highest five of the fifteen or twenty years immediately before
retirement.[25]

ADJUSTMENT OF BENEFITS AFTER RETIREMENT

Once a worker has retired with an initial benefit properly related
to his earnings record, further problems arise in keeping his benefit up to date with changing economic conditions.

Prices will change and productivity and real wages will continue
to increase after the worker retires. Since the average life expec-

[25] This step has been presented as a possible alternative to current procedures
by the present (1968) Commissioner of Social Security Administration, Robert M.
Ball; see his "Policy Issues in Social Security," *Social Security Bulletin*, Vol. 29,
No. 6 (June 1966), p. 7.

tancy at retirement is almost fifteen years, inflation can seriously erode the real value of any pension. For example, if prices rise by only 2 percent a year, the real value of a pension will be reduced by 18 percent after one decade and by 33 percent after two decades. There is no justification for permitting such changes in the general price level to reduce the real value of pension benefits. The hardships that inflation imposes on recipients of fixed incomes are generally acknowledged. The only question concerns the method by which these hardships should be prevented. Most countries rely on discretionary changes in benefits by the legislature. A few provide that benefits shall be automatically revalued each year to counteract price changes in the previous year. The United States has relied on the former method. Congress has periodically raised benefits in current payment status; the most recent increase was in 1967 when benefits were raised by 13 percent across the board.

The U.S. record in preventing inflation from eroding the real value of retirement benefits has been spotty. Increases in benefits have not fully offset the effects of inflation (see Chart v-3), so that retirees in most years (except those who retired in years immediately before a benefit increase became effective) have experienced a decline in the real value of their pensions. For example, in 1966 the 1954 retiree would have required benefits 8 percent higher than those he actually received in order to purchase the same goods and services that he was able to enjoy with his benefits in 1954; the corresponding increase for the 1959 retiree is 5 percent.[26] The enactment of Medicare and the 13 percent increase in OASDI benefits in 1967 were probably adequate to make up the erosion in the real purchasing power of the benefits since 1954. Nevertheless, since the process by which Congress amends social security is complex and lengthy, reasonably timely adjustments of benefits to every increase in the price level can hardly be expected.

No substantial argument—except cost—seems to exist against automatic adjustment in benefits to offset price changes. In the age of the computer, the administrative burden of such adjustment is no longer a serious obstacle. The only economic issue concerns the

[26] Saul Waldman, "OASDI Benefits, Prices, and Wages: 1966 Experience," *Social Security Bulletin*, Vol. 30, No. 6 (June 1967), p. 10.

Chart v-3. *Monthly Benefits*[a] *under OASDI for Persons Retiring in 1954 and 1959 Compared with Benefits Needed To Maintain Parity with Prices and Wages*

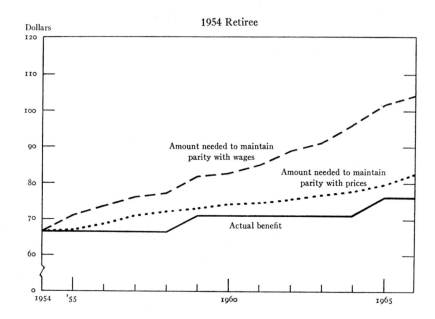

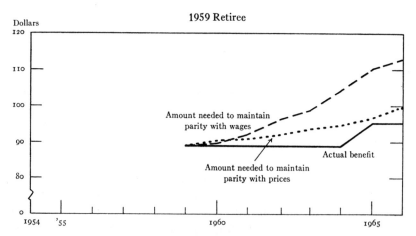

Source: Saul Waldman, "OASDI Benefits, Prices, and Wages: 1966 Experience," *Social Security Bulletin*, Vol. 30, No. 6 (June 1967), Table 1, p. 10.

a. Actual benefits are the average monthly benefits awarded to 1954 and 1959 retirees.

likelihood that automatic adjustment, like other escalator clauses, might tend to institutionalize inflation. It may be argued that, if price increases are automatically translated into higher money incomes, any shock to the price level—caused by, say, a rise in the price of imported raw materials or a brief spurt of demand—would trigger wage and pension increases, which would lead to further price increases, and so on. In other words, escalator clauses and automatic adjustment provisions may tend to perpetuate the price-wage spiral.

Nevertheless, failure to adjust benefits to compensate for price changes means that social security beneficiaries are expected to bear a large share of the burden of the inflation "tax." It is inconsistent to argue both that inflation is objectionable because it inflicts severe hardships on people with fixed incomes and that social security beneficiaries should not be protected against the inadequacies of economic policies which permit inflation to occur.

In some countries, social security benefits paid to retirees are adjusted for changes in money wages, which include the effect of productivity as well as price changes. This version of automatic adjustment is considerably more expensive than is adjustment for price changes only. In the United States, for example, automatic adjustment for price changes alone would have meant an increase of 23 percent in benefits for a 1954 retiree over the period 1954–66, while adjustment for changes in money wages would have meant a 56 percent increase over the same period. By comparison, his benefit actually increased by 14 percent.[27] The 13 percent increase enacted in 1967 was therefore adequate to more than offset the inflation in prices, but not the full increase in money wages (which includes productivity growth as well as the increase in prices).

In a growing economy, the OASDI program generates trust fund surpluses of tax receipts over benefit obligations. To the extent that surpluses in the trust funds help to determine the size of increases in benefits,[28] the probability that automatic adjustment

---

[27] *Ibid.*

[28] For the relationship between trust fund surpluses and benefit increases, see Chapter VII.

of benefits after retirement for money wage changes would fully absorb these surpluses is one of the chief arguments against it.

One of the most important disadvantages of the automatic-adjustment method when applied to the benefit structure is that the latter will tend to be rigidly "straight-jacketed" in the original form in which it was developed. . . . a gain results when earnings levels increase if the benefit formula is of a weighted nature. Similarly, additional financing is available to the system when the earnings base is raised. Under the automatic-adjustment method, such gains are necessarily distributed proportionately, whereas under the *ad hoc* method, they may be distributed in different manners (for instance, survivor benefits may be increased relatively more than retirement benefits), and it is thus possible to correct any anomalies or inequities in the program.[29]

This criticism applies to automatic adjustment with respect to either prices or wages, but it is more telling in the latter instance because the adjustments are larger and because it is difficult to think of a case in which it would be good social policy to reduce the real value of benefits for any group in order to permit them to increase for another.

Automatic adjustment for changes in money wages implies a judgment that retired workers should share fully in the productivity increase occurring after they leave the labor force. However, it may be argued that the preretirement income of the beneficiary is more likely to determine his style of life, which is, perhaps, a more relevant standard for setting old-age pensions. Furthermore, the desirability of additional public expenditures on social security must be weighed against other public spending and against private spending by taxpayers who would benefit from tax reductions (or smaller tax increases). Automatic adjustment of pensions with respect to changes in money wages would represent a permanent commitment that real pension benefits should rise just as fast as real wages. Whether or not such an expansion is desirable will de-

[29] Myers, "A Method of Automatically Adjusting the Maximum Earnings Base Under OASDI," p. 330.

pend at every point in time on the urgency of competing public and private wants. Even if it were desirable today to raise retirement benefits in line with increases in wages, it might not be desirable to do so in the future, when public and private expenditure alternatives will differ.

With adjustment of benefits to changes in money wages or to changes in prices, workers with identical wage histories who retired at different times would receive different benefits—a situation that might give rise to complaints about inequitable treatment. To abstract from price changes, which will be considered below, assume prices are constant. Consider two workers: A who retires at age 65 in 1955 and B who retires at age 65 in 1965. In each year of his working life, B received the same wages that A did ten years earlier (assume all earnings were within the wage base). A is awarded a benefit of $P a month in 1955, and B is awarded the same benefit in 1965. If real wages rise $100r$ percent between 1955 and 1965, A's pension in 1965 will be $P(1 + r)$, while B's will be $P. Undoubtedly, B would regard this as inequitable. But the differential is justified on the basis that A's income was earned earlier than B's and therefore was relatively higher on the income scale.

The same problem exists if benefits are adjusted for changes in prices only. In the foregoing example, if prices rose but productivity did not, A's pension (adjusted for price changes) in 1965 should be larger than B's, since B's earnings have a real value below A's numerically identical earnings by the amount of inflation that occurred in the relevant decade. Such apparent inequities are simply the consequences of a decision to adjust benefits of a retired person on the basis of events that occur after his wage history is closed.

On balance, the introduction of automatic adjustment of benefits after retirement to price changes seems desirable; and the case against adjustments to match increases in money wages is much stronger than the case for it. This conclusion presumes that the initial benefits at the time of retirement are based on earnings that are recent enough to reflect the individual's standard of living just prior to retirement.

"Blanketing-In"

The technical borders between eligibility and ineligibility for retirement benefits are sharp and narrow, and a considerable amount of money turns on which side of the border an aged person may be. For many years, under current law, a large number of aged persons will not be eligible for any public retirement benefits. Should this latter group—numbering 1.2 million people in 1966[30]—be awarded social security benefits, that is, be "blanketed-in" regardless of ineligibility by current standards?

OASDI and other government retirement systems covered only 70.7 percent of paid civilian employment in 1949. Since then, however, coverage of workers has become nearly universal (94.7 percent of paid employment in 1965); and eventually, nearly all aged persons will be eligible for benefits under one public program or another. But many of those who are now retired, and some persons yet to retire, worked in occupations before they were covered by social security or worked for too brief a time afterward to acquire fully insured status. The proportion of persons aged 65 or over who have received benefits in selected years beginning in 1940, and estimates for future years, are shown in Table v-3.

To be eligible for regular benefits, persons between the ages of 65 and 72 must be fully insured. Persons who reach age 72 before 1969 and are transitionally insured, and all persons aged 72 and over before 1968, are eligible for special reduced benefits—$40 for single persons, $60 for couples.[31]

[30] Unpublished estimate from the Social Security Administration.

[31] The benefits for noninsured persons are reduced by an amount equal to any public assistance payment or federal, state, or local pension. Eligibility for these benefits will require a growing number of quarters of coverage in 1968; the number of quarters required will cease to differ from ordinary eligibility requirements in 1970 for women and in 1972 for men. U.S. Department of Health, Education, and Welfare, Social Security Administration, *Social Security Handbook* (3d ed.; 1966), p. 33.

Table v-3. *Beneficiary Status of Population Aged 65 and Over, Selected Years, 1940-80*

Year	Number of Persons Aged 65 and Over (Millions)	Persons Receiving Social Security Benefits as Percentage of Aged Population		
		Total	Insured	Dependents
1940	9.0	2[a]	1[b]	1
1950	12.4[c]	21[a]	10	11
1955	14.5	43[a]	26	17
1960	16.7[c]	61[a]	43	18
1965	18.7	74[a]	51	23
1970[d]	20.4	79	57	22
1980[d]	24.3	84	63	21

Sources: Calculated from Robert J. Myers and Francisco Bayo, *Long-Range Cost Estimates for Old-Age, Survivors, and Disability Insurance System, 1966*, U.S. Department of Health, Education, and Welfare, Social Security Administration, Office of the Actuary, Actuarial Study No. 63 (1967), Tables 1, 9, and 5, pp. 22, 30, 26; Francisco Bayo, *United States Population Projections for OASDHI Cost Estimates*, Social Security Administration, Office of the Actuary, Actuarial Study No. 62 (1966), Table 11A, p. 25; U.S. Bureau of the Census, "Estimates of the Population of the United States, by Single Years of Age, Color, and Sex: 1900 to 1959," *Current Population Reports*, Series P-25, No. 311 (1965), pp. 13, 43; *Social Security Bulletin, Annual Statistical Supplement, 1965*, Table 38, p. 41; *Social Security Bulletin*, Vol. 30, No. 3 (March 1967), Table M-12, p. 33.
   a. The percentages overstate the proportion of aged persons receiving benefits since the beneficiary figures are as of December and the population figures are as of April 1 for 1950 and 1960, and as of July 1 for 1940, 1955, and 1965.
   b. January 1941 data were used as the first benefits were paid in January 1940.
   c. Census data (as of April 1).
   d. All projections are the mean of low-cost and high-cost assumptions made by the Social Security Administration. All data are estimated as of July 1.

PERSONS NOT ELIGIBLE FOR BENEFITS

Not much is known about those who are not eligible for regular benefits. The little that is known was learned mostly from the 1963 Survey of the Aged, which shows that those ineligible for benefits worked less, earned less, had lower total money income, and had fewer assets than beneficiaries in the same age group.[32] The

   [32] Lenore A. Epstein and Janet H. Murray, *The Aged Population of the United States: The 1963 Social Security Survey of the Aged*, U.S. Department of Health, Education, and Welfare, Social Security Administration, Office of Research and Statistics, Research Report No. 19 (1967), Tables 7.3 and 7.4, p. 336; Table 3.19, p. 303; and Table 4.2, p. 311. Information on all those ineligible for benefits is based on statistics for nonbeneficiaries aged 73 and over. Since the earnings test ceases to apply at age 72, all nonbeneficiaries who are that age or older may be assumed to be ineligible. Statistics on nonbeneficiaries between the ages of 65 and 72 cannot be used to infer the status of those ineligible for benefits, since this age group

differences were large: total money income of nonbeneficiaries was about two-thirds, and net worth from one-half to one-fourth, that of beneficiary units.[33] Among those ineligible for benefits were some relatively wealthy aged persons, particularly widows whose husbands had been employed in activities that were not covered at that time by social security.

Since 1963, the demographic and economic characteristics of nonbeneficiary units have probably changed markedly. One reason for this change is that the 1965 and 1966 amendments extended full or partial benefits to 1.2 million aged persons.[34] In addition, a large proportion of those ineligible for benefits were over 72 years of age when the survey was taken; and in the past five years, many have died. The evidence is insufficient for determining the financial status of those aged who are not eligible for benefits today; however, there is little doubt that the extension of eligibility in 1965 did not reach many of the poorest among the aged. Among aged nonbeneficiaries in the lowest third in 1962, 68 percent of the income of couples, 87 percent of the income of nonmarried men, and 68 percent of the income of nonmarried women came from public assistance or other public programs which would disqualify the recipient for the special age benefit or would cause the benefit to be reduced.[35] The transitional insured status did not affect previously ineligible aged persons under the age of 72. On the other hand, the income status of recent retirees has tended to be superior to that of past retirees.

In summary, those ineligible for retirement benefits in 1963 were, on the whole, poorer with respect to almost any standard than were beneficiaries. Many persons who were not eligible in 1963 have died since then; others receive benefits as a result of the 1965 and 1966 amendments.

---

includes many who are eligible to receive benefits but whose earnings reduce their benefits to zero.

[33] *Ibid.*, Tables 3.19 and 4.14, pp. 303 and 319.

[34] *Social Security Bulletin*, Vol. 28, No. 9 (September 1965), Table 1, p. 16, and Vol. 30, No. 6 (June 1967), Table M-13, p. 36. This figure does not include a small number of aged doctors who are not identified separately in the official statistics.

[35] Epstein and Murray, *The Aged Population of the United States*, Table 3.9, p. 294.

ARGUMENTS FOR AND AGAINST "BLANKETING-IN"

The blanketing-in of aged persons now ineligible for benefits has been opposed on several grounds. A major argument has been that blanketing-in would award benefits to persons who have not earned them by making contributions. But this argument is weak, even if the rationale of social security emphasized in Chapter IV is not accepted. First, the strict contributory principle has already been abandoned by providing special age-72 benefits to persons with no quarters of coverage and by financing these benefits out of general revenues. Second, as of January 1, 1968, a man aged 65 could be fully insured and eligible for the minimum benefit of $55 a month ($82.50 if married) with only $28 having been paid in payroll taxes. The family of a deceased worker would be eligible for survivor benefits if the man had worked for the minimum six quarters with a combined employer-employee contribution of as little as $26. Consequently, persons who have paid very modest amounts of taxes are insured and eligible for benefits, while persons who have worked in covered employment for a slightly shorter time are denied all benefits. This is a cruel and unnatural distinction, particularly since the small benefit amounts that depend on this distinction can make a substantial difference in the lives of the aged individuals concerned.

Similar arbitrary distinctions applicable to some disabled workers and to dependent survivors of some deceased workers prohibit the payment of benefits to many needy persons. Under present law, a disabled person receives benefits only if he has at least 20 quarters of coverage during the 40-quarter period prior to disability. Disability benefits are also paid to persons who become disabled before age 31 and were covered in at least half the quarters beginning at age 21. Survivors receive benefits only if the family head was either fully or currently insured. This means that, in some cases, survivors do not qualify for benefits because the deceased worker was covered for only five quarters when six were required. Clearly, the remaining disabled persons and dependent survivors who are not eligible for benefits are, in many cases, unfortunate individuals who live in utter destitution. In a universal social security system, disability and dependency alone should be sufficient to entitle a family to benefits.

Is further taxation justified to support the payment of cash benefits to groups in the population who have not attained the required insured statuses? There does not seem to be any reason in principle why full benefits should be paid to aged persons under age 72 with six or more quarters of coverage, and no benefits at all be paid to those with five or fewer quarters of coverage; nor why disability benefits should be denied to any worker who is disabled; nor why benefits should not be paid to dependent survivors of any deceased worker.

Furthermore, since in most states old-age assistance does not provide any aged household with sufficient income to lift it above the poverty threshold as defined by the Social Security Administration, it is wrong to deny special age-72 benefits to persons on public assistance. The chief reason for doing so is the practical consideration that most state welfare administrations include social security benefits in computing need. Payment of social security benefits without regard for assistance status therefore would merely transfer a portion of the cost of supporting the aged from the states to the federal government, but would not increase the income of the aged—since the special age-72 benefit (or any benefit likely to be paid to blanketed-in beneficiaries) is lower than old-age assistance benefits in all but a few states. Ironically, among old-age assistance recipients, the special age-72 benefit discriminates in favor of the less poor in all states where the basic assistance payment is larger than $40 a month ($60 for couples). Only those assistance recipients with sufficient outside income or wealth to have their benefits reduced below the level of the special age-72 benefit find it worthwhile to renounce public assistance and to accept social security.[36] The denial of special age-72 benefits to

[36] For example, suppose a state guarantees a minimum income of $75 a month under old-age assistance, and of two couples, A and B—both receiving old-age assistance—couple A with no outside income receives $75 in assistance, while couple B, with $70 of outside income, receives $5 of assistance. Couple A will be unwilling to give up its $75 assistance payment in exchange for the special $60 social security benefit. Couple B, on the other hand, will accept the $60 social security benefit in return for relinquishing the $5 assistance payment, and its total income will rise to $130.

public assistance recipients—a group of the aged which, on the average, is more needy than are the remaining aged who are eligible for benefits—is arbitrary and should be ended, with no offset, or only a partial offset, of public assistance benefits until the poverty threshold is reached.

Even if this extension in social security benefits were exactly offset by reductions in public assistance, the implicit intergovernmental transfer would be desirable. Such a change would be equivalent to a transfer from the federal government to the states of an amount equal to the states' savings on public assistance. This transfer would go for the most part to low income states where a relatively large proportion of the population is on assistance and to states with relatively generous welfare programs.

Social Security and Other Transfer Payment Programs

Most transfer payment programs with the objective of replacing earnings, such as public retirement programs and private pension plans, are not now coordinated with social security. As a result, some individuals may acquire eligibility under two or more programs where multiple entitlement was not intended; in other cases, the eligibility conditions may be so strict that mobile workers may not be eligible for benefits under any program.

The other social security objective—to guarantee a basic minimum income to the aged—brings the program into contact with other public programs designed to supplement the incomes of the poor. The largest of these are public assistance, including old-age assistance, and veterans' disability pensions.

THE PROBLEM OF OVERLAP

Social security and other public pensions. Federal, state, and local government retirement systems are typically independent of social security. They are separately financed, have different eligibility rules, provide substantially different benefits, and begin benefit payments at different ages. The benefit structure of each is constructed on the assumption that eligible workers will receive payments under one program only. Career soldiers differ in this respect from other government employees: they earn eligibility for both military pensions and social security simultaneously. Benefits under most government and private pension plans are usually payable at age 65, or after a stipulated number of years of service. For example, federal employees become eligible for reduced retirement benefits after 30 years of service (but not before age 55).

The lack of coordination between social security and other public retirement programs makes it possible for some beneficiaries to receive pensions under two or more programs.[37] For example, as noted above, government employees are frequently eligible for benefits at age 55, provided they have sufficient years of service. They may then become employed in private industry, earn social security coverage, and also achieve eligibility under a private pension plan. Similarly, a career military officer may retire after 20 years of service (perhaps at age 38), assured of both social security and military retirement benefits. In addition, he will have ample time to earn coverage under another government or private retirement program.

Whether or not multiple eligibility is desirable depends on the purpose of the program. Military retirement benefits and private pensions, which are designed to supplement social security, are used to recruit and retain employees with a special concern for retirement. Most government retirement systems, on the other hand, are designed to provide basic retirement benefits for career employees. Early retirement policies provide openings for younger people and avoid freezing older people into jobs which they can no longer discharge efficiently. However, the retired workers may acquire eligibility for social security, which will entitle them to the relatively generous benefits payable at the low end of the earnings scale.

Multiple eligibility is clearly contrary to the intent of the social security system. Disproportionate benefits for workers with low wage histories are justifiable only because such workers are assumed

[37] Data from the 1963 Survey of the Aged show that, at the end of 1962, 5 percent of all social security beneficiary units were also receiving pensions under government employee programs. Lawrence D. Haber and Rena Kling, *OASDHI Beneficiaries Receiving Government Pensions*, U.S. Department of Health, Education, and Welfare, Social Security Administration, Office of Research and Statistics, Note No. 2 (January 26, 1968), p. 1.

to have been unable to save adequately for retirement, and the same relative decline in living standards is assumed to be less tolerable than it is for workers who had higher incomes. These conditions do not apply to former civil servants whose earnings records compare more than favorably with those of the average social security beneficiary.

The inequities that may result are illustrated by the following hypothetical cases: (1) A person who worked 40 years as a federal employee and who earned a salary of $7,800 a year in his highest five years of service receives a pension of $5,948 a year at age 65 in 1968, or he may accept a reduced pension of $5,623 a year and on his death his surviving spouse will be entitled to a pension of 55 percent of the annuity before reduction. (2) A 30-year federal civil servant who retires at age 55 with a pension based on an annual salary of $7,800 receives at age 55 a pension of $4,388 a year ($4,219 if he wishes his spouse to have survivor benefits). If he then works at an annual salary of $7,800 for ten years in employment covered by social security, he and his wife will be eligible for benefits of $2,547 a year in addition to his civil service retirement benefit. His total benefits therefore will be $6,935 a year, almost two-thirds of which will be payable from age 55. If social security beneficiaries were allowed to disregard more than the lowest five years since 1950, social security benefits would be even larger. (3) A married worker who is covered by social security for 40 years at an annual salary of $7,800 will receive a benefit of only $3,876 a year, payable at age 65.

Such inequities may be removed in one of three ways. The first would be to universalize social security coverage and build other government pension programs on top of it. All workers would pay social security taxes, and all would be eligible for social security benefits. Governmental units that wished to use additional retirement benefits as an inducement for recruitment could adopt their own supplementary plans, as do private employers today. This solution is the most logical, but it would encounter stiff political resistance from representatives of government employees.

Second, social security benefits could be computed differently for beneficiaries entitled to benefits under another government program. For them, benefits might be set at a modest, flat proportion of average earnings. For example, if social security benefits were set at, say, 20 percent of average monthly earnings, the worker with dual entitlement in example (2) above (and his wife) would receive only $1,278 a year from social security.

Third, it would be possible to integrate the benefit structures by reducing social security benefits by the amount of other public retirement pensions received. To give some recognition to the employee's dual eligibility, the offset might be limited so that it would not reduce the social security benefit by more than, say, one-half or two-thirds, and so that the individual would carry over credit for coverage for the years in which he may have worked under a civil service plan. Other techniques could undoubtedly be devised to accomplish these objectives.

Social security and private pensions. While the benefits of public retirement programs are independent of social security, those provided under private pension plans ordinarily supplement it.[38] Such plans have been subject to criticism on a number of grounds. Many are not adequately funded, and some have not been able to meet their commitments. Many require workers to remain with a company for long periods before they receive benefit rights. Under most plans, credits are not portable; that is, workers cannot carry credits along with them from job to job.[39] As a result of these and other limitations, a relatively small proportion of retired workers are now eligible for private pensions, and by 1980 the proportion will still be under 35 percent.[40]

With regard to the future, two points should be mentioned. First, there is some indication that public policy is moving toward

[38] One of the requirements for federal tax exemption is that benefits paid by private pension plans should not be discriminatory; that is, they should not favor stockholders, officers, supervisors, and other highly paid employees. The regulations permit a benefit structure that presupposes the employee will receive social security benefits. In practice, this has been a very difficult provision to administer. See Merton C. Bernstein, *The Future of Private Pensions* (Free Press, 1964).

[39] These and other issues, together with recommended solutions, are discussed in President's Committee on Corporate Pension Funds and Other Private Retirement and Welfare Programs, *Public Policy and Private Pension Programs: A Report to the President on Private Employee Retirement Plans* (1965). See also Bernstein, *The Future of Private Pensions.*

[40] Daniel M. Holland, *Private Pension Funds: Projected Growth*, National Bureau of Economic Research, Occasional Paper 97 (Columbia University Press, 1966), p. 49.

the correction of certain defects in the private pension system and the development of minimum standards, at least for vesting and funding.[41] If these changes occur, the proportion of social security recipients with private pensions will rise. Second, even if the proportion remains small, the effect of private plans on the social security system may not be insignificant. Congress may conceive of an expansion of the private system as an appropriate or even preferred alternative to increasing benefits under the public system. Given the limitations of the private system, the result may be to encourage an inadequate pattern of replacement rates for social security unless some overlap arrangement is adopted. In the absence of such an arrangement, those who receive both social security and private pension benefits would enjoy high replacement rates. But for the majority receiving only social security benefits, the replacement rates might be significantly lower than they would have been in the absence of the private programs.

The problem of overlap arises because social security cannot adequately fulfill the earnings replacement objective in a world of rising money wages unless the maximum earnings level used in the benefit computation is continually raised. In the process, social security encroaches on earnings levels formerly covered only by private pension plans. Heretofore, this problem has not been serious, but it is certain to become more serious as the earnings limit under the public system is raised and benefits are liberalized.

The problem cannot be solved by permitting private pension plans to use the social security maximum earnings level as a floor. This would convert all private pensions to supplements to social security, a solution which is hardly practical. The denial of private pensions to low-paid workers would be unacceptable, since these workers sacrificed some wages to become eligible for their firm's or industry's pension program. In view of this past history, it will be necessary to require modification of present integration formulas to avoid disproportionate reductions in the private pensions of relatively low-paid wage earners as the social security earnings' ceiling and benefits increase.

[41] See President's Committee on Corporate Pension Funds, *Public Policy and Private Pension Programs*.

AID TO THE POOR

Present programs. Public assistance is payable to poor persons who fall into certain categories and who meet certain eligibility requirements that vary sharply from state to state. Aged persons may receive benefits under the old-age assistance program; nonaged survivors may receive benefits under aid to families with dependent children. Both groups may receive payments under aid to the blind or aid to the permanently and totally disabled, but these payments are small relative to those to the aged and to families with dependent children. In general, payments are higher and eligibility requirements are less strict for old-age assistance than they are for aid to families with dependent children. In both cases, however, the recipients' total money income and asset holdings must fall below certain highly variable amounts before payments can be received. In many states, relatives' responsibility clauses and residence requirements further limit eligibility.

As a result of these conditions, only two-fifths of all aged persons classified as poor by the Social Security Administration receive old-age assistance. In June 1967, old-age assistance payments averaged $68.05 a month, but they ranged from $39.15 in Mississippi to $101.65 in California.[42] They tend to be lowest in poor states where the incidence of poverty among the aged is highest. Social security benefits are included in computing total money income and, hence, reduce old-age assistance payments dollar for dollar when payments are below the state's maximum. But whether or not an aged social security beneficiary will receive supplemental old-age assistance depends importantly on his state of residence.

Veterans' disability pensions are payable to all veterans who are permanently and totally disabled, who are unemployable, and whose income is less than $1,800 a year ($3,000 a year, with dependents). In practice, any veteran over age 65 is eligible for a veterans' disability pension if, in addition to the income test, his estate

[42] *Social Security Bulletin*, Vol. 30, No. 10 (October 1967), Table M-24, p. 48; Ida C. Merriam, *Social Security Benefits and Poverty*, U.S. Department of Health, Education, and Welfare, Social Security Administration, Office of Research and Statistics, Note No. 6 (February 24, 1967), Table 1.

is less than roughly $10,000.[43] Upon reaching age 65, all veterans are presumed to be 90 percent disabled, so that actual disability of only 10 percent is all that has to be shown. Moreover, the 10 percent disability is regarded as the normal result of aging. Finally, a veteran unemployed at age 65 is presumed to be unemployable. When his income is computed, 10 percent of retirement benefits under any pension program are excluded. In determining income for couples, none of the earnings of the veteran's spouse is included, nor is the first $1,200 of income from rents, interest, profits, or dividends. The married veteran may escape the limitation on the size of the estate which disqualifies him from receiving benefits by transferring to his spouse any portion of an estate in excess of about $10,000. Veterans between the ages of 60 and 65 are assumed to be 50 percent disabled; hence, they must demonstrate 50 percent disability to receive benefits. Veterans between the ages of 55 and 60 are presumed to be 30 percent disabled (40 percent, if they can demonstrate 60 percent disability from one cause).

In general, it is more advantageous for veterans to claim veterans' disability pensions than it is to claim old-age assistance, since benefit levels for the former tend to be higher in most areas, eligibility requirements are less strict, and the veteran may establish eligibility through an affidavit, subject to sample check, rather than bring upon himself the full investigation of the welfare agency. In fiscal year 1967, $1.9 billion in veterans' disability pensions were paid.[44]

Alternative methods. Because the coverage of existing programs for the poor is so spotty and because benefits tend to be meager even for those covered, increasing attention has been given to the need for new programs or for complete restructuring of existing programs.[45]

Either a negative income tax or public assistance payable to all

[43] Veterans' disability pensions should not be confused with veterans' disability compensation, which is payable for service-connected disability without a means test.

[44] *The Budget of the United States Government, Fiscal Year 1969* (1968), p. 161.

[45] At the time the President signed the 1967 amendments to the Social Security Act, he created a Commission on Income Maintenance Programs to explore the broad range of suggestions that have been put forth for income support; see "Johnson's Social Security Statement," *New York Times,* January 3, 1968, p. 28.

the poor as a matter of right could end poverty among the aged, as well as the nonaged.[46] If either plan were adopted, social security could surrender the function of guaranteeing to beneficiaries an income floor and could concentrate on the function of providing earnings replacement. Then, the case for paying to workers with low wage histories benefits that are relatively larger than those paid to workers with high wage histories would disappear. Earnings replacement would call for benefits strictly proportional to earnings, while the negative income tax, or some similar program, would provide assistance to those with inadequate incomes. This division of two distinct functions between two programs would have a major advantage. The cost of any antipoverty program is multiplied many times if benefits are payable to all families regardless of income.[47]

But however favorable the long-run prospects for one or another sort of minimum income guarantee may be, a large-scale program of this kind seems many years away from public acceptance. In the interim, it is important to recognize that social security annually transfers larger cash benefits to people who are poor, or would be poor in the absence of the benefits, than does any other program. It is estimated that, for fiscal year 1968, $11.3 billion went to the aged poor alone, compared with roughly $7 billion under all public assistance programs which went to nonaged as well as aged poor in fiscal 1967.[48]

As an instrument for providing the poor with further assistance, however, across-the-board increases in social security have become inefficient: less than one-fifth of such increases accrues to them.[49] Selective changes in the system—increases in minimum benefits and widows' benefits, and improved benefits for nonmarried beneficiaries—would be more effective. Moreover, each of these suggested

[46] For a detailed discussion and analysis of negative income taxation, see Christopher Green, *Negative Taxes and the Poverty Problem* (Brookings Institution, 1967); and James Tobin, Joseph A. Pechman, and Peter M. Mieszkowski, "Is a Negative Income Tax Practical?" *Yale Law Journal*, Vol. 77, No. 1 (November 1967), pp. 1–27. (Brookings Reprint 142.)

[47] See Chapter IX for a method of integrating social security with a negative income tax.

[48] Merriam, *Social Security Benefits and Poverty*, Table 2; Appendix Table C-10, this volume.

[49] U.S. Department of Health, Education, and Welfare, Office of Assistant Secretary for Program Coordination, *Income and Benefit Programs* (1966).

changes has a kind of built-in obsolescence; as average wages, length of coverage, and life expectancy continue to rise, the proportion of workers affected will tend to decline.

Summary

The structure of benefits under the present social security program is deficient in a number of respects.

While benefits are paid largely on a family basis—as they should be—the pattern of benefits is unsatisfactory. The degree of protection of previous living standards provided by OASDI varies sharply among families of different size and composition. To improve the structure in this respect, benefits should be based on the total earnings of married couples up to the taxable maximum; the widow's benefit should be raised to 100 percent of the worker's benefit; the 50 percent "bonus" of married couples over the single person's benefit should be replaced by a single flat benefit for the spouse; and an additional payment of the same flat amount should be made to each dependent survivor, irrespective of the number. In addition, the minimum benefit should be increased substantially, and the family maximum should be discontinued.

It would not be desirable to continue to increase the maximum earnings that are subject to payroll tax—to which the maximum benefit is tied—without having an agreed policy regarding the appropriate cutoff point. A good practical rule might be to set the maximum at the median family income level, which in 1968 will approximate the maximum of $7,800 included in the 1967 amendments to the Social Security Act. Adjustments thereafter might be made annually on the basis of the average growth of the median family income, which was roughly 4.5 percent from 1956 to 1966; at this rate, the maximum would rise to about $10,600 by 1975. A 40 to 50 percent replacement rate at the maximum earnings level is a reasonable long-term goal.

In addition to adjusting the maximum earnings figure, benefits should be based on earnings in, say, the highest five years of the last fifteen or twenty years of earnings. As a result, retirement benefits would reflect increases in money wages during the worker's years of active employment. After the worker retires, benefits should be adjusted automatically on the basis of changes in some overall price index. Some countries adjust benefits after retirement on the basis of changes in average money wages. However, this type of adjustment prejudges the manner in which productivity increases are to be distributed to retired workers. It is better to avoid freezing the benefit structure in this way.

A major criticism of the social security system is that it excludes some aged and disabled persons and dependent survivors, whereas others receive benefits after only a few months of coverage, and still others have been blanketed-in. As a matter of permanent policy, minimum benefits should be extended to all disabled and aged people and to dependent survivors, regardless of the earnings history of the worker.

The social security system overlaps to some degree with other public retirement programs. Since the programs are not coordinated, higher total benefits are often paid to some persons who were covered by more than one program. These anomalies can be removed by universalizing social security and encouraging other government pension programs to provide only supplementary benefits; or by reducing social security benefits to a modest flat proportion of earnings (say, 20 percent) for those with coverage under another public retirement program; or by reducing social security benefits, up to a point, by the amount of other retirement income from a public program.

Public assistance programs supplement the social security program for those whose total income is inadequate to support minimum standards of living. It would be too inefficient and too expensive to raise social security benefits enough to end poverty among the aged, since this would require increased payments to all, regardless of income. It would also be inequitable, since there are millions of poor families other than the aged poor. The only completely satisfactory way to handle this problem is to adopt a negative income tax or to extend public assistance to all the poor. Either measure would automatically provide the necessary minimum income support for the aged. In the meantime, selective changes in the structure of social security benefits are much more effective than across-the-board increases in combating poverty.

CHAPTER VI

Social Security and Retirement

Decisions about when to retire, whether to do so abruptly or gradually, and whether or not to re-enter the labor force are basic questions in the economic life of most workers. Such decisions help to determine how much of life shall be devoted to work; therefore, they affect the dimensions of the retired population and the accompanying economic, social, and health problems.

Decisions concerning retirement depend on numerous factors. Business policies frequently make retirement mandatory. Private pension programs often stipulate that pensioners will lose benefits if they accept work in firms that compete with their previous employer. And, of course, retirement may be forced by ill health.

Within these limits, however, the terms upon which people can retire—the loss in earnings which they suffer from not working—are very important. Since social security is the dominant retirement system in the United States, it can influence the retirement decision, both directly, by altering the income choices that workers face, and indirectly, by helping to influence the other factors which determine the time of retirement. At the same time, social security is itself affected by the changes in attitudes caused by growing affluence.

Many people supported the Social Security Act of 1935 as a method of encouraging the aged worker to retire and thereby help to alleviate mass unemployment among younger workers. But by 1940, when the payment of benefits had begun, the problem was rapidly changing into one of labor shortage. The growth of retirement benefits since World War II—which has been a very prosperous period on the whole—has coincided with a sharp decline in participation in the labor force by the aged. Has this reduced participation been due to the more widespread eligibility for larger retirement benefits? Or have both lower participation and higher benefits resulted from economic growth? In general, do higher social security benefits encourage earlier retirement? What is the critical age or range of ages that should define the "aged" group? What is appropriate public policy in relation to the whole retirement issue? The resolution of these questions will have a significant effect on the welfare of the aged and, indeed, on who will be considered aged—whether the questions are resolved by purposeful or by haphazard decisions, or by making no decisions at all.

Impact of Social Security on Work Incentives

The social security system may cause less work effort by the aged and encourage early retirement for three reasons. First, the non-work-related income provided by Old-Age, Survivors, and Disability Insurance (OASDI) benefits makes retirement attractive for many workers. Second, the earnings test directly penalizes work effort. Third, OASDI may alter company retirement policies or produce other social and economic pressures that indirectly lead to withdrawal from the labor force. The evidence—though not conclusive—suggests that OASDI has weakened the work incentives of the aged.

SOME THEORETICAL POSSIBILITIES

Social security cuts the reduction in income that workers must face upon retirement, other things held constant. Assume that neither money income nor leisure is what economists term an "inferior" good. If a person's money income rises because he receives an OASDI retirement benefit, he prefers, all other things equal, to sacrifice some of his added income for less work (more leisure) rather than to keep all the income while working as hard as before. It follows that retirement benefits cause many aged workers to try to reduce their work effort. Furthermore, the larger the benefit relative to potential earnings, the stronger the effect in reducing the desired workload. This "income effect" of retirement benefits can be expected to vary among individuals: some would want to work as much as before; some would want to switch from full-time to part-time work; others would want to cease all employment.

The social security earnings test alters the choices just described by making at least partial retirement relatively more attractive for most workers. Effective in 1968, the earnings test permits workers to earn up to $1,680 a year without loss of benefits, but it reduces benefits by $1 for every $2 of annual earnings between $1,680 and $2,880, and by $1 for every $1 of earnings above $2,880. It is, in effect, a tax on earnings of either 0, 50, or 100 percent, depending on the amount of earnings, until benefits are reduced to zero. For those workers who can earn no more than $1,680, the earnings test is irrelevant, and the impact of social security on retirement is that described in the preceding paragraph. The earnings test affects only those persons who, in its absence, would have worked enough to earn more than $1,680. Anyone who would have retired because of the income provided by OASDI retirement benefits cannot be affected by the earnings test. However, among aged persons who would prefer to continue in employment after becoming eligible for retirement benefits, the earnings test has a potential independent effect on work effort. If such workers have substantial flexibility in adjusting their hours worked, and if reducing their work schedules does not greatly affect their rate of pay, the earnings test by itself would not be sufficient to cause full retirement, but rather only a partial reduction of hours worked and earnings.[1] For example, suppose that a self-employed professional who is eligible for annual social security benefits of $800 or more and who can fully adjust his work schedule would have worked enough, in the absence of the earnings test, to earn $250 a month, or $3,000 over

[1] Lowell E. Gallaway, *The Retirement Decision: An Exploratory Essay*, U.S. Department of Health, Education, and Welfare, Social Security Administration, Division of Research and Statistics, Research Report No. 9 (1965), p. 18, proves this proposition as part of a more general discussion of the impact of OASDI on work incentives.

the year. Given the earnings test, he will probably work less, since the last $120 ($3,000–$2,880) of earnings would not add to his income. His most likely reaction to the earnings test is to reduce his work effort partially to escape the 100 percent rate tax, but not to give up work altogether. On the other hand, an aged worker, employed by a large firm, may have to choose between continuation of full-time work, part-time work at a greatly reduced rate of pay, or retirement. In such cases, the earnings test can cause complete retirement. If the latter possibility is discounted, however, only 1.6 million out of the 17 million persons eligible for retirement benefits in 1966 appear to have been affected by the retirement test (Table VI-1).

The preceding discussion suggests that the earnings test may be important in explaining a fact observed in Chapter II: self-employed and professional workers, who control their own employment and have the greatest flexibility in adjusting hours worked and earnings, are less likely to retire than workers in other types of employment. In general, however, both the income effect of OASDI benefits and the earnings test can by themselves cause com-

Table VI-1. *Number of Persons Aged 65 and Over Affected by OASDI Retirement Test, 1966*

(In millions)

Retirement Test Status and Annual Earnings[a]	Number
Not affected by retirement test	15.4
Aged 72 and over	*8.7*
No earnings	*5.7*
Earnings of $1–$1,199	*1.0*
Affected by retirement test	1.6
Earnings of $1,200–$1,500	*0.2*
Earnings of $1,500–$2,700	*0.6*
Earnings over $2,700	*0.8*
Total eligible for cash benefits	17.0

Source: *Social Security Amendments of 1967*, Hearings before the Senate Committee on Finance on H.R. 12080, 90 Cong. 1 sess. (1967), Pt. 1, p. 241.
a. In 1966, workers could earn up to $1,500 a year without loss of benefits. Benefits were reduced $1 for every $2 of earnings between $1,500 and $2,700 and by $1 for every $1 of earnings above $2,700. Under the 1967 amendments to the Social Security Act, which are applicable beginning January 1, 1968, the corresponding breaking points were increased to $1,680 and $2,880, respectively.

plete retirement or, for persons who remain in the labor force, they can cause reduced work effort. The crude evidence available from historical and cross-section statistics does not permit separation of their individual effects; therefore, references to the impact of OASDI on work effort that are made henceforth in this discussion will apply to their combined effect.

OASDI may also encourage retirement because it sets the pattern for private and for state and local government retirement plans and, more generally, because it conditions both employer and employee attitudes toward "normal" retirement age. The basic difficulty in evaluating this aspect of social security is ignorance about the dominant direction of causation. The OASDI program may be a major causative factor in shaping employer policies and psychological attitudes toward aging. On the other hand, the program itself may simply reflect fundamental economic forces and public opinion as expressed through the political process.

Consider, for example, the following plausible explanation of the continuing trend toward early retirement. Assume that employers believe that they can reduce labor costs by laying off aged workers and hiring younger, healthier, better-educated replacements.[2] In the absence of a social security retirement program and given the constraint of widespread seniority practices, employers might be reluctant to fire old employees either for humanitarian reasons or for fear of undermining employee morale and arousing resentment. Under these conditions, social security may simply have reduced the major obstacles to the retirement of older workers by providing basic income support after retirement and by conditioning employee attitudes toward age 65 (and, more recently, age 62) as the normal retirement age. The fact that private pension plans can conveniently be designed as supplements to the OASDI program may have further reinforced the tendency to a common retirement age. Private pension plans designed for workers at age 65, which have been negotiated in a few key union contracts with major industries, may have set the standard for

---

[2] A recent study concludes that employers prefer younger workers to older workers at a given wage because they believe that productivity declines with age. Michael J. Brennan, Philip Taft, and Mark B. Schupack, *The Economics of Age* (Norton, 1967), pp. 206–09, 227–33.

workers in other industries.[3] This interpretation of recent economic history seems consistent in broad outline with present knowledge.

The validity of the hypothesis outlined above depends critically on the assumption that employers have strong economic reasons for retiring older workers; but although this is plausible and has some empirical support, it cannot be verified conclusively. Apart from this problem, the discussion is important in illustrating the difficulties of assigning causation to the role of OASDI. While the interpretation as stated places OASDI in an active causative role, two questions remain unanswered: first, whether or not the factors influencing OASDI legislation are largely independent of employers' and employees' preferences concerning retirement age, and, second, whether or not the trend toward early retirement would have occurred regardless of the retirement age established in the program.

In the sections that follow, evidence on retirement patterns will be considered, beginning with the presumption that OASDI is a major causative factor. The problems of distinguishing between the direct effects of OASDI—the income effect of benefits and the earnings test—and the indirect effects in shaping employer policies and employee attitudes will be passed over with little additional comment.

EVALUATION OF SOME EVIDENCE

As eligibility for social security benefits has increased, participation in the labor force by the aged has declined (Table VI-2). The decline in the participation rates for males 65 and over has dominated the overall trend since 1950. For aged females, the rate has remained quite stable, while the rate for females under 65 years of age has risen sharply. Several writers have observed this relationship, but they differ on the weight that can be assigned to OASDI in influencing the participation rate.[4]

[3] On the importance of key bargains for wage levels, see Otto Eckstein and Thomas A. Wilson, "The Determination of Money Wages in American Industry," *Quarterly Journal of Economics*, Vol. 76, No. 3 (August 1962), pp. 379–414.

[4] Clarence D. Long, *The Labor Force under Changing Income and Employment*, National Bureau of Economic Research, General Series No. 65 (Princeton University

Table VI-2. *Percentage of Aged Receiving OASDI Benefits and Participating in the Labor Force, at Five-Year Intervals, 1950–65*

	Percentage of Population Aged 65 and Over		
	Receiving OASDI	Participating in labor force	
Year	benefits	Male	Female
1950	16.4	45.8	9.7
1955	39.4	39.6	10.6
1960	61.6	33.1	10.8
1965	75.2	27.9	10.0

Sources: U.S. Department of Health, Education, and Welfare, Social Security Administration, *Social Security Bulletin, Annual Statistical Supplement, 1965*, Table 16, p. 14; *Manpower Report of the President* (1967), Table A-2, p. 202.

The independent effect of the recent growth of the OASDI is difficult to isolate, because other factors influencing the labor force activity of the aged were operative over the same time period. A decade ago, when evaluating similar though less pronounced evidence, Clarence D. Long observed that declines in labor force activity by the aged occurred before OASDI was created and that a short-run reversal in the long-run decline followed immediately after the first impact of OASDI and of expanded benefit payments by private pension funds in the 1940's. He concluded that ". . . social security and pensions were far from being the main force (though they doubtless helped) in bringing about the withdrawal of elderly persons from the labor market."[5] The evidence suggesting that OASDI has independently influenced retirement decisions is stronger today than at the time of Long's study, but his evaluation of the influence of other factors must still be considered. Among the many factors that may have caused the reduction in labor force participation by the aged were weak labor markets in the 1950's and the relatively low educational attainment of the

Press, 1958); Margaret S. Gordon, *The Economics of Welfare Policies* (Columbia University Press, 1963), pp. 31–40; Gertrude Bancroft, *The American Labor Force: Its Growth and Changing Composition* (Wiley, 1958), pp. 136–37; Gallaway, *The Retirement Decision*, pp. 24–46; Brennan, Taft, and Schupack, *The Economics of Age*, pp. 20–23.

[5] Long, *The Labor Force under Changing Income and Employment*, p. 163.

aged relative to younger workers during a period of rapid technical advance.[6]

Whatever the cause, age 65 had, by 1960, become a critical
watershed in the average working life in the United States. A
cross-section picture of the extent of labor force participation and

Table VI-3. *Percentage of Men and Women Aged 60 and Over in
the Labor Force and Working 35 or More Hours a Week, 1960*

	Men		Women	
Age	In labor force	At work 35 or more hours a week	In labor force	At work 35 or more hours a week
60	83	68	35	24
61	81	65	32	22
62	78	63	29	19
63	75	60	26	16
64	70	55	24	15
65	54	37	20	11
66	46	31	18	9
67	42	27	16	8
68	39	24	15	7
69	36	22	13	7
70–74	29	16	10	5

Source: Lenore A. Epstein and Janet H. Murray, *The Aged Population of the United States: The 1963 Social Security Survey of the Aged*, U.S. Department of Health, Education, and Welfare, Social Security Administration, Office of Research and Statistics, Research Report No. 19 (1967), Table 7.2, p. 335. Based on 1960 Census of Population data.

substantial employment as of the population census of 1960 is provided by Table VI-3. The sharpest drop in participation by males
occurred at age 65. In contrast, the data for females show a more
continuous and gradual downward pattern. A factor that may explain much of the difference between the patterns for aged males
and females is that in 1960 women, but not men, were able to retire at age 62 with actuarially reduced benefits. Thus, the evidence

[6] Gallaway, in *The Retirement Decision*, pp. 24–36, poses the problem of separat-
ing the effect of OASDI from these other important factors but does not convincingly
resolve it.

from Table vi-3 is consistent with the hypothesis that OASDI is a major factor in causing retirement. It is also consistent, of course, with the alternative hypothesis that other, more basic, factors influencing retirement age have caused the policies expressed by OASDI.

Another aspect of the effect of OASDI is its possible encouragement of part-time work by persons who remain in the labor force. Estimates of the work experience of the aged in 1962 (Table vi-4) reveal a shift to part-time work after age 65. The percentage of aged males and females with any work experience, and also the percentage working at full-time jobs, declined sharply with increasing age. The percentage usually working at part-time jobs, however, followed a different pattern, actually increasing for males aged 65 to 72 and declining very little for females, and then declining at later ages. In 1962, both men and women could retire at age 62 with permanently reduced benefits. Males aged 62–64 receiving reduced benefits in 1962 were a small and atypical group, however, so that comparisons of the whole 62–64 age group with the 65–72

Table vi-4. *Percentage of Men and Women Aged 62 and Over Working in 1962, by Work Experience and Age Groups*

Work Experience and Age Group	Men	Women
Usually full-time jobs[a]		
Aged 62–64	70	22
Aged 65–72	31	10
Aged 73 and over	10	3
Usually part-time jobs		
Aged 62–64	10	11
Aged 65–72	16	10
Aged 73 and over	12	3
All workers		
Aged 62–64	80	33
Aged 65–72	47	20
Aged 73 and over	23	6

Source: Lenore A. Epstein and Janet H. Murray, *The Aged Population of the United States: The 1963 Social Security Survey of the Aged*, U.S. Department of Health, Education, and Welfare, Social Security Administration, Office of Research and Statistics, Research Report No. 19 (1967), Table 7.3, p. 336. Figures are rounded and will not necessarily add to totals.

a. 35 or more hours a week.

age group do appear to be a valid approach to testing the impact of OASDI on labor force behavior.[7] The apparent shift to more part-time employment at age 65 does not prove anything conclusively by itself, but again it is behavior consistent with the hypothesis that OASDI has helped to induce full or partial retirement.

EFFECTS OF HIGHER BENEFITS

The impact of social security on retirement depends on both the level and availability of benefits. Since eligibility for social security benefits among those reaching age 65 is becoming virtually universal, the impact of the growth in coverage is primarily of historical interest. Of more importance for the future is the relative level of benefits. An increase in eligibility for benefits causes a sharp and dramatic change in the choices facing an aged person considering retirement; a modest rise in benefit levels relative to potential earnings has a similar but much weaker effect in altering choices and thus may have a wholly different quantitative effect on work incentives. In other words, even if the growth in eligibility for OASDI retirement benefits were to be accepted as the major factor explaining recent past trends in the labor force activity of the aged, the question of the quantitative effect of rising benefit levels on future labor force developments would still remain.

Unfortunately, the little evidence bearing on this point is even weaker than evidence on the effects of widened eligibility for benefits (Chart VI-1). The percentage of men aged 65–69 eligible for benefits who were receiving benefits at the beginning of a given year is a rough measure of at least partial withdrawal from the labor force, since the earnings test disqualifies most full-time workers from receiving benefits. The ratio of average annual benefit awards to median annual earnings is a measure of the attractiveness of benefit levels in retirement relative to earnings from continued work.[8] A comparison of only the terminal years 1950 and 1966 in

---

[7] See Erdman Palmore, "Work Experience and Earnings of the Aged in 1962: Findings of the 1963 Survey of the Aged," *Social Security Bulletin*, Vol. 27, No. 6 (June 1964), p. 5.

[8] Data for average benefit *awards* are given in Chart VI-1 rather than average annual benefits actually paid. The data for awards (which include benefits withheld) provide a better measure of changes in the level of retirement benefits for

Chart VI-1. *Percentage of Insured Males Aged 65–69 Receiving OASDI Benefits Compared with Ratio of Average Annual Benefit Awards to Median Annual Earnings, 1950–66*

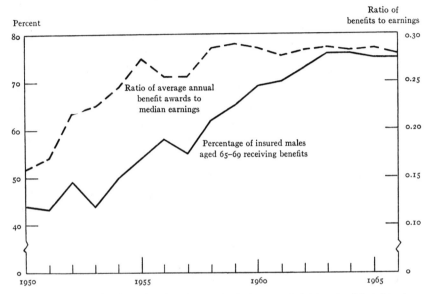

Sources: U.S. Department of Health, Education, and Welfare, Social Security Administration, *Social Security Bulletin, Annual Statistical Supplement, 1965,* Tables 31, 38, and 48, pp. 33, 41, 47; *Social Security Bulletin,* Vol. 30, No. 12 (December 1967), Table Q-6, p. 63, and various issues, 1955 and earlier years; Social Security Administration, unpublished data.

Chart VI-1 shows an apparent positive relationship between benefit levels and withdrawal from the labor force of men aged 65–69. If, however, only the period from 1958 to 1966 is considered, no relationship is apparent. The evidence is consistent with the hypoth-

workers reaching age 65. Estimates of the percentage of eligible workers receiving benefits in any year are given for the age group 65–69 in order to make these figures correspond as closely as possible to the benefit award figures and also because this group is the one that should be most responsive to changes in benefit levels. The general relationships shown are not greatly sensitive to this particular way of considering the problem.

Note that this measure of supply response differs considerably from labor force participation rates of the aged. The latter figure may be sensitive to increased eligibility for benefits while the measure used in Chart VI-1 is, to a first approximation, independent of the effects of changes in eligibility. To the extent that more general eligibility for benefits in the later years of the period caused the inclusion of persons different in important characteristics from the group eligible in the earlier years, the approximation is not a good one.

esis that higher benefit levels significantly reduce work effort, but it is also consistent with the hypothesis that both larger social security benefits and more frequent retirement have been due to growing average income. A further point is that the earnings test was liberalized several times during the period considered (see Appendix B); therefore, for this reason alone, the percentage of eligible workers receiving benefits may have risen somewhat over time.

International comparisons of relative benefit levels and labor force participation rates of the aged are also consistent with the hypothesis that higher benefit levels encourage retirement. Margaret S. Gordon reports a high inverse correlation between the labor force participation rates of males aged 65 and over and average benefits as a percentage of average earnings in fourteen industrialized countries in 1950.[9] Results based on 1960 data for nineteen countries confirm Gordon's results. Subject to a substantial degree of error, the data indicate that an increase of one percentage point in per capita social security benefits relative to average earnings reduces the participation rate of males aged 65 and over by approximately four-tenths of 1 percent (see Appendix D). The estimated impact on aged female participation rates is much weaker. The meager evidence on this point is not impressive; retirement is probably somewhat greater, the larger are retirement benefits provided by OASDI relative to average wages, but estimates of the quantitative importance of this effect must be regarded as very tentative.[10]

Early Retirement Benefits

Until 1956, retirement benefits were not paid before a person reached age 65. Beginning in November 1956 for women, and

[9] Gordon, *The Economics of Welfare Policies*, p. 35.

[10] Gallaway has attempted a quantitative measurement of the impact of OASDI benefit levels in the United States. His results are reported in *The Retirement Decision*, p. 36, and repeated in his "Negative Income Tax Rates and the Elimination of Poverty," *National Tax Journal*, Vol. 19, No. 3 (September 1966), p. 303, and also in his "The Aged and the Extent of Poverty in the United States," *Southern Economic Journal*, Vol. 33, No. 2 (October 1966), p. 217. For criticisms of these results see Michael K. Taussig, "Negative Income Tax Rates and the Elimination of Poverty: Comment," *National Tax Journal*, Vol. 20, No. 3 (September 1967), pp. 328–37; see also Gallaway's "Reply" to this comment in the same issue, pp. 338–43.

August 1961 for men, permanently reduced benefits were made available to workers retiring at age 62. A worker who retires before age 65 has his benefit permanently reduced by five-ninths of 1 percent for each month of the difference between his age when he receives his first benefit and when he reaches 65. Thus a worker who receives retirement benefits at the minimum age, 62, receives a benefit permanently reduced by 20 percent (thirty-six months times five-ninths of 1 percent) below the benefit payable at age 65. The amount of the reduction in benefits was calculated so as to permit payment of early benefits without raising the long-run costs of the benefits of early retirees.[11]

In 1965, about 62 percent of retirement benefit awards to men, and 73 percent to women, were reduced because of early retirement. Since 1956, the percentage of women applying for early retirement benefits has increased substantially, but no definite trend is yet apparent for men.[12] In 1965, the average benefit award to workers who retired at age 65 or later was $107 for men, while the average award for those who retired early was $78; for women, the corresponding amounts in 1965 were $83 and $61. The differences between reduced and unreduced benefits are due in part to the actuarial reduction and in part to the fact that early retirees tend to have lower previous earnings than persons who retire at age 65 or later.

The low benefits paid to early retirees has become a matter of great concern. The number of beneficiaries with permanently reduced benefits has increased rapidly to the point where in 1967 they were approximately one-third of all retired beneficiaries.

[11] The computation period for determining average monthly earnings differs somewhat for men and women if a worker retires before age 65. See Saul Waldman, "Old-Age Benefits for Workers Retiring before Age 65," *Social Security Bulletin,* Vol. 29, No. 2 (February 1966), p. 38.

[12] Figures cited in this paragraph are from Harry Shulman, "Reduced Benefit Awards to Retired Workers: Measuring Extent of Early Retirement," *Social Security Bulletin,* Vol. 29, No. 10 (October 1966), pp. 27–29, and also from *Social Security Bulletin,* Vol. 30, No. 3 (March 1967), Tables Q-5 and Q-6, pp. 46–47. Shulman derives the percentages from adjusted total award figures which exclude those awards not reflecting an actual choice between early and normal retirement. The adjusted data do not include (1) awards made when a disability benefit is converted to a retirement benefit, (2) awards made to persons aged 72 and over under the transitional insured status, and (3) those not involving retirement at the time the award is made. If the percentage with reduced benefits for early retirement were based on unadjusted totals, the figures for 1965 would be 43 for men and 60 for women.

Chart VI-2. *Percentage of Men Aged 60 to 68 in the Labor Force,
1961 and 1966*

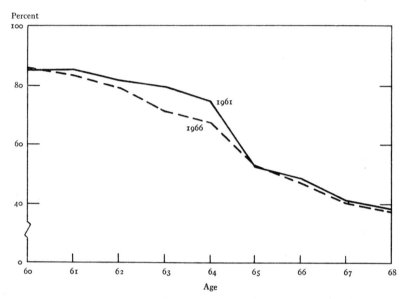

Source: U.S. Department of Labor, Bureau of Labor Statistics, unpublished estimates. These
estimates are not exactly comparable with published estimates or with the estimates based on
1960 Census data, which are shown in Table VI-3.

Many of them have little income other than social security and
are (with exceptions to be discussed) unfortunate in several other
respects. Early retirees tend to have had low earnings, to have been
subject to greater than average unemployment, and to be in bad
health.[13] In view of these facts, it may be somewhat surprising to
observe the apparently significant impact that early retirement under OASDI has had on retirement patterns in only five years (Chart
VI-2). Labor force participation rates for men aged 60–61 and 65–68

[13] The 1963 Survey of the Aged found that ". . . beneficiaries who were aged
62 to 64 at the time of the 1963 Survey were characterized by low incomes, low
employment rates, poor health, and very little voluntary retirement." Lenore A.
Epstein and Janet H. Murray, *The Aged Population of the United States: The 1963
Social Security Survey of the Aged,* U.S. Department of Health, Education, and
Welfare, Social Security Administration, Office of Research and Statistics, Research
Report No. 19 (1967), p. 108. See also Lenore A. Epstein, "Early Retirement and
Work-Life Experience," *Social Security Bulletin,* Vol. 29, No. 3 (March 1966), pp.
3–10, and *The Status of the Social Security Program and Recommendations for
Its Improvement,* Report of the Advisory Council on Social Security (1965), pp. 56–
58.

changed very little between 1961 and 1966, while those in the age bracket 62–64 dropped sharply. By 1966, the retirement pattern for aged men had become much more continuous and gradual. Despite the fact that benefits to early retirees are permanently reduced, the impact of early retirement provisions under OASDI has apparently been sufficient to alter significantly the retirement decisions of aged males. The decline in male participation rates occurred even though most of the early retirees receiving OASDI benefits reported in the 1963 Survey of the Aged that they were not well enough to be in the labor force.[14] Also, the decline occurred over a period in which the economy was expanding and overall unemployment rates were falling to low levels.[15] Had the economy been less prosperous in those years, male retirement ages might have fallen much more rapidly, following the pattern already observed for women.

Retirement Age and Related Issues

In 1935, the Social Security Act defined the aged population of the United States as those persons above age 65. The choice of this particular age—certainly a momentous decision—was apparently made without substantial consideration of alternatives. The desire to encourage retirement of the aged in order to create job openings for the young made selection of a low retirement age desirable, but cost considerations ruled out an age below 65. The choice was therefore shaped, at least implicitly, by the desire to remove as many persons as possible from the labor force, given the constraint of limiting the costs of the program within an acceptable range.[16]

[14] See Table VI-6 below.

[15] See Jacob Mincer, "The Short-Run Elasticity of Labor Supply," in Industrial Relations Research Association, *Proceedings of the Nineteenth Annual Winter Meeting* (1967), p. 227.

[16] This discussion is based on Wilbur J. Cohen, *Retirement Policies Under Social Security* (University of California Press, 1957), Chap. 2, pp. 17–20. Cohen does not believe that the Committee on Economic Security was influenced greatly by the goal of encouraging retirement as a means of reducing unemployment, but observes that this factor was important in obtaining widespread political support for the old-age aspects of the legislation.

The facts bearing on retirement age cited in the foregoing sections of this chapter suggest that OASDI has had a significant influence in standardizing the accepted end of working life at age 65. This is not of historical significance only. The impact of the enactment of early retirement amendments to OASDI, the great pressures to liberalize the benefits under existing early retirement provisions, and the prospect of pushing the minimum age down still further make it essential to face the issue of retirement age anew.

Aside from being very costly, a decision to lower the retirement age under OASDI would have far-reaching consequences, both economic and social, and would almost certainly be irreversible.

COSTS OF REDUCING THE RETIREMENT AGE

The cost of social security per active worker is a function of the average level of benefits actually paid and of the number of active members in the labor force supporting each retired person. This point may be illustrated by a somewhat extreme example: Assume that all persons in the United States in 1966 work from age 18 until they retire. A reduction in the hypothetical retirement age from 65 to 62, with average benefits and total production held constant, would increase the cost of social security per member of the working age population by roughly 30 percent. That is, the taxes required of each worker to finance one dollar of benefits for each retiree would increase from approximately 17 to 22 cents (Table VI-5). Similarly, if the age were lowered to 60 or to 55, the cost would be increased by more than 50 and 100 percent, respectively. The larger the ratio of the working, taxpaying population to the retired, beneficiary population, the lower are the costs of the program *at any given level of average benefits.* Another implication of the same point is that the larger the ratio, the higher is the level of average benefits *at any given level of average tax.* A lower retirement age under OASDI that encourages withdrawal from the labor force would, other things equal, lower the ratio of working taxpayers to retired beneficiaries, with two likely results. In the future, average benefit levels would probably be lower than they otherwise would have been. This would occur unless the working population

Table VI-5. *Ratio of Working Population to Population Over Various Hypothetical Retirement Ages, July 1, 1966*[a]

Hypothetical Retirement Age	Population Over Hypothetical Retirement Age (Thousands)	Working Population[b] (Thousands)	Ratio of Working Population to Population Over Hypothetical Retirement Age	Tax Required of Each Worker To Finance $1 of Benefits to Each Retiree
55	35,718	90,449	2.53	$0.40
60	26,387	99,780	3.78	0.26
62	23,052	103,115	4.47	0.22
65	18,457	107,710	5.84	0.17

Source: U.S. Bureau of the Census, "Estimates of the Population of the United States, by Age, Color, and Sex: July 1, 1966," *Current Population Reports*, Series P-25, No. 352 (1966), Table 1, p. 14.
a. Population figures represent the sum of total resident population and Armed Forces stationed outside the United States.
b. All persons between age 18 and the hypothetical retirement age are included in the working population

were willing to be taxed much more heavily to finance benefits than they would have been if the retirement age were not lowered. In addition, tax dollars would be diverted from other government programs to help finance OASDI retirement benefits. This second result would occur unless the taxpaying population became more willing to pay much greater total taxes as a consequence of earlier retirement or unless benefit levels were allowed to decline greatly.

Some combination of the following consequences of earlier retirement would have to come about: lower retirement benefits for a larger retired population, less government spending on other government programs, and lower after-tax incomes for the working population. The specific mix of these effects would depend on a political decision regarding the priorities of the claims of the groups affected. In addition, since lowering the retirement age would reduce production to the extent that it induced early retirement in a full employment economy, the actual cost would be higher than the transfer cost of the increased benefits. The quantitative importance of such an effect on economic growth is impossible to predict; it would depend on the extent to which the loss in output resulting from early retirement was offset by such factors as higher participation rates of married women and by gains in efficiency because of greater upward mobility of younger, more productive workers. How the burden of lower output would be shared by the retired and working populations would again be decided largely through the political process.

Social security has moved toward pre-age-65 retirement by allowing widows to receive reduced benefits at age 60 and full benefits at age 62, and by allowing men and women workers to retire at age 62 with reduced benefits. If unreduced benefits were payable at age 62 to present early retirees, the cost would be equivalent to about an 8.4 percent across-the-board increase in benefits.

Given the historical experience with age-65 retirement, it is reasonable to conclude that the average retirement age would decline over time if unreduced retirement benefits were made payable before age 65 and, therefore, that the costs to OASDI and to the economy would rise still more. Another reasonable conjecture is that pressures would develop to pay reduced benefits at, perhaps, age 60 or even age 55, thereby further lowering the average retirement age. There is no logical limit to this process; scores of bills, designed to provide more generous benefits to present early retirees and to extend full benefits to still younger persons, have already been introduced and strongly supported in Congress.

RATIONALE FOR EARLY RETIREMENT

Although the cost of early retirement is high, it is easy to understand the reasoning behind pressures to lower the age below the present limit of 65 and yet pay full benefits. As workers become older, unemployment tends increasingly to be long term, health deteriorates, and other misfortunes occur. To provide retirement benefits to a person aged 65 who may be quite vigorous, but to withhold them from someone aged 64 who is too feeble to work, seems arbitrary and cruel social policy.

In response to questionnaires in 1963 about their reasons for not working, most early retirees indicated that retirement was involuntary, that such reasons as poor health, compulsory retirement age, or unemployment and inability to find another job drove them out of the labor force (Table vi-6). Early male retirees gave ill health and unemployment as reasons for retirement much more often than did males who retired at age 65 or later. Mandatory retirement affected relatively few early retirees, indicating that in 1963 the standard retirement age was still 65 or older. The most important finding of this survey of early retirees is the high degree

Table vi-6. *Percentage Distribution of Retired Persons, by Reasons Given for Retirement, 1963*[a]

	Men		Women	
Reason for Retirement	Aged 62–64	Aged 65 and over	Aged 62–64	Aged 65 and over
Voluntary reasons	17	28	80	58
Preferred leisure	9	19	20	21
Other reasons	8	10	60	37
Involuntary reasons	83	72	64	63
Poor health	53	41	33	36
Compulsory retirement age	3	19	1	9
Laid off or job discontinued	19	8	15	8
Other reasons	8	4	15	10
Total	100	100	100[b]	100[b]

Source: Lenore A. Epstein and Janet H. Murray, *The Aged Population of the United States: The 1963 Social Security Survey of the Aged*, U.S. Department of Health, Education, and Welfare, Social Security Administration, Office of Research and Statistics, Research Report No. 19 (1967), Table 8.4, pp. 345–46. Figures are rounded and will not necessarily add to totals.

a. Retirement is defined to mean not working 35 hours or more a week for six or more consecutive months. All persons included in the survey were wage and salary workers who had retired after 1957.

b. Total is greater than 100 percent because multiple reasons were given.

of subjective disability among the aged, and especially among early retirees.

The reasons for retirement given in the 1963 survey confirm, in general, the results of earlier surveys, although there did appear to be evidence of an increase in voluntary retirement over that indicated in the previous decade.[17] In their important study of the aged, Peter O. Steiner and Robert Dorfman caution that results of questionnaires on reasons for retirement are difficult to interpret. For example, there is evidence that people tend to give poor health

[17] Epstein and Murray, *The Aged Population of the United States*, Chap. 8, pp. 101–05. See also Gordon, *The Economics of Welfare Policies*, p. 37.

as a reason for retirement as a "disguise for either lack of interest or unemployment."[18]

There are other reasons for skepticism about the finding that poor health is the predominant cause of the trend toward early retirement. As observed in Chapter II, more than two-thirds of all males aged 65 and over at the beginning of this century were physically capable of work. The contrast with the present is attributable to many factors: the early data are unreliable and, at best, are not fully comparable with more recent figures; the aged at the turn of the century were a much smaller and a younger group than the present aged; in the past, many more of the aged lived on farms and therefore had greater opportunities to reduce their work effort gradually as they underwent physical decline; and, probably most important of all, economic growth has steadily lessened the necessity for the aged to continue to work. Granted all the foregoing explanations, it seems reasonable to conclude that an additional factor affecting the trend toward early retirement has been a change in attitudes toward what constitutes bad health, a development with little apparent objective basis. Life expectancy at age 65 has improved in this century, although not as dramatically as life expectancy at birth.[19] It seems unlikely that the physical capability of the aged for work could have declined significantly at the same time. To determine the reasons why aged persons today consider themselves involuntarily retired because of poor health would require a study in social psychology far beyond the capabilities of ordinary questionnaires.

REDUCED BENEFITS FOR EARLY RETIREES

Many studies have shown that the problems of older workers are due to low incomes arising from inability to work. The recognition that such problems often arise before age 65 led to the introduction of early retirement benefits. Since the justification for early benefits is much the same as that for regular benefits, why should early retirees suffer permanently reduced benefits?

[18] Peter O. Steiner and Robert Dorfman, *The Economic Status of the Aged* (University of California Press, 1957), p. 43 (note 4), and p. 50.

[19] See U.S. Bureau of the Census, *Statistical Abstract of the United States, 1967* (1967), Tables 61 and 62, pp. 53, 54.

When Congress extended eligibility for early retirement benefits to men in 1961, the answer appeared to be simply cost. Congress even required that early retirement benefits for men be computed according to a somewhat stricter formula than that used in computing similar benefits for women, because it was estimated that equal treatment would involve a small additional long-run cost for the retirement program.[20] It was not concerned that the current dollar cost of benefits would rise, as it did, when reduced benefits were made available immediately to early retirees. Instead, it provided for permanently reduced benefits in order to keep the actuarial value of total benefits constant over the lifetime of retired workers. Thus, it appeared in 1956 and 1961 that a good thing—extending retirement benefits to persons who were in clear need of them—could be done at no expense and without endangering the "actuarial soundness" of social security.

The fallacy in this reasoning is obvious today. Many early retirees are at the bottom of the earnings and income scale and are disadvantaged in other respects as well. The early retirees themselves bear the real cost of this approach in the form of permanently reduced benefits until death.[21] The present unsatisfactory status of these unfortunate people can thus be traced directly to congressional concern regarding the actuarial costs of the program, instead of the income needs of the group.

Another possible long-run cost of early retirement (apparently ignored by Congress) is that it induces retirement by some workers who are not in need of early benefits. According to results of the questionnaires in 1963 on the reasons for retirement, 17 percent of the males who retired early did so voluntarily.[22] Almost 13

[20] Wilbur J. Cohen and William L. Mitchell, "Social Security Amendments of 1961: Summary and Legislative History," *Social Security Bulletin*, Vol. 24, No. 9 (September 1961), pp. 3–11, 33; and Marice C. Hart, "Old-Age, Survivors, and Disability Insurance: Early Retirement Provisions," *Social Security Bulletin*, Vol. 24, No. 10 (October 1961), p. 4.

[21] See the 1965 report of the Advisory Council on Social Security, *The Status of the Social Security Program and Recommendations for Its Improvement*, pp. 56–58, for a recent view of the problems of early retirees. In 1961, before disillusion set in, the view was different: "Under the provision making reduced benefits available at age 62, a man can weigh the amount of the benefit he can get against his physical condition, the availability of work, and his general financial situation and make the choice that seems best for him under all the circumstances." Cohen and Mitchell, "Social Security Amendments of 1961," p. 4.

[22] Epstein and Murray, *The Aged Population of the United States*, p. 345.

percent of the early retirees had maximum earnings in at least eight of the twelve years previous to retirement.[23] In other words, some workers aged 62 through 64 who in no apparent respect were disadvantaged relative to other workers were retiring early. Furthermore, early retirement for apparently voluntary reasons by workers without health problems or other handicaps increased sharply between 1963 and 1964. Almost one-third of all early male retirees in 1964 had a strong labor force attachment, according to the measures of continuous previous employment and earnings level.[24] Predictably, as employers and employees have had time to adjust to the early retirement provisions first effective in 1961, retirement patterns have moved in the expected direction.

The dilemma of providing early retirement benefits can be summarized simply: If benefits are reduced for those retiring early, some of the neediest retirees will receive pitifully small benefits, a result inconsistent with the fundamental objectives of social security. If benefits are not reduced (and, to a lesser degree, even if they are reduced), the retirement age will fall, adding considerably to the cost of the program. There is growing recognition that the problems of those under age 65 who cannot continue working are not adequately met by the present early retirement provisions.

The point that requires widespread public understanding is that the retirement program is the incorrect remedy for the problem at hand. The problem, for which public policy seeks an answer, is the *unemployability*, for one of many reasons, of aging workers.[25] To deal with the problem by expanding the social security retirement program to include continually younger workers is inherently inefficient since the problem begins in a smaller degree at quite early ages; there is no logical place to stop, once the retirement age is lowered.[26]

---

[23] Epstein, "Early Retirement and Work-Life Experience," p. 6.

[24] Unpublished data provided by the Social Security Administration.

[25] See Margaret S. Gordon, "National Retirement Policies and the Displaced Older Worker," in P. From Hansen (ed.), *Age with a Future* (Copenhagen: Munksgaard, 1964; distributed by F. A. Davis, Philadelphia), pp. 591–601. (University of California, Institute of Industrial Relations, Reprint 250.)

[26] Brennan, Taft, and Schupack observe that "a relatively high rate of nonparticipation begins to appear at about 45 years of age" (*The Economics of Age,* p. 204).

SOLUTIONS FOR THE PROBLEMS OF EARLY RETIREMENT

Two solutions, designed for the specific problems of the older worker, are needed. First, to provide cash benefits to those whose physical disability prevents them from working, the appropriate vehicle is not a retirement program which pays benefits to all, but a disability program which awards benefits to those whose problems provoke a genuine social concern. Eligibility for disability benefits for insured persons could be liberalized progressively with increasing age. A procedure analogous to that employed in determining eligibility for veterans' disability pensions might be appropriate. Permanent and total disability is a condition for benefits for veterans under age 55; 60 or 70 percent disability is a condition for benefits between the ages of 55 and 59; and 50 percent disability is required between the ages of 60 and 64. Alternatively, long-term unemployment might be taken as evidence of retirement among workers beyond specified ages. This procedure is followed in several Western European countries; for example, in the Federal Republic of Germany, unemployment for one year preceding application for benefits by persons aged 60 or older establishes eligibility for retirement benefits.[27]

Second, other programs need to be developed; cash benefits alone are an insufficient response to the problems. Health insurance is certainly one additional appropriate program that can and should be administered within the existing social security administrative structure. But other necessary programs, such as adult education, training, and rehabilitation, are beyond the scope of social security. Also outside the purview of social security are economic policies that assure full employment and price stability.

Steiner and Dorfman, writing a decade ago, pointed out that the problems of the aged could be traced, to a large degree, to deficiencies in health, education, and training that had their inception in middle-age or even earlier.[28] Their suggestion that these prob-

---

[27] U.S. Department of Health, Education, and Welfare, Social Security Administration, Office of Research and Statistics, *Social Security Programs Throughout the World, 1967* (1967), p. 80.

[28] Steiner and Dorfman, *The Economic Status of the Aged*, pp. 148–49.

lems be prevented through programs to help younger age groups has not yet influenced any important policy decisions. Public education and training programs should, perhaps, give more emphasis to the problems of aging; in this connection, continuing education seems particularly appropriate. The greater average duration of unemployment among older workers and the fact that long-term unemployment often merges into retirement suggest that the problem for many older workers is the obsolescence of skills. To the extent that this occurs, additional training or job counseling for workers in their fifties, or even their forties, would be desirable. More basic is the need to prevent poverty early in the life cycle, for poverty early in life is the root cause of bad health, lack of education and skills, and continued poverty later in the life cycle. The interrelationship between social security and other government programs in this respect has never been satisfactorily explored.

Along these same lines, but admittedly more speculative in nature, are suggestions for public policies that would distribute leisure more evenly over the working life, thereby improving the quality of work and leisure alike. At present, after completing their schooling, people usually work until age 65 or so, and then face perhaps twenty years of virtually complete idleness. This pattern seems grossly out of step with biological changes in physical capacity over the same time span. A gradual reduction in work effort with increasing age would seem to be a more desirable arrangement for most individuals.[29] Economic and social institutions that permit individuals gradually to reduce their work effort would probably be difficult and expensive to devise, but they seem eminently desirable long-run goals. Perhaps the long-run goal should be an institution as flexible in this respect as the family farm of a past era.

All these points bring us back to one final observation about the role of social security. To lower the age of eligibility for retirement benefits or to raise the benefits for retirees aged 62–64 would foreclose some of the most promising measures for dealing with the difficult problems of aging in our society. In view of ex-

[29] This basic idea, so-called "flexible retirement," is discussed by Lloyd Saville, "Flexible Retirement," in Juanita M. Kreps (ed.), *Employment, Income, and Retirement Problems of the Aged* (Duke University Press, 1963), pp. 140–77.

pected improvements in the health and longevity of the aged, extending the class defined as "aged" backward to include younger people would be perverse social policy. Indeed, persons reaching age 65 in the future will be increasingly better educated and employed in positions that call for mental rather than physical prowess. Their employment will be increasingly in the challenging professional and technical fields, in which work is preferable to leisure for many persons. Social priorities in other areas are not so low at this point that the government should undertake the extremely expensive task of subsidizing the leisure of healthy persons under age 65. To prevent relative deterioration of the income status of those now defined as aged is a sufficiently demanding goal for social security.

ENCOURAGEMENT OF LATER RETIREMENT

Social security now acts only as an inducement to early retirement. The retirement test, by curtailing benefits to those whose earnings exceed $1,680 a year, acts as a positive inducement to at least partial retirement, regardless of the beneficiary's health or desire for work. Past and expected improvements in the health of the aged suggest that the trend toward early retirement could be influenced by appropriate public policies. Measures to encourage voluntary continuation of work beyond age 65 are desirable for two reasons. First, *voluntary* decisions by aged persons to continue work result in improvement in their welfare. Second, improvement in the income status of the aged who are not workers becomes less costly, the smaller their number.

In considering ways by which workers could be given greater choice about when to retire, the discussion here will be limited to those changes which leave every aged person with choices at least as good as those available under the present program. Therefore, retirement at age 65 with benefits at least as high as those available today must remain one of the choices for every aged individual.

This limitation on acceptable changes in the present program means that any measure to encourage later retirement will be, to some extent, costly. The choice among policy measures should turn on their relative effectiveness in expanding freedom of choice about retirement for any given level of cost. Within the framework set forth above, three specific changes in the OASDI program deserve consideration. First, workers aged 65 and over could be exempted from the payroll taxes. Second, persons who work beyond age 65 could, on retirement, be paid permanently increased benefits —delayed retirement credits—just as persons who retire before age 65 are currently paid permanently reduced benefits. Finally, the earnings test as a condition for eligibility for benefits could be repealed or considerably relaxed.

For the purposes of evaluating these alternatives in terms of cost-effectiveness, regrettably little is known about how the aged would respond. In the short run, at least, there are reasons for skepticism that any of the measures would appreciably affect the labor force participation and intensity of work effort of the aged. If the surveys discussed previously in this chapter have any validity, many retired persons aged 65 and over do not feel able to work. Certainly many of the aged, especially widows aged 70 and over who have never worked, would not be influenced by any of the suggested policy changes. Given the present state of ignorance, the argument for a large commitment of funds to implement any one of the three measures is weak at this time. Nonetheless, in order to anticipate future developments, it is useful to consider each measure in brief outline.

Exempting workers aged 65 and over from OASDI payroll taxes. This alternative has the advantage of being relatively inexpensive; it would probably cost no more than $400 million a year to exempt both the employee and the employer share of the OASDI tax, or less than 2 percent of total 1967 OASDI revenues. The equity arguments for this alternative have some persuasiveness. Since retirees currently pay no taxes on social security benefits, it is difficult to justify OASDI taxes on earnings of aged persons who continue to work. The extra exemption, because of age, allowed for the personal income tax does not help at all in reducing the payroll tax burden of the aged who continue to be employed.[30] Exempting the employee's share of the payroll tax at age 65 would raise take-home pay, thereby making the prospect of continued

---

[30] For a discussion of the tax treatment of the aged, see Chapter VIII.

work more attractive for the aged worker. Exempting the employer's share of the tax would lower his costs of hiring aged workers at any given gross wage level. The possibility of wage discrimination by age to correspond with differences in productivity by age would enhance the employability of aged workers.

On the other side of the question, the cost of exempting aged workers from payroll taxes might increase significantly over time. In addition, no precedent exists for evaluating the administrative problems involved in implementing this measure as far as the employer share of the tax is concerned; it might be troublesome and even impossible for the Social Security Administration and for employers to single out the age 65 and over group of workers for tax purposes. The employee share of the tax, however, could be handled very easily by allowing the aged worker to claim a refund on his personal income tax return, a process that is currently used to refund employee overpayment of the OASDI tax.

This possibility obviously depends on continuation of the present method of financing social security. If the payroll tax were integrated with the personal income tax, the exemption of aged workers would have no meaning unless it were carried over into the income tax. However, this would be inconsistent with the objective of making social security benefits taxable in order to reduce the inequities in the present income tax. These points are discussed further in Chapter VIII.

Permanently increased benefits for late retirees. Delayed retirement credits in the form of permanently increased benefits for late retirees are a straightforward means of encouraging later retirement. Continuation of employment beyond age 65 would qualify a worker for increased retirement benefits upon cessation of work. While working, he would be subject to the earnings test. The credit could be given to workers in only those age groups where response to the credit was expected to be greatest. For example, credits might apply only to work between ages 65 and 71; beginning at age 72, the cessation of credits would coincide with the end of the earnings test. The amount of the credit could vary from token amounts to the actuarial rate, or even more. A worker's retirement benefit would have to be increased by about 9 percent for each year of employment beyond age 65 in order to keep the actuarial value of his benefits unaffected by his age of retirement. If the delayed retirement credit were made this large, changes in the average retirement age would no longer affect the actuarial costs of the OASDI program.

The delayed retirement credit would provide direct, tangible, monetary incentives for aged persons to continue work. When jobs were available, an aged worker could enter the labor force with the knowledge that any temporary loss in OASDI benefits because of the earnings test would be fully compensated by higher benefits when he again left the labor force. If the delayed credit were effective in encouraging mobility in and out of the labor force, the cyclical flexibility of the total labor force in the economy would be enhanced. Aged workers would be a source of additional skilled manpower when labor was scarce, but could leave the labor force at will to receive retirement benefits when job prospects were less attractive. The delayed retirement credit could be combined with exemption from OASDI payroll taxes after age 65 to make work for the aged much more remunerative than at present.

A delayed retirement credit would be very expensive if it were large enough to keep the present expected value of total benefits unchanged. The cost today would be equivalent to an increase of about 8.4 percent in benefits—the same as eliminating the earnings test. Given the uncertainty regarding the effectiveness of the credit in encouraging later retirement, a cost of this magnitude appears to be excessive. The cost could be scaled down as much as desired, of course, by limiting it to certain age groups or by cutting the amount, with some corresponding decrease in the effectiveness of its work incentive effect. Another possible reason for holding down the size of the credit would be the otherwise very high benefits payable to some persons working for several years past age 65.

Repeal of the earnings test. The cost of this measure would be exactly the same as that of paying late retirees permanently increased benefits in amounts which keep the actuarial value of total benefits constant for the program. In either case, changes in average retirement age would no longer affect the actuarial costs of the program. On any other grounds, repeal of the earnings test is an inferior alternative to a delayed retirement credit. The absence of an earnings test is inconsistent with the goals of social security. To pay benefits in addition to earnings is not to maintain past income levels, but rather to add to existing income levels which are frequently more than adequate. If the earnings test were repealed, benefits would be paid to the small minority of aged persons who are full-time workers with earnings that already give them very high incomes relative to the nonworking aged. To remove the earnings test would raise the cost of the OASDI program by about $2 billion a year at present benefit levels.[31] Surely better uses exist for limited government tax revenues than to pay very large amounts of benefits to the relatively affluent minority of the aged who would benefit by repeal of the test.

Pressures to liberalize or repeal the earnings test should be firmly resisted, despite its great unpopularity. Antipathy to the test is based on widespread misunderstanding of the objectives of social security and on assertions about its disincentive effects on the work effort of the aged. If the problem of work incentives is considered serious enough to warrant national concern, the foregoing discussion points to the need for pilot studies to test the effectiveness of delayed retirement credits of modest amounts or of exemption of aged workers from OASDI taxes. The heart of the issue concerning further relaxation of the earnings test is simply stated: There is no compelling reason for society to give people money simply because they attain some arbitrary age. If, as argued in Chapter IV, the appropriate objectives of social security (with respect to the aged) are the provision of income support to prevent destitution and the maintenance, after retirement, of a generous fraction of previous standards of living, the earnings test should stand in much its present form.

The discussion of the alternative measures directed toward encouraging later retirement leads to only one conclusion—the negative verdict that repeal of the earnings test is the worst of all possible alternatives. Given the present state of ignorance about the labor force behavior of the aged in general and, specifically, about the probable reaction of aged persons to any measure designed to encourage later retirement, it is premature to make a judgment

[31] *Social Security Amendments of 1967,* Hearings before the Senate Committee on Finance on H.R. 12080, 90 Cong. 1 sess. (1967), Pt. 1, p. 242.

that any one measure, or combination of measures, is preferable to all alternatives, including the alternative of no change at all. In view of the unsatisfactory state of knowledge at present, there is certainly a strong objection today to the implementation of any measure relating to the retirement decision that involves significant incremental costs for the OASDI program.

Summary

The social security system may encourage partial or complete retirement for several reasons. First, for persons who have reached retirement age, the retirement program directly reduces the incentives to continue work. In addition, the program may set the standard for other retirement programs and may condition social attitudes toward retirement age. The evidence suggests that the growth of OASDI has been one important factor in causing the sharp decline in the labor force participation of the aged since World War II.

Early retirement benefits have been made available to both men and women aged 62. These benefits are permanently reduced in order to keep constant the long-run costs of benefits. Payment of early retirement benefits has proved unsatisfactory for two reasons: first, it causes low benefits to be paid to very needy aged persons; second, it is still another aspect of the social security system that reduces the work incentives of the aged. More specific programs, such as extension of disability protection, are needed to meet the problem of unemployable, older workers who are under age 65.

Since the costs of social security vary so greatly with the relative size of the retired population, measures that might reverse the trend to early retirement should be given consideration. Two possible changes in the present program are, first, to exempt aged workers from OASDI taxes and, second, to pay permanently increased benefits—delayed retirement credits—to persons who work past age 65. The major problem with these measures is that their effectiveness, especially in the short run, might not be worth the costs involved. But both of these alternatives are preferable to any further relaxation of the earnings test.

CHAPTER VII

Costs and Benefits of Social Security

Estimating the relative costs and benefits of proposed changes in the social security system is an extremely complex undertaking. Estimates involve judgments about economic and demographic variables which must be predicted far into the future. Some changes in benefits cost little initially but are very expensive in the long run; others impose substantial costs initially, but these costs subsequently decline and average out to very little. Few individuals have any basis for judging how their own situation will be affected by any particular set of changes.

Alternative improvements in the benefit structure advance the major goals of social security in different degrees. For example, the long-run cost of an increase in the minimum benefit from \$55 to \$75 a month would be the same as the cost of an across-the-board increase of about 4 percent in all benefits. However, the cost of the increase in the minimum benefit would be quite high initially and decline over time, while that of the across-the-board change would rise in proportion to the increase in total benefits. Roughly 60 cents of every dollar of the increase in the minimum benefit would go to households classified as poor according to official standards. But adjustments in the minimum would not alter the earnings replacement rate at higher benefit levels. The across-the-board increase would direct only 15 to 20 cents of each additional dollar of increased outlays to poor households, but it would raise the replacement rate for all beneficiaries.[1]

[1] U.S. Department of Health, Education, and Welfare, Office of Assistant Secre-

149

In comparison with these two changes, raising widows' benefits would advance both the income support and the earnings replacement objectives—because widows are poorer than other beneficiary groups and because the need for protection of prior living standards is as great for them as it is for other survivors and for retired and disabled workers. On the other hand, an increase in benefit payments to wives would contribute less to attaining both objectives. Incomes of married couples tend to be higher relative to needs than are incomes of single persons. Also, wage replacement for couples is already generous relative to that of single retirees with similar preretirement standards of living.[2] Poor households would be helped more by an across-the-board increase.

The key to intelligent decision-making in social security is a recognition of the costs of particular modifications and of their contributions toward the desired goals. Since there is no objective method for settling disagreements about goals, disputes over the priority of particular changes would not be ended by accurate and relevant estimates of costs. But such estimates would enable policy decisions to focus on methods for using available resources most effectively to advance whatever goals emerge.[3]

Cost Estimates

The Office of the Actuary of the Social Security Administration prepares official estimates of social security costs. The major purpose of these estimates is to enable the Congress, the Executive Branch, and the public to compare the costs of various changes that would provide different kinds or amounts of benefits at different times, and to determine the level and phasing of taxes re-

tary for Program Coordination, *Income and Benefit Programs* (1966), p. 51, and authors' estimates.

[2] See Chapter V for a discussion of these issues.

[3] Methods of analyzing the benefits and costs of public expenditure programs have been receiving a considerable amount of attention in recent years. See Charles J. Hitch and Roland N. McKean, *The Economics of Defense in the Nuclear Age* (Harvard University Press, 1960); Robert Dorfman (ed.), *Measuring Benefits of Government Investments* (Brookings Institution, 1965); and Samuel B. Chase, Jr. (ed.), *Problems in Public Expenditure Analysis* (Brookings Institution, 1968).

quired to pay for these benefits. Several sets of estimates are prepared, each based on a different specialized set of assumptions. One particular set of estimates—the "long-range" estimates—is used to determine the "actuarial soundness" of the Old-Age, Survivors, and Disability Insurance (OASDI) program. By taking account of factors forecast far into the future, the long-range estimates are intended to provide the Congress and the public with a basis for considering the full price of any change in the system. An evaluation of the role of cost estimates in shaping social security policy must concentrate on the dominant role of the long-range estimates.

THE BASIS FOR LONG-RANGE ESTIMATES

The long-range cost estimates involve projections of many variables, ranging from population and labor force participation rates to the number of parents over age 65 who outlive OASDI insured children and the number of dependents of disabled workers.[4] Two estimates are made for each variable. One entails high costs and produces low revenues; the other entails low costs and produces high revenues. All projections of the first type are grouped together, yielding a "high-cost estimate"; those of the second type, grouped together, yield a "low-cost estimate." An "intermediate-cost estimate," calculated by a procedure that is roughly equivalent to taking the arithmetic average of the high-cost and low-cost estimates, is used in legislative work on social security.[5]

For these estimates, average money wages and prices are assumed to remain unchanged. An effort is made to project popula-

[4] For a full list of these variables, see Robert J. Myers, *Methodology Involved in Developing Long-Range Cost Estimates for the Old-Age, Survivors, and Disability Insurance System,* U.S. Department of Health, Education, and Welfare, Social Security Administration, Division of the Actuary, Actuarial Study No. 49 (1959), pp. 5–6.

[5] The actual procedure is to take arithmetic averages of high-cost and low-cost estimates of component items, such as projected number of beneficiaries, and then combine these component averages to obtain the final intermediate-cost estimate. See *The 1968 Annual Report of the Board of Trustees of the Federal Old-Age and Survivors Insurance and Disability Insurance Trust Funds,* H. Doc. 288, 90 Cong. 2 sess. (1968), p. 39 (hereafter referred to as Board of Trustees of OASDI Trust Funds, *1968 Annual Report*).

tion growth, however, and it is the uncertainty of the population forecasts that explains much of the difference between the high-cost and low-cost estimates.[6] The estimates are, therefore, a blend of static and dynamic projections, and cannot be interpreted as forecasts of expenditures, revenues, and trust fund developments.

Although the assumption that money wages will not grow is acknowledged to be unrealistic, it is defended officially on the ground that the intermediate-cost estimate is presented not as an absolute dollar amount but as a percentage of covered earnings. The costs of all future benefits for the next 75 years are presented in one summary measure: the level-cost rate. This measure is defined as "the constant combined employer-employee tax rate that, together with a tax on the self-employed of about 75 percent of such combined rate . . . , would exactly pay for future benefits and administrative expenses, after making allowance for the effect of the future interest earnings of the existing trust fund and for all other future interest earnings."[7]

The assumption of constant wages and prices is defended along the following lines:

If earnings levels rise, as they have in the past, the benefits and the taxable earnings base under the program will undoubtedly be modified. In fact, if all other assumed cost factors are closely followed by the experience, then increasing wage levels will automatically generate positive actuarial balances that can be used to increase benefit levels without changing the financing provisions. If such changes are made concurrently and proportionately with changes in general earnings levels, and if the experience follows all the other assumptions, the future year-by-year costs of the system as a percentage of taxable payroll would be the same as those shown [in the long-range intermediate cost estimate with the assumption of no growth in average earnings]. . . . However, the level-cost might not rise this much, or might even decline, if benefit adjustments do not fully reflect rising earnings. Again, the effect of such events can be observed in ample time to make any needed changes in the contribution schedule or any other appropriate changes in the system.[8]

A similar measure, the level-equivalent rate of contributions, is used to summarize the revenues that will be produced by scheduled tax rates. If these two measures of projected intermediate

[6] *Ibid.*, p. 38.   [7] *Ibid.*, p. 39.   [8] *Ibid.*, p. 44.

costs and revenues are sufficiently close to each other (within 0.3 percentage point) under a given schedule of taxes and benefits, the program is considered to be in "actuarial balance."[9] In other words, actuarial balance means that the taxes to be collected during the next 75 years plus accumulated interest on any balance in the reserve fund will be just sufficient to pay for the scheduled benefits.

ASSUMPTIONS

The official cost estimates are frequently regarded by nontechnicians as mathematically precise and neutral in influencing policy decisions. On the contrary, judgment is critically involved in every assumption, a circumstance which the Actuary has forthrightly stressed: ". . . the figures developed do not represent the widest possible range that could reasonably be anticipated, but rather our studied opinions as to a plausible range."[10] To observe that judgment plays a critical role in making projections into the future is not a criticism; knowledge of the future in most respects is too uncertain to permit analysts to dispense with judgment or, in some cases, simple guesses. The point is that the judgment built into the official cost estimates follows a consistent pattern of financial conservatism. This may be illustrated by the treatment of two crucial variables: population growth and change in real wages.

A critical factor influencing OASDI costs is the ratio of the aged beneficiary population to the working-age population, and this factor in turn depends, among other things, on future fertility and mortality rates. The lower the ratio of the aged population to the working-age population, the lower will be the costs of an old-age retirement program for the working population (see Chapter VI). Other things equal, lower fertility and lower mortality rates will in time increase the proportion of the aged population in the whole population by causing a relative decrease in the number of future

[9] Robert J. Myers, *Social Insurance and Allied Government Programs* (R. D. Irwin, 1965), p. 129.
[10] Robert J. Myers and Francisco Bayo, *Long-Range Cost Estimates for Old-Age, Survivors, and Disability Insurance System, 1966,* U.S. Department of Health, Education, and Welfare, Social Security Administration, Office of the Actuary, Actuarial Study No. 63 (1967), p. 5.

working-age people relative to the number of aged. Thus, lower fertility or mortality rates mean relatively high costs, and higher fertility or mortality rates relatively low costs, for any given benefit schedule.

Past forecasts by demographers of fertility rates have been very inaccurate. Reliable data are limited, and theory explaining changes in fertility is notably undeveloped. The Census Bureau, therefore, makes four population projections based on widely differing fertility assumptions, chosen so that actual experience will very likely fall somewhere in the range of the projections. Mortality rates, on the other hand, have remained within narrow ranges and, barring more spectacular advances in health care or environmental control than have occurred in recent years, the gradual upward trend in life expectancy is expected to continue. The Census Bureau therefore employs only one set of mortality assumptions in its population forecasts.[11]

When these considerations are kept in mind, the tendencies inherent in the cost estimates are evident. The low-cost estimate is based on fertility assumptions that fall roughly at the midpoint of the Census Bureau's range and on the same mortality assumptions that are used by the Census Bureau.[12] Thus, the demographic component of the low-cost estimate corresponds roughly to the median estimates of the Census Bureau. The high-cost estimate involves fertility estimates which lie well below the lowest fertility estimates of the Census Bureau and mortality rates that are lower than those assumed by the Census Bureau.[13] As a result, the high-

[11] For a description of Census Bureau practice, see U.S. Bureau of the Census, "Projections of the White and Nonwhite Population of the United States, by Age and Sex, to 1985," *Current Population Reports*, Series P-25, No. 345 (1966).

[12] In fact, the relationship is the reverse—the Census Bureau adopted the mortality assumptions of the Social Security Administration. Since publication of the last Census Bureau projections of population, the Social Security Administration has changed both its high and low mortality assumptions. The most significant change is an upward revision of the low mortality assumptions. The reason for the revision is that the downward trend in mortality leveled off in the mid-1950's; see U.S. Bureau of the Census, *Statistical Abstract of the United States, 1966* (1966), Table 65, p. 55.

[13] U.S. Bureau of the Census, "Projections of the White and Nonwhite Population of the United States"; and Francisco Bayo, *United States Population Projections for OASDHI Cost Estimates*, U.S. Department of Health, Education, and Welfare, Social Security Administration, Office of the Actuary, Actuarial Study No. 62 (1966), pp. 10–16.

cost estimate involves demographic assumptions that lead to higher OASDI costs than would result from incorporation of any combination of assumptions used by the Census Bureau. Since the intermediate-cost estimate, on which legislative planning is based, is an average of the high- and low-cost estimates, it is implicitly based on demographic assumptions which produce costs roughly as high as the assumptions that the Census Bureau regards as a limiting case. The low-cost estimate, although not used in legislative work, incorporates demographic assumptions that are near those which would be derived if the midpoint of the various Census Bureau assumptions were taken.[14] Differences in the mortality and fertility rates are not the only source of variation between the low- and high-cost estimates, although they are among the most important.

Two basic reasons are given for the use of such low fertility (high-cost) rate projections.[15] First, it is argued that birth rates will continue to decline because of increased use of birth-control devices. This judgment is plausible; but because numerous other forces are at work as well, it is difficult to predict the outcome. Second, it is argued that it is better to overestimate than to underestimate costs:

In addition, the population projections that are presented in this study were prepared to serve as a basis for estimating the cost of the Old-Age, Survivors, Disability, and Health Insurance system. Since the use of high-fertility assumptions tends to underestimate the cost of the system, we believe it would be preferable to project birth rates that are reasonable and yet are not too optimistic about the future cost of the program.[16]

If social security were merely a private insurance firm, such conservatism about the future might be well advised. Private insurors must have sufficient funds on hand at all times to pay off all accrued liabilities, for they cannot allow themselves to depend on fu-

---

[14] But according to the low-cost estimate, OASI is 6.2 percent overfinanced; that is, taxes are 6.2 percent higher than would be necessary to produce revenues the present value of which would equal benefits. DI is overfinanced by 11.8 percent. See Board of Trustees of OASDI Trust Funds, *1968 Annual Report*, p. 43.

[15] See Bayo, *United States Population Projections for OASDHI Cost Estimates*, p. 8.

[16] *Ibid.*

ture premium income to meet their liabilities on a cash basis as they come due. Social security, on the other hand, has behind it the full financial resources of the federal government and is not, therefore, bound by a test of *actuarial* soundness. This point is explicitly recognized in official explanations of the long-range cost estimate.[17] But once this distinction is recognized, the argument for adopting anything but the most reasonable assumptions in making social security cost estimates is weak. The federal government runs no risk of bankruptcy; future deviations from predictions of social security costs should involve equally likely chances that tax rates will have to be raised or lowered.

A second, and more basic, expression of the tendency toward financial conservatism in the long-range cost estimate is the assumption that average taxable money wages will not increase. To be more precise, it is assumed that average wages for men and women taken separately will not change. Since a rise in female participation rates, relative to male participation rates, is projected, the assumption is that average wages of all workers will actually fall.[18] That average money wages will increase is virtually certain;[19] and the range within which the actual increase is likely to fall is narrower than the plausible range for population growth.

Future increases in wages will occur unless there is no rise in productivity per worker and in prices. To assume that average money wages remain constant is to assume an economy in which productivity stagnates and the price level remains unchanged, an assumption which is universally rejected by economists today.[20]

---

[17] House Committee on Ways and Means, *Actuarial Cost Estimates for the Old-Age, Survivors, Disability, and Health Insurance System as Modified by the Social Security Amendments of 1967*, 90 Cong. 1 sess. (1967), p. 4 (hereafter referred to as House Committee on Ways and Means, *Actuarial Cost Estimates for OASDHI*).

[18] Myers and Bayo, *Long-Range Cost Estimates*, p. 6.

[19] Average annual earnings per full-time employee increased by 3.5 percent a year from 1929 to 1947 and by 4.5 percent from 1947 to 1965. See U.S. Department of Commerce, Office of Business Economics, *The National Income and Product Accounts of the United States, 1929–1965; Statistical Tables* (1966), Table 6.5, pp. 106–09. Average wages in covered employment grew at slightly lower rates in recent years.

[20] A recent study concludes, "It seems reasonable to believe that the relatively higher rate of productivity increase after 1947 will be sustained or increase moderately in the years ahead." *Productivity, Prices, and Incomes*, Materials prepared by the Committee Staff for the Joint Economic Committee, 89 Cong. 2 sess. (1967), p. 21.

The assumption that past growth rates will continue in the future is much more plausible.

A careful explanation of the implications of rising earnings now accompanies the official figures; and short- and medium-range estimates incorporating assumptions of rising earnings are provided as supplements to the long-range estimates. However, as observed earlier, the long-range estimates dominate decision-making in social security. In the most recent case, when the Administration in 1967 presented to the Congress proposals for improvements in OASDI benefits, the estimates for the existing program and for proposed changes were all based on the usual long-range estimates incorporating the level-earnings assumption.[21]

The relationship of this assumption to the interpretation of the long-range estimates was clearly stated years ago:

. . . nearly everyone has taken these estimates as estimates of the cost of the *existing* old age insurance program. Actually, they are estimates of the cost of a program with an escalator clause which automatically adjusts benefits in such a way as to offset exactly the effects of the rising wage level. Aside from the confusion created by this inadequately explained assumption, its validity is highly questionable; in the past . . . adjustments in the benefit level have not been proportionate to the rise in the wage level. . . . Actually, . . . there are many other possible bases for adjustment of benefits in an expanding economy. The pat formula assumed by the actuaries tends to conceal the major problem of choice facing policymakers. It would be much less misleading to present an estimate based on the existing benefit formula and a rising wage level, with a clear warning that periodic adjustments in the benefit formula should be expected.[22]

The assumption of unchanged money earnings in actuarial calculations virtually guarantees that social security will be "overfinanced." Both benefit commitments and taxes increase as earnings increase, but taxes increase much more than benefits because the

[21] See *President's Proposals for Revision in the Social Security System,* Hearings before the House Committee on Ways and Means on H.R. 5710, 90 Cong. 1 sess. (1967), Pt. 1.

[22] Charles C. Killingsworth and Gertrude Schroeder, "Reply," *Quarterly Journal of Economics,* Vol. 66, No. 2 (May 1952), p. 295; for the original paper in which these issues were discussed, see their article, "Long-Range Cost Estimates for Old-Age Insurance," *Quarterly Journal of Economics,* Vol. 65, No. 2 (May 1951), pp. 199–213. See also Robert J. Myers, "Long-Range Cost Estimates for Old-Age Insurance: Comment," *Quarterly Journal of Economics,* Vol. 66, No. 2 (May 1952), pp. 286–93.

benefit formula is progressive (that is, the replacement rate is higher for low-earnings histories than for high-earnings histories) and because benefits, which are determined in part on the basis of past, lower-earnings records, lag behind increases in earnings and payroll taxes.[23]

The magnitude of overfinancing that results from the assumption of unchanged earnings may be illustrated simply. Table VII-1

Table VII-1. *OASDI Taxes, Benefits, and Surpluses, 1967, and Projections under Alternative Estimating Procedures, 1980 and 1985*

(In millions of dollars)

	Payroll Taxes		Benefits		Current Surplus[a]	
Calendar Year	Constant-earnings assumption[b]	Increasing-earnings assumption[c]	Constant-earnings assumption[b]	Increasing-earnings assumption[c]	Constant-earnings assumption[b]	Increasing-earnings assumption[c]
1967 (actual)	25,518	25,518	21,418	21,418	+3,942	+3,942
1980 (estimated)	40,368	55,886	36,348	38,423	+5,972	+23,579
1985 (estimated)	42,979	62,686	41,195	44,108	+4,768	+29,597

Source: *The 1968 Annual Report of the Board of Trustees of the Federal Old-Age and Survivors Insurance and Disability Insurance Trust Funds*, H. Doc. 288, 90 Cong. 2 sess. (1968), Tables 21, 22, and 23, pp. 41, 42, 46.
    a. Current surplus equals payroll taxes plus interest on the trust fund minus the sum of benefit payments, administrative expenses, and transfers to the railroad retirement account for the year.
    b. Intermediate-cost estimate of the Social Security Administration, which assumes that earnings remain constant.
    c. Average total earnings of covered workers are assumed to increase at an annual rate of 3 percent; other assumptions are the same as for the constant earnings method.

gives estimates of payroll taxes and benefits for 1980 and 1985 under, first, the usual intermediate-cost assumption of level earnings and, second, the assumption that average earnings of covered workers grow by 3 percent each year. This rate of increase is much below the trend in recent years[24] and consequently understates the difference between estimates based on the level-earnings assumption and estimates based on plausible assumptions. Another factor that tends to understate the difference is the assumption that the level of maximum covered earnings will remain un-

[23] Myers and Bayo, *Long-Range Cost Estimates*, p. 18.
[24] See footnote 19, p. 156.

changed as average earnings grow—which, of course, is unrealistic. However, the estimates under the assumption of increasing earnings are also unrealistic, principally because the surpluses caused by rising earnings could not be tolerated for even five years, much less fifteen or twenty. Such hypothetical surpluses are useful illustrations of what actually happens repeatedly—not long after every amendment to the Social Security Act.

The defense of the level-earnings assumption is that this procedure leaves a margin of safety in financing the program. When earnings rise, the OASDI program develops a surplus. But in the assumptions made to estimate costs, the only concern appears to be that the program might run a deficit; in other words, it is implicitly held that, within limits, only underestimates of the costs of the program have bad consequences while overestimates are relatively harmless. As previously observed, this consideration is relevant only for a private insurance carrier, but it is not applicable to a public program.

The cost estimates tend to be overstated also by the use of an artificially low interest rate on trust fund balances. The intermediate-cost estimate now assumes an interest rate of 3.75 percent, which is below all borrowing rates of the federal government and much below that of private borrowers (even issuers of tax-exempt securities). The use of an interest rate that is 0.5 percent higher would enable benefits to be raised by about 3 percent within the limits of "actuarial soundness." This would be enough to raise widows' benefits from 82.5 percent to 100 percent of the benefits of retired workers, with no increase in taxes.[25]

The tendency to underestimate revenues relative to costs in the long-range cost estimates does not necessarily affect the growth of the system. On the one hand, the relative overstatement of costs at each point in time makes any given schedule of benefits seem more expensive than it really is. This factor is likely to deter a request for increases in benefits (even though the increases may not affect

---

[25] The importance of the interest rate is discussed at somewhat greater length in Henry J. Aaron, "Benefits Under the American Social Security System," in Otto Eckstein (ed.), *Studies in the Economics of Income Maintenance* (Brookings Institution, 1967), pp. 58–60.

the system for many years), since every Congress and President share a distaste for raising taxes. For example, there is at present widespread sentiment in Congress that payroll taxes should not exceed 10 percent. If it had been recognized in 1967 that benefits could have been increased considerably more than the actuarial calculations indicated without having to raise above 10 percent the total OASDI payroll tax rate on covered earnings, some benefit adjustments that were rejected might have been enacted.

On the other hand, the development of cash surpluses every couple of years as the result of overfinancing generates pressures for increased benefits. Each time that the Social Security Act is amended, a new, higher benefit schedule is enacted together with a schedule of taxes that is just sufficient to keep the program in "actuarial balance." Typically, the cost estimates project a rough balance between social security revenues and expenditures for the succeeding year or two.[26] Then large trust fund surpluses are scheduled, to be offset only in the distant future when large interest earnings on the trust fund, combined with current taxes, will be called upon to meet current benefits. The large surpluses materialize much sooner, however—frequently within a year or two. And, for the reasons stated above, the program shows signs of being overfinanced according to the long-range estimates. When the surpluses inherent in the old benefit and tax structures become evident to all, the pressures for a new, higher benefit schedule become politically irresistible. New cost estimates are made, and the cycle is complete.

Which of these two effects of the present method of making cost estimates is likely to predominate is difficult to determine. The Social Security Administration apparently feels that the use of an increasing-earnings assumption in its official cost estimates would lead to exorbitant benefit commitments. In defense of the level-earnings assumption, it is argued that ". . . the possibility of future

---

[26] The 1967 amendments do project combined surpluses for the OASI and DI trust funds of $1.9 billion and $4.2 billion for 1968 and 1969, respectively. However, these compare with surpluses estimated less than a year earlier of $4.2 billion and $7.5 billion, respectively. See House Committee on Ways and Means, *Actuarial Cost Estimates for OASDHI*, pp. 9–10, and *The 1967 Annual Report of the Board of Trustees of the Federal Old-Age and Survivors Insurance and Disability Insurance Trust Funds*, H. Doc. 65, 90 Cong. 1 sess. (1967), pp. 28–35.

increases in earnings levels should be considered only as a safety factor and not as a justification for adjusting benefits upward in anticipation of such increases."[27] As argued in Chapter V, this concern over committing *all* the incremental taxes estimated from an expected future growth in the economy is a legitimate one; options about future benefit improvements should be left open. The real issue, as brought out by Killingsworth and Schroeder in the passage quoted above (p. 157), is whether the long-range estimates do not actually hinder Congress in determining priorities between alternative benefit improvements, increases in other expenditures, and tax cuts in a growing economy. On the basis of the considerations raised here, we believe that the long-range cost estimates do not provide the information that would best enable Congress and the public appropriately to choose among the alternatives.

PRESENTATION OF THE ESTIMATES

The costs of most government expenditures on goods and services and most transfer payments are presented as dollar totals incorporated in the budget proposed by the President. Before appearing publicly, these requests to Congress for spending authority have passed through several stages of departmental and executive office review in which the desirability of each expenditure, and particularly of each increase in expenditure, is weighed in comparison with other outlays or increases in outlays. In addition, estimates of some program costs for the succeeding five years are compiled as part of the planning-programming-budgeting system, so that implications of present programs for future budgets can be reviewed centrally before the rush of the annual budget cycle commences.[28]

Social security expenditures and revenues occupy a special position in the budget planning process, in two important respects. First, social security benefit payments and taxes pass through a trust fund; neither is subject to annual budget review or to

[27] House Committee on Ways and Means, *Actuarial Cost Estimates for OASDHI*, p. 28.

[28] The planning-programming-budgeting system was introduced in the budget for fiscal 1969. For a description, see David J. Ott and Attiat F. Ott, *Federal Budget Policy* (2d ed.; Brookings Institution, 1968), Chap. 8.

congressional appropriations.[29] Second, the method of presenting
social security costs as a percentage of covered payroll makes it difficult to compare (*a*) the current costs of alternative changes in
the OASDI benefit structure with each other or (*b*) the cost of
changes in expenditures on social security with the cost of changes
in expenditures on other programs.

The long-range cost estimates are clearly inadequate for evaluating the OASDI program relative to other federal government programs. Even if realistic assumptions were adopted, the level-cost estimates cannot be easily compared with the dollar estimates for
other programs. The Social Security Administration does present
—at least every year—more realistic and useful estimates of the cost
of benefits over the succeeding five years (short-range estimates)
and over the succeeding fifteen or twenty years (medium-range estimates).[30] Unlike the long-range estimates that are the basis of
policy decisions about benefits, the short- and medium-range estimates assume that earnings grow (at a very modest rate) over the
time period in question.

For evaluating specific changes in OASDI relative to changes in
other government programs, however, even the short- and medium-
range estimates have serious shortcomings. They generally show
expected trends in future benefits and taxes for the entire OASI
and DI programs, whereas what is needed for most budget decisions
are estimates of specific, alternative structural changes in the programs. In addition, the short-range estimates—which, because of
their limited time-horizon, are potentially the most useful for
budget planning—give realistic approximations of future developments in OASDI only if *scheduled* benefits and taxes do not change
over the succeeding five years. But scheduled benefits and taxes
are constrained by the requirement of "actuarial balance," which
in turn is based on the long-range estimates that assume constant
earnings. As indicated above, when earnings grow, the OASDI
program develops a surplus. Thus the short-range estimates show,
as they should under an increasing-earnings assumption, that the
OASDI trust funds will grow rapidly; the most recent estimate is

[29] Issues relating to the use of the trust fund device are discussed in Chapter VIII.
[30] The latest such estimates are presented and discussed in the Board of Trustees
of OASDI Trust Funds, *1968 Annual Report,* pp. 26–38, 45–47.

that they will rise from $26.3 billion in 1967 to $59.3 billion in 1972.[31] But since vast surpluses would not be permitted to develop, the short-range estimates of benefits and taxes are clearly not relevant for budget planning purposes.

The same basic point applies to the problem of evaluating any one change in the OASDI benefit structure relative to some alternative change. With present estimates, the task of making accurate comparisons of the costs of alternative improvements in benefits is extremely arduous. For example, the costs of the various components of the President's 1967 social security proposals were presented in both level-cost terms and dollar terms for the first year.[32] Although certain proposals (such as the increase in the minimum benefit or in special age-72 benefits) would impose substantial initial costs, there was no indication that these costs would diminish with time, or that the costs of other proposals (for example, the across-the-board increases in benefits) would impose added costs that would grow in pace with total benefits.[33] Since the cost estimates are based on the assumption of constant earnings, they tend to overstate the cost of items for which outlays as a percentage of covered payroll are expected to diminish, relative to the cost of items for which outlays as a percentage of covered payroll are expected to remain the same or to rise. Thus, for example, the level-cost in 1967 of raising the minimum benefit from $44 to $70, in addition to the proposed 15 percent across-the-board increase, was roughly equal to the cost of a 4 percent across-the-board increase in benefits. If the long-range estimates recognized the virtual certainty of increased earnings, it would be clear that a once-and-for-all increase in minimum benefits would not be even this costly. In

[31] *Ibid.,* Tables 14 and 18, pp. 30, 36.
[32] See *President's Proposals for Revision in the Social Security System,* Hearings, pp. 98, 117, 128–84.
[33] The best estimates of the cost of components of the benefit structure are short-range estimates of the dollar values of various benefit changes five years in the future. See, for example, *Social Security Amendments of 1967,* Report of the House Committee on Ways and Means on H.R. 12080, H. Rept. 544, 90 Cong. 1 sess. (1967), Table VI, p. 92. Unfortunately, these estimates are given for only a very narrow range of alternative changes. Furthermore, as pointed out above, they are based on benefits scheduled in a program that is actuarially balanced under the assumption of constant earnings. Consequently, they are unrealistic, because as earnings grow, large surpluses will develop and Congress will raise benefits.

fact, however, there were no separate estimates of the relative cost of the increases in minimum benefits and the across-the-board increases. At no point in the public presentation of the Administration's program to the Congress was the cost of raising the minimum stated, either in level-cost or in dollar terms.[34]

To summarize: within social security, the cost of alternative benefit features cannot, in general, be conveniently compared. In fact, two benefit changes with equal level-costs typically are not equally costly at a given rate of interest if the distribution of their costs as a percentage of covered payroll over time is not identical. On the basis of present methods of estimate, the cost of benefit changes that involve outlays which increase as a percentage of payroll over time will be understated relative to benefit changes whose costs decrease as a percentage of payroll over time.

OASDI ESTIMATES IN BUDGET PLANNING

Short-term estimates of costs of OASDI are needed for two distinct budgetary purposes: first, for determining stabilization policies and, second, for planning the allocation of funds in the budget among alternative programs in the years immediately ahead. For both purposes, dollar estimates of both benefits and costs, prepared with as much precision as possible, are required. Costs expressed as a percentage of covered payroll (as in the long-range estimates) are no help for these purposes. The forecasts should be based on plausible assumptions for all relevant variables, including changes in money wages. As observed previously, short-range and some medium-range cost estimates are now based on assumptions of increasing earnings. These estimates should be expanded to include costs of alternative changes in the components of the benefit structure;

[34] Estimates of the costs of individual components of a benefit-increase package are subject to the difficulty that they depend on the order in which the estimates are taken. In regard to the 1967 Administration proposals to raise benefits by 15 percent across the board and to raise the minimum from $44 to $70, the cost of raising the minimum depends on whether it is computed before inclusion of the 15 percent increase or after. Since a 15 percent increase would move some benefits above $70 and would move all other smaller benefits closer to that figure, the cost of raising the minimum to $70 would be larger if it were computed before than if it were computed after taking account of the 15 percent benefit increase.

and in presentations to the Congress of plans for new improvements in benefits, they should be given at least as much prominence as the long-range estimates are given. These steps are essential for integrating the OASDI system into effective budget planning.

Long-range cost estimates should be continued as guides to long-range policies and costs, but they too should be prepared on the basis of plausible assumptions regarding each relevant variable, rather than on the basis of assumptions which systematically lead to overfinancing of the system. Long-range cost estimates do serve a useful purpose in helping the government to recognize today the long-run consequences of proposed changes. For example, a change in the computation period for average monthly earnings to the highest ten years of earnings would add only trivially to cash outlays for benefits as of 1968 but would involve a massive long-run commitment of social security funds. The extent of such a commitment should be made clear by careful long-range estimates, which take account realistically of long-run economic trends. If these trends are not taken into account, the estimates cannot fully serve their purpose. In the absence of any persuasive arguments to the contrary, the possibility of overestimating the costs of the program should be given as much weight as the possibility of underestimating them. Realistic assumptions about economic growth and a greater recognition of the uncertainties of future fertility and mortality developments are essential.

Even if these necessary changes are made, the role of very long-range estimates in determining amendments to the benefit structure should be deemphasized. In view of the vast uncertainties about economic and demographic factors 75 years hence, it should be acknowledged that, even with the use of the best forecasting techniques, estimates over a shorter span of years are more relevant to decisions about priorities in improving benefits. It would be more realistic to plan changes in the program over a 25-year time horizon.[35] Moreover, the long-range cost estimates would be

[35] Movement toward a shorter time horizon in making cost estimates for OASDI would be consistent with recent trends. The present 75-year period for the OASDI long-range estimates is itself a revision of an earlier time horizon which extended indefinitely into the future. Moreover, cost calculations for the new hospital insurance system under social security extend only 25 years into the future, on the ground that long-range estimates are much more difficult to predict. See House

more meaningful if they were presented in relation to total estimated national income rather than in terms of the actuarial balance principle. This would permit appraisal not only of the social security program itself but also of the outlays of this program relative to other projected outlays in both the public and the private sector.

Cost Estimates and Individual Equity

Many of the inequities of the benefit structure discussed in Chapter V are perpetuated primarily by cost considerations. But the problem of cost is compounded by widespread confusion about the individual equity implications of the social security retirement program. A number of calculations have recently been made to show that payments to social security by new entrants into the labor force will be much greater than the retirement benefits that they can expect to receive subsequently.[36] These calculations have influenced the views of some members of Congress and others who have begun seriously to question the fairness of the social security system as it is developing in the United States.[37] Much of the con-

---

Committee on Ways and Means, *Actuarial Cost Estimates for OASDHI*, p. 17; see also Advisory Council on Social Security Financing, *Financing Old-Age, Survivors, and Disability Insurance* (1959), p. 15. In view of past difficulties in predicting accurately economic and demographic developments, any distinction between OASDI costs and hospital insurance costs in this respect can hardly be justified.

[36] These calculations are reviewed by John A. Brittain, "The Real Rate of Interest on Lifetime Contributions Toward Retirement Under Social Security," in *Old Age Income Assurance*, Compendium of Papers on Problems and Policy Issues in the Public and Private Pension System, Pt. III: *Public Programs*, 90 Cong. 1 sess. (1967), pp. 109–14. Brittain's paper is the first to treat the problem with rigor. It provides the conceptual basis for the discussion in this section and for the calculations presented in Appendix A. See also the papers in the same volume by Colin D. Campbell and Rosemary G. Campbell, "Cost-Benefit Ratios under the Federal Old-Age Insurance Program," pp. 72–84, and Yung-Ping Chen, "Inflation and Productivity in Tax-Benefit Analysis for Social Security," pp. 85–108.

[37] *President's Proposals for Revision in the Social Security System*, Hearings. The leitmotiv of these Hearings is the concern about the equitable treatment of young workers, especially those with maximum taxable earnings. See, in particular, pp. 329–41. See also the minority views expressed in *Social Security Amendments of 1967*, Report of the Senate Committee on Finance to Accompany H.R. 12080, Report No. 744, 90 Cong. 1 sess. (1967), pp. 339–40.

cern about individual equity is based on acceptance of the most naive form of the insurance analogy for social insurance—that every individual should receive at least the full amount of his "contribution" in retirement.

The discussion in Chapter IV explains why such an oversimplified view of the principle of individual equity is not a suitable criterion for making judgments about the social security system. However, if the program inflicted severe penalties on many workers—if workers were able to obtain substantially higher yields from personal investments than from social security—it would be necessary to examine whether these transfers in combination with transfers resulting from other taxes and government expenditures were equitable or efficient. This broad view of the equity issue transcends existing social security institutions and raises complex problems.[38] But for the discussion below and in Appendix A, the present benefit-tax framework for social security is accepted.

Based on present scheduled tax rates and benefit formulas, it is a simple matter to show that, under reasonable assumptions, the value of total employee and employer taxes paid by young workers entering the labor force today (plus interest) will greatly exceed the value of their *presently* legislated retirement benefits. If, instead, the total taxes scheduled for each worker were invested in savings accounts and the accumulated savings were used to buy an annuity at retirement, the annuity income would be far greater than retirement benefits scheduled in the *present* social security law. If there were a reasonable probability that the taxes and benefits scheduled in the present law were even roughly accurate forecasts of actual taxes and benefits in the future, it would be correct to conclude that OASDI is unfair to young workers.

The fallacy in this argument is that the presently scheduled taxes and benefits will *not* remain unchanged. As indicated earlier in this chapter, the tax schedules and benefits in the present law were constrained by the requirement that the program should be "actuarially balanced" over the next 75 years under the assumption that average money earnings will not grow. Not surprisingly, on these assumptions, scheduled benefits are meager relative to

_____

[38] See Chapter IX for our long-range proposals to reform the present social security structure in the light of the principles discussed in Chapter IV.

scheduled taxes for young workers today. Expectations of positive returns on personal investments—the implicit alternative to the OASDI retirement program in all comparisons—are based on past experience of a constantly growing economy in which investment in more plant and equipment per worker has had very high real returns. If average earnings should remain unchanged, the "return" on social security taxes would be very poor indeed, just as the return on almost every personal investment would be poor in a static economy.

An estimate of the relationship between taxes and benefits requires a realistic projection of the growth of earnings. One reasonable assumption is that money earnings per worker will rise at the same rate as in the past.[39] For illustrative purposes, assume that average money earnings per covered worker will grow at 4 percent a year, a rate that reflects a 2.5 percent annual increase in productivity per worker and a 1.5 percent annual increase in the price level. The implications of adopting this assumption in place of the assumption that earnings will not change can best be seen by contrasting estimates of the relationship between taxes and benefits under each assumption.

The figures in Table VII-2 represent the value of OASDI retirement benefits as a percentage of total taxes to be paid by an individual who enters the labor force on January 1, 1968, at age 22, and who earns average manufacturing wages thereafter until retirement at age 65. Taxes include the taxes paid by both the employer and employee. An interest rate of 3.75 percent (the rate used in the official long-range estimates) is used to accumulate taxes and to discount retirement benefits until the individual reaches the assumed retirement age. Estimates in column 1 are based on the assumption that the taxes and benefits scheduled in the present social security law remain unchanged in the future,

[39] Average hourly earnings in manufacturing grew at 4.4 percent a year from 1929 to 1965, at 4.3 percent a year from 1947 to 1965. The consumer price index rose at a rate of 1.7 percent a year from 1929 to 1965, at 1.9 percent a year from 1947 to 1965. Average real wages—average money earnings (in manufacturing) deflated by the consumer price index—grew at 2.6 percent a year from 1929 to 1965, at 2.4 percent a year from 1947 to 1965. Productivity per worker—nonfarm output per man-hour—grew at 2.3 percent a year from 1929 to 1965, at 2.8 percent a year from 1947 to 1965. *Productivity, Prices, and Incomes*, Table II.15, p. 97; Table III.25, p. 128; Table IV.3, p. 137.

Table vii-2. *Present Value of OASDI Retirement Benefits as a Percentage of Present Value of Taxes for Workers Entering Labor Force January 1, 1968*[a]

Sex and Marital Status	Assuming Unchanged Earnings (1)	Assuming 4 Percent Growth in Earnings (2)
Single male	49	72
Single female	57	85
Couple	82	123

a. All estimates assume that (a) worker enters labor force in January 1968 at age 22 and has earnings of $6,000 (approximate average manufacturing earnings for production workers in 1967) (U.S. Bureau of the Census, *Statistical Abstract of the United States, 1967* [1967], Table 334, p. 237); (b) worker retires at age 65 with average life expectancy; (c) interest rate is 3.75 percent; (d) taxes and benefits are based on the Social Security Act as amended through 1967; (e) employee bears the burden of the employer as well as the employee tax.

Estimates in column 1 assume no growth in earnings. Estimates in column 2 assume (a) 4 percent growth in annual earnings; (b) same replacement rate as that scheduled today for worker with average annual earnings of $6,000; (c) adjustment of benefits after retirement by 1.5 percent a year to partially compensate retirees for assumed inflation. Further details and assumptions for these calculations are given in Appendix A.

and that there is no change in the individual's money wages. Estimates in column 2, on the other hand, are based on the assumption that money wages will rise at an average annual rate of 4 percent. In addition, these estimates require further assumptions about corresponding increases in the taxable maximum wage base, variations in the replacement rate, adjustment of benefits after retirement to compensate for price increases, and other factors. (These and other technical details are discussed in Appendix A.) Even without detailed discussion of the technical problems of dealing with the assumption of growth in earnings and benefits, the dramatic differences in the estimates in columns 1 and 2 lead to the unshakable conclusion that growth in the economy cannot be ignored in this type of individual equity calculation.[40] Once the consequences of the assumption of unchanged earnings are fully understood, the need for more tenable assumptions for projection purposes is obvious.

For documentation of this point with historical evidence, consider the estimates shown in Table vii-3. The figures in both columns show the value of benefits as a percentage of the value of

[40] It should also be noted that the estimates in column 2 of Table vii-2 are based on very conservative assumptions with regard to the adjustment of benefits and taxes to growth. On balance, benefits are understated relative to taxes.

Table VII-3. *Present Value of OASDI Retirement Benefits as a Percentage of Present Value of Taxes for Workers First Covered in January 1937, at Age 34, and Retiring on December 31, 1967*[a]

Sex and Marital Status	Assuming 1937 Maximum Taxable Earnings, and Taxes and Benefits as of 1939 Amendments (1)	Actual Experience Reflecting Changes in Law since 1939 and Expected Changes after 1967 (2)
Single male	95	337
Single female	112	402
Couple	163	583

a. All estimates assume interest rate of 3.75 percent. Estimates in column 1 assume worker had constant earnings equal to $3,000 from 1937 to 1967 and that his taxes and benefits were based on social security law as of 1939 amendments. Estimates in column 2 assume that worker had maximum taxable earnings in each year between 1937 and 1967 and also that the worker's initial benefit in January 1968 will be increased thereafter by 1.5 percent a year to partially compensate retiree for annual inflation. Otherwise, estimates in column 2 are based on actual taxes and benefits. Further details and assumptions for these calculations are given in Appendix A.

taxes for individuals who were first covered by OASDI at age 34 in January 1937 and who retired on December 31, 1967. Figures in column 1 are based on the assumption that scheduled taxes and benefits as of 1940 would remain unchanged; in other words, the unchanged-average-earnings assumption is applied retrospectively in precisely the same way that it is today applied by some writers. Figures in column 2 are based on actual experience and thus reflect the several changes in the social security law that have come as a response to the growth of the economy since 1940.

As the estimates in Table VII-3 suggest, past and present retirees have fared well under the OASDI program. Comparisons of the estimates in columns 1 and 2 show that predictions of the experience of present retirees based on scheduled taxes and benefits in the 1939 law under the assumption that 1937 maximum taxable earnings would remain unchanged would have greatly understated the actual value of the benefits relative to taxes. Today's young workers will pay OASDI taxes over a longer period than did present retirees, but it does not necessarily follow that they must fare badly under the program. Given reasonable assumptions about the future growth of the economy, and the continued willingness of Congress to keep benefits up to date with changes in earnings levels, there is no reason to believe that social security will inflict severe inequities on the great majority of present young workers.

The benefit structure can be adjusted in many different ways to keep retirement benefits up to date with growth in average money earnings. As argued in Chapter V, partial automatic adjustment of the benefit formula is preferable to the *ad hoc* adjustments that Congress has enacted belatedly in the past in reaction to the growth of the economy. The precise method of adjustment is less important, however, than the willingness, expressed through effective political decisions, to legislate repeatedly the benefit increases that will be needed time after time to maintain the value of benefits relative to higher levels of real and money incomes.

Summary

Estimates of benefits and costs of the social security program must take into account a large number of variables, many of which are difficult to predict. The official long-range cost estimates used by the Congress in considering new legislation are based on conservative demographic and economic assumptions that tend to overstate the true costs of improvements in the benefit structure. The most unrealistic of these assumptions is that money wages will remain unchanged.

The use of such conservative estimates leads to overfinancing of the social security system as earnings rise. Payroll tax receipts increase faster than benefits, mainly because benefits—which are based in part on past earnings—lag behind any increase in earnings. As a result, each social security bill provides for a schedule of benefits and taxes that generate very large surpluses shortly after enactment. These surpluses encourage Congress to raise benefits, but payroll taxes are also raised at the same time to preserve "actuarial balance." New surpluses providing further room for benefit adjustments are thus ensured for the future, and the cycle is repeated.

The use of conservative assumptions exaggerates the cost of upward adjustments in benefits and thus tends to moderate increases in benefits. On the other hand, recognition of the imminence of large surpluses in the trust funds creates pressures for new benefit increases. But whatever their effect on the level of benefits, the actuarial long-range estimates would be more useful in the government budgeting process if they were based on realistic assumptions for all relevant variables, particularly changes in money wages. It would also be more realistic to require estimates of costs over a much shorter time period—perhaps 25 years—than over 75 years, the period now incorporated in the actuarial calculations. Moreover, to permit an evaluation of the social security program in relation to other programs, the long-range costs should be compared with projected national income rather than presented in terms of actuarial balance.

A major impediment to action toward improving the benefit structure is the calculation of rates of return on the taxes of today's younger workers. Like the official long-range estimates, such calculations assume no changes in scheduled taxes and benefits, and no future increases in money wages. When reasonable assumptions regarding increases in benefits and earnings are made, the calculations are seen to be erroneous. Most individuals will be treated fairly under social security as long as benefits continue to be raised to keep in step with a growing economy.

CHAPTER VIII

Financing Social Security

The best method of financing the Old-Age, Survivors, and Disability Insurance (OASDI) program depends crucially on what the nation regards as the rationale of the system. The discussion in previous chapters has emphasized that the system is a combination of taxes on the currently employed and transfers to certain retired, disabled, and dependent surviving persons. There is only a remote connection between the payroll taxes paid by the worker and the benefits that he or his family will receive. If the trust funds continue to be financed on a current basis, the currently employed will be taxed enough to pay for the benefits of those who are retired and disabled and who are dependents of deceased workers. The earnings received by workers during their working careers establish rights to receive benefits which the currently employed agree to provide out of their incomes.

The use of past earnings to establish the right of the individual and his family to benefits is widely accepted. But the desirability of using the payroll tax for financing purposes depends on its merits relative to alternative financing sources, not on the need for maintaining a relationship between earnings and benefits. The appropriate comparison is with the individual income tax, which is the basic source of federal funds for other purposes. In this chapter, the question of whether the payroll tax measures up to the income tax as a major source of revenue will be considered, and alternative methods of financing social security will be discussed.

Evaluation of the Payroll Tax

The major features of the payroll tax have been described in Chapter III. The tax is levied at equal rates on employers and employees. The maximum combined OASDI rate—7.6 percent in 1968 on earnings up to $7,800—is scheduled to run to 10.0 percent in 1973. The rate including the tax for hospital insurance is 8.8 percent in 1968 and will rise to 11.8 percent in 1987. The OASDI tax on self-employed persons, approximately one and one-half times the rate applying to employees, is limited to a maximum of 7 percent, which becomes effective in 1973; the tax including hospital insurance will rise to 7.9 percent in 1987.[1]

The payroll tax is the third largest federal tax, ranking behind the individual income tax and the corporation income tax. In fiscal year 1967, individual income tax receipts amounted to $61.5 billion, corporation tax receipts to $34.0 billion, and payroll tax receipts to $31.5 billion.[2] Because both the rate and base have been increased frequently in recent years, receipts from the payroll tax have grown much faster than those from either the corporation or the personal income tax.

The revenue potential of each tax may be better understood by comparing the tax bases—taxable income for the individual and corporation income taxes, and taxable earnings for the social security payroll tax.[3] Rough estimates for the calendar year 1967 are as follows:

Tax	Estimated Tax Base, 1967 (Billions of Dollars)
Individual income tax	330
Corporation income tax	75
Social security payroll tax	360

[1] Self-employed persons pay social security tax if their net earnings are at least $400 a year. The health insurance tax rate for the self-employed is 50 percent of the combined employer-employee rate.

[2] See Appendix Table G-3. Payroll tax receipts include taxes collected for health and unemployment insurance.

[3] A taxable earnings maximum of $7,800 is assumed. The actual taxable maximum for 1967 was $6,600.

In other words, one percentage point yielded approximately $3.3 billion under the individual income tax, $3.6 billion under the payroll tax, and $750 million under the corporation income tax.

To compare any tax with other sources of revenue, it is necessary first to determine who bears the tax. Then judgments can be made about its equity and economic effects. The major features of the payroll tax that bear scrutiny are its incidence, regressivity, contribution to stabilization policy, and effects on the allocation of resources, including its impact on personal and public saving.

INCIDENCE

The popular assumption is that (*a*) the employee share of the payroll tax is borne by the wage earner and (*b*) the employer share is shifted forward to the consumer in the form of higher prices. Most economists do not believe that there is any difference in the incidence of payroll taxes legally levied on employees and employers. They believe that a major share of a payroll tax is borne by the wage earner, and some believe that all of it rests on him.[4]

The OASDI (or payroll) tax is virtually a universal tax levied at a proportional rate on wages and salaries up to $7,800. Since the tax is levied on payrolls in practically all occupations and industries, workers cannot, in general, move elsewhere in order to avoid it.[5] The ultimate incidence of such a tax depends on the assumptions made regarding labor and product markets. A payroll tax does not make labor more productive, so that employers have no reason to pay higher total labor costs after imposition of the tax. While they very likely are unable to reduce wages immediately after imposition of the tax, they can do so effectively over time by not increasing wages as much as they would have if the tax had not

[4] See, for example, Seymour E. Harris, *Economics of Social Security; The Relation of the American Program to Consumption, Savings, Output, and Finance* (McGraw-Hill, 1941), Pt. II; Richard A. Musgrave and others, "Distribution of Tax Payments by Income Groups: A Case Study for 1948," *National Tax Journal*, Vol. 4, No. 1 (March 1951), pp. 23–25; and Tax Foundation, Inc., *Economic Aspects of the Social Security Tax* (Tax Foundation, Inc., 1966), pp. 42–50.

[5] The exceptions are persons engaged in part-time domestic service, employees of some nonprofit organizations, and ministers who have not elected to be covered. It is hardly likely that there is much movement into such pursuits to avoid the payroll tax.

been introduced. However, they might be unable to restrain the growth of earnings in this way if wage earners should react to reduced earnings by leaving the labor force or by reducing the number of hours worked (that is, if the supply of labor were responsive, to some extent, to wages net of payroll taxes). Employers would then have to bid up gross wages to attract additional workers or to keep those they have; wages would rise as a result of the tax (though not necessarily by the exact amount), and less labor would be employed.

The total supply of labor is generally regarded as inelastic with respect to small changes in wages; the size of the labor force seems to depend primarily on demographic factors.[6] If this is true, the reduction in take-home pay that results from higher payroll taxes will not induce wage earners to withdraw from the labor force. The same number of workers will be seeking the same number of jobs, wages gross of payroll tax will remain unchanged, and the workers will bear the full burden of the tax in lower net wages.

This argument is independent of whether or not the worker regards the payroll tax as a *quid pro quo* for later benefits. But if he does, he will, of course, accept the lower after-tax wage when the payroll tax is imposed and not alter his behavior in the labor market. In these circumstances, the elasticity of the supply of labor with respect to wages would have no bearing on the incidence of the tax because the worker would not regard the tax as reducing his wages. The tax would be regarded as a user charge, the supply of labor would be unchanged, net earnings would fall by the amount of the tax, and the full burden would certainly be borne by the wage earner.

In practice, wages are frequently fixed in the short run by contract or custom and cannot be reduced immediately. Producers will treat an increase in payroll taxes as they would any other in-

[6] Cyclical factors may cause short-run variations in the labor force, but the extent of the cyclical influence is uncertain. See Jacob Mincer, "Labor-Force Participation and Unemployment: A Review of Recent Evidence," in Robert A. Gordon and Margaret S. Gordon (eds.), *Prosperity and Unemployment* (Wiley, 1966), pp. 73–112. For an analysis of the factors influencing the supply of labor over the long run, see Clarence D. Long, *The Labor Force under Changing Income and Employment*, National Bureau of Economic Research, General Series No. 65 (Princeton University Press, 1958).

crease in labor cost and will attempt either to pass on the additional expense through higher prices or to replace labor with capital goods, or both. The higher prices will cause a reduction in sales, and output and employment will be lowered unless the government maintains real demand at the old level through monetary and fiscal policies. Relative prices and employment and output in specific industries will change. If money demand does not expand enough, total output and employment will fall. Thus, while the burden of the payroll tax probably falls on the worker in the long run, the short-run effect of imposing the tax will vary with conditions in product and labor markets.

The above analysis assumes income-maximizing behavior and certainty in labor markets. It takes no account of the possibility that changes in payroll taxes may affect the results of collective bargaining between large firms and labor unions. Labor unions may resist any cut in real wages of their members as payroll taxes are increased, and may succeed in inducing management to grant a larger wage increase after imposition (or increase) of the payroll tax. In such circumstances, part or all of the payroll tax may be shifted to the consumer. Critics of this view argue that, if such market power exists, labor and management can exercise it to raise prices and wages before the tax is imposed. Nevertheless, the possibility that the adoption of a new payroll tax, or an increase in an old one, may be the occasion when labor and management try to exercise this power cannot be dismissed.

Very few empirical studies of the effect of the payroll tax on wages are available for resolving these theoretical complexities. John A. Brittain concluded (on the basis of a cross-section analysis) that, at any given level of productivity, industries in countries with relatively high employer payroll taxes pay a basic wage that is relatively lower by about the same amount.[7] This evidence suggests that the full burden of payroll taxes—whether levied on employers or employees or both—rests on the workers.

It is sometimes alleged that, even if wage earners bear the em-

[7] Brittain, "The Real Rate of Interest on Lifetime Contributions Toward Retirement Under Social Security," in *Old Age Income Assurance,* Compendium of Papers on Problems and Policy Issues in the Public and Private Pension System, Pt. III: *Public Programs,* 90 Cong. 1 sess. (1967), pp. 112–14. (Brookings Reprint 143.)

ployer tax, it does not follow that each worker bears the tax in exact proportion to his earnings that are subject to tax. The argument appears to be that, because of the complexities of the OASDI tax, the employer tax cannot be "credited to each particular employee on the basis of the amount he paid."[8] The complexities referred to—for example, that the employer tax may be paid twice by a person who has two jobs whereas an employee pays tax only up to a maximum each year, or that the tax on self-employment income is smaller than the tax on employment income—may have some differential impact on the allocation of the particular types of labor involved. Nevertheless, it would be erroneous to assume that the tax is not borne by wage earners in these cases. Distribution of the total tax on employment income by the amounts paid by employees and of the tax on self-employment income by the amounts paid by the self-employed is only a rough indication of the incidence of the tax; if the data were available, an estimate of the impact of the "complexities" of the tax could be made.

Finally, the present differential between the combined employer-employee tax on wages and salaries and the self-employment tax is based on the assumption that workers bear only about half of the tax paid by the employer. As stated above, the combined OASDI tax rate on payrolls is 7.6 percent in 1968, and the rate on self-employment income is 5.8 percent. Beginning in 1973, the rates will be 10 percent and 7 percent, respectively. Such differentials cannot be justified if substantially all of the burden of the payroll tax is borne by the workers.

REGRESSIVITY

When considered relative to wages alone, the payroll tax is clearly proportional up to the $7,800 taxable limit, and regressive thereafter. Since this tax is earmarked to finance benefits that are paid largely to persons in the lower income classes, the entire tax-transfer system embedded in OASDI is regarded as highly progressive; that is, the net contribution to income is highest in the very lowest

[8] *President's Proposals for Revision in the Social Security System,* Hearings before the House Committee on Ways and Means on H.R. 5710, 90 Cong. 1 sess. (1967), Pt. 1, p. 331.

income classes, declines until it reaches a "break-even" point where the benefits equal total taxes paid, and then becomes a net tax payment in the highest income classes.[9]

This view of the income distribution effect of OASDI overlooks one of its major characteristics: the tax is levied on one group in the population, and the benefits are received by another group. Aggregation of taxes and benefits by income classes therefore gives a misleading picture of the distribution of the real burden and benefits of the taxes and transfers. At any given time, the tax is proportional or regressive with respect to the incomes of those who are subject to tax; and the benefits accrue largely to persons with little other income. These relationships are shown in Charts VIII-1 and VIII-2, which compare the taxes and transfers with the incomes of the relevant groups.[10]

From the point of view of the generation receiving transfers, OASDI benefits are probably two-thirds or more of family money income for families with total income of less than $2,000 (Chart VIII-1); they decline to 2 percent or less for families in the upper income groups.[11] Thus, taken by themselves, the transfers are highly progressive. This progressivity is due principally to the lack of outside income by the aged, the disabled, and surviving beneficiaries in the lower income classes, and also to the benefit formula.

The picture on the tax side is quite different. Under the assumption of backward shifting of the employer tax, OASDI taxes are slightly progressive with respect to ordinary income up to $7,000 or $8,000, and regressive thereafter (Chart VIII-2). This pattern of tax incidence reflects the changing importance of taxable earnings as incomes rise. In the lower part of the income scale, the ratio of taxable earnings to total income rises; the ratio begins to fall at higher levels because the payroll tax applies only up to a maximum ($7,800) and because property income which is not subject to pay-

[9] For the year 1970, John J. Carroll's projections indicate a "break-even" level of $3,000 based on the social security system under the 1958 amendments. See his *Alternative Methods of Financing Old-Age, Survivors, and Disability Insurance* (University of Michigan, Institute of Public Administration, 1960), Chap. 6, pp. 114–30. At current tax rates and benefits, the break-even level is higher.

[10] See Appendix E for a statement of the methods used to prepare the tax estimates.

[11] Chart VIII-1 is intended to be illustrative only. In the absence of official data, it was based on rough estimates prepared by the authors.

Chart VIII-1. *Schematic Relationship between OASDI Benefits and Total Family Income, for Families with OASDI Benefits, 1965*

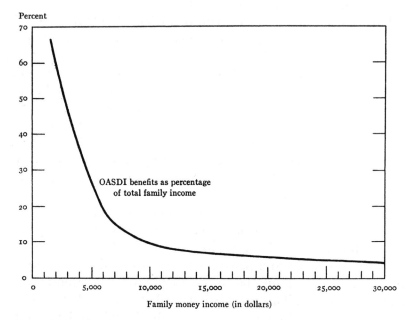

Source: Authors' estimates.

roll tax becomes increasingly important as incomes rise above this point. Even elimination of a limit on taxable earnings would not remove the element of regressivity in the top brackets. Calculations based on a file of 100,000 federal income tax returns for the year 1964 indicate that regressivity sets in at about $9,000 of total income under a flat tax on all earnings.[12]

The distribution of the payroll tax burden is somewhat more progressive than an equal-yield proportional tax on consumption, while the income tax is, of course, much more progressive than the payroll tax. If it is assumed that the employer tax is shifted to the consumer, the OASDI tax is approximately as regressive as a consumption tax.

The increases in rates already scheduled for future years will have a significant impact on the tax payments of the lowest income groups. In 1987, the payroll tax for social security, disability, and

[12] See Appendix E for method of calculation.

Chart VIII-2. *Effective Tax Rates, by Income Level, of a 5 Percent Payroll Tax*[a] *on Employers and Employees and of Alternative Methods of Raising the Same Revenue*

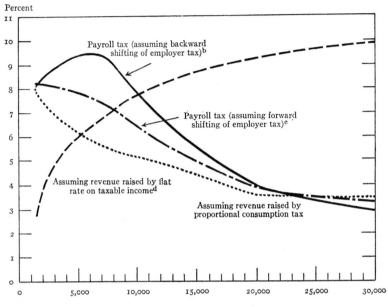

Percent

Payroll tax (assuming backward shifting of employer tax)[b]

Payroll tax (assuming forward shifting of employer tax)[c]

Assuming revenue raised by flat rate on taxable income[d]

Assuming revenue raised by proportional consumption tax

Ordinary income (in dollars)[e]

Source: Appendix E.

a. Tax is 7 percent for the self-employed. Maximum earnings subject to tax are $7,800 as specified in the 1967 amendments to the Social Security Act.

b. Employer and employee taxes are assumed to be borne by the employee; self-employment tax is assumed to be borne by the self-employed.

c. Employer tax is distributed in proportion to consumption by income class; employee tax and self-employment tax are assumed to be borne by the employee or the self-employed.

d. The tax is applied to taxable income as defined in the Internal Revenue Code for 1965.

e. Ordinary income is adjusted gross income exclusive of capital gains and losses, plus excluded sick pay and dividends.

health care will reach a maximum of $920.40 (Table VIII-1). Payroll taxes will exceed the 1965–67 income tax liability for a single person with an income of less than $6,275, a married couple with an income of $7,535, and a married couple with two children and an income of $8,860. At 1964 income levels, a 10 percent tax on wages and salaries up to $7,800 (and a 7 percent tax on self-employment income up to $7,800) would have been higher than the income tax for 57 percent of the individuals and married couples filing federal income tax returns, and $1.5 billion would have been paid by persons officially classified as living below poverty

Table VIII-1. *Maximum Combined Employer-Employee Taxes and Maximum Tax on Self-Employed under the OASDI and Health Insurance Programs, 1967 and Later Years*

(In dollars)

Year	Maximum Employer-Employee Tax			Maximum Tax on Self-Employed		
	OASDI	Health insurance	OASDI and health insurance	OASDI	Health insurance	OASDI and health insurance
1967	514.80	66.00	580.80	389.40	33.00	422.40
1968	592.80	93.60	686.40	452.40	46.80	499.20
1969–70	655.20	93.60	748.80	491.40	46.80	538.20
1971–72	717.60	93.60	811.20	538.20	46.80	585.00
1973–75	780.00	101.40	881.40	546.00	50.70	596.70
1976–79	780.00	109.20	889.20	546.00	54.60	600.60
1980–86	780.00	124.80	904.80	546.00	62.40	608.40
1987 and after	780.00	140.40	920.40	546.00	70.20	616.20

Source: Based on data in Appendix Table B-8.

levels (Appendix Table F-1). The tax burden on the low-paid worker is somewhat smaller if the employer tax is shifted forward to the consumer.

The payroll tax is grossly inferior to the individual income tax in its treatment of people with equal incomes as well as in the relative burden it imposes on people with different incomes. Income alone does not differentiate a man's ability to pay; his family responsibilities are also important. Making ends meet on an income of $3,000 is much more difficult for a man with a wife and two children than it is for a single person without dependents. Major health expenditures and casualty losses also affect ability to pay. The individual income tax takes such differences into account through the personal exemptions and deductions, which are subtracted before arriving at income subject to tax.

By contrast, the payroll tax is levied on gross wages without any allowance for family size. Thus, in 1968 a wage earner with earnings of $3,200 pays $243.20 as social security tax (less if the employer tax is assumed to be partly shifted forward) whether he is single or a family man. For a couple with two children, the official "poverty-line" income is $3,335; that is more than twice the poverty-line income for a single person.[13] Also, the payroll tax takes no account of unusual medical expenses, whereas the income tax permits deductions for expenses that exceed 3 percent of income. There is no way of improving the payroll tax in these respects, short of broadening the tax base to include other income and introducing exemptions and deductions.

CONTRIBUTION TO STABILIZATION POLICY

The payroll tax is much less sensitive than the federal individual income tax to fluctuations in national income and employment. Since the payroll tax is regressive while the personal income tax is progressive, the yield of the payroll tax (with tax rates assumed constant) usually fluctuates proportionately less, and the personal income tax usually fluctuates proportionately more, than personal income over a business cycle. Although regressive, the payroll tax does not have perverse flexibility during the business cycle—that is, it does not *increase* automatically when incomes decline, and vice versa—but it responds considerably less than the income tax to changes in economic activity. For example, between 1962 and 1965, when the gross national product increased by 22 percent, the OASDI tax rose by 15 percent and the individual income tax rose by 37 percent (after allowance for the 1964 tax cut).[14] Thus the payroll tax is a relatively poor automatic stabilizer; it is less than half as responsive as the income tax to changes in income. Although not every feature of the federal tax system need be highly responsive to changes in income, the effect of the

[13] Chart V-2, p. 92.
[14] Gross national product was taken from *Survey of Current Business*, Vol. 46, No. 7 (July 1966), Table 1.3, p. 12, and Vol. 47, No. 7 (July 1967), Table 1.3, p. 14. The OASDI tax response was assumed to be proportional to the increase in taxable earnings, shown in *Social Security Bulletin*, Vol. 30, No. 9 (September 1967), Table Q-3, p. 48. The individual income tax was taken from U.S. Treasury Department, Internal Revenue Service, *Statistics of Income—1962; Individual Income Tax Returns* (1965), Table A, p. 4, and *Statistics of Income—1965; Individual Income Tax Returns* (1967), Table 1.1, p. 1. The effect of the 1964 tax cut, as estimated by Joseph A. Pechman, "Individual Income Tax Provisions of the Revenue Act of 1964," *Journal of Finance*, Vol. 20, No. 2 (May 1965), p. 261, was to lower individual income tax liabilities by 19.5 percent.

payroll tax on the built-in flexibility of the entire system is significant since social security taxes alone now raise roughly $30 billion a year, or 19 percent of total federal revenues. Payroll taxes to finance the unemployment insurance system raise these figures to $33 billion and 21 percent, respectively.[15]

Scheduled increases in tax rates, which are enacted many years before the increases become effective, have several times produced perverse fiscal policies. Perhaps the most serious was when the payroll tax first became effective on January 1, 1937. The tax of 2 percent on payrolls—almost 1 percent of personal income in 1937—went into effect five months before the onset of a severe business contraction.[16] In the years since World War II, increases in the OASDI tax became effective in the midst of the 1953–54 recession, only a few months before the onset of recessions in 1957 and 1960, and during the slowdown of the growth in output in early 1967.

By contrast, the benefit side of the social security trust accounts have contributed to economic stability. First, older workers tend to fall back on OASDI when they cannot find employment during slack periods. Second, benefits have generally been raised along with or shortly after tax increases, thus offsetting the deflationary impact of the tax increases. Since 1961, stabilization policy has been given considerable weight in the timing of tax and benefit increases, with the result that changes which would have been made on the basis of long-term considerations were accelerated or delayed by several months.

On balance, because of increases in benefits and despite the regressivity of the taxes and the inappropriate timing of tax rate increases, the social security system has contributed to the nation's stability since the end of World War II. Nevertheless, this contribution could have been enhanced if an elastic source of revenue,

---

[15] The *Budget of the United States Government, Fiscal Year 1969* (1968), p. 539.

[16] The social security tax and the accompanying railroad retirement tax yielded $700 million in 1937, and personal income amounted to $74.1 billion; see U.S. Department of Commerce, Office of Business Economics, *The National Income and Product Accounts of the United States, 1929–1965; Statistical Tables* (1966), Tables 1.9 and 3.8, pp. 12, 58. The 1937–38 recession began in May 1937; see Geoffrey H. Moore, *Measuring Recessions*, National Bureau of Economic Research, Occasional Paper 61 (1958), p. 260.

like the personal income tax, had been substituted for the payroll tax. Even with the payroll tax, the overall effect would have been more satisfactory if the timing of the tax rate increases had been more flexible. Such flexibility could have been achieved if the connection between tax rate changes and benefit increases had been loosened.

EFFECTS ON ALLOCATION OF RESOURCES

A major standard for judging the suitability of any tax is its effects on economic efficiency. Most taxes tend to change the allocation of resources from what it would be without the taxes, but some change it more than others. The major considerations in this connection are the effects of the payroll tax on the use of labor, personal saving, and incentives.

The use of labor. If the preceding analysis of incidence is correct, the payroll tax has very little effect on the use of labor. Since it is almost a general tax, there is little incentive for wage earners to seek jobs in which they might avoid the tax. Moreover, as already indicated, if the supply of labor is not very responsive to the level of wages, the imposition of the tax does not significantly affect the amount of labor employed. The payroll tax, therefore, affects the allocation of resources only to the extent that the tax is a burden on consumption or profits. Any part of the payroll tax not shifted backward on workers would increase the cost of labor relative to that of capital goods. Its effect would be very much like the investment tax credit, accelerated depreciation, or other measures which reduce the price of capital relative to that of labor.

To the extent that the employer bears some portion of the payroll tax, perhaps its major effect on the use of labor would result from its differential impact between (*a*) high-paid and low-paid workers and (*b*) workers who tend to move from one job to another and those who do not. Because the tax is applied only to earnings below a specified limit, it decreases the cost of high-paid labor relative to that of low-paid labor, if the tax is not fully borne by workers. Similarly, since the employer tax is levied at a flat rate on taxable earnings of any employee whether that employee has been taxed before or not, employers may pay more tax on account

of workers with multiple jobs during the year than they do on account of employees with one job. For example, an employer pays
taxes only on the first $7,800 of earnings of any individual worker.
For a job that pays an annual wage of $15,600, the employer pays
twice as much tax if he hires two different individuals for half the
year than if he hires one individual for the whole year. Employer
reluctance to assume such additional labor costs may tend to discourage mobility among workers. For the same reason, employers
are encouraged somewhat to pay overtime rather than to hire additional workers.

The direction of these effects on the use of labor is clear. Their
magnitudes are unknown, but there is no evidence to suggest that
they are large.

Personal saving. Before the enactment of the social security program, individual savings and a scattering of group retirement
plans were the major protection against the loss of earnings resulting from retirement, death, or disability. It is sometimes suggested
that social security encourages individuals to set aside a smaller
amount of personal savings on the ground that it removes a major
reason for saving. On the other hand, the availability of social security may well provide an incentive for individuals to save more:
with major hazards already covered, other savings goals may appear to be within reach.

The available evidence suggests that, over the long run, individuals covered by government and industrial pension plans tend to
save more than those who are not covered.[17] How net saving by
beneficiaries has been affected is not known. Between 1929 and
1960–67, personal savings rose from 5.0 percent to 5.9 percent of
disposable income; at the same time, many other factors had a significant influence on the savings ratio.[18] Moreover, the effect of so-

[17] See Roger F. Murray, "Economic Aspects of Pensions: A Summary Report," in
Old Age Income Assurance, Pt. V: *Financial Aspects of Pension Plans,* pp. 69–78;
Phillip Cagan, *The Effect of Pension Plans on Aggregate Saving: Evidence from a
Sample Survey,* National Bureau of Economic Research, Occasional Paper 95 (Co-
lumbia University Press, 1965); and George Katona, *The Mass Consumption Society*
(McGraw-Hill, 1964), Chap. 19, pp. 182–202.

[18] *Economic Report of the President,* February 1968, Table B-15, p. 226, and *Economic Indicators,* Prepared for the Joint Economic Committee by the Council of
Economic Advisers, 90 Cong. 2 sess. (July 1968), p. 5.

cial security on *national* saving must take into account its impact on government saving as well as on personal saving. The government's contribution to saving as a result of the social security system is discussed below in the section on trust funds.[19]

Work incentives. The payroll tax does not apply to earnings above the maximum taxable level. By contrast, the individual income tax—which is levied at graduated rates ranging up to 70 percent—is alleged by a few writers to have a significant effect on incentives because it tends to reduce rewards for greater effort.[20]

Taxation is only one of the many factors affecting work incentives. To isolate the unique effect of the tax factor from the available statistical record or from the results of direct interviews with taxpayers is an extremely difficult task. No evidence suggests that income taxation has greatly reduced the amount of labor performed by workers and managers. Work habits are not easily changed, and most people cannot vary hours of work or the intensity of their efforts in response to variations in tax rates. According to a recent survey, ". . . the loss of annual output due to work disincentives caused by the progressive income tax is of negligible proportions."[21]

Moreover, the direction in which the effect of high tax rates operates is not even clear on theoretical grounds. On the one hand, the personal income tax tends to reduce incentives by reducing the net returns from additional work effort. The social security tax has a similar effect up to the taxable maximum. On the other hand, both personal income and payroll taxes may provide a greater incentive to obtain more income because they cut down on the income left over for spending.

While there is some evidence regarding the effect of the progressive income tax on work incentives, there is no evidence at all of the effects of the payroll tax. Economists today can only guess at the impact of a 10 percent tax on persons at or below poverty lev-

[19] See pages 204–12.

[20] Otto Eckstein, "Financing the System of Social Insurance," in William G. Bowen and others (eds.), *The American System of Social Insurance: Its Philosophy, Impact, and Future Development* (McGraw-Hill, 1968).

[21] Robin Barlow, Harvey E. Brazer, and James N. Morgan, *Economic Behavior of the Affluent* (Brookings Institution, 1966), p. 3; see their Chapter 10, pp. 129–50, for the detailed evidence.

els of income. In any case, the differences between the two taxes in their effects on incentives are likely to be small.

SUMMARY EVALUATION

In the long run, both the employer and the employee payroll tax are probably borne by the worker. The payroll tax, to the extent that it is not borne by the worker, tends to encourage the use of high-paid labor at the expense of low-paid labor, and also to discourage the mobility of workers. It probably has relatively little effect on the total supply of labor. The yield of the payroll tax is less responsive to changes in income than the yield of the income tax, and thus has less built-in flexibility. The major destabilizing influence of the payroll tax resulted from bad timing of increases in the tax rate rather than from the nature of the tax. Although the income tax is sometimes alleged to discourage work incentives, there is little indication that it has had a substantial effect on effort among those who are subject to the rates in the higher brackets.

Considered as a complete system, OASDI taxes and benefits redistribute income from middle- and high-income employed persons, who tend to be savers, to low-income inactive persons, who tend to spend all or most of their incomes. However, net personal savings have not declined relative to disposable income despite the great expansion of the social security program in the last three decades.

The regressivity and other inequities of the payroll tax, rather than its stabilization and allocative-efficiency effects, are the grounds for considering it inferior to the personal income tax. The major differences that exist between the two taxes—the exemptions, the personal deductions, and the broader income concept under the personal income tax—argue in favor of the personal income tax rather than the payroll tax. The payroll tax bears too heavily on low-income persons and on those with heavy family responsibilities.

Methods of General Revenue Financing

Since the income tax is the major source of federal revenues, reliance on the general funds of the Treasury would automatically substitute income taxation for payroll taxation. Several different approaches may be taken to introduce general revenue financing into the social security system. In the following discussion, it is assumed that the financial operations of social security will continue to be carried out through the trust funds and that the system will continue to be operated approximately on a pay-as-you-go basis, so that the reserves will be maintained at about current levels.

The different methods by which general revenues could be channeled to social security may be grouped under the following four headings: integration of the payroll tax with the income tax; allowance for personal exemptions from the payroll tax, the cost of which would be paid by the general fund; introduction of a government contribution from the general fund; and integration of OASDI with a liberalized public assistance system or some variant of the negative income tax.

INTEGRATION OF PAYROLL TAX WITH INCOME TAX

Integration of the payroll tax with the individual income tax would involve conversion of the payroll tax into a withholding tax for income tax purposes. It would not necessarily involve any change in the payroll tax, the end of earmarking, or modification of the practice of accumulating the payroll tax in the trust funds. Individuals would receive credit—dollar for dollar—against their income taxes for the amount of payroll taxes paid.

The operation of the integrated tax for a person with an income of $3,000 and another with an income of $10,000 is illustrated in Table viii-2. Both individuals are assumed to be married and to have two children. It is assumed that the $3,000 income consists entirely of earnings subject to the payroll tax and that the $10,000 income includes $1,000 of property income. For simplicity, the employee payroll tax rate is assumed to be 5 percent for earnings up to $7,800. The income tax rates are those applicable to 1967, and amounts withheld for income tax purposes are assumed to be at the rates prescribed by the Internal Revenue Code.

The individual with the $3,000 income is subject to income tax withholding of $4 and pays a payroll tax of $150. He will

Table VIII-2. *Illustration of Method of Integrating the Payroll Tax with the Individual Income Tax for a Married Person with Two Children*

	Assumed Income	
Method of Integration	$3,000[a]	$10,000[b]
Full integration[c]		
Income tax liability[d]	$ 0	$1,114
Total amounts withheld	154	1,296
Income tax[e]	4	906
OASDI[f]	150	390
Year-end adjustment		
Refund	154	182
Balance of tax due	—	—
50 percent integration[c]		
Income tax liability[d]	0	1,114
Total amounts withheld	79	1,101
Income tax[e]	4	906
OASDI[f]	75	195
Year-end adjustment		
Refund	79	—
Balance of tax due	—	13

a. Includes only earnings subject to payroll tax.
b. Includes $1,000 of property income; remainder is earnings subject to payroll tax and income tax withholding.
c. Under full integration, the entire payroll tax is credited against the income tax; under 50 percent integration, half the payroll tax is credited.
d. Rates applicable to 1967. It is assumed that taxpayer uses standard deduction.
e. Amounts withheld are computed on the basis of the monthly withholding tables shown in Section 3402 of the Internal Revenue Code.
f. Payroll tax is assumed to be 5 percent on earnings up to $7,800.

receive a refund of the entire amount after he files his return following the end of the year. The $10,000 individual pays a payroll tax of $390 and is subject to $906 of withholding for income tax purposes. His income tax liability is $1,114, so that he is entitled to a refund of $182 at the end of the year.

The integration technique can be applied in a partial form to the payroll tax, as shown in the lower half of Table VIII-2. It would be possible, for example, to integrate half the payroll tax with the income tax. This would reduce to $79 the refund paid to the $3,000 income recipient, and the recipient of the $10,000 income would owe $13.

Whether or not integration would require an increase in other taxes to offset a loss of revenue would depend on overall fiscal requirements. Integration of the payroll tax with the income tax would be an appropriate method of reducing taxes if tax reduction were in order. In 1967, the OASDI payroll tax amounted to roughly 8 percentage points applied to the individual income tax base, or about 40 percent of individual income tax liabilities.

Integration could be limited to the employee tax, or applied to the combined tax paid by employees and employers. The latter alternative may be defended on the ground that the employee probably bears the burden of the employer tax as well as his own. On the other hand, integration does not necessarily require a change in the status of the employer tax. It could be continued as a separate tax, or replaced by another tax (for example, by a flat-rate tax on total payrolls, by an increased corporation income tax, or by a new value-added tax).

The integration proposal does not affect the financial arrangements surrounding social security itself. The payroll tax would continue to be paid into the trust funds. The practice of translating the cost of increased benefits into payroll tax equivalents could also be continued, but the increased tax would in effect be converted to an income tax through integration.

Integration could apply to all or part of the presently scheduled payroll taxes or to future increments of the payroll tax. Thus, the integration device is extremely flexible and could be used to achieve any desired distribution of the burden of social security financing between the payroll tax and the income tax. Moreover, it would require no disruption of the institutional structure of social security financing.

EXEMPTIONS FROM PAYROLL TAX

Another method of improving the distribution of the burden of the social security tax is to allow workers personal exemptions in the payroll tax computation. This revision would mean that all individuals with incomes below the exemption levels would not be

subject to tax, and that the proportional payroll tax would be converted to a progressive tax, up to the maximum taxable level of
earnings.[22]

Exemptions could be provided either on an employee basis—one
exemption per covered worker—or on a family basis as is now done
under the personal income tax. Since income tax withholding already takes personal exemptions into account, it would be simpler
to use the income tax exemptions (plus the minimum standard deduction) for payroll tax purposes.[23] This would make it possible
to combine the income tax and payroll tax withholding, and to relieve employers from any additional burden of compliance.[24] Alternatively, payroll tax deductions could continue as now, and adjustments could be made annually on personal income tax returns.

Adjustment when the employee files his final return and enters
the correct amount of his exemptions seems the better alternative.
Since this type of information is already entered on computer
tapes for administrative and audit purposes, the additional calculations needed to make the adjustments for the trust funds would
not be difficult or costly, whereas the additional reporting required by current adjustment would be regarded by employers as
an unnecessary burden and they would doubtless oppose it. Furthermore, the exemptions reported by employees to their employers are frequently different from those eventually taken on final returns, so that the calculations based on employer reports would be

[22] Since the payroll tax is levied at a flat rate, the effect of the exemption would
be the same as a tax credit equal to the payroll tax rate times the value of the
exemption.

[23] The minimum standard deduction is $200 for the taxpayer, plus an additional
$100 for each exemption on his return, up to a maximum of $1,000. This device,
which was enacted under the Revenue Act of 1964, was designed to relieve those
with low incomes from tax without granting additional exemptions to those in
higher brackets. For a discussion of the minimum standard deduction, see Joseph A.
Pechman, *Federal Tax Policy* (Brookings Institution, 1966), pp. 69–72.

[24] At present, employers are given the option of using tables that list the amount
of tax to be withheld or of computing for each employee the amount to be withheld. The latter method—called the "percentage method" because it involves applying actual tax rates to income less the personal exemptions and the standard deduction—is used by large firms that employ computers for accounting purposes. If
payroll taxes and withholding taxes were combined, the rates for the percentage
method would need to be revised, just as they are when individual income tax rates
are changed.

only an approximation. On the other hand, many employees subject to social security are not required to file income tax returns. Except for evasion, those who do not file presumably are not taxable. Accordingly, this procedure would increase the number of returns filed each year.

The cost of family-based exemptions and a minimum standard deduction identical to those in the personal income tax is over 40 percent of a payroll tax on wages and salaries up to $7,800. The cost is relatively large because the exemption and the standard deduction would be given not only to those who are relieved from the payment of taxes but also to taxpayers with incomes above the exemption levels. Of the total loss in revenue, only about one-eighth is accounted for by the tax rebate to persons who are not subject to federal income tax.[25]

However, the cost could be reduced to about 5 percent of the payroll tax by denying the exemptions and the minimum standard deduction to those with incomes above the value of the exemptions and deductions. But if this were done, a troublesome "notch" problem would be created just above the exemption levels. For example, with a 5 percent payroll tax, the exemption and minimum standard deduction—amounting to $3,000—would provide relief worth $150 to a married person with two children.[26] Yet another individual with earnings of $3,001 would—because of the additional dollar of income—be required to pay a payroll tax of $150.05.

Such a problem could be avoided by various devices. The simplest, but in some ways the least attractive, would be to limit the amount of payroll tax to the amount of earnings in excess of the exemptions plus the minimum standard deduction.[27] For example, a married worker with two children and earnings of $3,100 would pay $100 of payroll tax. The 5 percent tax would take hold beginning at $3,157.89; at this point, the payroll tax would be $157.89, which is exactly equal to the amount of earnings in excess of

[25] See Appendix F for the methods used to prepare these estimates.

[26] The exemption is $600 per capita and the minimum standard deduction is $200 for the taxpayer plus an additional $100 for every exemption on his return.

[27] Technically, the payroll tax would be the lower of (a) 5 percent of earnings up to the taxable maximum or (b) the amount of earnings in excess of the exemptions plus the minimum standard deduction.

Table VIII-3. *Illustrative Tax Liabilities as a Percentage of Various Earnings under a 5 Percent Payroll Tax and a Personal Exemption*

Earnings (Dollars)	5 Percent Tax with No Exemptions	5 Percent Tax with Exemption[a]		
		Exemption available to all taxpayers	Exemption restricted to low-income taxpayers	
			By notch rate of 100 percent[b]	By notch rate of 50 percent[c]
Married person with two children[a]				
1,000	5	—	—	—
2,000	5	—	—	—
3,000	5	—	—	—
3,100	5	0.2	3.2	1.6
3,200	5	0.3	5.0	3.1
3,300	5	0.5	5.0	4.5
3,400	5	0.6	5.0	5.0
3,500	5	0.7	5.0	5.0
4,000	5	1.2	5.0	5.0
5,000	5	2.0	5.0	5.0
6,000	5	2.5	5.0	5.0
7,000	5	2.9	5.0	5.0
7,800	5	3.1	5.0	5.0
Single person with no dependents[a]				
500	5	—	—	—
600	5	—	—	—
700	5	—	—	—
800	5	—	—	—
900	5	—	—	—
950	5	0.3	5.0	2.6
1,000	5	0.5	5.0	5.0
1,500	5	2.0	5.0	5.0
2,000	5	2.8	5.0	5.0
3,000	5	3.5	5.0	5.0
4,000	5	3.9	5.0	5.0
5,000	5	4.1	5.0	5.0
6,000	5	4.2	5.0	5.0
7,000	5	4.4	5.0	5.0
7,800	5	4.4	5.0	5.0

a. Exemption is the same as under the present income tax law—$600 per capita. In addition, taxpayer would be allowed the minimum standard deduction. Total allowance is $3,000 for married person with two children and $900 for single person.

b. The payroll tax would be (a) 5 percent of earnings up to $7,800 or (b) the amount of earnings in excess of the exemption plus the minimum standard deduction—whichever is the lower.

c. The payroll tax would be (a) 5 percent of earnings up to $7,800 or (b) one-half of earnings in excess of the exemption plus the minimum standard deduction—whichever is the lower.

$3,000. The disadvantage of this type of notch provision is that the tax rate is 100 percent for the range to which it applies. However, with a low tax rate, the range is narrow and applies to a relatively small number of persons. The disincentive effects are hardly likely to be significant in such circumstances, but may be a source of irritation in a few cases.

Another device would be to limit the tax to some fraction, say 50 percent, of earnings in excess of the exemption level. This would reduce the tax rate to 50 percent and extend to $3,333.33 the range over which the notch provision would apply.[28]

The difference between the three exemption approaches is illustrated in Table VIII-3, which compares a flat 5 percent payroll tax and a payroll tax with the same personal exemptions and minimum standard deduction allowed under the present individual income tax. Exemptions limited to low-income taxpayers are also shown, with two different notch provisions—one with a 100 percent and the other with a 50 percent rate. For purposes of illustration, the taxes are computed for a married person with two children and for a single person without dependents. The essential difference among the three approaches is that the traditional type of exemption reduces the tax burdens at all earnings levels, whereas the limited exemption confines the relief to taxpayers with low income.

CONTRIBUTION FROM GENERAL REVENUES

The probability that a contribution from general revenues would ultimately be required to help finance the social security system has been acknowledged from the beginning. In 1935, the Committee on Economic Security predicted that benefits would exceed annual receipts by 1965, and recommended that the federal government should begin then to make contributions.[29] The 1938 and

[28] Alternatively, the *exemption* could be tapered off by reducing it, say, by 50 cents for every dollar of earnings in excess of the exemption level. This method widens the range over which the notch provision applies, but is similar in all other respects to the method described in the text.

[29] *Report to the President of the Committee on Economic Security* (1935), pp. 31–32. The prediction proved unusually accurate in terms of timing, although the type of general revenue financing enacted in 1965 was not that envisaged in the early

1948 Advisory Councils also strongly supported a contribution from general revenues.[30] A government contribution was incorporated in the Social Security Act under the Revenue Act of 1943, when the scheduled rate reductions were postponed, but this provision was eliminated in the 1950 amendments.[31] Since then, proposals for general revenue financing have been made from time to time, but Congress has not acted on them.

Even though the need for some general revenue financing has been recognized for a long time, there is no agreement on the formula that might be used. Two suggestions have been considered in the past:

1. The Committee on Economic Security contemplated a contribution from general revenues to cover the deficit arising from the payment in the early decades of annuities that exceeded the employer-employee contributions plus accumulated interest. The deficiency for these "past-service credits" could be met by a government contribution made from the beginning of the program or introduced at a later date when the payroll tax had been stabilized.[32]

2. Some people view the benefit structure as a two-tiered combination of (a) minimum benefits for the lowest-paid workers and (b) the portion of the benefit structure above the minimum. This division suggests that the minimum should be paid out of general revenues (since low-paid workers contribute only a small portion of their benefits) and the remainder out of payroll taxes.

Both suggestions are based to a substantial degree on the contributory principle. It need hardly be pointed out that it would be

stages of social security. The 1965 legislation provided for general revenues (a) to finance hospital insurance benefits for aged persons who were neither fully insured nor railroad retirement beneficiaries and (b) to match the monthly premiums paid by individuals who elected the supplementary medical insurance. There was another departure from payroll tax financing in 1966, when general revenues were appropriated to finance the cost of special OASDI benefits to persons aged 72 before 1968 and who had less than three quarters of coverage.

[30] Advisory Council on Social Security, *Final Report, December 10, 1938*, S. Doc. 4, 76 Cong. 1 sess. (1939), pp. 6–7, 24–27; and *Old-Age and Survivors Insurance*, A Report to the Senate Committee on Finance from the Advisory Council on Social Security, S. Doc. 149, 80 Cong. 2 sess. (1948), pp. 45–46.

[31] P.L. 235, Title IX, Section 902 (1944); and P.L. 734, Title I, Section 109(a) (1950).

[32] Robert M. Ball, "What Contribution Rate for Old-Age and Survivors Insurance?" *Social Security Bulletin*, Vol. 12, No. 7 (July 1949), p. 5.

virtually impossible to devise a formula that is likely to be applicable for more than a brief period of time. As benefits change, the required payment from general revenues would necessarily be altered. In other words, since benefits are not set on the basis of contributions, any one formula is bound to require periodic amendment.[33]

A simple, general revenue contribution does not attack the main shortcoming of the payroll tax—that is, its excessive burden on workers with low income. To relieve these workers of this burden, any general revenue formula would need to be accompanied by a personal exemption for payroll tax purposes.

INTEGRATION WITH A NEGATIVE INCOME TAX

Considerable thought has been given in recent years to the relationship between the welfare system and the income tax system. The traditional method of helping poor families has been through public welfare and other direct transfer payments. Most of these welfare programs reach specific categories of poor persons; except for general relief, which is inadequate almost everywhere, and the unemployed parent program under aid to families with dependent children, which at mid-1967 reached approximately 60,000 families in 22 states,[34] they provide no assistance to families headed by able-bodied workers who, for reasons of background, training, or temperament, do not participate effectively in the modern industrial economy. Old-age assistance, for example, is designed to assist only the aged poor.

In a fundamental respect, welfare may be regarded as an extension of the income tax system; public assistance is in effect an extension of progression into the lowest brackets, with negative rather than positive rates. Recognition of this relationship has stimulated great interest in the possibility of merging the two systems through the "negative income tax."

Under this concept of progression, a "break-even" level would be designated as the dividing line between those who receive pay-

[33] Other countries have decided on various arbitrary formulas to set the contribution from general revenues, but there is no discernible pattern (see Appendix Table c-8).

[34] *Welfare in Review*, Vol. 5, No. 8 (October 1967), Table 7, p. 41.

ments and those who do not. If the income of a tax unit is below the break-even level, the unit would not pay a tax but, instead, would receive a payment from the government. This payment would be computed by applying a negative tax rate (or rates) to the shortfall of the unit's income below the break-even level. For example, if the rate is 50 percent and the break-even level is $3,000, a family with an income of $1,000 would receive $1,000 (i.e., half of the difference between $3,000 and $1,000) as the negative tax allowance (Table VIII-4).

Table VIII-4. *Illustrative Negative Tax Allowances for a Family of Four, on Assumption of a Break-even Level of $3,000 and a Negative Tax Rate of 50 Percent*

(In dollars)

Annual Income	Negative Tax Allowance	Disposable Income[a]
0	1,500	1,500
500	1,250	1,750
1,000	1,000	2,000
1,500	750	2,250
2,000	500	2,500
2,500	250	2,750
3,000	0	3,000

a. Annual income plus negative tax allowance.

There are many variants of the negative income tax, and it is not the purpose here to discuss their relative merits or the various problems of administration and compliance.[35] The following characteristics of the negative income tax are significant from the standpoint of social security policy: (*a*) the allowances would go to all persons with income below the break-even level, regardless of their age, employment status, or source of income; (*b*) the allowances would be adjusted to family size as well as to income; (*c*) expenditure of the funds by the recipients would not be sub-

[35] For a comprehensive discussion, see Christopher Green, *Negative Taxes and the Poverty Problem* (Brookings Institution, 1967); and James Tobin, Joseph A. Pechman, and Peter M. Mieszkowski, "Is a Negative Income Tax Practical?" *Yale Law Journal*, Vol. 77, No. 1 (November 1967), pp. 1–27. (Brookings Reprint 142.)

ject to scrutiny by the government; and (d) the allowances would not be given in the spirit of the dole—the system is structured to avoid the stigma associated with the receipt of government assistance.

The characteristics of the negative income tax are very similar to those of the social security system—with the important exception of the income test which is implicit in the negative income tax. Social security benefits are adjusted to family size, are not subject to government scrutiny when spent, and are given as a matter of right. As previously indicated, minimum social security benefits are pitifully inadequate for households with no other income. If a negative income tax were enacted, the aged poor should be eligible for its benefits just as other groups in the population would be. The only question is whether the two systems should be operated side by side or be formally integrated.

If the negative income tax were operated independently, family units receiving social security benefits would presumably be eligible to file for negative income tax allowances. They would report their income, including social security benefits, and receive a supplementary payment geared to this level of income. If their social security benefits exceeded the break-even level, they would automatically become ineligible for a negative income tax allowance. Except for the fact that the aged poor would receive two checks, this system presents no particular problems of administration.

On the other hand, there is much to be said for integrating the two systems to avoid duplication. If there were two independent systems, the aged poor who are eligible for social security would receive larger transfer payments than the aged poor who are not eligible. For example, assume a break-even level of $1,500 for a family of two and a negative tax rate of 50 percent. A married couple receiving a social security benefit of $900 a year and no other income would receive a supplementary negative income tax allowance of $300 [0.5($1,500 − $900)]; thus its disposable income would be $1,200 ($900 from social security and $300 from the negative income tax). Another couple not eligible for social security would receive a negative income tax allowance of only $750 [0.5($1,500)]. Thus, the first family would have $450 more of disposable income.

It probably would be desirable to handle negative income tax allowances of the aged through the social security system. Those who are not eligible for social security could be blanketed-in, and reimbursement for the cost of their benefits—as well as the cost of the supplementary payments to those with social security benefits lower than negative income tax allowances—would be made to the trust fund from the general fund of the federal government.

The cost of negative income tax payments to the aged poor would be relatively small, compared with the total cost of a negative income tax. For example, with (a) break-even levels of $1,500 for an unrelated individual or family head and $500 for each additional member of the family and (b) a negative tax rate of 50 percent, the total cost of the negative income tax would be about $6.1 billion based on 1964 incomes. Of this amount, about one-fourth would go to families headed by a person aged 65 or over.[36]

It is probably impractical to raise social security benefits in the short run to levels high enough to avoid the need for any supplementary assistance from a negative income tax to persons over age 65. To accomplish this objective, minimum social security levels would have to be raised to the minimum allowances paid under the negative income tax. This would be inefficient in terms of the objectives of income maintenance, since the additional benefits would be paid whether or not the recipient had income from other sources. Moreover, an increase in the minimum social security benefits would generate pressures for increases of benefits above the minimum, and it is unlikely that these would go to needy aged persons. It is clear, therefore, that the aged poor could be aided more effectively and at lower overall cost by a negative income tax than through increases in minimum social security benefits. Increases in the minimum social security benefits must be regarded as a "second best" solution, inferior to the introduction of a negative income tax but superior by far to the present distribution of benefits.

Although there are many practical problems,[37] the Social Secu-

---

[36] Green, *Negative Taxes and the Poverty Problem,* Tables 9-1, 9-3, and D-1 (line 11), pp. 141, 147, and 190.
[37] See Tobin, Pechman, and Mieszkowski, "Is a Negative Income Tax Practical?"

rity Administration should be able to administer, at reasonable costs, a negative income tax for all aged persons. General revenue financing would automatically be introduced into the system if the additional cost were paid by the general fund. Like a direct general fund contribution, however, this method would not in itself solve the problem of the impact of the payroll tax on low-income workers.

The use of general fund financing is often criticized on the ground that benefits might be lower than they would be if the financing came entirely from an earmarked tax.[38] The available statistical evidence suggests that, compared with countries relying on general revenue financing, countries using payroll taxes have somewhat higher old-age benefits and smaller benefits for other transfer programs, but *total* benefits seem to be unaffected by the type of financing (see Appendix D). In the United States, resistance to increases in benefits—particularly to beneficiaries with low earnings histories—has become noticeably stronger as the payroll tax rate approaches 10 percent. It is impossible to predict what effect general revenue financing might eventually have on the system. Regardless of the outcome, however, this consideration should carry little weight in the decision. The purpose is not to maximize benefits, but to set them at levels that meet the basic objectives of the program and conform with other priorities in the public and private sectors. The question of general revenue financing should be considered on its merits, and not on the basis of an uncertain forecast of its effect on the level of benefits.

Taxation of Aged Persons

A graduated income tax with allowances for personal exemptions and heavy medical expenses automatically allows for special circumstances of the individual taxpayer. Nevertheless, the federal income tax imposes smaller liabilities on the aged than on the nonaged with the same total income. All persons over 65 years of age have an additional exemption of $600, pay no tax on their

[38] See Eckstein, "Financing the System of Social Insurance," in *The American System of Social Insurance.*

social security or railroad retirement pensions, and receive a tax credit on other retirement income up to $1,524 ($2,286 for couples filing jointly).[39] These provisions affect only those aged persons with sufficient incomes to be taxable, and they benefit to only a very modest extent the aged who are officially classified as poor.

The federal tax treatment of the aged is relevant to social security policy because it is expensive. The desirability of these tax advantages should be weighed against the desirability of other benefits for the aged or nonaged which could be provided at similar cost. In 1964, the special exemption for age and the tax credit for retirement income cost about $740 million (Appendix Table F-2), and the exclusion of social security benefits from the tax base cost another $1.6 billion, or a total of $2.3 billion.

The extra exemptions for age are supported on the ground that aged taxpayers have less ability to pay than other members of the community. While the aged may be relatively poor (see Chapter II), it does not follow that aged persons with a given income and other deductions have less ability to pay than do nonaged persons with the same income. In general, the available data show that the budget needs of the aged are not greater than those of younger taxpayers,[40] and this is particularly true now that Medicare has been enacted. Another argument for extra exemptions is that the aged find it difficult to adjust to lower incomes after retirement. However, the graduated income tax partially adjusts for this change. For example, the tax of a married person whose taxable income falls from $25,000 to $8,000 at retirement drops from $6,020 to $1,380.

The omission of social security and railroad retirement benefits from the tax base dates from the 1930's when tax rates were low and exemptions were high; it mattered little then whether benefits were subject to tax or not. As incomes grew and social security was extended, others who were not eligible for social security pleaded

---

[39] Until the end of 1966, the aged were also allowed to deduct all their medical and dental expenses, instead of only the excess over 3 percent allowed to other taxpayers. This benefit was eliminated because of the federal program for health insurance for the aged enacted in 1965.

[40] See sources cited in Table v-1, p. 83.

for similar treatment. As a result, a 20 percent credit against tax for the first $1,200 of retirement income (other than social security benefits) was enacted in 1954. In 1962, the maximum income subject to the credit was raised to $1,524; in 1964, the credit was set at 17 percent for that year and at 15 percent beginning with 1965 (to correspond with the general rate reductions enacted for those years), and the limit on income subject to it was raised to $2,286 on joint returns (to allow for the 50 percent supplementary social security payment to a husband on behalf of his wife).

Aside from the objection that special tax relief is questionable in general, the objection to these provisions is that they give the greatest tax advantage to higher income persons among the aged. At 1964 income levels, 47 percent of the $2.3 billion revenue cost of the retirement income credit, the special exemption, and the exclusion of OASDI benefits went to the aged with incomes above $5,000 (who constituted less than 20 percent of all aged).[41] Thus, a disproportionate amount of relief is given to those aged persons who do not need such help.

In principle, it would be fairer to remove the additional exemption for age and make all retirement income taxable. The additional revenue could be used to good advantage to raise social security benefits. An opportune occasion for removing the exemption would be at the time of integration of the payroll tax with the personal income tax.

Presidents Kennedy and Johnson recommended revisions in the tax treatment of the aged that were designed to improve the distribution of the tax benefits between high- and low-income persons, but not to recover the revenue loss. In 1963, President Kennedy proposed that the extra exemption for the aged and the retirement income credit be replaced by a credit of $300 against tax at all income levels. To avoid double benefits, the credit would have been offset by an amount equal to the taxpayer's bracket rate times one-half the social security and railroad retirement benefits (the portion presumed to be attributable to the employer's contribu-

[41] Derived from Appendix Table F-2; *Statistics of Income—1964; Individual Income Tax Returns* (1967), Table 27, p. 89; and U.S. Bureau of the Census, *Statistical Abstract of the United States, 1965* (1965), Table 19, p. 24.

tion). These proposals would have reduced the taxes of persons over 65 years of age by more than $300 million, annually.[42]

In 1967, President Johnson proposed that a special exemption of $2,300 for aged single persons and $4,000 for aged married couples be substituted for the special provisions. These special exemptions were to be offset dollar-for-dollar when the income of the aged began to exceed $5,600 for single persons and $11,200 for married persons, but they were not to fall below one-third of the social security and railroad retirement benefit (on the ground that few, if any, individuals would have "contributed" that much for a long time to come).[43] The net reduction of taxes for the aged under this plan would have been close to $60 million a year.

Neither the Kennedy nor the Johnson proposal was enacted by the Congress, despite the net tax reductions offered in the interest of tax reform. The pressures for retaining the present distribution of tax benefits outweighed the arguments of the Treasury for greater equity. Despite the double rebuff, the need for tax reform in this area remains. If the level and structure of social security benefits are to be liberalized and improved, there is little justification for maintaining tax benefits that are both costly and inequitable.

The Trust Funds

The financial operations of the social security system are handled through the OASI trust fund and the DI trust fund. The former was established on January 1, 1940, on the recommendation of the 1938 Advisory Council;[44] the latter was created—with virtually no public comment—on August 1, 1956, when disability benefits were made a part of the social security program (contributions began on January 1, 1957).[45] Some modifications of present OASDI fi-

[42] *Revision of Our Tax Structure,* Message from the President of the United States Transmitting Recommendations Relative to a Revision of Our Tax Structure, H. Doc. 43, 88 Cong. 1 sess. (January 24, 1963), pp. 12–13.

[43] *President's Proposals for Revision in the Social Security System,* Hearings, Pt. 1, p. 198.

[44] Advisory Council on Social Security, *Final Report, December 10, 1938,* pp. 6–7, 26.

[45] *The 1967 Annual Report of the Board of Trustees of the Federal Old-Age and*

nancing arrangements would directly affect trust fund receipts, while others would involve taxes or transfers outside the social security framework.

METHOD OF OPERATION

Social security taxes are collected by the federal Internal Revenue Service and are paid into the Treasury as internal revenue collections. These taxes are automatically transferred to the trust funds through a "permanent" congressional appropriation. The first transfer is made on the basis of estimated tax receipts; periodic adjustments are later made to correct the original estimates to the extent that they differ from the taxes actually payable on the basis of reported earnings.[46]

In addition to taxes, the receipts of the trust funds include interest on the investments held by the funds and reimbursements from the general fund for the noncontributory credits for military service and for benefits to noninsured persons aged 72 and over.[47] Disbursements from the funds include benefit payments, administrative expenses, and transfers to the railroad retirement account.[48]

The trust funds are permitted to invest only in bonds issued by the federal government. These bonds are of two types: (a) direct interest-bearing obligations or obligations guaranteed by the fed-

---

Survivors Insurance and Disability Insurance Trust Funds, H. Doc. 65, 90 Cong. 1 sess. (1967), pp. 1, 9.

[46] Exact amounts cannot be transferred initially because social security and income taxes withheld are not separately identified by the employer on the report he submits with his monthly or semimonthly payment to the Treasury depositary. The exact computations are based on the quarterly earnings reports submitted by employers and on the information supplied by the self-employed with their annual federal income tax returns.

[47] These reimbursements covered (a) credits of $160 a month granted for military service between September 16, 1940, and December 31, 1956, and (b) benefits to persons aged 72 or over before 1968 who were blanketed into the social security system in 1966. See Chapter III, pp. 37–38, 40.

[48] The transfers to the railroad retirement account represent the cost of the financial interchange provisions between OASDI and the railroad retirement trust fund (see Chapter III, p. 46). Small reimbursements are also made annually by the trust funds to the Department of Health, Education, and Welfare for the cost of vocational rehabilitation services furnished to disability insurance beneficiaries and to disabled adults receiving benefits on the basis of disabilities that have continued since childhood.

eral government as to both principal and interest; and (b) special
public-debt obligations created exclusively for the trust funds.
The funds may purchase federal debt obligations in the open market or when they are issued. The interest on the special debt obligations must equal the average market yield on all federal debt
outstanding with a maturity of four or more years, but need
bear no relation to the interest rate currently being paid by the
federal government.

A summary of the transactions of the trust funds through the
end of 1967 is given in Table viii-5. As of December 31, 1967, the
accumulated assets of the trust funds were about $26 billion, most
of which is accounted for by the excess of taxes collected over benefits paid. Interest on investments has been relatively small, accounting for about 6 percent of total benefits paid; on an annual

Table viii-5. *Summary of Operations of Old-Age and Survivors
Insurance and Disability Insurance Trust Funds through December 31, 1967*

(In billions of dollars)

Item	Old-Age and Survivors Insurance Trust Fund	Disability Insurance Trust Fund	Total
Income	202.0	14.0	216.0
Taxes (less refunds)	191.3	13.4	204.7
Reimbursements for noncontributory credits for military service	0.2	*	0.2
Interest on investments	10.5	0.6	11.1
Disbursements	177.8	12.0	189.8
Benefit payments	170.4	11.1	181.5
Administrative expenses	3.8	0.7	4.5
Transfers to railroad retirement account	3.6	0.1	3.7
Payments for vocational rehabilitation services	—	*	*
Fund on December 31, 1967	24.2	2.0	26.3

Sources: *The 1968 Annual Report of the Board of Trustees of the Federal Old-Age and Survivors Insurance and Disability Insurance Trust Funds*, H. Doc. 288, 90 Cong. 2 sess. (1968), Tables 14 and 18, pp. 30, 36. Figures are rounded and will not necessarily add to totals.
* Less than $50 million.

basis, it has been little more than 3–4 percent of annual benefits in recent years.[49]

NATURE OF TRUST FUNDS

The trust funds were created to provide security for the receipts accumulated by the social security system. Investment in private securities was rejected in order to avoid large-scale ownership of private firms by a government agency and "to provide the greatest possible security for the funds. . . ."[50] Originally, the Old-Age and Survivors Insurance (OASI) reserve was expected to total $46 billion in 1980, but it has never exceeded much more than half that amount.[51]

The idea of a reserve fund was borrowed from private insurance. As indicated in Chapter III, the 1935 legislation was predicated to a large extent on the principle of "individual equity," that is, that benefits would bear a significant relationship to amounts contributed by each employee, plus accumulated interest. But this policy was partially abandoned in 1939, following the advice of the 1938 Advisory Council. It is curious that the Council, even though it recommended a substantial reduction in the reserve fund, proposed the transfer of reserves to a trust fund. This fund was to be regarded as a "contingency fund to insure ready payment of benefits at all stages of the business cycle and under varying conditions. . . ."[52] The 1959 Advisory Council endorsed the use of a trust fund for contingency purposes, but gave no guidance as to its ultimate size, except to say that interest on a fund of fixed size "will meet a decreasing proportion of benefit costs."[53] The 1965 Advisory Council was the first to suggest the present policy—that the trust fund should be large enough to maintain the program's solvency in the face of severe recession conditions,

---

[49] Appendix Table G-2.

[50] Ida C. Merriam, *Social Security Financing*, Social Security Administration, Federal Security Agency, Division of Research and Statistics, Bureau Report No. 17 (1953), p. 29.

[51] *Ibid.*, and Appendix Table G-2.

[52] Advisory Council on Social Security, *Final Report, December 10, 1938*, p. 25.

[53] Advisory Council on Social Security Financing, *Financing Old-Age, Survivors, and Disability Insurance* (1959), p. 20.

which were defined as those that would prevail if in one year there should be a drop of 5 million in the number of people with covered earnings.[54]

The record does not indicate clearly what the Advisory Councils had in mind when they recommended the trust fund device for contingency purposes. Through the accumulation of bonds, the payment of benefits is guaranteed to the extent that the federal government will continue to pay principal and interest on the bonds; the trust fund itself does not provide any additional assurance that such federal payments will be made. Nor could the existence of a trust fund prevent the Congress from lowering benefits, if it were determined to do so.

The purpose of the reserve—apart from its accumulation in a trust fund—can be inferred more easily from the record. After recommending the creation of a "reasonable" reserve, the 1938 Advisory Council stated, "It is desirable that the payment of benefits should not be dependent upon quick congressional action in levying emergency taxes to meet deficits or in sudden raising of contribution rates when disbursements exceed current tax collections or normal appropriations to the system."[55]

Thus, the reserve was intended to provide for continuity of payment if Congress failed to act quickly to appropriate additional funds when current tax receipts fell sharply. A sharp decline in business activity would reduce the flow of payroll tax receipts. In such instances, the reserve could be used to make up any short-run deficiencies; without a reserve, a congressional appropriation would be necessary. Thus, the reserve turns out to be a device to implement the intention of Congress to continue to pay the statutory benefits even when payroll receipts drop sharply and unexpectedly.

But the trust fund is not the only device available to Congress to accomplish this objective. As long as funds are "permanently" appropriated by Congress for a specific purpose, expenditures for that purpose would be made regardless of the condition of the budget. The trust fund may be an additional psychological safeguard to prevent a future Congress from undermining the social

[54] Advisory Council on Social Security, *The Status of the Social Security Program and Recommendations for Its Improvement* (1965), p. 20.

[55] Advisory Council on Social Security, *Final Report, December 10, 1938*, p. 25.

security system, but it is neither a necessary nor a sufficient condition for meeting this objective. This is not to say that the trust funds should be eliminated; on the other hand, they should not be regarded as a significant element in the system. The major determinant of the policy toward the accumulation of a reserve should be its effect on the overall fiscal policy of the federal government.

IMPACT ON ECONOMIC STABILITY AND GROWTH

The accumulation of assets in a reserve has both a short-run and a long-run impact. The short-run impact depends on the timing of the surpluses or deficits in relation to cyclical disturbances. The long-run impact depends on the effects of the surpluses or deficits on national saving and investment.

Economic stability. The impact of the social security system on economic stability depends not only on the balance of receipts and expenditures but also on changes in benefit and tax schedules. In addition, it depends on the degree to which surpluses or deficits in the social security trust funds are offset by other fiscal actions.

Through 1956, the OASI trust fund showed a surplus every year. Since 1957, except for moderate short-term movements, both the OASI and DI trust funds have not, on balance, added significantly to their reserves. Total reserves of $26.3 billion at the end of 1967 compared with $23.0 billion in the funds ten years earlier. During the period 1937–41, trust fund accumulation was undesirable in the light of the high unemployment then prevailing. Most of the period 1942–56 was characterized by high employment and inflation, except for the recession years 1948–49 and 1953–54. Social security surpluses contributed, on balance, to economic stability during that period. The social security trust funds alternated between small cash deficits and small surpluses between 1957 and 1965. Then in 1966 and 1967, when prices rose and economic policy was restrictive, surpluses of $2.5 billion and $3.9 billion, respectively, reinforced general policy. However, the impact of social security on economic stability must also be evaluated in terms of the changes from year to year or from quarter to quarter. As noted earlier, some perverse changes in social security taxes have occurred during recessions or the initial stages of recovery. There is little doubt that, until recent years at least, other opportunities to delay or advance social security tax changes in order to reinforce economic policy have not been taken, because tax rate increases were scheduled for many years ahead.[56]

An appraisal of the impact of social security financing on economic stability in the past is handicapped because there is no way of knowing whether economic policies would have been better or worse without social security, since the absence of the ameliorating or aggravating effects of social security surpluses or deficits might have led to policies different from those actually adopted. On the other hand, if other taxes and expenditures would have been unchanged in the absence of the trust funds, overall fiscal policy would have suffered. Since great emphasis was placed in the 1940's and 1950's on the administrative budget—which excluded the trust funds—the latter interpretation seems to be the more reasonable one.[57]

The more recent emphasis in federal fiscal policy on the consolidated budget and the national income accounts budget—both of which include the trust funds—suggests an improvement in orientation by taking into account the trust funds.[58] Nevertheless, there is no guarantee that the balance of social security receipts and expenditures will automatically contribute to economic stability. From an economic standpoint, failure to take into account the effect of the trust funds is clearly an error, but this could easily be remedied by the use of appropriate budget concepts for fiscal policy planning without making any changes in the social security trust funds. The 1967 President's Commission on Budget Concepts recommended

[56] On the other hand, scheduled tax increases have been deferred at times when an increase in taxes would have been stabilizing. The most egregious example was the decision made during World War II not to allow the increase from 2 percent to 4 percent in the payroll tax rate, which had been scheduled under the 1939 law to take effect in 1943.

[57] For an analysis of the effect of lending and credit programs (some of which are conducted through trust funds), see George F. Break, *Federal Lending and Economic Stability* (Brookings Institution, 1965).

[58] The national income budget excludes loan transactions; it is similar to the consolidated budget in most—but not all—other respects. For a comparison of the various budget concepts, see David J. Ott and Attiat F. Ott, *Federal Budget Policy* (2d ed.; Brookings Institution, 1968), Chap. 2. See also *The Budget of the United States Government for the Fiscal Year Ending June 30, 1968* (1967), pp. 9–10, 394–402.

the adoption of a comprehensive consolidated budget statement to achieve this objective, and the President implemented this suggestion in his budget for fiscal year 1969.[59]

Economic growth. Although economists differ in their views about the size of the contribution of increments in private investment to economic growth, it is generally accepted that growth will be faster if the rate of investment rises. Most economists agree that, if full employment can be maintained, government can contribute to investment by running budget surpluses. Such surpluses add to national saving and provide the resources needed for private investment.[60]

It follows that the social security trust funds can affect the nation's growth if, apart from their effects on the nation's ability to maintain full employment, they add to or subtract from national saving over the long run. This will depend on whether the funds are running surpluses or deficits; the former add to saving, the latter reduce it. The accumulation of balances exceeding $23 billion through 1957 in the two trust funds (OASI and DI) added to saving, which increased the resources available for investment. Since then, however, there has been little net accumulation, and a pay-as-you-go policy has been followed for social security. This suggests that the trust funds will neither add to nor detract from the growth rate in the future, unless they exercise favorable or perverse cyclical influences on the stability of the economy.

We conclude that the trust fund device is of little significance for determining social security policy or aggregate economic pol-

[59] See the *Report of the President's Commission on Budget Concepts* (October 1967) and *The Budget of the United States Government, Fiscal Year 1969* (1968), pp. 8–10, 464–82.

[60] National saving is the difference between national output and the consumption expenditures of consumers and government; investment is also that part of national output which is not consumed. Thus, national saving is equal to private investment. For a discussion of this relationship and its implications for growth policy, see Herbert Stein and Edward F. Denison, "High Employment and Growth in the American Economy," *Goals for Americans,* Report of the President's Commission on National Goals and Chapters Submitted for the Consideration of the Commission (Prentice-Hall, 1960), pp. 163–90; and Arnold C. Harberger, "Taxation, Resource Allocation, and Welfare," in John F. Due (ed.), *The Role of Direct and Indirect Taxes in the Federal Revenue System,* A Conference Report of the National Bureau of Economic Research and Brookings Institution (Princeton University Press, 1964), pp. 62–70.

icy. Perhaps the only argument for continuing the trust fund as an institution is that the public might misinterpret any action to alter its apparent character. The trust fund arrangement is part of the image of social security and has had an important role in making it acceptable to the people.[61] The public might construe any major changes in the trust fund as an indication of congressional intention to renege on its commitment to provide retirement and disability benefits as a matter of right.[62] As long as OASDI is permitted to develop to complete maturity with an adequate benefit structure and fair taxes to finance it, there would be no reason to abandon the trust fund idea.

Summary

Although the payroll tax performed an important role in paving the way to acceptance of a comprehensive social security system, it leaves much to be desired as the main—let alone, the only—source of financing. It lacks the built-in flexibility of the individual income tax and is particularly burdensome on the poor. In the long run, both the employer and employee payroll taxes are probably paid by the workers.

Social security benefits are heavily weighted in favor of the poor, but the burden of the tax levied to support these benefits is borne by a different group of people, many of whom will receive no cash benefits for three or four decades. Those who have incomes below minimum acceptable levels are unable to pay for retirement benefits many years in the future. This problem can be remedied only by relying on the individual income tax to finance benefits in whole or in part. Since the individual income tax is the main source of federal revenues, reliance on general revenues would automatically substitute income taxation for payroll taxation.

A number of methods are available for introducing general revenue financing. One method is to allow a full or partial credit

[61] See Chapter IV.

[62] However, few people seem to have any doubts about the continued payment of veterans' benefits, which are funded through the annual appropriations process.

for the payroll tax against the personal income tax liability of the individual. Another is to introduce a personal exemption into the payroll tax. Still another is to provide for a contribution from general revenues, based on the principle that the federal government should reimburse the trust funds for (a) past service credits of individuals who did not contribute fully to the system during its early days or (b) the transfer element in the minimum social security benefit. Finally, if a negative income tax were enacted, the allowances of the aged poor might be administered by the Social Security Administration, with payment for the additional cost being made from the general fund.

Some of the funds to provide general revenues might be obtained by removing the income tax benefits of the aged (that is, the special $600 exemption for those over 65, the exclusion of social security and railroad retirement benefits from the income tax base, and the special credit for other retirement income). These provisions cannot be justified on grounds of tax equity, and they are open to the objection that they are of greatest benefit to the aged in the highest income classes.

Although the trust funds have been a feature of the social security system for more than a quarter of a century, they are not an essential part of it. A reserve fund—as distinct from a trust fund—may be useful to permit payment of benefits under emergency conditions without congressional authorization. The question of general versus payroll tax financing is also independent of the trust fund device. The accumulation of reserves helped to promote national saving during the early postwar period, at a time when short-run stabilization policy called for budget surpluses. Although the trust funds have been destabilizing on several occasions—largely through inadvertence—there is no reason why their effect on the economy should be disregarded. Increasing use of the new consolidated budget, which includes the trust funds as well as the regular agencies of the federal government, should help toward an improvement of federal fiscal policies.

CHAPTER IX

Agenda for Reform

A number of major aspects of the social security system in the United States—its benefit structure, its relationship to the retirement decision, methods of determining its costs, and its financing—have been examined in the preceding chapters. Explicit or implicit recommendations for changing the system have been presented; these recommendations comprise an agenda for reform, which is set forth in this summary chapter.

The proposals are presented in three dimensions. The first disregards the historical development and the present institutional setting of social security; it would create a full-scale income maintenance system for the aged which achieves the objectives of social security and is also consistent with the nation's decision to eradicate poverty in all groups. We regard this system as superior to any alternative, and recommend it as a long-term goal. But it would be very expensive, since it involves a complete reform of the transfer system to all the nonaged as well as the aged, and would be highly controversial.

Accordingly, a second set of more modest proposals, to improve social security within the present framework, is presented. These take account of the structure of social security today and of the institutions to which people have become accustomed. Because these proposals involve certain inefficiencies which are inherent in any set of proposals that builds on the present structure, they would probably be more expensive than the portion of the first set of proposals which would apply only to the aged.

Finally, a list of immediate and urgently needed changes that would be consistent with the longer-term goals is presented for consideration in the next round of social security legislation. Some of these proposals impose very small costs, especially in the near future; in the aggregate, they impose no greater costs than those incurred by the typical benefit increases in recent years.

Total Reform

The basic dilemma in considering reform of the social security system is that the United States has attempted to solve two problems with one instrument—how to prevent destitution among the aged poor and how to assure to people, having adequate incomes before retirement, benefits that are related to their previous standard of living. The earnings replacement function calls for benefit payments without an income test. Basic income support, on the other hand, can be carried out most efficiently if payments are confined to households with low income.

Two separate systems are needed to accomplish the two functions at the lowest cost. The earnings replacement function should continue to be performed by a social security system. Social security would become strictly wage-related, with the replacement rate roughly the same at all earnings levels between subsistence and the median earnings level. The income support function should be transferred to a negative income tax system or to a comprehensively reformed system of public assistance. With a good negative income tax, dependents' allowances would be unnecessary under social security. The payroll tax might be retained, but it should be used only as a withholding mechanism for the individual income tax.

Negative income tax or public assistance allowances, payable to *all* households with incomes below specified levels or break-even points, would close a portion of the gap between household incomes from all sources and these specified levels. The minimum allowance provided by the negative income tax—the product of the break-even levels and the negative tax rate—should be at least equal to a minimum subsistence standard of living for families of all sizes. The allowances for the aged could be administered by the

Social Security Administration, but financed from general revenues.

For the aged, the proposed system would require two calculations—one for the retirement benefit based on past earnings, the other for the negative income tax based on total money income. The beneficiary unit would be entitled to choose the most advantageous benefit. Choice of the negative income tax would require the unit to waive the earnings-related benefit, and to be subject to the negative income tax rate on all its income, not including the basic negative income tax allowance. Choice of the earnings-related benefit would mean that the unit would pay positive income tax rates on all its income *including* the benefit. Inclusion of the earnings-related benefit in taxable income for positive income tax purposes reflects the view, expressed in Chapter IV, that social security benefits are transfers and that taxes levied to finance them should not be regarded as "contributions."

The following example illustrates how the negative income tax would operate in conjunction with the earnings-related benefit. Assume that aged persons are granted an earnings-related retirement benefit equal to 50 percent of past average family earnings. Assume also that the basic negative income tax allowance is set at $1,800 for a married couple, and that all other income for those electing to receive the allowance would be subject to a negative tax rate of 50 percent. For couples with no other income, the negative income tax allowance would not be elected when past average earnings exceeded $3,666 and the retirement benefit, therefore, exceeded $1,833. At this benefit level, the tax under the positive income tax system for a married couple with no dependents is $33,[1] leaving a net benefit after tax of exactly $1,800.

On the other hand, a couple with $1,000 of other income would choose to receive an earnings-related retirement benefit when its past average earnings were $2,828 and its retirement benefit was $1,414. The positive income tax on $2,414 of total income would

---

[1] This and the following example assume that the couple uses the standard deduction to compute taxable income and is permitted to have only two exemptions (not four as under present law). The tax of $33 is found in the simplified table for persons receiving incomes of less than $5,000, which allows for the standard deduction.

be $114, which yields an after tax income of $2,300. The negative income tax would be 50 percent of other income, or $500; this amount plus the $1,800 negative income tax allowance would also yield an after tax income of $2,300. This illustrates the most attractive feature of the negative income tax approach: as total income—including the retirement benefit—increases, the negative income tax payment is reduced and ultimately disappears.

The advantage of the dual system is its efficiency and flexibility. Either part of the system could be altered independently of the other. At present, any effort to improve social security with respect to the income support function typically requires substantial improvements with respect to the earnings replacement function. For example, a program to raise minimum benefits to help the aged poor must in practice be joined with a general benefit increase, thereby making the cost of aiding the poor seem greater than it is. This is aggravated, of course, by the fact that the present system supplements income regardless of the income status of the beneficiary; in many instances, higher minimum benefits would be paid to individuals with adequate incomes. Under the proposed system, the earnings-related benefit could be set at any desired percentage of past earnings; negative income tax allowances to those with low earnings histories would be sufficient to keep incomes above poverty levels. Thus, policymakers and the public could identify immediately the cost of performing the two distinct functions of the system.

Partial Reform

In view of the controversial nature of the negative income tax and the great political appeal of social security in its present form, the prospects of total reform in the foreseeable future seem dim. Accordingly, this section presents a set of proposals that would remove the most serious shortcomings of the present social security system, while leaving its basic structure intact. These proposals, which should be regarded as medium-term goals to be attained perhaps over the next one or two decades, would be consistent with the more comprehensive reform measures discussed above.

1. There is an urgent need to provide more realistic income

support for the aged who are poor, and more equitable replacement incomes for those who are more fortunate. Toward this end, the minimum benefit should be raised and the benefit formula should reflect preretirement standards of living as indicated by *family* earnings and the size of the beneficiary unit. The basic benefit formula should be $90 a month plus 30 percent of average earnings up to the median family income level. All households should be assumed to have average monthly earnings of at least $100 for the purposes of the benefit calculation. To reflect the effect of family size on living standards (as explained in Chapter V), approximately $30 a month should be added to the basic benefit for each dependent.

With the proposed formula, the minimum benefit for single workers would be $120 a month, and for couples, $150 a month. At average annual earnings of $7,800, which is the taxable earnings ceiling under current legislation, the benefit would be $285 a month for single retirees, $315 for couples. This relatively simple formula would assure all aged persons sufficient retirement income to prevent poverty; and for retirees who had had maximum taxable earnings, the replacement rates would be 44–48 percent. Families with equal standards of living before retirement would receive benefits that would enable them to have roughly equal standards after retirement, although lower than preretirement standards.

This formula would provide substantial increases in benefits to one- and two-person beneficiary households, with the largest increases reserved for widows and past recipients of low earnings. Family units of four or more persons (typically survivors) would also qualify for large increases. Only the benefits of three-person households with high earnings histories would not be increased. Such households might be given the option of using a past benefit formula if it would give them higher benefits.

Payment of a flat amount for each dependent departs significantly from present practice. This proposed treatment is a strict application of the standard-of-living approach combined with a simple, linear benefit formula. As noted in Chapter V, the benefit formula could be altered to relate the dependents' benefits to earnings, as under present law. To do so would require either that the principle of relating post- to preretirement living standards be rejected or that, as average earnings increase, the increase in wage-related benefits for single persons be smaller than the increase for married couples.

2. The combined earnings of husband and wife should be included in average earnings for the purpose of computing benefits, since living standards of couples with relatively modest earnings, which would be partially replaced by social security at retirement, depend on the combined earnings of the couple. Benefits of couples in which the wife worked would reflect the earnings of the wife to the extent that her husband's earnings fell short of the maximum earnings level.

3. The present practice of basing benefits on earnings since 1951 (after dropping out the lowest five years) will result in increasingly inadequate benefits as earnings histories lengthen. It gives too much weight to years in which past wages, because of inflation or growth of productivity, were much below the wage levels prevailing in years in which benefits are paid.

To remedy this defect, earnings should be adjusted to reflect the relative earnings level of the household in each year in which income is earned. Alternatively, average earnings might be computed on the basis of the highest five years. The first method is preferable, because it gives appropriate credit for the high earnings early in life of those whose earnings do not keep pace with the national average. Nevertheless, the latter method is a good substitute and has the advantage of simplicity. Either of the two approaches is superior to present practice.

4. The benefit formula should continue to exclude earnings above specified levels. Under the 1967 amendments this level is $7,800, which is close to the median family income for 1968 and seems reasonable. This level should be adjusted upward no faster than the rise in median family income. On the assumption that the rate of growth of median family income will be the same as the growth between 1956 and 1966, the annual adjustment would average 4.5 percent a year, and the maximum earnings level for calculating benefits would rise to almost $10,000 in five years, $12,000 in ten years, and $23,500 in twenty-five years.

On the basis of the standard-of-living approach, the earnings ceiling for the computation of couples' benefits should be higher than that for the computation of single persons' benefits by an amount equal to the extra income that couples require to achieve a given living standard. Such a differential could be achieved gradually by allowing the earnings base for couples to rise by the rate of growth of family income while allowing that for single beneficiaries to rise by the rate of change of prices only.

Revision of the benefit formula in this way would permit elimination of the maximum limit on family benefits. The family maximum denies to large surviving families benefits that would provide the same relation between living standards before and after eligibility as that to which smaller families are entitled. The present practice of setting a family maximum below officially determined poverty thresholds for large families, but two or three times that threshold for small families, cannot be justified. Elimination of the maximum family benefit would be feasible only if the benefits for wives and other dependents were set at a flat dollar amount in accordance with the first recommendation; otherwise, total benefits would become excessive for very large families.

5. Benefits, once awarded, should be adjusted automatically for changes in the consumer price index. The alternative of annual or biennial adjustment through congressional action is cumbersome, and historical experience indicates that discretionary changes are unsatisfactory. Past increases in benefits already awarded have tended to be smaller than the rate of price inflation. Any additional improvements in benefits already awarded should not be made automatically, but should remain open to legislative discretion.

6. The social security system should be extended to all government employees. Government employees' pension programs, like industrial pension programs, should be supplementary to the basic social security retirement system. This would avoid the inequities that arise through dual or multiple entitlements. Even if integration along these lines is not considered feasible, civil service workers whose period of employment is insufficient to provide adequate benefits might be given transferable credits to the social security system for the period of their employment, thereby providing a guarantee that government employment would always produce a

benefit as least as large as the same employment would produce under social security.

7. With the improvement in health and gradually increasing longevity, there is no need to encourage early retirement in our economy. Accordingly, benefits to early retirees should not be paid in the future. The permanently reduced benefits paid to early retirees already receiving benefits should, on the other hand, be increased to the present unreduced benefit level. The problems of those who are too young to qualify for old-age benefits, but who are unable to work, should be met through the disability program or unemployment compensation, or both. Under these programs, full benefits should be available for those just under age 65 who are unable to work, even if they are not totally disabled in a medical sense. These changes would reduce the incentive to retire before age 65 for those who can continue to work, while more adequate benefits would be provided to those over age 65.

8. There should be no further increase in the amount of earned income permitted without loss of benefits. The greater outlays occasioned by increases in this amount accrue to persons whose economic status on the average is superior to that of beneficiaries who do not work. Since there are large social benefits to be derived from work after age 65, late retirees might be given a "delayed retirement credit" (that is, higher pensions on any earnings history) as a substitute for a less stringent retirement test. The size of the credit should not be based on actuarial considerations.

9. Long-range actuarial calculations should be de-emphasized in determining social security policy. To reflect the future burdens of social security benefits on the economy, the long-range estimates should be based on the assumption that earnings will continue to increase, and they should be evaluated in terms of the relationship of projected costs to the national income rather than in terms of the actuarial balance concept now used. Short-range estimates, based on the same forecasts of economic trends that are used by the President in his annual Economic Report and Budget Message, should be emphasized in planning changes in the benefit and tax structure and in coordinating such changes with the government's overall fiscal policy.

10. The payroll tax is the most burdensome tax levied by the

federal government on the poor in the United States, and it should eventually be replaced by income taxes. The payroll tax on employees should be regarded as part of the withholding tax under the individual income tax, with overpayments to be refundable after the individual files his final income tax return. The employer's tax should be replaced by general revenues. There should be no difference in taxes paid by wage and salary workers and by the self-employed. These changes would remove the inequities, both vertical and horizontal, in the payroll tax. The payroll tax might be retained as a withholding tax to focus attention on social security and on the fact that support of the current aged by the working population establishes the claim of the latter group for future support. The payroll tax is not essential for this purpose, since a portion of the individual income tax earmarked for social security would do just as well. But the payroll tax is well entrenched and could be retained as an accounting convention.

If these changes were adopted, it would matter little for taxpayers whether the payroll tax were levied on each worker's earnings or on each family's earnings. The adjustment to a family unit basis of taxation would be made on the final income tax return. If the changes were not adopted, households with more than one earner should be entitled to claim a refund of payroll taxes paid on family earnings in excess of the earnings ceiling used in the benefit computation. Alternatively, one of the other devices discussed in Chapter VIII for tempering the regressivity of the payroll tax—an exemption and minimum standard deduction in the payroll tax itself, for example—might be adopted, although these devices are less effective, or more cumbersome, or both.

A comparison of the benefits payable under the system just described with benefits under the 1967 amendments is shown in Table IX-1. Each household is assumed to become eligible for benefits in 1968, and to have had during 1967 the earnings shown in the first column (which are assumed to have increased since 1956 at the rate of 4 percent a year). Every beneficiary unit would receive at least as much under the proposed changes as it receives under current legislation. Most beneficiaries would receive large increases. These increases would accrue mostly to single retirees, widows, and large surviving families with low earnings histories. They

Table IX-1. *Comparison of Social Security Monthly Benefits for 1968 Retirees under Current Legislation and Proposed Formula*[a]

(In dollars)

Earnings in 1967		Single Retiree		Retired Couple		Surviving Widow and Two Children		Aged Widow		Surviving Widow and Five Children	
Annual	Monthly	Current legislation[b]	Proposed formula	Current legislation[b]	Proposed formula	Current legislation[b]	Proposed formula	Current legislation[b]	Proposed formula	Current legislation[b]	Proposed formula
800	67	55.00	120.00	82.50	150.00	82.50	180.00	55.00	120.00	82.50	270.00
1,800	150	81.10	131.66	121.70	161.66	121.70	191.66	67.00	131.66	121.70	281.66
2,800	233	99.30	154.80	149.00	184.80	154.40	214.80	82.00	154.80	154.40	304.80
3,800	317	116.20	177.97	174.30	207.97	206.40	237.97	95.90	177.97	206.40	327.97
4,800	400	134.30	201.11	201.50	231.11	262.40	262.40[c]	110.80	201.11	262.40	351.11
5,800	483	150.00	218.89	225.00	248.89	311.20	311.20[c]	123.80	218.89	311.20	368.89
6,800	567	156.00	227.69	234.00	257.69	329.60	333.60[c]	128.70	227.69	329.60	377.69
7,800	650	156.00	228.00	234.00	258.00	329.60	333.60[c]	128.70	228.00	329.60	378.00

a. Earnings are assumed to grow at the rate of 4 percent a year. Average monthly earnings (AME) under current legislation computed for 1956–67; AME's under proposed formula were computed on the basis of the highest five years.
b. Benefits as provided under the 1967 amendments to the Social Security Act.
c. Beneficiary would have lower benefits under the proposed formula, and would choose option of having benefits computed as under present law. Benefits under the proposed formula are $261.11, $278.89, $287.69, and $288.00 for earnings in last year of $4,800, $5,800, $6,800, and $7,800, respectively.

would arise principally because the standard-of-living approach is more favorable to single persons and large, multi-person families than is the current benefit formula. The increases indicated for workers with low-earnings histories and for their families also reflect the judgment that additional expenditures on raising minimum benefits are justified as a "best buy," directing a large fraction of added outlays to needy households.

Table IX-1 assumes that the new benefit formula would go into effect in 1968. The change in benefits would increase the costs of social security by roughly 50 percent in 1968, but by smaller percentages in later years. Such an increase is not practical in the short run, nor is it desirable in view of other urgent demands on the federal budget. Average benefits under current legislation will tend to increase as earnings rise. Consequently, the figures in Table IX-1 should be interpreted as indicating the *relative* change in benefits among family size and income categories that would occur over the long run if the proposed formula were adopted, and not as a comparison between actual benefits under the two formulas as they might be ten or twenty years hence.

Proposals for Immediate Legislative Action

The reform proposals just described would considerably alter the distribution of benefits, but would provide nearly all beneficiaries with substantially increased benefits and reduce the benefits of no one. Consequently, they are expensive and can be achieved only gradually over many years.

In the next round of social security legislation, more modest changes should be enacted to move the system in the desired direction. Such changes would stress adjustments in the minimum benefits and in the benefits paid to widows and survivors. These urgently needed changes would impose costs no greater than past increases in benefits.

1. Because the payroll tax is inequitable, the income tax law should be amended to provide refunds of social security taxes paid

by individuals whose earnings do not exceed their personal exemptions plus the minimum standard deduction: the refunds would accrue almost entirely to households classified as poor. This change in the law would cost approximately $0.7 billion if the refunds were confined to the employee tax.[2] The entire cost of this urgently needed reform for the poor could be recovered by terminating the special tax benefits now accorded to aged households under the federal income tax legislation, and which accrue disproportionately to those with relatively high incomes.

Whenever a cut in federal taxes becomes appropriate, it should be implemented at least in part by allowing some fraction of the remaining social security taxes to be treated as withheld individual income taxes. The fraction chosen would depend on the amount of the tax cut desired to be allocated in this form. This change should be borne by the general revenue sources of the Treasury so that revenues allocated to the OASDI trust funds would be unaffected.

2. The family should be adopted as the unit whose earnings are relevant to the computation of benefits. This could be done by enacting a deadline after which no new benefits to retired couples could be based on separate earnings histories of the husband and wife. After the deadline, benefits would be based on total family earnings. This reform would entail no current costs. Over the longer run some costs would develop, since the saving to the system which arises because wives' benefits are smaller relative to their taxes than are benefits of single women would be lost.

3. Since the income needed by a widow to attain a given standard of living is not less than that needed by a person who was never married, the widow's benefit should be raised to 100 percent of the worker's benefit. This change would be approximately as costly as a 3 percent across-the-board increase in benefits.

4. To move toward a more realistic floor of support, the minimum benefit should be raised to $75 a month for single retirees and $105 for couples. This change would impose the same costs as an across-the-board increase of about 4 percent in benefits. Fur-

---

[2] See Chapter VIII for a discussion of methods of avoiding a "notch" problem for those with incomes just above their exemptions and minimum standard deduction.

ther increases in the minimum benefit should follow later, unless, in the interim, more comprehensive and efficient methods of establishing a floor under income were adopted.

5. To provide for growth in benefits as the economy expands, newly awarded benefits should be computed on the basis of average earnings in the ten years of highest earnings. All benefits in current payment status should be recomputed on this basis for present beneficiaries who would profit from the change. This would involve only minor short-run costs, because the maximum computation period for any retired worker was only twelve years (nine years for women) as of January 1968. In the long run, the costs of this change would become large, but these costs could be financed with the revenue produced by constant tax rates applied to a constantly growing tax base.

6. To prevent the erosion of benefits by inflation, benefits in current payment status should automatically be adjusted for price changes. If this adjustment were combined with a provision that also adjusted the earnings base automatically for price changes, the net change in costs would be negligible.

7. To reflect the added expenses which large families must incur to achieve the same living standards as smaller families, additional survivor benefits of $30 a month per dependent should be paid to households with more than two surviving children, and the family maximum should be eliminated. The cost of this change would be small.

8. To help move social security toward the standard-of-living approach to the computation of benefits (as described in Chapter V), a permanent ceiling on the benefits payable to wives and other dependents should be established, with the proviso that no benefits in current payment status would be reduced by such a change. This ceiling should be substantially below the $105 ceiling on wives' benefits contained in the present law. The limit on wives' and dependents' benefits could be approached by raising benefits for single persons more rapidly than those of couples so that the spouses' benefits gradually become relatively smaller.

9. To reduce the incentive to stop working prematurely, early retirement benefits should not be awarded in the future. However, persons genuinely incapable of work should not be penalized; un-

reduced benefits should be extended to such persons to meet their special problems.

10. To encourage the continued employment of healthy, aged persons who wish to continue working, experiments with modest delayed retirement credits should be conducted, perhaps restricted at first to persons aged 65–67.

The history of social security is one of success. From small beginnings in the midst of economic depression and unemployment, it has grown enormously to occupy a pre-eminent position among domestic programs. In 1967, when budget stringencies forced retrenchment on most domestic programs, Congress nonetheless raised annual social security benefits by $4 billion. Thus, earlier fears that political opposition would destroy the program now seem oddly out of place. The survival of social security as a permanent American institution is no longer in question; the relevant issues today concern the optimal marginal improvements in the program that will determine its future effectiveness. This book has attempted to deal with these issues and thus to provide perspectives for evaluating alternative improvements in social security relative both to one another and to improvements in other public programs.

APPENDIXES

APPENDIX A

Individual Equity Calculations
for the OASI Retirement Program

This appendix compares the present values of Old-Age and Survivors Insurance (OASI) retirement benefits with the taxes paid by the beneficiaries when they were employed. The calculations disregard disability, survivor, and medical benefits (other than survivor benefits paid to widows of retired persons) of the social security program, as well as other government taxes, transfers, and exhaustive expenditures on goods and services. While the relevance of these calculations to the policy issues discussed in this volume is open to serious question (see Chapters IV and VII), similar estimates are being made by other writers and are being accepted uncritically by many who are not familiar with the underlying assumptions. The purpose of this appendix is to explain the assumptions and methodology and to present alternative benefit-tax ratios that are more plausible, in the light of past experience, than those which have been advanced heretofore.

The Benefit-Tax Model

The benefit-tax ratios are usually computed as follows: First, the total taxes paid by both employee and employer on the former's covered wages are accumulated at some assumed rate of interest. Second, upon the worker's retirement at age 65, the accumulated savings are used to purchase a life annuity that provides monthly payments equal to the value of OASI monthly retirement benefits. Third, the accumulated taxes are compared with the annuity value of the benefits. If the present expected value of the annuity, as calculated by this procedure, is at least as great as the present expected value of accumulated OASI taxes, the individual receives his "money's worth" from the OASI retirement program.

The notation used is as follows:

T = accumulated value of total taxes at compound interest at retirement

B = discounted value of expected benefit stream

$V = (B/T)$100

$b_{y,m}$ = family monthly benefit for year y, month m

y = years after retirement at age 65 (0 at age 65, 1 at age 66, and so on)

m = the month of year y (1 for January, 2 for February, and so on)

$n = 12y + m$

$100i$ = monthly rate of discount or rate of interest (in percent)

$P^M_{y,m}(P^F_{y,m})$ = probability that a male (female) aged 65 will live through age y, month m

k,m = age of worker in k years, m months after he begins work (a,0 when he enters labor force; 65,0 when he retires)

$w = 12(65 - k) - m$ = number of months between age k,m and worker's sixty-fifth birthday

$t_{k,m}$ = tax for age k, month m.

For a male, the present expected value of any month's benefit at retirement is $b_{y,m}P^M_{y,m}/(1+i)^n$. The total value of benefits at retirement (ignoring the very small probability of living beyond age 99) is

$$B = \sum_{y=0}^{34} \sum_{m=1}^{12} \frac{b_{y,m}P^M_{y,m}}{(1+i)^n}.$$

Since a widower receives $66\frac{2}{3}$ percent, and a widow receives 55 percent, of a couple's benefit, the value of a couple's benefit may be expressed as follows:

$$B = \sum_{y=0}^{34} \sum_{m=1}^{12} \left[\frac{0.667 b_{y,m}P^M_{y,m}(1 - P^F_{y,m}) + 0.55 b_{y,m}P^F_{y,m}(1 - P^M_{y,m}) + b_{y,m}P^M_{y,m}P^F_{y,m}}{(1+i)^n} \right].$$

The value at retirement of a month's taxes is $t_{k,m-1}(1+i)^w$. The value of the total tax stream at retirement is

$$T = \sum_{k=a}^{64} \sum_{m=1}^{12} t_{k,m-1}(1 + i)^w.$$

For purposes of these calculations, it is assumed that workers and their spouses survive until retirement. This assumption permits survivors benefits and that portion of taxes which finance them to be ignored. It must be noted, however, that the social security "program" is in reality an inseparable package, and that the assumption used here can be justified only on the grounds of convenience.

If V is equal to or greater than (less than) 100, the value of a worker's retirement benefits equals or exceeds (is less than) the value of his taxes *at the assumed interest rate.*

THE ASSUMED INTEREST RATE

The interest rate used to obtain the value of taxes accumulated up to retirement is of great importance. Benefit-tax calculations have no meaning independent of the rate of interest, and the results of such calculations are sensitive to the choice of a particular rate. The correct interest rate is the rate that best approximates the relevant alternatives in the private market for the average individual. That is, values of V are "good" or "bad" only relative to outcomes that individuals could typically expect if they saved on their own volition.

The interest rate should be interpreted in two senses in the following discussion. On the one hand, it represents hypothetical rates of return on additional private savings that investors could obtain if they invested the amounts that they pay as social security taxes. On the other hand, it represents the "time preference" of social security taxpayers. Time preference is the return which people would require if they were to save more voluntarily. For some people, time preference is so high that they save nothing voluntarily and even dissave at high rates of interest.

The appropriate rate of interest to use in evaluating the costs or benefits of a government program is one of the most difficult conceptual problems in economics and is a subject on which economists differ sharply.[1] The problem of choosing the appropriate rate of discount

[1] The disagreement among economists about the proper interest rate to be used in benefit-tax calculations is best illustrated by the exchange between Otto Eckstein and Jack Hirshleifer in "A Survey of the Theory of Public Expenditure Criteria," "Comments," and "Reply by Mr. Eckstein," *Public Finances: Needs, Sources, and Utilization,* National Bureau of Economic Research (Princeton Univer-

where benefits and taxes are income related is even more complex, since there is abundant reason to believe that the rate of time preference and the real rate of return which investors can obtain differ systematically with income. Low-income recipients do little or no saving and, indeed, many dissave, suggesting strongly that their time preference considerably exceeds the real rates of return, of perhaps 3 or 4 percent, which they can obtain. High-income recipients usually have access to somewhat higher rates of return and save far more. Although it may be suspected that time preference at the margin is higher for the poor than for the well-to-do, the available data do not, unfortunately, permit empirical support of this proposition. The problem is further complicated because one of the justifications for social security is the need to override observed preferences of households on the question of whether or not to save.[2] Since there is no basis for selecting one interest rate, the present calculations will be based on a range of rates varying from 3 to 10 percent.

OTHER ASSUMPTIONS

Further simplifying assumptions were needed to make the calculations manageable:

1. The worker enters the labor force on January 1 of the year he begins work, works continuously until December 31 of the year he retires, and is covered continuously by OASI while he works. No account is taken of possible periods of unemployment. Moderate unemployment in any individual work history reduces tax liabilities, but may not reduce benefits. In extreme cases, the worker, when computing average earnings, may be compelled to include years of zero earnings that are due to prolonged unemployment. On the whole, if unemployment were taken into account, V would probably be higher.

2. Each worker retires on the eve of his (her) sixty-fifth birthday (which is December 31) and, if the worker is married, the age of the

sity Press, 1961), pp. 453–63, 495–501, 503–04. John A. Brittain has dealt with this problem by calculating the real rate of interest implicit under certain assumptions about OASDI taxes and benefits in a growing economy. His procedure in effect calculates the rate of interest and rate of discount that produces a value of V of unity. See "The Real Rate of Interest on Lifetime Contributions Toward Retirement Under Social Security," in *Old Age Income Assurance*, Compendium of Papers on Problems and Policy Issues in the Public and Private Pension System, Pt. III: *Public Programs*, 90 Cong. 1 sess. (1967), pp. 109–32. (Brookings Reprint 143.)

[2] See Chapter IV, pp. 56–58, 61–65.

husband or wife is also 65. Taxes paid by the secondary worker or benefits to which she (he) may be entitled on her (his) own earnings history are ignored. Since secondary earners add relatively more to the family social security tax bill than they do to family benefits, ignoring them overstates the ratio of benefits to taxes in households with more than one earner. Also, workers who retire well before age 65 receive higher benefits relative to taxes, other things equal, than do workers who retire at age 65 or later. If the present downward trend in the average retirement age continues, the use of the age 65 retirement assumption leads to an understatement of the true values of V for young workers in the labor force today.[3] Furthermore, since it is assumed that both husband and wife are the same age, the present value of retirement benefits of a retired male worker aged 65 who is married to a younger woman is overstated in these calculations, but that of survivors benefits is understated.

3. Benefit-tax calculations for current retirees utilize estimates of present mortality rates, which are assumed to remain constant over the lifetime of current retirees. Any improvement in mortality experience for this group would imply a higher value of V. Official projections of mortality rates through the year 2000 are used for current younger workers, and are assumed to level off at that date. The value of retirement benefits for future retirees is computed for both high mortality and low mortality assumptions; the benefit figure used in these estimates is the mean of these two figures.[4]

4. Employer and employee taxes are included in the value of accumulated taxes for any worker. This is approximately one-third greater than the taxes paid by the self-employed, and V for the self-employed would be correspondingly larger than that computed for workers. If the payroll tax is partly or fully shifted forward rather than backward to

[3] The average retirement age for males retiring at the present time with *unreduced* benefits is about 67. See Robert J. Myers, "Analysis of Whether the Young Worker Receives His Money's Worth Under Social Security," memorandum in *President's Proposals for Revision in the Social Security System*, Hearings before the House Committee on Ways and Means on H.R. 5710, 90 Cong. 1 sess. (1967), Pt. 1, p. 332.

[4] Present mortality rates were derived from U.S. Department of Health, Education, and Welfare, Public Health Service, *United States Life Tables: 1959–61*, Vol. 1, No. 1 (1964), Tables 2 and 3, pp. 10–13. Mortality rates for the year 2000 are derived from Francisco Bayo, *United States Population Projections for OASDHI Cost Estimates*, U.S. Department of Health, Education, and Welfare, Social Security Administration, Office of the Actuary, Actuarial Study No. 62 (December 1966), Table 6, p. 14. The present calculations make use of estimates by John A. Brittain, who used data from the U.S. Department of Health, Education, and Welfare sources cited in this footnote.

the worker, the value of accumulated taxes actually paid by workers is overstated and V is understated.

5. Only retirement benefits are included in the value of benefits, on the assumption that the disability program is self-supporting and that OASI survivor benefits other than those paid to widows of retired workers and the taxes paid to finance them can be excluded from the calculations. It is assumed that the value of these other benefits is 20 percent of the total employee and employer taxes paid. Isolation of the retirement aspects of OASI in this way is admittedly artificial and unsatisfactory.[5]

6. The value of benefits is computed separately for single males, single females, and for married couples. According to a recent estimate by Robert J. Myers, 81 percent of all men aged 65 are married.[6] The couple's benefit is probably much closer, therefore, to the average retirement benefit than is the benefit of either the single male or the single female.

7. No explicit account is taken of administrative costs, which have averaged about 2 percent of total benefits paid by the OASI trust fund.

Estimated Benefits and Costs

In evaluating V for social security, both historical experience and the anticipated future course of the current system are of interest. Since continuation of social security in identically its present form is extremely unlikely, the values of V under more plausible assumptions about the future course of the system are of major interest.

[5] To be more specific, this is in effect an assumption that the survivor and disability programs do not exist and that, in the event of the death of a worker before age 65, the value of his accumulated taxes is forfeited to the program and helps to pay for retirement benefits. In private correspondence with the authors, Robert J. Myers, the Chief Actuary of the Social Security Administration, has clarified the implications of this assumption and estimated that 77.2 percent of the OASDI contribution rate would be needed to finance retirement benefits, given the above interpretation. Mr. Myers also has pointed out to the authors that such a separation of the OASDI program is not valid, since widows' benefits payable in old age cannot be allocated between the survivors and old-age parts of the total program.

[6] Hearings on H.R. 5710 (cited in footnote 3 above), p. 332. An alternative approach, one adopted by Myers, is to assume that all workers have an equal probability at the time they enter the labor force of being married by retirement age. This assumption permits calculation of the value of retirement benefits as a weighted average of single persons', survivors', and couples' benefits.

HISTORICAL EXPERIENCE

Social security has been a superb investment for workers who have retired in recent years. The ratio of benefits to taxes paid, V, for workers

Table A-1. *Social Security Benefits as a Percentage of Taxes for 1968
Retirees: Actual Experience*[a]

Annual Earnings and Family Status	Interest Rate[b] (Percent)			
	3	3.75	5	6
Worker First Covered in 1937[c]				
Maximum taxable earnings, 1937–67				
Single male	391	337	261	212
Single female	470	402	308	248
Couple	681	583	447	360
One-half average manufacturing earnings, 1937–67				
Single male	568	494	392	324
Single female	682	590	462	379
Couple	988	856	672	552
Worker First Covered in 1951[d]				
Maximum taxable earnings, 1951–67				
Single male	532	475	393	339
Single female	639	567	464	397
Couple	926	821	675	578
One-half average manufacturing earnings, 1951–67				
Single male	704	629	522	450
Single female	847	751	616	526
Couple	1,226	1,088	894	766

a. The initial 1968 benefits for all estimates are based on the annual earnings histories of each worker and the benefit formula as of 1968. Benefits are assumed to increase by 1.5 percent a year after 1968. Current mortality estimates are used in computing the value of benefits. Benefits provided in the 1967 amendments to the Social Security Act are assumed to have been payable beginning January 1968.
b. Interest rate is twelve times the i in the benefit equation and in the tax equation on pages 232–33.
c. Worker is assumed to have begun paying social security taxes January 1, 1937, and to have retired at age 65, December 31, 1967.
d. Worker is assumed to have begun paying social security taxes January 1, 1951, and to have retired at age 65, December 31, 1967.

who were initially covered in 1937 and 1951, and who retired on December 31, 1967, after having either maximum taxable earnings or one-half average manufacturing earnings in every year during which they were covered by social security, substantially exceeds 100 (Table A-1). In these calculations benefits are assumed to rise by 1.5 percent a year after retirement, enough to offset an expected modest rate of increase in prices. If the adjustment for inflation were larger, social security would be even a better buy than that implied by Table A-1.

PROJECTED FUTURE EXPERIENCE

Values of V based on benefits and taxes scheduled under the 1967 amendments to the Social Security Act are shown in Table A-2. In columns 1 and 2, no growth of earnings is assumed; in columns 3 and 4, benefits and taxes are adjusted for assumed increases in earnings. The low values of V for interest rates of either 3.75 percent (column 1) or 6 percent (column 2) mean that very few young persons would receive benefits worth as much as the taxes they pay if social security were frozen in its present (1968) form. The estimates in columns 1 and 2 are typical of similar calculations by other writers, the results of which serve as the basis for the allegation that the OASI retirement program penalizes young workers.[7] These estimates, like the assumptions on which they are based, are completely unrealistic.

To obtain more realistic figures, the following changes in the benefit calculations are made in order to keep benefits in line with higher earnings.

First, average money earnings and taxable maximum earnings are assumed to grow at an annual rate of 4 percent. Aside from the fact that Congress has raised the taxable maximum periodically in discrete steps, this assumption has a sound historical basis, at least since 1950.[8]

Second, to keep the benefit formula up to date, it is assumed for the calculations shown in columns 3 and 4 of Table A-2 that the present replacement rate applicable to a worker with given earnings in 1968 remains constant as earnings grow. That is, the replacement rate at

[7] The results are roughly similar, for example, to those presented by Robert J. Myers in "The Value of Social Security Protection in Relation to the Value of Social Security Contribution" and "Analysis of Whether the Young Worker Receives His Money's Worth Under Social Security," in Hearings on H.R. 5710 (cited in footnote 3 above), pp. 330–41, after allowance is made for Myers' assumption that the employer's share of taxes should be excluded from the calculation.

[8] Appendix B discusses the history of legislative changes in the maximum taxable earnings.

Table A-2. *Projected Social Security Benefits as a Percentage of Taxes for Young Workers First Covered in 1968: Unchanged Earnings Assumption and Increasing Earnings Assumption*[a]

1968 Annual Earnings and Family Status	Unchanged Average Earnings Assumption		4 Percent Increase in Average Earnings Assumption	
	Interest rate (percent)		Interest rate (percent)	
	3.75 (1)	6 (2)	3.75 (3)	6 (4)
$7,800				
Single male	46	20	68	34
Single female	54	24	80	40
Couple	77	34	115	57
$6,000				
Single male	49	22	72	36
Single female	57	26	85	42
Couple	82	37	123	62
$3,000				
Single male	63	28	93	47
Single female	74	32	110	54
Couple	106	48	159	79
$1,500				
Single male	90	41	134	68
Single female	105	47	157	78
Couple	153	68	228	114

a. Worker is assumed to enter labor force at age 22, January 1, 1968, and to retire at age 65. Under unchanged earnings assumption, benefits are assumed to remain constant after retirement; under increasing average earnings assumption, benefits are assumed to be increased by 1.5 percent a year after retirement.

each relative position on the earnings scale is assumed to remain unchanged as earnings grow.[9]

[9] For example, consider a worker who enters the labor force January 1, 1968, on his 22nd birthday and has covered earnings in 1968 of X dollars, and assume that the present benefit formula provides a replacement rate of r for average monthly earnings of $(X/12)$ dollars. His monthly retirement benefit, according to the present benefit formula, is $r(X/12)$ dollars. For an assumed annual growth rate of $100j$ percent for average money earnings, the worker will have an annual stream of X, $X(1+j)$, $X(1+j)^2$, ..., $X(1+j)^n$ over $n+1$ years. His average monthly earnings at retirement after $n+1$ years of work, on the assumption that the taxable maximum

Third, the initial benefit level at retirement is increased by 1.5 percent a year after retirement, to offset the effect of moderate price increases.[10]

The assumption that earnings will grow and that the social security program will be adjusted in response to this growth slightly weakens the conclusion that social security is unfair to the young worker today. It must be remembered, however, that the values of V in columns 3 and 4 in Table A-2 are calculated under the most conservative assumptions —assumptions which almost certainly guarantee that the OASI retirement program will be heavily overfinanced. The social security program is in actuarial balance with presently scheduled benefits and taxes under the assumption of no growth in average money earnings. When earnings grow, the program with a *given* benefit formula and tax structure becomes overfinanced for two reasons: (1) The benefit formula is progressive with respect to covered earnings. As earnings grow, more and more earnings histories fall in brackets having the lowest replacement rates. Therefore, benefits fall relative to taxes, which are proportional to earnings. (2) Benefits are based on the earnings history of the retired worker while taxes are levied on current earnings. As earnings grow, the social security system collects more taxes immediately but incurs greater benefit obligations only on a deferred basis.[11]

---

also increases at j percent a year and, as provided in the current law, that his lowest (first) five years of earnings can be dropped from the computation, will be

$$\frac{X(1+j)^5 + X(1+j)^6 + \ldots + X(1+j)^n}{12(n-4)} = \left(\frac{X^*}{12}\right) \text{ dollars.}$$

The assumption of a constant replacement rate for this worker means that the benefit structure is altered each year to assure that his initial monthly benefit is set equal to $r(X^*/12)$ in the benefit-tax calculations.

An unrealistic aspect of this assumption is that workers are implicitly assumed to remain frozen in their *relative* earnings position. For a discussion of the equity problems in OASDI that result from differences in lifetime earnings profiles, see Henry J. Aaron, "Benefits Under the American Social Security System," in Otto Eckstein (ed.), *Studies in the Economics of Income Maintenance* (Brookings Institution, 1967), pp. 61–72.

[10] This assumption has substantial historical justification. Saul Waldman, "OASDI Benefits, Prices, and Wages: A Comparison," *Social Security Bulletin*, Vol. 29, No. 8 (August 1966), pp. 19–23, 30, and "OASDI Benefits, Prices, and Wages: 1966 Experience," *Social Security Bulletin*, Vol. 30, No. 6 (June 1967), pp. 9 ff.

[11] These factors are discussed more fully in Robert J. Myers and Francisco Bayo, *Long-Range Cost Estimates for Old-Age, Survivors, and Disability Insurance System, 1966*, U.S. Department of Health, Education, and Welfare, Social Security Administration, Office of the Actuary, Actuarial Study No. 63 (January 1967), pp. 18–19.

Under the assumptions in columns 3 and 4 of Table A-2, it is almost certain that social security will be overfinanced because tax collections will soar (especially since the taxable maximum is assumed to increase) while increased benefits will not be payable until far into the future. Only if demographic trends turn out to be much more unfavorable for the costs of social security than expected today would the system not be overfinanced.

A simple, plausible adjustment in the conservative assumptions underlying columns 3 and 5 of Table A-2 yields much larger values of V. Assume that the annual earnings of a worker rise from X in year 0 to $X(1 + j)^n$ in year n. Instead of assuming that the replacement rate applicable to the average monthly earnings $(X^*/12)$ of this worker at retirement is identical to the replacement rate applicable to average monthly earnings of $(X/12)$ under the present law, assume that replacement rates change proportionately with changes in earnings levels. That is, if a replacement rate r applies to a present average monthly earnings level of $(X/12)$, at retirement r will apply to an average monthly earnings level of $(X/12)(1 + j)^n$. Since replacement rates vary inversely with earnings, and since $(X^*/12)$ is considerably smaller than $(X/12)(1 + j)^n$, a replacement rate greater than r would be applicable to $(X^*/12)$ and, therefore, benefits payable on any given earnings history would be considerably higher. This is particularly true if, as under the present method of computing average monthly earnings (AME), only five years of lowest earnings are dropped in computing $(X^*/12)$.

Even this modest adjustment in the benefit-tax calculation under an increasing earnings assumption significantly increases the values of V (see Table A-3). The figures in Tables A-4 through A-6, discussed below, are calculated on the basis of adjusted replacement rates.

VARIATION OF V WITH THE RATE OF GROWTH OF EARNINGS

Whether a worker entering the labor force today will receive retirement benefits worth as much as his social security taxes depends on the future rate of growth of the economy. To illustrate the effect of alternative rates of growth, the top half of Table A-4 presents estimates of V under the assumed growth rates of average money earnings of 2.5 and 5 percent, as well as 4 percent which most closely approximates past trends. The other assumptions are a 2.5, 4, and 5 percent rate of growth of the taxable maximum, respectively, proportionate adjustment of initial replacement rates, and a 1.5 percent annual increase in benefits after re-

Table A-3. *Projected Social Security Benefits as a Percentage of Taxes for Young Workers First Covered in 1968: Effects of Proportional Changes in Replacement Rates Applied to Increasing Earnings Base*[a]

1968 Annual Earnings and Family Status	Interest Rate (Percent)	
	3.75 (1)	6 (2)
$7,800		
Single male	82	41
Single female	96	48
Couple	140	70
$6,000		
Single male	90	46
Single female	106	53
Couple	155	77
$3,000		
Single male	129	65
Single female	152	76
Couple	220	110
$1,500		
Single male	144	73
Single female	170	84
Couple	247	122

a. Assumptions identical to those used for columns 3 and 4 in Table A-2, except for the differences in calculation of initial replacement rates discussed in text, p. 241. Worker is assumed to enter labor force at age 22, January 1, 1968, and to retire at age 65. Earnings are assumed to grow at 4 percent a year, and benefits are assumed to be increased by 1.5 percent a year after retirement.

tirement. The estimates show the expected result that, other things equal, a higher rate of growth of earnings leads to higher values of V.

VARIATION OF V WITH BENEFIT ADJUSTMENTS
AFTER RETIREMENT

It is reasonable to expect that relatively high rates of growth of money earnings will be accompanied by relatively high rates of inflation, and that relatively high rates of inflation in turn will lead to a relatively large adjustment of benefits after retirement. The estimates shown in the bottom half of Table A-4 illustrate how such an assumption affects the values of V. These figures are based on the same as-

Table A-4. *Projected Social Security Benefits as a Percentage of Taxes under Alternative Rates of Growth of Earnings and of Adjustment of Benefits after Retirement*[a]

1968 Annual Earnings and Family Status	Earnings Growth Rate (Percent)		
	2.5 (1)	4 (2)	5 (3)
All Benefits Increased by 1.5% after Retirement			
$7,800			
Single male	46	56	64
Single female	54	66	74
Couple	78	96	108
$6,000			
Single male	50	62	71
Single female	59	72	83
Couple	86	106	121
$3,000			
Single male	70	88	104
Single female	81	103	120
Couple	118	150	176
$1,500			
Single male	88	100	108
Single female	102	116	125
Couple	149	168	182
Benefits Increased by 1%, 1.5%, and 2% after Retirement[b]			
$7,800			
Single male	44	56	66
Single female	52	66	78
Couple	76	96	112
$6,000			
Single male	49	62	74
Single female	56	72	86
Couple	82	106	126
$3,000			
Single male	67	88	108
Single female	78	103	126
Couple	114	150	183
$1,500			
Single male	85	100	112
Single female	98	116	130
Couple	143	168	190

a. Worker is assumed to enter labor force at age 22, January 1, 1968, and to retire at age 65. Calculations are based on a 5 percent rate of interest. Replacement rates are assumed to change proportionately with changes in earnings levels. A growth rate of 2.5, 4, and 5 percent, respectively, is assumed for the taxable maximum.
b. The 1 percent figure applies to column (1), the 1.5 percent to column (2), and the 2 percent to column (3).

sumptions as in the top half except for the different assumptions about the benefit adjustment after retirement. Somewhat arbitrarily, it is assumed in column 1 that a 2.5 percent rate of growth of money earnings is accompanied by a rate of increase of benefits after retirement of only 1 percent a year; that, in column 2, a 4 percent rate of growth of money earnings is accompanied by an annual benefit adjustment after retirement of 1.5 percent; and that, in column 3, a 5 percent rate of growth of money earnings is accompanied by an annual benefit adjustment after retirement of 2 percent. Again, the results show that the greater the rate of adjustment of benefits after retirement, the higher is the value of V.

VARIATION OF V WITH AGE OF ENTRY INTO LABOR FORCE

Late entry into the labor force greatly reduces social security taxes paid, usually without a corresponding decrease in retirement benefits. The effect of the age of entry on the values of V that a worker can expect is illustrated by the estimates in Table A-5. Column 2 is the same as column 2 in Table A-4; it is based on the assumptions of a 4 percent rate of growth for earnings, a 4 percent rate of growth for the taxable maximum, proportionate adjustment of replacement rates with growth in earnings, a 5 percent rate of interest, a 1.5 percent annual increase in benefits after retirement, and age 22 for entry into the labor force. Columns 1 and 3 in Table A-5 differ from column 2 only in that the ages for entry into the labor force are assumed to be 18 and 26, respectively.

The positive relationship of V with age of labor force entry demonstrated in Table A-5 is an important factor qualifying the apparent progressive relationship of V with earnings. Age of entry depends on, among other factors, the number of years of schooling of an individual. People who receive college undergraduate and graduate training enter the labor force later in life than those who do not go beyond high school. In turn, earnings are a function of the length of schooling; to a significant degree, late entrants into the labor force have relatively high earnings. This means that the apparent progressivity of the benefit formula is offset to some degree by systematic differences in the age of entry by persons at different earnings levels. Thus, V for a single male worker who enters the labor force in 1968 at age 22 and always has maximum taxable earnings is only 56 percent, compared with 88 percent for a person who enters the labor force at the same age with earnings always at one-half average manufacturing earnings ($3,000 in 1968); if the first worker enters the labor force at age 26 while the latter enters at age 18,

Table A-5. *Projected Social Security Benefits as a Percentage of Taxes, for Different Ages of Entry into Labor Force*[a]

1968 Annual Earnings and Family Status	Age of Entry into Labor Force		
	18 (1)	22 (2)	26 (3)
$7,800			
Single male	50	56	64
Single female	58	66	74
Couple	85	96	108
$6,000			
Single male	56	62	70
Single female	64	72	82
Couple	94	106	120
$3,000			
Single male	79	88	100
Single female	92	103	116
Couple	134	150	170
$1,500			
Single male	88	100	112
Single female	104	116	131
Couple	150	168	190

a. Worker is assumed to enter labor force on January 1, 1968, and to retire at age 65. Based on assumptions of a 4 percent a year rate of growth of earnings and maximum taxable earnings, a 1.5 percent annual increase in benefits after retirement, and a 5 percent rate of interest. The replacement rate is adjusted proportionately for changes in earnings.

the differential narrows considerably—64 percent for the high earner and 79 percent for the low earner.

PROGRESSIVITY OF LIFETIME REDISTRIBUTION OF INCOME

Social security combines a regressive payroll tax on the working-age population with a system of transfers that is progressive relative to the incomes of the retired population. Some writers prefer to consider the question of the progressivity or regressivity of the social security program on the basis of its effect on the lifetime distribution of income for a given individual or group of individuals.[12] However, the lifetime in-

[12] See, for example, Elizabeth Deran, "Income Redistribution Under the Social Security System," *National Tax Journal*, Vol. 19, No. 3 (September 1966), pp. 276–85. The author correctly identifies many of the complicating factors that are discussed in the text.

come distribution approach leads to ambiguous conclusions regarding the progressivity of the retirement program.

The estimates in Table A-5 show, in the first place, that the apparent progressive pattern of V by earnings level may be offset, to some extent, by differences in the age of entry into the labor force that have a regressive impact on the values of V. Persons at different ends of the earnings scale differ in other important respects as well. Persons with high earnings are more likely to be married and have longer life

Table A-6. *Projected Social Security Benefits as a Percentage of Taxes, for Interest Rates of 5 and 10 Percent*[a]

1968 Annual Earnings and Family Status	Interest Rate (Percent)	
	5	10
$7,800 Single male	56	11
$1,500 Single male	100	19

a. Worker is assumed to enter labor force January 1, 1968, at age 22 and to retire at age 65. Based on assumptions of a 4 percent a year rate of growth of earnings and maximum taxable earnings, a replacement rate adjusted proportionately for changes in earnings, and a 1.5 percent annual rate of growth in benefits after retirement. Except for interest rates, assumptions are identical to those used in calculating estimates in Table A-3.

expectancies.[13] Both of these factors probably make social security significantly less progressive than it first appears.

The most fundamental difference may be the inverse variation of rates of time preference with income. The fact that many poor persons dissave rather than save, and are willing to borrow at rates of interest well above 10 percent, suggests that their high rate of return on their social security "investment" is not sufficient to compensate them for their loss of income resulting from the payroll tax. At very high rates of time preference, the individual's subjective valuation of retirement benefits relative to foregone taxes is very small. Table A-6, for example, shows V for individuals at the extremes of the earnings scale for two different rates of interest, 5 and 10 percent. These results indicate that the apparent progressivity of OASI depends critically on the assumption that rates of time preference do not differ significantly between the relatively well-off and the poor. In short, the degree of net progres-

[13] See discussion in Chapter II.

sivity of OASI, as measured by its effects on the lifetime distribution of individual or group income, is uncertain.

VARIATIONS OF V WITH IMPROVEMENTS IN THE BENEFIT STRUCTURE

The estimates in Table A-2, based on assumptions concerning the growth in earnings and maximum taxable earnings, assume no change in present replacement rates. It has been observed that this set of assumptions virtually guarantees that social security will be overfinanced on a long-range actuarial basis and that large annual cash surpluses will be generated for the trust funds. The estimates in Table A-3 assume only a modest increment in benefits over those in Table A-2, and represent only one possible improvement in future benefits relative to taxes for workers in social security.

The range of possible improvements in the benefit structure is infinite. The history of social security suggests that, when earnings grow and cause the program to be overfinanced on both a long-range actuarial basis and a current cash basis, Congress will make use of the surpluses to legislate an improved benefit formula. Moreover, Congress has thus far not been content to limit improvements in the benefit structure to those that can be financed with unchanged *scheduled* tax rates, but has instead consistently approved costly benefit changes that necessitate rate increases (see Appendix B). In short, individual equity calculations that ignore the possibility of future improvements in benefits probably greatly understate the true values of V for young workers in the labor force today.

Estimates in Table A-7 are based on a range of assumed future improvements in the benefit structure. In common with previous estimates, the procedure for calculating these estimates is to assume a 4 percent annual rate of growth for money earnings from 1968 into the indefinite future and a corresponding 4 percent rate of growth for maximum taxable earnings. To obtain the estimates in column 1, it is again assumed, as for the estimates in Table A-2, that replacement rates remain unchanged as earnings grow; but instead of following the present method of computing average monthly earnings (AME), the computation period for AME is assumed to be the highest *ten* years of earnings. In column 2, the computation period is assumed to be the highest *five* years of earnings. In column 3, the replacement rates are assumed to be 25 percent higher than the corresponding rate applicable to each earnings history in column 2. It is strikingly evident that any of these three

Table A-7. *Projected Social Security Benefits as a Percentage of Taxes under Alternative Improvements in the Benefit Structure*[a]

	Average Monthly Earnings		
1968 Annual Earnings and Family Status	Based on highest 10 years of earnings (1)	Based on highest 5 years of earnings (2)	Based on highest 5 years of earnings and 25 percent increase in replacement rates (3)
$7,800			
Single male	75	82	102
Single female	87	95	120
Couple	125	137	172
$6,000			
Single male	79	86	108
Single female	92	101	126
Couple	134	147	184
$3,000			
Single male	102	112	140
Single female	118	130	162
Couple	173	190	237
$1,500			
Single male	146	160	200
Single female	170	187	233
Couple	248	272	340

a. Worker is assumed to enter labor force at age 22, January 1, 1968, and retire at age 65. Based on 5 percent rate of interest. Earnings and maximum taxable earnings are assumed to grow at 4 percent a year. Benefits are increased by 1.5 percent a year after retirement.

assumed improvements in the benefit structure would give present entrants into the labor force generally satisfactory values of V under social security.

The estimates in Table A-7 may well be overstatements of the future ratio of benefits to taxes under social security. Any of the improvements assumed in computing these estimates would be costly, and possibly could not be financed out of tax rates now scheduled for social security. If taxes were revised *immediately* to finance these improvements, the resulting values of V would, of course, be much lower.

On the other hand, the estimates of V in Table A-7 are not *necessar-*

ily overly optimistic. First, favorable demographic trends—much higher than expected birth rates, for example—could make future improvements in social security much less costly than now projected. Second, and more fundamental, if significant improvements in the benefit structure occur gradually over the next 40 or 50 years, present young workers in the labor force will share fully in better benefits but to only a limited extent in higher taxes. To take an extreme example: if a given benefit increase is legislated on the eve of a worker's retirement, he shares fully in higher benefits but pays *no* additional taxes. This example is not farfetched, for the history of social security is replete with cases of workers sharing in general benefit increases immediately after retirement.

Finally, some previous estimates of V (for example, Table A-2, columns 3 and 4) have been based on assumptions that guarantee that social security will be *overfinanced*. Therefore, they understate the probable true values of V. The estimates in Table A-7 are based on assumptions that might make social security *underfinanced;* and, therefore, they may overstate the probable true values of V. The very large gap between the values computed in the two sets of estimates is a measure of the substantial degree of uncertainty about future demographic, economic, and political developments. One set of estimates cannot be shown conclusively to be more realistic than the other.

Conclusions

Two major conclusions emerge from the calculations in this appendix. First, there is no substantial basis for the view that young workers of today will be treated badly under OASI. If past trends in economic growth continue in the future, the current young generation of workers will be in a position to receive retirement benefits equal to or greater than the value of their OASI taxes, both benefits and taxes being estimated over a reasonable range of interest rates. This finding does not imply that *every* individual is guaranteed his money back under OASI, but the question of such a guarantee is irrelevant.

Second, benefit-tax calculations for workers now entering the labor force have little, if any, value beyond demonstrating that some previous calculations are misleading. The relationship of OASI benefits to OASI taxes over the lifetime of a worker now entering the labor force depends on decisions that will be made well into the twenty-first century. Once the assumption of a level average of money earnings is abandoned, as it should be, the range of plausible assumptions about the future course of the economy is unlimited. Yet the results depend critically on the choice of such assumptions, a choice that cannot be verified objectively. The results also depend critically on demographic developments and political decisions in the twenty-first century; and it is even more difficult to project these far in advance than it is to project economic developments. Acceptance of the inability to narrow the range of uncertainty in making individual equity calculations is another compelling argument for not using them as the basis for policy decisions in shaping the OASI retirement program.

APPENDIX B

History of Social Security Legislation*

Programs established in accordance with the Social Security Act have expanded enormously and undergone considerable change in coverage, benefits, and tax rates since the Act was passed in 1935. Coverage has been broadened to include virtually all employees, the self-employed and, finally, professionals including lawyers and doctors. Only retirement benefits were contemplated in 1935; but benefits for dependents and survivors were added in 1939, disability insurance in 1956, and hospital and medical insurance for persons aged 65 and over in 1965. The requirements for attaining insured status, and thus qualifying for various benefits, have gradually been relaxed. Benefits have been increased on several occasions. Additional earnings without loss of benefits have been permitted. To finance the enormous growth of Old-Age, Survivors, Disability, and Health Insurance (OASDHI), the combined employer-employee tax rate on an individual's earnings was increased—in several steps—from 2 percent in 1937 to 8.8 percent in 1967 and 1968 (scheduled to reach 11.8 percent in 1987), and maximum taxable earnings were raised—also in several steps—from $3,000 in 1937 to $7,800 in 1968.

Coverage

The 1935 Social Security Act specified that the old-age insurance program should include all workers under age 65 who were engaged in commerce and industry (except railroads) in the continental United States, Alaska, Hawaii, and on American vessels. Under legislation enacted in

* Prepared by Alicia Munnell. Except as noted, the material in this appendix is based on data taken from sources shown for the accompanying tables.

1939, coverage was expanded slightly by eliminating the "under 65" age restriction. During the 1940's, railroad workers were, in essence, included in the survivor benefits portion of the old-age insurance program, and World War II veterans who died within three years after discharge were given fully insured status.

The major expansion in coverage occurred in 1950 (Table B-1). Regularly employed farm and domestic workers were included, and for the first time the program was extended beyond employees to include the nonfarm self-employed (except professionals). Certain state and local government employees and employees of nonprofit institutions were given the option of joining the program. This same 1950 legislation also expanded geographical coverage by including the inhabitants of Puerto Rico and the Virgin Islands, and Americans employed outside the United States by American employers.

The 1954 legislation expanded coverage significantly. Additional farm and domestic workers were included, and compulsory coverage was extended to self-employed farmers and to self-employed professionals, except those in medicine and law. Further elective coverage was granted to state and local government employees (except firemen and policemen) already under other retirement systems, and to ministers.

The main extension of compulsory coverage in 1956 was to change the gratuitous status of the armed forces, set forth in the 1950 legislation, to a regular contributory coverage. Legislation in 1956 also expanded the coverage of self-employed to include all professionals except doctors of medicine.

By 1956, coverage had been extended to practically all persons gainfully employed other than federal government employees (who are covered by the federal Civil Service Retirement System) and railroad workers (who are covered by the Railroad Retirement Act). Subsequent legislation resulted in certain minor extensions. In 1958, 1960, and 1961, there were small increases in coverage to state and local government employees. The 1960 Act extended coverage to the inhabitants of American Samoa and Guam; and American citizens employed by foreign governments and by international organizations in the United States were covered for the first time. The inclusion in 1965 of self-employed doctors of medicine and interns meant that coverage of the working population by the OASDHI or some other government retirement program was virtually complete. Coverage was extended to certain small categories of state and local government employees under the 1967 amendments. The coverage basis of ministers was revised; coverage became compulsory unless the minister should opt out on grounds of conscience or religious principle.[1]

Benefits

There have been three major trends in legislation affecting OASDHI benefits. First, new types of benefits have transformed the original simple retirement plan of 1935 into a much more extensive set of programs. Second, the requirements for becoming fully insured have been gradually liberalized, and several less rigorous categories of insured status have been established to permit payment of some benefits to persons with limited periods of coverage. Third, the method of calculation has become more generous, resulting in larger average benefit payments.

TYPES OF BENEFITS

The old-age insurance section of the 1935 Social Security Act provided primarily for monthly retirement benefits to insured workers at age 65. Any worker who contributed but was not fully insured by retirement would receive a lump-sum refund of his contribution plus an allowance for interest. (This provision was eliminated in 1939.) There were also provisions for a lump-sum death payment (Table B-2).

The 1939 legislation greatly expanded the scope of the old-age insurance program by adding monthly benefits for the dependents and survivors of insured workers. Dependents' benefits were provided for the family of a retired worker. To the worker's retirement benefits, 50 percent additional benefits were added (subject to a maximum family benefit) for a wife aged 65 or a child under 18. Monthly survivor benefits were also provided for an insured worker's widow aged 65 or over, dependent parents aged 65 or over, children under 18, and a widowed mother with a child under 18.

Further categories of dependents and survivors were added in 1950. The wife's benefit was extended to cover a wife under 65 years of age

---

[1] The major groups still remaining outside OASDHI (other than federal civilian employees and railroad workers who are covered by their own programs) are domestic workers earning less than $50 a quarter from a single employer, self-employed persons whose net earnings for the taxable year are less than $400, employees of state and local governments not covered by a federal-state agreement, and employees of certain nonprofit organizations for whom elective coverage has not been arranged.

with a child under 18. For an aged dependent husband of a retired woman worker, an additional 50 percent of the wife's retirement benefit was provided. Survivor benefits were extended to a dependent widower aged 65 or over and to a dependent divorced wife of a deceased worker if she had an eligible child.

Additional, though minor, groups of dependents and survivors were included in the 1956 Act. Wives of retired workers between the ages of 62 and 65 were made eligible for permanently reduced benefits. A child over 18 became eligible for dependent and survivor benefits if he were disabled before age 18. The age at which a widow and a female dependent parent of a deceased worker could receive benefits was lowered to 62.

The 1956 legislation, however, did provide a significant improvement in protection by initiating monthly payments (after a six-month waiting period) to workers between the ages of 50 and 64 who had been permanently and totally disabled. In 1958, benefits were extended to include the dependents of disabled workers; and in 1960, the 50-year age restriction was eliminated so that all workers under 65 and their dependents are eligible for disability insurance.

The minimum retirement age was lowered to 62 for women in 1956 and for men in 1961, and benefits were permanently reduced by $5/9$ percent for each month under 65. Thus, a worker retiring at age 62 receives benefits smaller by 20 percent than the benefits he would be paid if he retired at age 65.

In 1961, reductions to age 62 were extended to dependent husbands and dependent male survivors, but the husbands' benefits were permanently reduced if claimed before age 65. Further age reductions in 1965 allowed a widow to start receiving reduced benefits at 60. Also, in 1965, two new minor classes of dependents and eligible survivors were added —namely, aged, divorced women if the marriage lasted 20 years and children aged 18 through 21 if attending school.

The most dramatic feature of the 1965 legislation was the addition of health insurance to the existing old-age, disability, and survivors insurance. Insured workers over age 65 and certain other aged persons were made eligible for the hospital and related benefits provided by the new program. These benefits include the following: (1) inpatient hospital care for 90 days for each illness, with $40 deductible and $10 coinsurance a day after 60 days; (2) 100 post-hospital days in an extended care institution, with $5 coinsurance a day after 20 days; (3) outpatient services with $20 deductible and 20 percent coinsurance; and (4) 100 post-hospital home visits. Also available on an elective basis (with no insured status required) at a charge of $3 a month initially is additional medical insurance to cover 80 percent of physician and related expenditures with $50 deductible a year. The 1967 amendments provided each Medicare beneficiary with a lifetime reserve of 60 days of hospital care after the 90 days covered in a "spell of illness" have been exhausted. There would be $20 coinsurance for each such added day of coverage.[2]

Benefits for disabled widows and widowers were introduced by the 1967 amendments. Widows and widowers of certain deceased insured workers who become totally disabled not more than 7 years after the spouse's death are eligible for disability benefits between the ages of 50 and 62. Benefits amount to 50 percent of the primary insurance amount if first awarded at age 50, increase gradually to 82.5 percent for persons first receiving benefits at age 62.

QUALIFICATIONS FOR INSURED STATUS

As prerequisites for various types of benefits, the social security laws require that a person shall have attained "insured status." There are five classifications of "insured." The term "fully insured" was introduced in 1939 to identify those persons eligible for monthly retirement benefits at age 65. In addition, a less rigorous classification, "currently insured," relaxed the minimum requirements so that a young deceased worker's family could be eligible for survivor benefits without the worker being fully insured. With the proposed introduction of the "disability freeze" (omitting periods of extended total disability in the calculation of average monthly earnings) in 1954, the classification "insured for disability" was included in the legislation. The 1965 Act included two additional classifications: "transitionally insured" and "insured for hospital benefits." The details of these different insured classifications are summarized in Table B-3 and discussed below.

Fully insured. The 1935 Act required that workers, to be fully insured, have $2,000 of cumulative wage credits and have been employed in each of five years. In 1939, the basis was changed from wage credits to quarterly periods of coverage. To become fully insured, the worker had to be covered for one-half of the quarters after 1936 (or after age 21) to retirement (or death); the minimum coverage required was 6 quarters, and the maximum was 40.

In 1950, the starting year was changed—primarily for newly covered

[2] Herman M. Somers and Anne R. Somers, *Medicare and the Hospitals: Issues and Prospects* (Brookings Institution, 1967), contains an analysis of the program, which is beyond the scope of the present volume.

groups—from 1936 to 1950 and a worker had to be covered for one-half of the period after 1950 (or after age 21) to retirement. Quarters earned before 1951 could also be counted.

In 1960, the coverage required was reduced from one-half to one-third of the quarters after 1950 (or after age 21) to retirement, disability, or death. In 1961, the coverage required was further reduced—to only 1 out of every 4 quarters during the same period. In all cases, quarters earned before 1951 could be counted, and the minimum requirement remained at 6 quarters—as specified in 1939. With the 1961 legislation, calculations pertaining to insured status for women were based on the period after 1950 (or after age 21) to age 62 (or death), while for men the terminal point was left at age 65.

Currently insured. Currently insured status was introduced in 1939 to provide for the survivors of a young deceased worker; even today, it applies for the most part to requirements for survivor insurance. To meet the requirements, a worker must be insured for 6 of the 13 quarters immediately preceding death, retirement, or disability, including the quarter of that event.

Insured for disability. The qualifications for disability insured status, established in the 1954 Act, require that a person must be covered in one-half of the last 40 quarters, including the quarter when disability occurred. In 1965, the minimum was lowered to 6 quarters for those who become blind at an early age. The 1967 amendments allow a worker who becomes disabled before age 31 to qualify for disability insurance if he worked in one-half the quarters between age 21 and the time he is disabled, or alternatively if he works in covered employment in 6 of the last 12 quarters.

Transitionally insured. The category transitionally insured—a very minor category added in 1965—provides small retirement and survivor benefit payments to certain aged workers and their wives and widows. Essentially, the requirements are the same as those for fully insured, but the minimum coverage required is 3 quarters and the worker must attain age 72 before 1969.

Insured for hospital benefits. With the beginning of health insurance in 1965, the classification "insured for hospital benefits" was established. A worker can achieve this status in four ways: (1) by being fully insured or the dependent or survivor of a fully insured person; (2) by working in covered employment for three-fourths of the period from 1966 to age 65; (3) by reaching age 65 before 1968; or (4) as a railroad retirement beneficiary. Under these lenient requirements, almost all persons currently attaining age 65 can qualify for the hospital insurance program.

CALCULATION OF BENEFITS

Benefits are derived in two steps. First, the worker's average monthly wage over a specified period is calculated; and second, a table included in the law is used to determine, on the basis of the worker's average monthly earnings, his primary insurance amount—the amount his benefit would be at or after age 65. Since the average monthly wage concept was introduced in 1939, generous allowances have been made to exclude years of low earnings. To this gradually increasing base, higher and higher rates have been applied; and in 1950, when coverage was extended, a new starting date (1951) for the computation was provided. Between 1950 and 1967 both the minimum and the maximum benefit have almost tripled (Table B-4).

The 1935 Social Security Act included a formula for calculating benefits based on a worker's cumulative wages; but before any benefits were paid, this formula was replaced by another incorporated in the 1939 legislation, which based payments on the average monthly wage (Table B-5).The average was calculated for the period after 1936 (or after age 21) to age 65 (or death). Primary insurance amounts were calculated by taking 40 percent of the first $50 of the average monthly wage and 10 percent of the next $200 and increasing the total by 1 percent for each year that the worker was employed in covered employment and received at least $200 in wages. A minimum benefit of $10 a month and a maximum family benefit of $85 were included in the legislation. This method of calculating benefits was used until April 1952 when it was replaced by the formula included in the 1950 Act.

This formula based the calculation of the average monthly wage on the period after 1950 and increased the benefit rates to 50 percent of the first $100 and 15 percent of the next $200. The same legislation eliminated the provision of a 1 percent increase in benefits for each year of coverage. The 1950 formula was employed for only 5 months. In September 1952, it was replaced by a formula in the 1952 Act, which raised to 55 percent the benefit rate on the first $100.

Legislation in 1954 brought major changes in the formula. The average wage used as a basis was increased by allowing the 4 (or 5 if there were at least 20 quarters of coverage) years of lowest earnings to be omitted in computing the average. (In 1956, the law was changed so that the lowest 5 years could be omitted in all cases.) Also, the "disability freeze" was instituted in 1954, which permitted periods of extended total disability to be omitted in the calculation of the average monthly wage. The benefit rates were increased to 55 percent on the first $110 and 20 percent on the next $240. The minimum benefit was raised from $25 to $30 a month, and the maximum family benefit was set at $200 instead of $168.75.

Legislation in 1958 increased benefit rates still more: 58.85 percent was applied to the first $110 and 21.4 percent to the next $290. The minimum benefit was raised to $33, and the maximum family benefit was increased to $254.

Minor changes in the computation of the average monthly wage were made in 1960 and 1961. The 1960 revision allowed workers who continued working past the minimum retirement age to substitute years of higher earnings after this point for earlier years of low earnings in calculating the average. The 1961 legislation retained age 65 as the terminal point for calculating the average monthly wage for men, although age 62 had been instituted as the terminal point for women by the 1956 legislation. The minimum benefit was raised in that year to $40.

The 1965 legislation raised the benefit rate on the first $110 to 62.97 percent and on the next $290 to 22.9 percent, and set a 21.4 percent rate on the next $150. These new rates meant that primary benefits did not reach a maximum until the average wage was $550. The minimum benefit was set at $44 a month and the maximum family benefit at $368.

A 13 percent increase in benefits was included in the 1967 legislation, and the average monthly earnings included in benefit calculations were increased to $650. The benefit rates were raised to 71.16 percent on the first $110, 25.88 percent on the next $290, 24.18 percent on the next $150, and 28.43 percent on the last $100 of average monthly wage.

The preceding details of the benefit formula apply solely to the computation of the worker's primary insurance amount. After 1939, benefits were also provided for dependents of retired workers and for survivors, and after 1958 they were provided for dependents of disabled workers. These additional benefits—the so-called secondary benefits—are expressed as percentages of the primary benefits. For two distinct reasons, they have increased greatly since 1940. First, the basis on which they are calculated—namely, the worker's primary insurance amount—has increased; second, nearly all survivor benefit rates have become larger fractions of the worker's primary benefit (Table B-6).

In addition to monthly payments, the 1935 Act included lump-sum death benefits. The formula was based on cumulative wages so that the beneficiary would receive 3.5 percent of the worker's cumulative wage credits minus any benefits that might have been paid before the worker's death. This formula was applied in 1937–39, but it was superseded by 1939 legislation which set the death benefit at 6 times the primary insurance amount; it then remained unchanged until 1950 when it was reduced to 3 times the primary benefit. In 1954, the maximum was set at $255.

The Earnings Test

The original 1935 Social Security Act required complete retirement from all employment as a condition of eligibility for benefits. This severe restriction has been modified on several occasions, so that presently a worker can earn $1,680 a year (or $140 of wages in any month) without any loss of benefits.

One of the advantages of old-age insurance discussed at the time of the 1935 legislation was that it would encourage aged workers to retire and, as a result, more jobs would be available for younger men. Consequently, it was determined that a worker must completely withdraw from the labor force to qualify for benefits and must be required to forfeit an entire month's benefit whenever he engaged in active employment in that month.

In 1939, before the earnings test of 1935 was ever applied to actual beneficiaries, the law was relaxed slightly to permit earnings of $14.99 a month without any loss of benefit. The amount was raised to $50 in 1950 and to $75 in 1952. In all cases, any earnings in excess of these stated amounts resulted in the loss of all benefits for the month in question (Table B-7).

The earnings test as of 1952 resulted in substantial inequities. First, only earnings from covered employment were included in the restrictions; second, workers who earned slightly more than $75 in some months, but well below that amount in others, suffered a severe loss of benefits. To remedy these difficulties, the 1954 legislation placed the wage test on an annual basis, just as self-employed income had been treated in 1950 and 1952. The annual limit on all earnings covered and uncovered was raised to $1,200; for each additional $80, one month's benefit was withheld. However, a worker could still be paid benefits for any month in which he earned wages of less than $80 and did not engage in substantial self-employment. Therefore, a person retiring in the middle of a year was eligible for benefits as soon as his monthly wages fell below $80 regardless of his annual income. The 1958 legislation increased this monthly limit from $80 to $100 a month.

In 1960, very different treatment of earnings in excess of $1,200 was enacted. For earnings between $1,200 and $1,500 only $1 of benefits was withheld for every $2 of earnings; above $1,500 of earnings, $1 of benefits was withheld for each $1 of earnings. The 1961 legislation raised to $1,700 the upper limit of the range (making it $1,200–$1,700) to which the 50 percent reduction in benefits would apply. The 1965 Act allowed even larger earnings by raising the lower limit to $1,500 and having the 50 percent reduction in benefits apply to earnings over the range from $1,500 to $2,700; for earnings above $2,700, $1 in benefits was withheld for each dollar earned. Also in that year, the monthly limit on wages, without loss of benefits, was raised to $125. In 1967, the annual limit again was raised, to $1,680, and the 50 percent reduction was applied to earnings between $1,680 and $2,880. There was a comparable rise, to $140, in the monthly limit on wages.

Under the present legislation, the results of the earnings test are as follows: Assume an individual is entitled to a social security benefit of $80 a month. If his earnings from employment are between $0 and $1,680, then his total income can vary between $960 ($0 from earnings and 12 × $80 from social security) and $2,640 ($1,680 from earnings and $960 from social security). As his earnings from employment rise to the $1,680 to $2,880 range, his total income can vary from $2,640 ($1,680 from earnings and $960 from social security) to $3,240 ($2,880 from earnings and $360 from social security). However, when earnings grow from $2,880 to $3,240, there is no increase in total income ($2,880 from earnings plus $360 social security or $3,240 from earnings and no social security income).

The 1950 legislation set an age limit of 75, after which there would be no restrictions on earnings. In 1954, the age was reduced to 72.

Financing

According to the 1935 legislation, the contributions from employer-employee payroll taxes were to exceed benefits in the early years and to result in the accumulation of a large trust fund. With the 1939 amendments, emphasis shifted from the accumulation of a large reserve toward a pay-as-you-go basis of financing accompanied by the formation of a small contingency fund. In 1950, the legislation provided for the accumulation of a slightly larger reserve than had been envisioned in 1939. It was estimated that current contributions on the basis of the 1950 tax schedule plus interest earned on trust fund holdings would be sufficient to finance all benefits in perpetuity. Also, it was estimated that annual surpluses of taxes and interest over benefits would lead to an accumulation of a reserve of $83 billion in the 1990's.[3]

[3] John J. Carroll, *Alternative Methods of Financing Old-Age, Survivors, and Disability Insurance* (University of Michigan, Institute of Public Administration, 1960), p. 38.

In each of the amendments since 1950, Congress has reasserted its intention that the OASDI system should be self-supporting. In practice, benefits have been paid primarily out of current tax contributions, representing essentially a transfer from the young, working, tax-paying population to those persons who have become eligible for old-age, disability, and survivor benefits.

In 1935, a schedule of combined employer-employee tax rates was established; it began with a 2 percent tax through 1939, then was to increase in four steps of 1 percent each, to level off at 6 percent in 1949. These taxes were to be levied on the first $3,000 of a worker's annual earnings. Under legislation in the 1940's the 2 percent tax rate was extended through 1949. The 1950 Act provided a revised tax schedule, with a rate of 3 percent through 1953 and increases in four steps thereafter, to reach a maximum of 6.5 percent in 1970. The 1950 Act also increased maximum taxable earnings to $3,600. The 1954 Act extended the schedule to reach a maximum rate of 8 percent in 1975, and it raised the worker's maximum taxable earnings to $4,200.

With the enactment of disability insurance in 1956, an extra ½ percent flat rate was added to the 1954 schedule to finance these additional benefits. Another increase of ½ percent was applied in 1958, and the rate increases were reduced from 5-year to 3-year intervals, to attain a maximum rate of 9 percent by 1969. Also, this legislation increased the tax base from $4,200 to $4,800. Legislation in 1961 added ¼ percent to the existing rate structure and set a new maximum rate at 9¼ percent, to be attained in 1968.

The introduction of health insurance in 1965 resulted in a revised schedule, with the combined tax rate to reach 11.3 percent in 1987. This schedule included a tax for health insurance, which was 0.7 percent initially and was scheduled to reach 1.6 percent in 1987. The tax for disability benefits was raised from 0.5 to 0.7 percent.

The revised tax schedule included in the 1967 legislation raised maximum taxable earnings to $7,800. The total OASDHI tax rate is scheduled to rise from 8.8 percent in 1968 to 11.8 percent in 1987 and thereafter (see Table B-8). Disability insurance accounts for 0.95 percent of the total rate, while the tax for health insurance increases from 1.2 percent in 1968 to 1.8 percent in 1987.

The expansion in programs, the increases in tax rates, and the larger maximum taxable earnings have resulted in a growth in maximum combined social security taxes paid by employers and employees from $60 in 1937 to $706.40 in 1968.

The preceding description of rates applies to salaried workers. The self-employed were first brought under the coverage of social security in

1950, and at that time their tax rate was established as three-fourths of the combined employer-employee rate (rounded to the nearest $\frac{1}{10}$ percent as of 1961). In 1965, a maximum tax rate of 7 percent—to be reached in 1973—was set for the self-employed for old-age, survivors, and disability insurance. The tax rate for hospital insurance was established at one-half of the employer-employee rate.

Although the payroll tax has been the primary method of financing, there have been minor alternatives, on occasion. In 1946, appropriations from general revenues were authorized to reimburse the OASI trust fund for noncontributory survivor insurance provided to certain World War II veterans. Small amounts were transferred from the general fund until the middle of 1950, when legislation provided that any additional costs from the 1946 provision be borne by the trust fund. Finally, in 1956, the 1950 law was reversed, and it was ruled that the trust funds be reimbursed annually for any costs arising before 1956 from the 1946 or subsequent legislation providing noncontributory credits to veterans. Nevertheless, there were no further transfers made from general revenues until the Secretary of Health, Education, and Welfare ruled, in 1965, on the annual amount owed to the trust funds. The first reimbursements of $78 million and $16 million were made to the OASI and DI trust funds, respectively, for fiscal year 1966. Furthermore, in the 1967 amendments, transfers from the general fund were provided to finance deemed additional covered earnings of military personnel. In 1965, appropriations from general revenues were authorized to finance hospital insurance benefits for those individuals not fully insured, and to match funds collected from the voluntary contribution of $3 a month by participants in the medical insurance program that supplements the hospital insurance program. The benefits provided by a 1966 amendment, which granted $35 a month to certain persons who were, generally, never covered by OASDI, but who attained age 72 before 1968 ($52.50 for a husband and wife when both are eligible), are also financed from general revenues. These special age-72 benefits to noninsured individuals were increased from $35 to $40 a month ($52.50 to $60 for couples) by the 1967 legislation.

Table B-1. *History of Compulsory Coverage under Social Security Legislation, 1935–67*

Year of Legislation	Groups[a]	Areas[b]
1935	All workers under age 65 in commerce and industry (except railroads)	United States including Alaska, Hawaii, and American vessels
1939	Workers over age 65 in commerce and industry (except railroads)	No change
1946	Railroad workers covered, in effect, for survivor benefits[e]	No change
1950	Regularly employed farm workers Regularly employed domestic workers Nonfarm self-employed (except professionals) Federal civilian employees (not under retirement systems) Americans employed outside United States by American employers	Puerto Rico and Virgin Islands added
1954	Farm self-employed Additional farm workers Additional domestic workers Professional self-employed (except those in medicine and law)	No change
1956	Members of armed forces Lawyers, dentists, doctors of osteopathy, veterinarians, naturopaths, optometrists, chiropractors, and farm landlords who materially participate in farming activities	No change
1960	Americans employed in United States by foreign governments and international organizations Parents working (not at domestic service or casual labor) for a child	Guam and American Samoa added
1965	Self-employed doctors of medicine Medical interns Recipients of tips (subject to employee tax only)	No change
1967	Ministers[d]	No change

Sources: Robert J. Myers, "Old-Age, Survivors, Disability, and Health Insurance Provisions: Legislative History, 1935–65" (leaflet, U.S. Department of Health, Education, and Welfare, Social Security Administration, July 1965); Social Security Administration, *Social Security Handbook* (1966), p. 200; *Summary of Social Security Amendments of 1967*, Joint Publication of Senate Committee on Finance and House Committee on Ways and Means, 90 Cong. 1 sess. (1967), p. 3.

a. Groups included in 1935 Social Security Act plus those specified under subsequent legislation.

b. Areas included in 1935 Social Security Act plus those specified under subsequent legislation.

c. Railroad workers are covered under a separate retirement program which operates on similar principles and is closely related to Old-Age, Survivors, and Disability Insurance (OASDI). For survivor benefits, railroad and other earnings are combined to determine eligibility and amount. In 1951, the two systems were brought even closer together by placing workers with less than 10 years of railroad service under OASDI for all benefits.

d. Ministers are covered on a compulsory basis unless the minister opts out on grounds of conscience or religious principle

Table b-2. *History of Benefits Provided by Social Security Legislation, 1935–67*

Type of Benefit and Recipient	Year of Legis- lation	Age Requirement	Required Insured Status of Worker[a]
	Retirement Benefits		
Retired worker			
Male	1935	65 or over	Fully
	1961	62 or over[b]	Fully
Female	1935	65 or over	Fully
	1956	62 or over[b]	Fully
50 percent additional benefits for dependents			
Wife[c]	1939	65 or over	Fully
	1956	62 or over[b]	Fully
Child	1939	Under 18	Fully
	1956	Any age if disabled be- fore 18	Fully
	1965	18–21 if attending school	Fully
Wife, with eligible child[d]	1950	None	Fully
Dependent husband	1950	65 or over	Fully and currently
	1961	62 or over[b]	Fully and currently
	1967	62 or over[b]	Fully
Divorced dependent wife (if marriage lasted 20 years)	1965	62 or over[b]	Fully
$35 payment to retired worker	1965	72 or over	Transitionally[e]
$40 payment to retired worker	1967	72 or over	Transitionally[e]
$17.50 payment to worker's wife	1965	72 or over	Transitionally[e]
$20 payment to worker's wife	1967	72 or over	Transitionally[e]
	Survivor Benefits		
82.5 percent of worker's benefit			
Widow	1939[f]	65 or over	Fully
	1956	62 or over	Fully
	1965	60 or over[bg]	Fully
Dependent divorced widow	1965	60 or over[b]	Fully
Dependent widower	1950	65 or over	Fully and currently
	1961	62 or over	Fully and currently
	1967	62 or over[g]	Fully
Dependent parent[h]			
Male	1939[i]	65 or over	Fully
	1961	62 or over	Fully
Female	1939[i]	65 or over	Fully
	1956	62 or over	Fully

Table B-2. *(continued)*

Type of Benefit and Recipient	Year of Legis-lation	Age Requirement	Required Insured Status of Worker[a]
Survivor Benefits (continued)			
75 percent of worker's benefit Widow, with eligible child[d]	1939	Under 65	Fully or currently
Divorced widow, with eligible child[d]	1950	None	Fully or currently
Child	1939[j]	Under 18	Fully or currently
	1965	18–21 if attending school	Fully or currently
Child disabled before 18	1956	None	Fully or currently
$35 to worker's widow	1965	72 or over	Transitionally[e]
$40 to worker's widow	1967	72 or over	Transitionally[e]
Lump-sum death benefit	1935	None	Fully or currently
Disability Benefits			
Disabled worker	1956	50–64	Fully, currently, and for disability
	1958	50–64	Fully and for disability
	1960	Under 65	Fully and for disability
Disabled widow (or widower)	1967	50–62[g]	Fully (or fully and currently)
50 percent additional benefits Wife	1958	62 or over[b]	Fully
Child	1958	Under 18 (also over 18 if disabled before 18)	Fully
	1965	18–21 if attending school	Fully
Wife, with eligible child[d]	1958	None	Fully
Dependent husband	1958	65 or over	Fully and currently
	1961	62 or over[b]	Fully and currently
Divorced dependent wife (if marriage lasted 20 years)	1965	62 or over[b]	Fully

265

Table B-2. *(concluded)*

Type of Benefit and Recipient	Year of Legis- lation	Age Requirement	Required Insured Status of Worker[a]
Medical Benefits			
Hospital and related benefits	1965	65 or over	Fully or for hospital
Supplementary medical benefits	1965	65 or over (voluntary)	None

Sources: Robert J. Myers, "Old-Age, Survivors, Disability, and Health Insurance Provisions: Legislative History, 1935–65" (leaflet, U.S. Department of Health, Education, and Welfare, Social Security Administration, July 1965), and *Social Insurance and Allied Government Programs* (R. D. Irwin, 1965); Social Security Administration, *Social Security Handbook* (1966) and *Social Security Programs in the United States* (1966); *Summary of Social Security Amendments of 1967*, Joint Publication of Senate Committee on Finance and House Committee on Ways and Means, 90 Cong. 1 sess. (1967), pp. 1–3; 81 Stat. 821.

a. See pages 255–56 for explanation of various types of insured status.

b. Benefits permanently reduced: (1) for insured worker the benefit is reduced by 5/9 percent for each month before age 65; (2) for widow the benefit is reduced by 5/9 percent for each month before age 62; (3) for dependent wife or husband the benefit is reduced by 25/36 percent for each month before age 65.

c. A maximum of $105 was introduced for the wife's benefit by the 1967 legislation.

d. Except when child is eligible only because of attending school at age 18–21.

e. In addition, the Prouty Amendment of 1966 further liberalized eligibility requirements for persons over age 72 by providing $35 ($52.50 for a husband and wife both of whom are eligible) for *noninsured* workers if (1) they reached age 72 before 1968 or (2) they had three quarters of coverage for each year after 1966 and before age 72. Wilbur J. Cohen, Robert M. Ball, and Robert J. Myers, "Social Security Payments to Non-insured Persons," *Social Security Bulletin*, Vol. 29, No. 9 (September 1966), pp. 5–6. These benefits and those for the transitionally insured were raised to $40 for single beneficiaries and $60 for couples by the 1967 legislation.

f. 1939–60: Survivors received 75 percent of worker's benefits.

g. The 1967 amendments provided benefits to certain disabled widows and widowers (or surviving disabled divorced wives) of deceased insured workers between the ages of 50 and 62. To be eligible, the beneficiary must become totally disabled not later than 7 years after the death of the spouse. If the benefit is first awarded at age 50, it amounts to 50 percent of the primary insurance amount. This percentage increases gradually until it reaches 82.5 percent for those persons first receiving benefits at age 62.

h. If there are two parents, each receives 75 percent.

i. 1939–August 1950: 50 percent of worker's benefit; September 1950–1960: 75 percent of worker's benefit.

j. 1939–August 1950: 50 percent of worker's benefit; September 1950–1960: 75 percent of worker's benefit for first child, 50 percent of worker's benefit for other children.

Table B-3. *History of Requirements for Coverage Specified by Social Security Legislation, 1935–67*

Year of Legislation	Basis	Amount	Time Period	Minimum	Maximum
			Fully Insured[a]		
1935	Wage credits	$2,000	Some employment in each of 5 years	$2,000	—
1939	Quarters of coverage	One-half	After 1936 (or after age 21) to age 65 (or death)	6	40
1950	Quarters of coverage	One-half	After 1950 (or after age 21) to age 65 (or death)[b]	6	40
1960	Quarters of coverage	One-third	After 1950 (or after age 21) to age 65 (or death)[b]	6	40
1961	Quarters of coverage	One-fourth	Men: After 1950 (or after age 21) to age 65 (or death)[b]	6	40
			Women: After 1950 (or after age 21) to age 62 (or death)[b]	6	40
			Currently Insured[c]		
1939	Quarters of coverage	6 of 12	Preceding death	6	—
1946	Quarters of coverage	6 of 13	Including quarter of death	6	—
1950	Quarters of coverage	6 of 13	Including quarter of death or retirement	6	—
1954	Quarters of coverage	6 of 13	Including quarter of death, retirement, or disability	6	—
			Insured for Disability		
1954	Quarters of coverage	20 of last 40	Including quarter of disability	20	—
1965	For the blind: quarters of coverage	One-half	From after age 21 to disablement	6	—
1967	For workers disabled before age 31: quarters of coverage	One-half *or* 6 of last 12	From after age 21 to disablement	6	—
			Including quarter of disability	6	—
			Transitionally Insured[d]		
1965	Quarters of coverage	One-fourth	Men: From 1951 (or after age 21) to age 65 (or death)[b]	3	—
			Women: From 1951 (or after age 21) to age 62 (or death)[b]	3	—
	and age	72	Before 1969		
			Insured for Health Benefits		
1965	All persons fully insured under OASDHI, their dependents, and survivors				
	or quarters of coverage	Three fourths	From 1966 to age 65	None	—
	or age	65	Before 1968	None	—
	or railroad retirement beneficiary				

Source: See Table B-2.
a. See pages 255–56 for a description of fully insured status.
b. Quarters of coverage earned before 1951 can be counted.
c. See page 256 for a description of currently insured status.
d. Special category for persons attaining age 72 before 1969.

267

Table B-4. *History of Primary Insurance Amounts Provided by Social Security Legislation, 1939–67*[a]

(In dollars)

Average Monthly Wage	Monthly Primary Insurance Amount, by Year of Legislation							
	1939[b]	1950	1952	1954	1958	1961	1965	1967
25	10.00	20.00	25.00	30.00	33.00	40.00	44.00	55.00
50	20.00	25.00	27.50	30.00	33.00	40.00	44.00	55.00
100	25.00	50.00	55.00	55.00	59.00	59.00	63.20	71.50
150	30.00	57.50	62.50	68.50	73.00	73.00	78.20	88.40
200	35.00	65.00	70.00	78.50	84.00	84.00	89.90	101.60
250	40.00	72.50	77.50	88.50	95.00	95.00	101.70	115.00
300	40.00	80.00	85.00	98.50	105.00	105.00	112.40	127.10
350	40.00	80.00	85.00	108.50	116.00	116.00	124.20	140.40
400	40.00	80.00	85.00	108.50	127.00	127.00	135.90	153.60
450	40.00	80.00	85.00	108.50	127.00	127.00	146.00	165.00
500	40.00	80.00	85.00	108.50	127.00	127.00	157.00	177.50
550	40.00	80.00	85.00	108.50	127.00	127.00	168.00	189.90
600	40.00	80.00	85.00	108.50	127.00	127.00	168.00	204.00
650	40.00	80.00	85.00	108.50	127.00	127.00	168.00	218.00
Minimum benefit	10.00	20.00	25.00	30.00	33.00	40.00	44.00	55.00
Maximum benefit								
Individual	60.00	80.00	85.00	108.50	127.00	127.00	168.00	218.00
Family	85.00	150.00	168.75	200.00	254.00	254.00	368.00	434.40

Sources: 1939–54, calculated from benefit formulas presented in Table B-5; 1958–61, U.S. Department of Health, Education, and Welfare, Social Security Administration, unpublished memorandum; 1965, Social Security Administration, *Social Security Handbook* (1966), pp. 120–23; 1967, Public Law 90–248, 90 Cong., H.R. 12080, January 2, 1968 (1968), *An Act*, pp. 4–6. Minimum and maximum benefit data from Robert J. Myers, *Social Insurance and Allied Government Programs* (R. D. Irwin, 1965), p. 49; *Social Security Handbook*, pp. 120–23; 81 Stat. 821.

a. "Primary insurance amount" denotes the amount payable to a retired worker and on which the benefits of his dependents and survivors are based, or the basis for benefits payable to survivors of worker who dies before retirement.

b. Under the 1939 legislation, all benefits were increased by 1 percent for each year of coverage. This provision was discontinued by the 1950 legislation.

Table B-5. *History of Benefit Formulas for Primary Insurance Amounts Provided by Social Security Legislation, 1935–67*

Year of Legislation	Basis	Formula
1935	Cumulative wages	$\frac{1}{2}$ % of first $3,000 *plus* $\frac{1}{12}$% of next $42,000 *plus* $\frac{1}{24}$% of next $84,000
1939	Average monthly wage after 1936	40% of first $50 *plus* 10% of next $200 *plus* increase of total by 1% for each year of coverage
1950	Average monthly wage after 1950	50% of first $100 *plus* 15% of next $200
1952	Average monthly wage after 1950	55% of first $100 *plus* 15% of next $200
1954	Average monthly wage after 1950 (excluding 4 or 5 years of lowest earnings)	55% of first $110 *plus* 20% of next $240
1958	Average monthly wage after 1950 (excluding 5 years of lowest earnings)[a,b]	58.85% of first $110 *plus* 21.4% of next $290
1965	Average monthly wage after 1950 (excluding 5 years of lowest earnings)[b,c]	62.97% of first $110 *plus* 22.9% of next $290 *plus* 21.4% of next $150
1967	Average monthly wage after 1950 (excluding 5 years of lowest earnings)[b,c]	71.16% of first $110 *plus* 25.88% of next $290 *plus* 24.18% of next $150 *plus* 28.43% of next $100[d]

Sources: Robert J. Myers, "Old-Age, Survivors, Disability, and Health Insurance Provisions: Legislative History, 1935–65" (leaflet, U.S. Department of Health, Education, and Welfare, Social Security Administration, July 1965); *Actuarial Cost Estimates for the Old-Age, Survivors, Disability, and Health Insurance System as Modified by the Social Security Amendments of 1967*, House Committee on Ways and Means, 90 Cong. 1 sess. (1967).
a. After the 1956 legislation, workers were allowed to exclude the 5 years of lowest earnings.
b. As a result of 1956 legislation, computation of average monthly earnings for women was based on years up to age 62.
c. The 1960 legislation permitted workers past statutory retirement age to substitute high earnings after this age for earlier years of low earnings.
d. The intent of the 1967 amendments was to move away from the three-part formula toward a two-part formula, but this was not consistent with the objective of raising benefits by a uniform percentage.

Table B-6. *History of Benefits to Dependents and Survivors Provided by Social Security Legislation, 1939–67*

Type of Beneficiary or Payment	Benefits as Percentage of Primary Insurance Amount, by Year of Legislation[a]						
	1939	1950	1956	1960	1961	1965	1967
Dependents of retired and (after 1958) disabled workers							
Wife, aged 65	50	**	b	**	**	**	c
Child, under 18	50	**	**	**	**	**	**
Dependent husband, aged 65	—	50	**	**	b	**	c
Wife, child present	—	50	**	**	**	**	**
Child, disabled before 18	—	—	50	**	**	**	**
Child, 18–21, attending school	—	—	—	—	—	50	**
Wife, divorced after 20 years, aged 65	—	—	—	—	—	50	**
Survivors							
Widow, aged 62[d]	75	**	**	**	82.5	e	f
Widow, divorced after 20 years, aged 62	—	—	—	—	—	82.5e	**
Dependent widower, aged 62[g]	—	75	**	**	82.5	**	f
Dependent parent							
Male, aged 62[h]	50	75	**	**	82.5[i]	**	**
Female, aged 62[d]	50	75	**	**	82.5[i]	**	**
Mother, child present[j]	75	**	**	**	**	**	**
Divorced widow, eligible child	—	75	**	**	**	**	**
Child under 18	50	75, 50k	**	75	**	**	**
Child, disabled before 18	—	—	75, 50k	75	**	**	**
Child, 18–21, attending school	—	—	—	—	—	75	**
Lump-sum death payment	600	300	l	**	**	**	**

Sources: Robert J. Myers, "Old-Age, Survivors, Disability, and Health Insurance Provisions: Legislative History, 1935–65," (leaflet, U.S. Department of Health, Education, and Welfare, Social Security Administration, July 1965); *Summary of Social Security Amendments of 1967*, Joint Publication of Senate Committee on Finance and House Committee on Ways and Means, 90 Cong. 1 sess. (1967), pp. 1–2.
** No change.
a. See footnote a to Table B-4 for definition of primary insurance amount.
b. Eligible for permanently reduced benefit at age 62.
c. Under the 1967 Act, maximum of $105 was introduced for the wife's or dependent husband's benefit.
d. 1939–56, aged 65; after 1956, aged 62.
e. Eligible for permanently reduced benefit at age 60.
f. Benefits can be paid to certain disabled widows and widowers of deceased insured workers between the ages of 50 and 62. If the benefit is first awarded at age 50, it amounts to 50 percent of the primary insurance amount. This percentage increases gradually until it reaches 82.5 percent for persons first receiving benefits at age 62.
g. 1950–61, aged 65; after 1961, aged 62.
h. 1939–61, aged 65; after 1961, aged 62.
i. If there are two parents, then 75 percent each.
j. Widow under 62, except when child is eligible only because of school attendance at ages 18–21.
k. 75 percent for oldest child; 50 percent for others.
l. Under the 1954 Act, maximum of $255 was introduced.

Table B-7. *History of Social Security Legislation on Earnings Test, 1935–67*

Year of Legislation	Earnings Permitted[a]	Deductions in Benefits	Age at Which Restriction Ends
1935	None	Loss of entire benefit for any month in which wages are earned	—
1939	$14.99 a month	Over $14.99, loss of entire month's benefits	—
1950	$50 a month	Over $50, loss of entire month's benefits	75
	Self-employed: $600 a year	One month's benefit withheld for each $50 over $600	75
1952	$75 a month	Over $75, loss of entire month's benefit	75
	Self-employed: $900 a year	One month's benefit withheld for each $75 over $900	75
1954	$1,200 a year	One month's benefit withheld for each $80 over $1,200, but benefits are paid for any month when wages do not exceed $80 and the worker does not engage in substantial self-employment	72
	or $80 in wages a month	Over $80 a month, the annual test applies	
1958	$1,200 a year	One month's benefit withheld for each $80 over $1,200, but benefits are paid for any month when wages do not exceed $100 and the worker does not engage in substantial self-employment	72
	or $100 in wages a month	Over $100 a month, the annual test applies	
1960	$1,200 a year	$1,201–$1,500: $1 reduction for $2 earned. Over $1,500: $1 reduction for $1 earned. Same monthly test as 1958	72
1961	$1,200 a year	$1,201–$1,700: $1 reduction for $2 earned. Over $1,700: $1 reduction for $1 earned. Same monthly test as 1958	72
1965	$1,500 a year	$1,501–$2,700: $1 reduction for $2 earned. Over $2,700: $1 reduction for $1 earned	72
	or $125 in wages a month	For any month when earnings do not exceed $125, benefits will be paid; over $125 a month, the annual test applies	
1967	$1,680 a year	$1,681–$2,880: $1 reduction for $2 earned. Over $2,880: $1 reduction for $1 earned	72
	or $140 in wages a month	For any month when earnings do not exceed $140, benefits will be paid; over $140 a month, the annual test applies	

Sources: Robert J. Myers, *Social Insurance and Allied Government Programs* (R. D. Irwin, 1965), and "Old-Age, Survivors, Disability, and Health Insurance Provisions: Legislative History, 1935–65," (leaflet, U.S. Department of Health, Education, and Welfare, Social Security Administration, July 1965); *Summary of Social Security Amendments of 1967*, Joint Publication of Senate Committee on Finance and House Committee on Ways and Means, 90 Cong. 1 sess. (1967), p. 2.

a. Legislation for 1935–52 refers to covered earnings; legislation for 1954-67 refers to all earnings.

Table B-8. *Tax Rates under Social Security Legislation, 1937–68 (Actual) and 1969–87 Onward (Scheduled)*

(Rates in percentages)

Year	Maximum Taxable Earnings	Employer-Employee Combined Tax Rate				Self-Employed Tax Rate		
		OASI[a]	DI[b]	HI[c]	Total	OASDI[d]	HI[c]	Total
		Actual						
1937–49	$3,000	2	—	—	2	—	—	—
1950	3,000	3	—	—	3	—	—	—
1951–53	3,600	3	—	—	3	2.25	—	2.25
1954	3,600	4	—	—	4	3	—	3
1955–56	4,200	4	—	—	4	3	—	3
1957–58	4,200	4	0.5	—	4.5	3.375	—	3.375
1959	4,800	4.5	0.5	—	5	3.75	—	3.75
1960–61	4,800	5.5	0.5	—	6	4.5	—	4.5
1962	4,800	5.75	0.5	—	6.25	4.7	—	4.7
1963–65	4,800	6.75	0.5	—	7.25	5.4	—	5.4
1966	6,600	7	0.7	0.7	8.4	5.8	0.35	6.15
1967	6,600	7.1	0.7	1.0	8.8	5.9	0.50	6.4
1968	7,800	6.65	0.95	1.2	8.8	5.8	0.6	6.4
		Scheduled						
1969–70	7,800	7.45	0.95	1.2	9.6	6.3	0.6	6.9
1971–72	7,800	8.25	0.95	1.2	10.4	6.9	0.6	7.5
1973–75	7,800	9.05	0.95	1.3	11.3	7.0	0.65	7.65
1976–79	7,800	9.05	0.95	1.4	11.4	7.0	0.7	7.7
1980–86	7,800	9.05	0.95	1.6	11.6	7.0	0.8	7.8
1987 on	7,800	9.05	0.95	1.8	11.8	7.0	0.9	7.9

Source: See Table B-5.
a. Old-age and survivors insurance.
b. Disability insurance.
c. Health insurance.
d. Old-age, survivors, and disability insurance

APPENDIX C

Foreign Social Security Systems*

More than three-fourths of the countries in the world have public programs which provide long-term assistance for old-age or disability and for the survivors of deceased workers. Such programs are found in all European countries, Canada, the United States, Mexico, 19 of the 23 nations of Central and South America, 24 of the 39 African countries, 8 of the 11 Middle East countries, and 11 of the 24 nations in Asia and Oceania.

About 70 of the 93 countries with programs of old-age, disability, and survivor benefits have social insurance systems; the remaining countries have either universal pension or social assistance programs.[1] While most of these 70 countries rely solely on social insurance programs, 5 of

* Prepared by Alicia Munnell. The material in this appendix is based on the comprehensive survey of the world's social security programs prepared by the Social Security Administration. See U.S. Department of Health, Education, and Welfare, Social Security Administration, Office of Research and Statistics, *Social Security Programs Throughout the World, 1967* (1967). For changes that have taken place since the publication of *Social Security Programs Throughout the World, 1967*, see U.S. Department of Health, Education, and Welfare, Social Security Administration, Office of Research and Statistics, Note 1, *Recent Foreign Social Security Developments* (1968).

[1] The three classifications of systems for old-age, disability, and survivor benefits— social insurance, universal pension, and social assistance—take different forms in different countries and are difficult to define with precision, but they provide a useful basis for distinguishing the most common approaches to social security. Social insurance systems are generally considered as compulsory programs financed by contributions of employees and/or employers, and, in some countries, of the government, with benefits linked to past contributions to or coverage under the program. Universal pension systems usually cover all persons, and benefits are determined by demographic factors rather than contributions to the system. They are usually financed by taxes on the employer or the employee, or both, with supplemental contributions by the government. Under social assistance systems, benefits are based on need and are paid from general government funds.

273

them—Canada, Denmark, Finland, Norway, and Sweden—maintain a universal pension plan to provide the basic benefits and use the insurance program for supplementary pensions reflecting the individual's prior earnings. The primary system in Australia, Barbados, Guyana, Saudi Arabia, South Africa, and Trinidad and Tobago is a social assistance program where benefits are paid to any citizen who qualifies under a means or income test.

Most European systems predate the U.S. Social Security Act of 1935 (see Table c-1). The programs in Denmark and Germany date back to the late nineteenth century. Those in New Zealand and Australia also have early beginnings; their first laws were passed in 1898 and 1908, respectively. Most of the countries in North and South America first enacted social security legislation between 1920 and 1945; and the majority of those in Asia started programs in the 1950's. In Africa, most of the emerging countries passed their first public insurance legislation within the last ten years.

In total, almost one-half of the 93 countries have passed their first law since 1950. In addition, extensive changes have been introduced in other countries, so that more than one-half of the social insurance programs now in existence were actually started after 1950.

Coverage

Because of administrative and financial constraints, only partial coverage is characteristic of most countries. Generally, the older the program, the more extensive the coverage. Gradually, as the system matures, the program goes beyond industrial and commercial employees to include farm workers and the self-employed in commerce, agriculture, and the professions.

By definition, a universal pension is extended to everyone within the country, although most nations have a residency requirement and many will not provide pensions to aliens without a reciprocal agreement. Social assistance programs extend potential coverage to all residents, but restrict benefits to those who demonstrate need.

Social insurance coverage varies greatly. The most extensive coverage is in Israel, Japan, the Netherlands, Switzerland, and the United Kingdom. In these countries, virtually all residents are included, since the law explicitly covers the nonemployed as well as all employed and self-employed persons.

Practically all employed and self-employed persons are covered in the United States and about 20 other countries; in addition, benefits are available for some nonemployed. The United States, along with a few other countries, is unusual in that most of its population is covered under one basic system. In most of the countries, however, various groups are covered under separate systems that function simultaneously; for example, France and Italy have separate systems for the self-employed, and Austria, Belgium, the Federal Republic of Germany, and Luxembourg have distinct programs for wage earners and for salaried employees,[2] as well as for the self-employed (see Table c-2).

All but the self-employed are included in the programs in a second large group of nations, while both the self-employed and agricultural workers are excluded in a third group (including Iran, Ireland, Portugal, and Turkey) which limits coverage to industrial and commercial employees.

Certain occupations are generally treated separately (Table c-2). Public employees, for instance, are almost always covered under a special system; probably the reason is that government workers generally have a retirement plan at the time that social insurance legislation is enacted. Seamen, railroad workers, and miners also come under separate programs very frequently. These special systems are almost always more generous both in terms of benefits and in requiring less rigorous qualifying conditions.

Coverage becomes generally more extensive with economic development and growth. In Europe, every country but one includes all employees in industry, commerce, and agriculture, and four-fifths also include at least some self-employed. In the Americas, twelve countries include agricultural workers in addition to industrial and commercial employees. Of the numerous programs in Africa, only twelve include persons in agriculture; and in Asia, only four include agricultural workers. In addition, in both Africa and Asia the programs apply to only a few persons because of the large agricultural population, the small amount of wages paid, the low level of literacy, and the paucity of reliable records.

Benefits

EMPLOYMENT AND RESIDENT REQUIREMENTS

For persons who are covered by a country's social insurance system, there are still certain qualifications to be met before they are eligible

---

[2] As a rule, the provisions for wage earners and salaried employees are more or less identical. The separation of coverage of these groups is usually for historical or political reasons.

Table c-1. *Year of Enactment of First Major Legislation for Old-Age, Disability, and Survivor Insurance Programs, Countries throughout the World*

Before 1900	Hungary, 1928
Europe	Poland, 1927
Denmark, 1891	Union of Soviet
Germany, 1889	Socialist Republics, 1922
New Zealand, 1898	
	1930–39
1900–1909	Central and South America
Australia, 1908	Barbados, 1937
	Ecuador, 1935
Europe	Peru, 1936
Austria, 1906	
Czechoslovakia, 1906	Europe
Iceland, 1909	Finland, 1937
Ireland, 1908	Greece, 1934
United Kingdom, 1908	Norway, 1936
	Portugal, 1933
1910–19	Yugoslavia, 1937
Europe	
France, 1910	United States, 1935
Italy, 1919	
Luxembourg, 1911	*1940–49*
Netherlands, 1913	Africa
Rumania, 1912	Algeria, 1949
Spain, 1919	
Sweden, 1913	Asia
	Japan, 1941
1920–29	Turkey, 1949
Africa	
South Africa, 1928	Central and South America
	Argentina, 1944
Canada, 1927	Costa Rica, 1941
	Dominican Republic, 1947
Central and South America	Guyana, 1944
Brazil, 1923	Panama, 1941
Chile, 1924	Paraguay, 1943
Cuba, 1921	
Uruguay, 1928	Europe
	Albania, 1947
Europe	Switzerland, 1946
Belgium, 1924	
Bulgaria, 1924	Mexico, 1942

Table c-1. *(concluded)*

1950–59	*1960–67*
Africa	Africa
Burundi, 1956	Central African Republic, 1963
Congo (Kinshasa), 1956	Congo (Brazzaville), 1962
Guinea, 1958	Gabon, 1963
Libya, 1957	Ghana, 1965
Morocco, 1959	Ivory Coast, 1960
Rwanda, 1956	Kenya, 1965
United Arab Republic, 1950	Liberia, 1961
Asia	Mali, 1961
Ceylon, 1958	Mauritania, 1965
China (Mainland), 1951	Niger, 1965
China (Taiwan), 1950	Nigeria, 1961
India, 1952	Tanzania, 1964
Iran, 1953	Uganda, 1967
Iraq, 1956	Upper Volta, 1960
Israel, 1953	Zambia, 1965
Malaysia, 1951	Asia
Philippines, 1954	Lebanon, 1963
Singapore, 1953	Saudi Arabia, 1962
Syria, 1959	Vietnam (North), 1961
Central and South America	Central and South America
Bolivia, 1956	Colombia, 1961[a]
Nicaragua, 1955	Haiti, 1965
Trinidad and Tobago, 1951	Jamaica, 1965
Europe	Venezuela, 1966
Cyprus, 1956	
Malta, 1956	

Source: U.S. Department of Health, Education, and Welfare, Social Security Administration, Office of Research and Statistics, *Social Security Programs Throughout the World, 1967* (1967), and Note 1, *Recent Foreign Social Security Developments* (1968).
a. Actual application delayed until 1966, and still under study at end of year.

277

Table c-2. *Workers Covered under Social Insurance Systems, Selected Countries, 1967*[a]

| Country | Workers Covered by Basic Social Insurance System | | Agriculture | | Self-employed | Workers under Separate Systems |
	Employees in industry and commerce	Public employees	Wage and salaried	Self-employed		
Argentina	**	—	—	—	**	Public employees, agricultural workers, railroad workers, seamen, and several other occupations
Austria	**b	—	**	—	—	Public employees, nonagricultural self-employed, agricultural self-employed, miners, and notaries
Belgium	**b	—	**	**	**	Public employees, railway employees, miners, and seamen
Brazil	**	—c	—c	—c	**	Public employees and seamen
Canada	**c	**c	**c	**c	**c	None
Chile	**	—	—	—	**d	Public employees, railroad workers, seamen, and about 30 other occupations
Cyprus	**	**	**	**	**	None
Denmark	**	|—	**	—	|—	Public employees
Ecuador	**	**e	—	—	**	Salaried employees in banking, insurance, and government
Finland	**	—	**	—	—	Public employees, seamen, and seasonal workers
France	**	—	—	—	—	Public employees, agricultural employees, agricultural self-employed, nonagricultural self-employed, railroad workers, miners, seamen, and public utility employees
Germany, Federal Republic	**bf	—	—	—	—	Public employees, self-employed artisans, self-employed farmers, and miners
Greece	**	—	—	—	**g	Public employees and workers in agriculture
Iran	**	—	—	—	—	Public employees
Ireland	**h	—	—	—	—	Public employees
Israel[i]	**	—	**	**	**	Public employees
Italy	**	—	**	—	—	Public employees, self-employed farmers, self-employed artisans, railway workers, industrial managers, journalists, seamen, and members of liberal professions

278

Country					Groups covered under special or separate systems
Luxembourg	**b	—	—	**	Public employees, self-employed artisans, self-employed merchants, self-employed farmers, railroad employees, miners, and members of liberal professions
Mexico	**	**	**	**	Public employees, petroleum workers, and railroad employees
Netherlands[i]	**	—	**	**	Public employees
Norway[k]	**	—	**	**	Public employees, railway workers, seamen, fishermen, and forestry workers
Panama	**	**	**	**	None
Paraguay	**	—	**	**	Public employees, railroad workers, and bank employees
Peru	**b	**l	**	**b	None
Portugal	**	—	—	**	Public employees, railway employees, fishermen, and employees in liberal professions
Spain	**	—	—	**	Public employees, agricultural employees and small farmers, domestic servants, and seamen
Sweden	**c	**	**c	**c	Public employees
Switzerland[i]	**	**	**	—	None
Turkey	**	—	—	**	Public employees, railroad workers, and miners
Union of Soviet Socialist Republics	**	—	—	**	Members of collective farms
United Kingdom[i]	**m	**	**	**	None
United States	**	**	**	—	Public employees and railroad workers
Uruguay	**	—	**	**	Public employees, teachers, rural workers, domestic servants, bank employees, notaries, and members of liberal professions

279

Source: U.S. Department of Health, Education, and Welfare, Social Security Administration, Office of Research and Statistics, *Social Security Programs Throughout the World, 1967* (1967).

** Indicates group covered.

a. For explanation of social insurance system and other social security programs, see page 273, footnote 1. See Tables c-3, c-4, and c-5 for coverage, residency, citizenship, and financial requirements for these programs.   b. Separate systems for wage earners and salaried employees.   c. Low-income workers are excluded.   d. Only the self-employed in urban areas whose annual income is not above Santiago minimum wage.   e. Manual government workers are under the main program, salaried government employees fall under a separate system.   f. Salaried employees earning over $5,400 a year are excluded.   g. Certain self-employed workers in urban areas.   h. Nonmanual workers earning over $3,360 a year are excluded.   i. All residents are covered.   j. The welfare pension and the national pension programs together include all adult citizens.   k. All employees and self-employed persons earning over "base amount" and born after 1898.   l. The only agricultural workers covered are tenants on cotton and rice farms.   m. Coverage optional for married women, and for self-employed and nonemployed persons whose income is below $728 a year.

for benefits. Most of the social insurance programs impose a minimum period of coverage (Table c-3), which can vary from as few as three years (for example, Norway, Sweden, and the United Kingdom) to as many as forty-five years (Belgium). However, reduced pensions often are available to persons who have not completed the full qualifying period. Also, as in the United States, there are alternative methods of attaining insured status for newly covered workers.

The qualifications under universal pension plans are much less rigorous (Table c-4). There is a residency requirement which varies from one year in Denmark to ten years in Canada and New Zealand. Denmark, Iceland, and Sweden also require citizenship.

The social assistance systems in Australia, Finland, New Zealand, and South Africa require a minimum period of residency and, in addition, either a means or an income test (Table c-5).

AGE

In addition to employment and residency requirements, there are age requirements for pensions. Most pensions are awarded at age 60 or 65; however, the requirement varies from age 50 to age 70 (Table c-6). About half of the countries have the same retirement age for men as for women; the others allow women to retire (usually five years) earlier. Awards are often permitted before normal retirement age if (1) a worker is willing to accept a permanently reduced benefit; (2) he has been employed in dangerous or arduous labor; (3) he is involuntarily unemployed just prior to his pensionable age; (4) he has been covered for a very long period, such as 35 years.

OTHER QUALIFYING CONDITIONS

Countries with a universal pension program require only an age test to qualify. The social assistance programs always require either an income or, more often, a means test.

Under the social insurance systems, the most common requirement for a pension is substantial retirement by the beneficiary (Table c-6). In Canada, Israel, Nicaragua, the Philippines, the United Kingdom, and the United States the retirement requirement is waived after the pensioner reaches a certain age. Several countries (for example, France, the Federal Republic of Germany, Ireland, Italy, Luxembourg, the Netherlands, Norway, Sweden, and Switzerland) allow the pensioner to continue in full-time employment at his present job and at the same time receive his pension.

SIZE OF BENEFIT

Pensions can be of two types: (1) a benefit dependent on previous earnings and period of coverage and (2) a flat amount awarded to all qualifying persons.

Generally, pensions are directly related to an individual's earnings record and are calculated on the basis of an average of recent earnings. This method prevents pensions from depending on earnings in an atypical year or in years long before retirement when average earnings may have been relatively low. Countries that use lifetime earnings or an average over a long period usually try to make some adjustment, such as revaluing earlier wages or omitting years of low earnings, to take into account the upward trend in wages. The programs in Austria, Belgium, Canada, France, the Federal Republic of Germany, Norway, Sweden, Switzerland, and Turkey all have a provision for the automatic revaluation of recorded prior wages (Table C-7).

Flat pensions, where the size of the benefit does not vary with earnings, are paid in almost all countries with a universal pension plan. They are also typical of areas formerly or currently under British influence (such as Cyprus, Ireland, and Israel) as well as of the United Kingdom itself.

Benefits for dependents are usually set as a percentage of the worker's benefit; the percentage may be as much as 50 percent or more for a wife or dependent husband. Survivor benefits are generally expressed as a fraction of the pension which was or would have been paid to the deceased; under almost all programs, a widow receives between 50 and 75 percent of her spouse's pension. Some plans also pay pensions to dependent widowers, and many include benefits for orphans.

FINANCING

For the most part, the existing social insurance programs are compulsory contributory programs. They are usually financed by extra budgetary funds raised from special taxes and set aside in special funds separate from other accounts (Table C-8).

The most common form of financing is the tripartite arrangement where contributions come from employees, employers, and the government.[3] Next are programs where the government does not partici-

---

[3] Although the law calls for the government to contribute, it does not comply in many countries, particularly those in Latin America.

pate. In a few countries, the social insurance tax is paid exclusively by the employer.

In the tripartite financing program, the insured person usually pays a certain percentage of earnings which is generally matched by the employer, who is taxed a certain percentage of his payroll. Often there is a maximum amount of earnings on which an individual can be taxed. The government can participate in the program in a number of ways. It can (1) match a portion of the combined employee-employer contribution, in which case its contribution would be expressed as a percentage of covered earnings, (2) pay a fixed percentage of benefit expenditures, (3) contribute a lump-sum amount annually, or (4) be committed to financing any deficit caused by an excess of outgo over income.

In Argentina, Canada, France, Iran, Peru, Portugal, Turkey, and the United States, contributions from the workers and their employers finance all the benefits. In Finland and Sweden, benefits are financed entirely by the employer.

A few nations (Cyprus, Denmark, Ireland, Japan, and the United Kingdom) levy a flat tax in terms of a fixed monetary amount that varies primarily with the age and sex of the insured person, but remains constant for all levels of earnings.

The financing of the universal pension plans is primarily by means of general revenues, frequently augmented by contributions from the personal income tax (Table c-9).

The assistance programs in Australia, Finland, and South Africa are financed almost entirely from government general revenues. In New Zealand, receipts from personal income and corporation income taxes finance most of the programs (Table c-10).

Table c-3. *Years of Coverage Required for Full Old-Age Benefits under Social Insurance Systems, Selected Countries, 1967*[a]

Country	Years of Coverage Required[b]
Argentina	5[c]
Austria	15 (1 within last 3)
Belgium	[d]
Brazil	5
Canada	None
Chile: Wage earners—men	15
women	10
Salaried employees—men	35
women	20
Cyprus	3
Denmark	5
Ecuador	25[e]
Finland	None
France	30
Germany, Federal Republic	15
Greece	16 plus 225 days each year after 1961
Iran	10
Ireland	3
Israel	5
Italy	15
Japan: Welfare pension	20
National pension	10–25
Luxembourg: Wage earners	10
Salaried employees	5
Mexico	10
Netherlands	Every year, age 15–64
Norway	3
Panama	15
Paraguay	15
Peru: Wage earners	20
Salaried employees	15
Portugal	5
Spain	3 in last 7
Sweden	3
Switzerland	Every year since 1948 (or age 21)
Turkey	14
United Kingdom	3
United States	10

Sources: U.S. Department of Health, Education, and Welfare, Social Security Administration, Office of Research and Statistics, *Social Security Programs Throughout the World, 1967* (1967), and Social Security Administration, unpublished data.

a. For explanation of social insurance system, see page 273, footnote 1.

b. Whenever requirements were given in days, weeks, months, or quarters, they were translated into years (rounded to the nearest whole year) for purposes of comparability.

c. For full pension, there is a requirement of 30 years for men and of 27 years for women.

d. Requirement is stated in terms of years of employment. For full old-age benefits, the worker must have been employed in every year since 1926 or for a total of 45 years for men and 40 years for women.

e. Twenty-five years required for retirement at age 60; 30 years at age 55; 15 years at age 65; 10 years at age 70; 35 years for retirement at any age.

Table c-4. *Residence and Citizenship Requirements for Old-Age Benefits under Universal Pension Systems, Countries with Such Systems, 1967*[a]

Country	Years of Residency	Citizenship
Canada	Last 10, or 40 adult years	No
Denmark	Last 1	Yes
Finland	5	No
Iceland	Last 5, or 10 years since age 16	Yes[b]
New Zealand	Last 10[c]	No
Norway	Last 5[d]	No
Sweden	Last 5	Yes[b]

Source: See Table c-3.
a. For explanation of universal pension system, see page 273, footnote 1.
b. Unless there is a reciprocity agreement with the worker's country of nationality.
c. Twenty years required if the worker was a nonresident in 1938.
d. Aliens must have 15 years after age 20.

Table c-5. *Residence, Citizenship, and Financial Requirements for Old-Age Benefits under Social Assistance Systems, Selected Countries, 1967*[a]

Country	Years of Residency	Citizenship	Financial Status
Australia	10 (continuous)	No	Limited means
Finland	5 (continuous)	No	Limited means
New Zealand	Last 10[b]	No	Limited income
South Africa	5 out of last 10[c]	No	Limited means

Source: See Table c-2.
a. For explanation of social assistance system, see page 273, footnote 1
b. Twenty years required if the worker was a nonresident in 1938.
c. Aliens must have 25 years out of the last 30.

Table c-6. *Age Requirements and Other Qualifying Conditions for Full Old-Age Benefits, Selected Countries, 1967*

| Country | Age | | Other Qualifying Conditions |
	Men	Women	
Argentina	55[a]	50[a]	Complete retirement
Australia	65	60	Means
Austria	65	60	Substantial retirement
Belgium	65[a]	60[a]	Substantial retirement
Canada			
Universal pension	68[b]	68[b]	None
Insurance pension	68[b]	68[b]	Substantial retirement[e]
Chile			
Wage earner	65	55	None
Salaried employee	65[d]	55[d]	Complete retirement
Cyprus	65	65	None
Denmark			
Universal pension	67	62	Income
Insurance pension	67	67	None
Ecuador	55	55	Substantial retirement
Finland			
Universal pension	65	65	None
Assistance pension	65	65	Means
Employer pension	65	65	Retirement (from insured employment)
France	60	60	None
Germany, Federal Republic	65[e]	65[e]	None
Greece	62	57	Substantial retirement
Iceland	67	67	None
Iran	60	55	Retirement (from insured employment)
Ireland	70	70	None
Israel	65	60	Substantial retirement[f]
Italy	60	55	None
Japan			
Welfare pension	60	55	None[g]
National pension	65	65	Income
Luxembourg	65[h]	65[h]	None

Table C-6. *(concluded)*

Country	Age Men	Age Women	Other Qualifying Conditions
Mexico	65	65	Retirement (from insured employment)[i]
Netherlands	65	65	None
New Zealand			
Universal pension	65	65	None
Assistance pension	60	60	Income
Norway			
Universal pension	70	70	None
Supplementary pension	70	70	None
Panama	60	55	None
Paraguay	60	60	None
Peru			
Wage earner	60	60	Partial retirement
Salaried employee	60	55	Complete retirement
Portugal	65	65	Retirement (from insured employment)[e]
South Africa	65	60	Means
Spain	65	65	Complete retirement
Sweden			
Universal pension	67[a]	67[a]	None
Supplementary pension	67[a]	67[a]	None
Switzerland	65	62	None
Turkey	60	55	Retirement (from insured employment)
United Kingdom	65	60	Retirement[f]
United States	65[a]	65[a]	Substantial retirement[j]
Uruguay	50	50	Retirement (from insured employment)

Source: See Table C-2.
a. Reduced pensions available at earlier age.
b. The age requirement will be gradually reduced to 65 years in 1970 and thereafter.
c. Earnings test eliminated after age 70.
d. Or after 35 years of contribution for men and 30 years for women.
e. Payable at age 60 if unemployed 1 year, or if woman with 10 years of employment in last 20 years.
f. Test eliminated after age 70 for men and age 65 for women.
g. Pension reduced by 20 percent if there is no retirement.
h. Earlier retirement permitted with more years of contribution.
i. Retirement not necessary if pension plus earnings is below prior earnings.
j. Earnings test eliminated after age 72.

Table c-7. *Bases for Calculation of Old-Age Benefits, Selected Countries, 1967*

Country	Basis of Calculation	Revaluation of Recorded Prior Wages	Benefits Adjusted to Price Changes
	Social Insurance Pensions		
Argentina	Average earnings last 12 months	–	–
Austria	Average earnings last 5 years (or during ages 45–50)	*	–
Belgium	Average lifetime earnings	*	*
Brazil	Average earnings last 12 months; additional 1 percent of earnings for each year of contribution	–	–
Canada	Average earnings since 1966	*	*
Chile	Average earnings last 5 years	–	*
Cyprus	Flat pension ($5 a week)[a]	–	–
Denmark	Years of contribution	–	*
Ecuador	Average earnings highest 5 years; additional 1.25 percent of earnings for each year of contribution beyond 5	–	*
Finland	Earnings last 2 years; length of coverage	–	*
France	Average earnings last 10 years	*	*
Germany, Federal Republic	"Assessed wages"; years of contribution	*	–
Greece	Average earnings last 2 years; additiona 1 to 2.5 percent of pension for each 300 days of contribution beyond 3,000 days	–	–
Iran	Average earnings last 2 years; years of contribution	–	–
Ireland	Flat pension ($8 a week)[a]	–	–
Israel	Flat pension ($22 a month)[a]	–	*
Italy	Lifetime contributions	–	–
Japan			
Welfare pension	Average lifetime earnings; years of coverage	–	–
National pension	Years of contribution	–	–
Luxembourg	Flat pension ($37 a month)[a]; increments based on lifetime insured earnings	–	*
Mexico	Average earnings last 250 weeks; additional 1 percent of earnings for each year of contribution beyond 500 weeks, and additional increment of 2 percent of earnings for each year of work after age 65	–	–
Netherlands	Flat pension ($67 a month)[a]	–	*
Norway	Average earnings; years of contribution	*	*
Panama	Average earnings last 10 or 15 years;[b] additional 1 percent of earnings for each year of contribution beyond 120 months	–	–
Paraguay	Average earnings last 3 years; additional 1 percent of pension for each 50 weeks of contribution beyond 780 weeks	–	–
Peru			
Wage earners	Last year's earnings; years of contribution	–	–
Salaried employees	Average earnings in last 3 or 5 years; years of contribution beyond 60 months	–	–

Table C-7. *(concluded)*

Country	Basis of Calculation	Revaluation of Recorded Prior Wages	Benefits Adjusted to Price Changes
Social Insurance Pensions (concluded)			
Portugal	Average lifetime earnings; additional 2 percent of earnings for each year of contribution beyond 10 years	–	–
Spain	Legal wage for each occupation	–	–
Sweden	Average earnings; years of coverage	*	*
Switzerland	Flat pension ($234 a year)[a] plus increments according to average annual contribution	*	–
Turkey	Average earnings highest 7 of last 10 years; additional 1 percent of pension for each year of insurance beyond age 60	*	–
United Kingdom	Flat pension ($11 a week)[a] pius graduated pension based on total contributions	–	–
United States	Average earnings after 1950 (excluding 5 years of lowest earnings)	–	–
Uruguay	Average earnings last 5 years	–	*
Universal Pensions			
Canada	Flat pension ($69 a month)[a]	–	*
Denmark	Flat pension ($16 a month)[a]	–	*
Finland	Flat pension ($18 a month)[a]	–	*
Iceland	Flat pension ($53 a month)[a]	–	*
New Zealand	Flat pension ($70 a month)[a]	–	–
Norway	Flat pension ($63 a month)[a]	–	*
Sweden	Flat pension ($81 a month)[a]	–	*
Social Assistance Pensions			
Australia	Amount determined by means test	–	–
Denmark	Amount determined by income test	–	*
Finland	Amount determined by means test	–	*
New Zealand	Amount determined by income test	–	–
South Africa	Amount determined by means test	–	–

Source: See Table C-2.

* Indicates country revalues wages in accordance with overall growth of wages or adjusts benefits to price changes, or both.

a. Dollar amounts are based on exchange rates in effect in 1967. The figures, which appear quite small when compared with benefits in the United States, may give a false impression of the significance of the programs. For a more meaningful comparison of relative benefit levels for selected countries, see Table III-4, p. 51.

b. Whichever is more favorable.

Table C-8. *Financing Social Insurance Systems, Selected Countries, 1967*

Country	Employee	Employer	Self-Employed	Government Contribution	Maximum Monthly Taxable Earnings (U.S. Dollars)[a]
	Taxes on Wages and Salaries (in percent)				
Argentina	11[b]	15[b]	11[b]	None	None
Austria	8-8.25[c]	8-8.25[c]	8	26.5 percent of total expenditures of system	239
Belgium	4.25-5.5[d]	6-7[d]	4.25	Annual lump-sum subsidies	192
Brazil[e]	8	8	8	8 percent of covered earnings plus 5 percent of corporate income tax yield	5 times highest minimum wage
Canada	1.8	1.8	3.6	None	4,625 a year
Chile[e]	6-7.5[f]	7.5-12.5[f]	10	Subsidies toward automatic adjustments	None
Ecuador[e]	5	7	5	40 percent of cost of pensions	450
Finland	None	5	Not covered	None	—
France[e]	6	15	6	None	219
Germany, Federal Republic	7	7[g]	7	Annual subsidy of 20-33⅓ percent of cost of system	350
Greece	2.25	5.75	2.25	Excess of cost over revenue	173
Iran[h]	5	13	Not covered	None	325
Israel[i]	1.4	2.3	3.7 of income	0.37 percent of covered earnings and 100 percent of income-test supplements	183
Italy	6	9.65	6	About 45 percent of cost of system	None
Japan (welfare pension)					
Men	2.75	2.75	Not covered	20 percent of benefit costs	168
Women	1.95	1.95	Not covered	20 percent of benefit costs	168
Minors	3.35	3.35	Not covered	25 percent of benefit costs	168
Luxembourg	6	6	6	100 percent of basic pensions, 50 percent of administrative costs, and any deficit	428

Country			Special rates		
Mexico	1.5	3.75		20 percent of employer contribution	6.40 a day
Netherlands[j]	10.2[k]	None	Special rates 10.2	100 percent of contribution of exempted poor and excess of cost of system over revenue	293
Norway	4	7	5.4	1.3 percent of taxable earnings	504
Panama[e]	5	7	Not covered	1.1 percent of covered earnings	None
Paraguay[h]	6	13	Not covered	1.5 percent of earnings	None
Peru	2[l]	2	Not covered	None	None
Portugal[e]	5.5	8	Not covered	None	140
Spain[e]	3.9[m]	12.1	Not covered	Subsidy	95
Sweden	None	8.5[n]	8.5	None	811 a year
Switzerland	2.2	2.2	4.4 of income[o]	Annual subsidies about 25 percent of cost of system	None
Turkey	5	6	Not covered	None	11.10 a day
United States	3.9	3.9	5.9	None	6,600 a year
Uruguay	12–18[p]	24	12–18[p]	Allocations from various taxes, but not paid regularly in the past	None

Flat Rate Taxes (in U.S. dollars; weekly rates unless otherwise noted)

Country			Special rates		
Cyprus[q]					
Men	0.34	0.34	0.45	0.34 an employee, 0.22 self-employed	—
Women	0.17	0.17	0.22	0.17 an employee, 0.11 self-employed	—
Denmark					
Supplementary	0.26	0.52	Not covered	None	—
Invalid (annual rate)	None	2.07	Not covered	None	—
Ireland[r]					
Industrial workers					
Male	1.03	1.03	Not covered	{Excess of cost over revenues (about 33⅓	—
Female	0.88	0.98	Not covered	{ percent)	
Agricultural workers					
Male	0.71	0.71	Not covered	{Excess of cost over revenues (about 33⅓	—
Female	0.55	0.68	Not covered	{ percent)	

291

Table c-8. *(concluded)*

Country	Employee	Employer	Self-Employed	Government Contribution	Maximum Monthly Taxable Earnings (U.S. Dollars)[a]
	Flat Rate Taxes, concluded (in U.S. dollars; weekly rates unless otherwise noted)				
Japan (national pension)					
Age 20–34[s] (monthly rate)	0.56	None	0.56	Subsidy equal to 50 percent of contributions	—
Age 35–59[s] (monthly rate)	0.70	None	0.70	100 percent cost of assistance	—
United Kingdom[r,t]					
Male	1.43[u]	1.60	2.22	Amount equal to 25 percent of flat contributions (33⅓ percent for self- and nonemployed); lump-sum subsidy; 100 percent of cost of income-test pension	50.40 a week[t]
Female	1.24	1.39	1.84		50.40 a week[t]

Source: See Table c-2.

a. Dollar amounts are based on exchange rates in effect in 1967. The figures, which appear quite small when compared with benefits in the United States, may give a false impression of the significance of the programs.

b. These rates apply to industry and commerce. Taxes for other occupations vary from 5 to 12 percent for the insured person and from 3.5 to 16 percent for the employer.

c. Employees and employers pay 8.25 percent on wages and 8 percent on salaries.

d. Employees pay 5.5 percent on wages and 4.25 percent on salaries, and employers pay 7 percent on wages and 6 percent on salaries.

e. Contributions also finance sickness and maternity benefits, and, for Spain, unemployment benefits and family allowances.

f. Employees pay 6 percent on wages and 7.5 percent on salaries. Employers pay 7.5 percent on salaries and 12.5 percent on wages.

g. Employer pays the tax for any employee whose earnings are below 10 percent of ceiling.

h. Contributions also finance sickness, maternity, and work-injury benefits.

i. Nonemployed persons also contribute 3.7 percent of their income.

j. Contributions also finance work-injury pensions.

k. Nonemployed persons also contribute 10.2 percent of their income.

l. Salaried employees contribute 1 percent of their salaries.

m. Of legal wage for particular occupation.

n. Applies only to wages between $108 and $811.

o. This tax is also paid by the nonemployed.

p. According to level of earnings, sex, and age when first covered.

q. Contributions also finance sickness, maternity, work-injury, and unemployment benefits.

r. Contributions also finance sickness, maternity, and unemployment benefits.

s. This tax is paid by the nonemployed as well as employees, although low-income persons are exempted.

t. In addition to the flat rate tax, there is a 4.25 percent tax for employers and employees on weekly wages between $25.20 and $50.40.

u. Nonemployed men pay $1.69 a week; nonemployed women, $1.32 a week.

Table c-9. *Financing Universal Pension Systems, Countries with Such Systems, 1967*

Country	Taxes on Income and Wages — Insured person	Taxes on Income and Wages — Employer	Government Contribution	Maximum Taxable Earnings (U.S. Dollars)[a]
Canada	4 percent of taxable income	3 percent of income subject to corporate income tax	Yield of 3 percent manufacturers' sales tax	2,775 a year
Denmark	3 percent of taxable income[b]	None	About 83 percent of cost	None
Finland	1.5 percent of taxable income	1.5 percent of payroll	None	None
Iceland[c]	$60–89 a year[d]	$0.64 an employee a week	54 percent of cost	—
New Zealand[e]	7.5 percent of gross income	7.5 percent of net corporate income	Excess of cost over revenues (about $33\frac{1}{3}$ percent)	None
Norway[f]	4 percent of wages and salaries	7 percent of payroll	1.3 percent of taxable earnings	504 a month
Sweden	4 percent of taxable income	None	70 percent of cost	5,790 a year

Source: See Table c-2.
a. Dollar amounts are based on exchange rates in effect in 1967. The figures, which appear quite small when compared with benefits in the United States, may give a false impression of the significance of the programs.
b. Low-income persons exempted from tax.
c. Contributions also finance maternity benefits.
d. Depending on marital status and sex. Payable by all residents aged 16–66, except married women.
e. Contributions also finance the social assistance program in addition to sickness, maternity, and unemployment benefits and family allowances.
f. This contribution also finances the social insurance system.

Table c-10. *Financing Social Assistance Systems, Selected Countries, 1967*

Country	Taxes on Payrolls and Income — Insured person	Taxes on Payrolls and Income — Employer	Government Contribution	Maximum Taxable Earnings
Australia	None	None	100 percent	—
Finland	1.5 percent of taxable income[a]	1.5 percent of payroll[a]	85 percent	None
New Zealand[b]	7.5 percent of gross income	7.5 percent of net corporate income	Excess of cost over revenues (about $33\frac{1}{3}$ percent)	None
South Africa	None	None	100 percent	—

Source: See Table c-2.
a. The major share of the proceeds of these taxes goes toward financing the universal pension.
b. These contributions also finance the universal pension in addition to sickness, maternity, and unemployment benefits and family allowances.

APPENDIX D

International Comparisons

This appendix presents details on two sets of international comparisons referred to in the text: (1) the determinants of social security expenditures (Chapter III); and (2) social security and labor force participation (Chapter VI).

Determinants of Social Security Expenditures

The fact that social security programs have sprung up on roughly similar lines in every advanced industrial country suggests that similar forces may be operating which make enactment of social security attractive. A previous study by Aaron,[1] based on 1957 data, found evidence consistent with the following hypotheses:

1. The age of a social security program is a major factor determining the size and adequacy of social security outlays. The age of the program reflects in part attitudes and circumstances which led to early enactment of social security and in part the rising costs of pension programs as coverage is extended and deepened. Particularly in the case of old-age benefits, many years had to elapse under most systems before workers were entitled to full benefits.

2. Social security outlays are larger in wealthy than in poor countries, but the response of these outlays to higher income is less than proportionate.

3. The greater the amount of social security costs met through

[1] Henry J. Aaron, "Social Security: International Comparisons," in Otto Eckstein (ed.), *Studies in the Economics of Income Maintenance* (Brookings Institution, 1967), pp. 13–48.

general revenues, the smaller are outlays as a fraction of national income. The use of earmarked taxes may insulate social security from competition with other national outlays.

4. Social security outlays and household saving rates are negatively correlated. Whether public saving reduces the need for private saving or a strong tradition of private saving reduces the need for public saving was not clear.

5. The adequacy of old-age benefits is inversely related to the proportion of the total population over retirement age. In countries with a relatively large aged population, one reaction apparently has been to reduce benefits per aged person in comparison with per capita income.

6. Total expenditures on social security and the adequacy of benefits tend to be greater in countries where the government is generally active, as indicated by expenditures for other purposes than social security.

These hypotheses were re-examined in the light of 1960 data. Each hypothesis, except the fourth, received added support, although support for the third was considerably less robust than that based on the earlier data.

Each additional decade under social security is associated with roughly a 2.5 point increase in the ratio of all social security expenditures to national income (Tables D-1 and D-2); with about a 1.6 point increase in the ratio of benefits for the aged to national income (Equations 3-14 and 3-15 in Table D-3); and with about 0.13 point in the ratio of aged benefits per capita to national income per capita (Table D-4, Equations 4-5 and 4-6). The greater the proportion of the total population that is aged, the larger are total benefits for the aged as a fraction of national income, but this variable is highly correlated with the age of the system, D_s, and its coefficient loses significance in regressions when D_s is an independent variable.[2] The adequacy of benefits for the aged, however, is lower in those countries where the proportion of the total population over retirement age is relatively high. Each increase of one percentage point in this proportion is associated with a decline of about 3.5 points in the ratio of per capita aged benefits to per capita national income (Equations 4-3 through 4-6). Each percentage point difference in the proportion of national income spent on programs other than social security is associated directly with a difference of about 0.32–0.40 point in social security outlays as a percentage of national income

[2] For a list of variables and their abbreviations, see page 298.

(Equations 1-6 and 1-8), 0.15–0.20 point in outlays for the aged as a percentage of national income (Equations 3-12 through 3-15), and 2.59–2.84 points in the ratio of aged benefits per capita to national income per capita (Equations 4-3 to 4-6).

Added support for the first and second hypotheses is gained by examining the impact of the age of the system and of per capita national income on the dollar level of per capita total social security expenditures. When both independent variables are included in the equation, each additional decade in the age of the system is associated with about a $24 increase, and each additional $100 of per capita national income results in approximately a $10 gain in per capita social security expenditures (Table D-5, Equation 5-3).

The fourth hypothesis, that savings rates and social security outlays are negatively correlated, is not supported by these regressions. The null hypothesis—that they are unrelated—cannot be rejected since the t values in Equations 1-2, 1-7, 2-2, 2-7, 2-9, 3-6, 3-10, and 3-15 are all insignificant, although in each case the coefficient is negative.

The third hypothesis, that general revenue financing (E_t) is associated with lower social security outlays, has received more attention than any of the other statistical findings of the earlier study because of the obvious relevance of that hypothesis to social security policy in the United States. In the results reported here, the coefficient of E_t is negative and significant in regressions in which old-age benefits as a fraction of national income is the dependent variable; but the coefficient is insignificant when all social security expenditures as a fraction of national income is the dependent variable. This result suggests that the use of general revenue financing for social security does not affect the level of *total* social security outlays but tends to result in a different composition of outlays, with relatively more spent on such other social welfare programs as family allowances and health benefits and relatively less on the aged.

Other results are roughly consistent with findings from the earlier Aaron study, and readers seeking a more detailed discussion are directed to that source.

Social Security and Labor Force Participation

In Chapter VI, evidence was presented to support the hypothesis that an increase in social security retirement benefits causes the aged to reduce their work effort. One piece of evidence comes from the multivariate regression analysis of data from 19 countries;[3] these data, except as noted below, are for the year 1960. The dependent variable used to measure work effort is labor force participation of (a) the total population over age 65 and (b) the male population over age 65. Independent variables are per capita income, the population over the social security retirement age as a percentage of the total population, and average social security old-age benefits as a percentage of average earnings in manufacturing.

The following hypotheses were tested in the regressions presented in Table D-6:

1. Other things equal, a higher level of per capita income causes the aged to reduce their work effort, on the ground that leisure is not an inferior good for most aged persons.

2. Other things equal, a higher percentage of the total population over the social security retirement age is associated with less work effort by the aged, on the ground that the retirement age defines the group that a particular society considers too old to be in the labor force. That is, it is expected that a low retirement age—say, 60—would generally be associated with a large percentage of the population over the retirement age; in such a country, the labor force participation of persons over age 65 is expected to be lower than in a country with a higher retirement age.

3. Other things equal, a higher level of retirement benefits relative to earnings causes the aged to reduce work effort on the ground that the difference between earnings and benefits is the opportunity cost of retirement.

The regression results (Table D-6) are consistent with these hypotheses. All slope coefficients are negative, as expected, and statistically significant. Labor force participation of both the total aged population and the male aged population appears to be inversely related to the relative level of retirement benefits, but the results are stronger for males alone than for both males and females together.[4]

[3] These countries are Australia, Austria, Belgium, Canada, Denmark, Finland, France, Federal Republic of Germany, Iceland, Japan, Netherlands, New Zealand, Norway, Portugal, Spain, Sweden, Switzerland, United Kingdom, and United States.

[4] The reader is cautioned that the sample is small and proper measurement of the variables in a regression across countries is very difficult; therefore, care must be taken in interpreting the results.

Description of Variables

In the following list, numbers in parentheses refer to sources listed on page 299.

TABLES D-1 THROUGH D-5

A_b	= Average old-age benefits as a percentage of national income per capita; $A_b = A_y/P_r$
A_y	= Percentage of national income spent on payments to the aged in 1960 (1) (3)
D_a	= Dummy variable indicating the number of years since old-age insurance was introduced (4)
D_s	= Dummy variable indicating the number of years since the first social security program was introduced (4)
D_w	= Dummy variable indicating participation in past wars
E_p	= Social security expenditures per capita in 1960, measured in U.S. dollars at the current exchange rate (1)
E_t	= Expenditures on social security out of general revenues as a percentage of national income (1) (3)
E_y	= Social security expenditures as a percentage of national income in 1960 (1) (3)
G_y	= Government expenditures other than welfare as a percentage of national income in 1960 (1) (3)
L	= Male life expectancy at birth (5)
N_y	= Social security expenditures net of benefits to war victims as a percentage of national income; $N_y = E_y - W_y$
P_r	= Percentage of total population over retirement age (4) (5)
P_r*	= Percentage of total population over age 65 (5)
S	= Household saving as a percentage of personal expenditures plus savings (3)
W_y	= Percentage of national income spent on payments to war victims (1) (3)
y	= Rate of growth of gross national product, 1955–60 (3)
Y_p	= National income per capita in 1960 (3) (5)

TABLE D-6

P_r	= Percentage of total population over retirement age in 1960 (1961 when only that year was available) (4) (5)
Y_p	= Per capita national income in U.S. dollars for 1960 (5) (6) (Entered into regressions as index with Norway = 100)
B	= Old-age benefits in U.S. dollars divided by the population over retirement age (1) (5) (6)
W	= Average annual wages in manufacturing in 1960 (1963 for Spain) in U.S. dollars (2)
B/W	= Ratio of per capita benefits to wages
$LFP(T65+)$	= Percentage of total population over age 65 classified as "economically active" in 1960 or 1961 (1962 for France) (2)
$LFP(M65+)$	= Percentage of male population over age 65 classified as "economically active" in 1960 or 1961 (1962 for France) (2)

APPENDIX D   299

Sources

1. International Labour Office, *The Cost of Social Security, 1958–1960* (1964).
2. International Labour Office, *Year Book of Labour Statistics, 1966* (1967).
3. United Nations, Department of Economic and Social Affairs, Statistical Office, *Yearbook of National Accounts Statistics, 1965* (1966).
4. U.S. Department of Health, Education, and Welfare, Social Security Administration, Office of Research and Statistics, *Social Security Programs Throughout the World, 1967* (1967).
5. United Nations, Department of Economic and Social Affairs, Statistical Office, *Demographic Yearbook*, annual issues, 1961–65.
6. United Nations, *Statistical Yearbook, 1965* (1966).

Table D-1. *Determinants of Social Security Expenditures as a Percentage of National Income (E_y), Regression Results, 1960*[a]

Equation	Constant Term	Age of System D_s	Household Saving S	General Revenue Financing E_t	Other Government Expenditures G_y	Percentage of Population over 65 P_r^*	Past Wars D_w	Coefficients of Determination R^2	$\bar{R}^2$
I-1	−.00855	.00248‡ (5.4479)						.6341‡	.5911‡
I-2	−.00604	.00251‡ (5.2101)	−.04273 (.2930)					.6361‡	.5678‡
I-3	−.00922	.00256‡ (5.0235)		−.08026 (.3989)				.6377‡	.5698‡
I-4	−.02747	.00244‡ (6.5214)					.00238‡ (3.0770)	.7701‡	.7270‡
I-5	−.01524					1.41033‡ (4.3596)		.5279‡	.4723‡
I-6	−.08045	.00263‡ (7.3812)			.42196‡ (3.5065)			.7931‡	.7543‡
I-7	−.02192	.00252‡ (6.5575)	−.11384 (.9626)				.00253‡ (3.1962)	.7835‡	.7258‡
I-8	−.07814	.00257‡ (8.3186)			.32848‡ (2.9857)		.00172† (2.5543)	.8558‡	.8174‡

a. Figures in parentheses are t values.
† Indicates statistical significance at the 95 percent level.
‡ Indicates statistical significance at the 99 percent level.

Table D-2. *Determinants of Social Security Expenditures Net of Benefits to War Victims as a Percentage of National Income* (N_y), *Regression Results, 1960*[a]

Equation	Constant Term	Age of System D_s	Household Saving S	General Revenue Financing E_t	Past Wars D_w	Other Government Expenditures G_y	Percentage of Population over 65 P_r^*	Coefficients of Determination	
								R^2	$\bar{R}^2$
2-1	−.01221	.00242‡ (5.8156)						.6655‡	.6261‡
2-2	−.00702	.00249‡ (5.7251)	−.08839 (.6718)					.6747‡	.6137‡
2-3	−.01287	.00250‡ (5.3868)		−.07863 (.4286)				.6693‡	.6073‡
2-4	−.02612	.00239‡ (6.3866)			.00175† (2.2559)			.7462‡	.6986‡
2-5	−.02141						1.40658‡ (4.8104)	.5765‡	.5267‡
2-6	−.08175	.00257‡ (8.3076)				.40814‡ (3.9069)		.8288‡	.7967‡
2-7	−.01916	.00250† (6.5960)	−.14276 (1.2253)		.00193† (2.4806)			.7693‡	.7078‡
2-8	−.08036	.00253‡ (8.5459)			.00104 (1.6088)	.35159‡ (3.3278)		.8540†	.8151‡
2-9	−.07449	.00257‡ (8.3231)	−.05918 (.5984)		.00115 (1.6782)	.33225† (2.9474)		.8576‡	.8068‡
2-10	−.08202	.00237‡ (4.7168)				.37274† (2.9214)	.16625 (.5090)	.8317‡	.7868‡

a. See notes to Table D-1.

Table D-3. Determinants of Social Security Expenditures on the Aged as a Percentage of National Income (A_y), Regression Results, 1960[a]

Equation	Constant Term	Age of System D_s	Household Saving S	General Revenue Financing E_t	Past Wars D_w	Other Government Expenditures G_y	Percentage of Population over 65 P_{r^*}	Age of Old-Age Insurance System D_a	Benefits for War Victims W_y	Growth Rate of GNP y	R^2	$\bar{R}^2$
3-1	-.03357	.00137‡ (5.0672)									.6017‡	.5548†
3-2	.01242							.00083† (2.6177)			.2873	.2034
3-3	-.02247						.72773‡ (3.6441)				.4386†	.3725†
3-4	-.03339	.00108† (2.8801)					.25935 (1.1124)				.6303‡	.5609‡
3-5	-.02966						.58520† (2.8243)	.00049 (1.6992)			.5244†	.4352†
3-6	-.02224	.00138‡ (4.8590)	-.02269 (.2633)								.6034	.5290‡
3-7	-.02548	.00159‡ (5.9905)		-.22738† (2.1645)							.6919‡	.6341‡
3-8	-.03421	.00132‡ (5.9589)			.00144‡ (3.0462)						.7479‡	.7006‡
3-9	-.02854	.00129‡ (5.2340)							1.35811‡ (2.1715)		.6923‡	.6346‡
3-10	-.02325	.00163‡ (5.7915)	-.03863 (.4942)	-.23245† (2.1501)							.6968‡	.6160‡
3-11	-.06135					.19627† (2.4203)	.74318‡ (3.8489)			.50853† (2.4122)	.6573‡	.5650‡
3-12	-.05701	.00144‡ (6.0068)				.19001† (2.6040)		.00039 (1.5145)			.7090‡	.6544‡
3-13	-.05778	.00165‡ (7.2983)		-.21870† (2.4538)		.21749† (2.9070)					.7923‡	.7370‡
3-14	-.05935	.00158‡ (8.2213)		-.22813‡ (3.1032)		.17332† (2.9125)			1.20975† (2.7017)		.8635‡	.8148‡
3-15	-.05229	.00163‡ (8.5110)	-.07601 (1.2944)	-.16555† (1.8023)		.15241‡ (2.5205)			1.46398‡ (3.0537)		.8791‡	.8233‡
3-16	-.03408	.00140‡ (6.5370)			.00123† (2.7021)						.7928‡	.7375‡

a. See notes to Table D-1.

Table D-4. *Determinants of the Ratios of Average Old-Age Benefits to National Income per Capita (A_b), Regression Results, 1960*[a]

Equation	Constant Term	Age of System D_s	Percentage of Population over Retirement Age P_r	Other Government Expenditures G_y	Household Saving S	Male Life Expectancy at Birth L	Coefficients of Determination	
							R^2	$\bar{R}^2$
4-1	.08230	.00750† (2.3932)					.2520	.1640
4-2	.21055	.01145‡ (3.5818)	−3.24929† (2.4414)				.4550†	.3528†
4-3	−.22063	.01273‡ (5.2772)	−3.52538‡ (3.5362)	2.59441‡ (3.6983)			.7149‡	.6389‡
4-4	−.24751	.01257‡ (5.0027)	−3.54463‡ (3.4535)	2.65863‡ (3.6058)	.28445 (.4233)		.7185‡	.6180‡
4-5	.15647	.01338‡ (5.0369)	−3.55415‡ (3.4921)	2.76669‡ (3.6246)		−.00644 (.6479)	.7232‡	.6244‡
4-6	.14271	.01323‡ (4.7986)	−3.57632‡ (3.4088)	2.84384‡ (3.5355)	.31026 (.4514)	−.00670 (.6541)	.7275‡	.6017‡

a. See notes to Table D-1.

Table D-5. *Determinants of per Capita Social Security Expenditures (E_p), Regression Results, 1960*[a]

Equation	Constant Term (U.S. dollars)	Per Capita National Income Y_p	Age of System D_s	Coefficients of Determination	
				R^2	$\bar{R}^2$
5-1	26.49189		1.92625† (2.1977)	.2213	.1296
5-2	31.90573	.09081‡ (4.0813)		.4949†	.4355†
5-3	−105.02546	.10221‡ (7.6897)	2.41253‡ (5.7210)	.8342‡	.8031‡

a. See notes to Table D-1.

Table D-6. *Determinants of Labor Force Participation for Aged Total Population [LFP(T65+)] and for Aged Male Population [LFP(M65+)], Regression Results, 1960*[a]

Equation	Constant Term	Percentage of Population over Retirement Age P_r	Per Capita National Income Y_p	Ratio of per Capita Benefits to Wages B/W	Coefficients of Determination R^2	$\bar{R}^2$
		Total Population Aged 65 and Over				
6-1	.43136	−.89261† (2.2231)	−.06698† (2.5722)	−.25326† (2.7105)	.5942‡	.4860‡
6-2	.34483		−.06649† (2.2870)	−.27496† (2.6504)	.4605†	.3593†
		Male Population Aged 65 and Over				
6-3	.79385	−1.86350† (2.7907)	−.13378‡ (3.0893)	−.41291† (2.6573)	.6518‡	.5589‡
6-4	.61321		−.13275† (2.5687)	−.45821† (2.4845)	.4710†	.3718†

a. See notes to Table D-1.

Burden of the Payroll Tax and of Alternative Revenue-Raising Methods

This appendix describes the methods used to estimate the burden of the payroll tax by income levels under different shifting assumptions and of alternative methods of raising the same revenue, as presented in Chart VIII-2 and Table E-1. The calculations were prepared on the basis of a file of approximately 100,000 federal individual income tax returns for the year 1964.[1]

The payroll tax rates were assumed to be 5 percent each for employees and employers, and 7 percent for the self-employed. These are the OASDI payroll tax rates that will be effective for 1973 and after under the 1967 amendments to the Social Security Act. Also, as under the 1967 amendments, $7,800 was assumed to be the maximum taxable earnings. Tax liabilities were calculated for each return in the file, and the results were weighted and accumulated to obtain aggregates by income class. Effective rates were obtained by dividing the computed tax liabilities by "ordinary income," which is adjusted gross income as defined in the Internal Revenue Code exclusive of capital gains and losses, plus the dividend and sick pay exclusions.

Taxes were allocated to each sample unit on the basis of the following assumptions:

1. The employer and employee taxes are borne entirely by the employee. In this case, the tax was computed by applying the combined

[1] For a description of the file, see Joseph A. Pechman, "A New Tax Model for Revenue Estimating," in Alan T. Peacock and Gerald Hauser (eds.), *Government Finance and Economic Development* (Paris: Organisation for Economic Co-operation and Development, 1965). (Brookings Reprint 102.)

employer-employee tax rate of 10 percent (7 percent for the self-employed) to earnings of up to $7,800, as reported on the tax returns.

2. The employer tax is shifted forward to the consumer in the form of higher prices. The employee tax and the self-employment tax were allocated to the earner; the employer tax was allocated to each sample unit on the basis of the estimated amount consumed. Consumption at various income levels was estimated by applying to money income before tax the ratio of consumption to income of single consumers and family nonfarm units, obtained from a special tabulation by the U.S. Treasury Department of the 1960–61 Bureau of Labor Statistics expenditure survey.[2]

3. An amount equivalent to the total revenue resulting from the tax on earnings paid by employers, employees, and the self-employed is raised by the individual income tax levied at a flat rate on taxable income as defined in the Internal Revenue Code for the year 1965.

4. An amount equivalent to the total revenue resulting from the tax on earnings paid by employers, employees, and the self-employed is raised by a general consumption tax. As in 2 above, consumption was estimated on the basis of the 1960–61 Bureau of Labor Statistics expenditure survey.

[2] U.S. Department of Labor, Bureau of Labor Statistics, Survey of Consumer Expenditures, 1960–61, *Consumer Expenditures and Income,* various volumes.

Table E-1. *Effective Rates on Income of a 5 Percent Payroll Tax on Employers and Employees[a] and of Alternative Methods of Raising the Same Revenues, by Income Classes, 1964*

(In percentages)

| Ordinary Income Class[b] | Effective Rate of Payroll Tax | | Assuming Revenue Is Raised by Flat Rate Tax on Taxable Income[e] | Assuming Revenue Is Raised by Hypothetical Proportional Consumption Tax |
	Assuming backward shifting of employer tax[c]	Assuming forward shifting of employer tax[d]		
$1,000– 2,000	8.1	8.2	2.7	8.0
2,000– 3,000	8.4	7.8	4.3	7.0
3,000– 4,000	8.9	7.9	5.1	6.7
4,000– 5,000	9.3	7.8	5.8	6.2
5,000– 6,000	9.4	7.7	6.2	5.9
6,000– 7,000	9.5	7.6	6.5	5.6
7,000– 8,000	9.4	7.5	6.9	5.4
8,000–10,000	8.4	6.8	7.4	5.3
10,000–15,000	6.3	5.6	8.3	4.8
15,000–25,000	3.9	3.8	9.3	3.5
25,000 or more	1.5	2.6	10.7	3.5
All classes[f]	5.9	5.9	5.9	5.9

Source: Special tabulation based on a sample of approximately 100,000 federal individual income tax returns for the year 1964.

a. Self-employed are also included (the tax on the self-employed is 7 percent).

b. Ordinary income is adjusted gross income exclusive of capital gains and losses, plus excluded sick pay and dividends.

c. Maximum earnings subject to tax is $7,800. Employer and employee taxes are assumed to be borne by the employee; self-employment tax is assumed to be borne by the self-employed.

d. Maximum earnings subject to tax is $7,800. Employer tax is distributed in proportion to consumption by income class; employee tax and self-employment tax are assumed to be borne by employee or the self-employed.

e. The tax is applied to taxable income as defined in the Internal Revenue Code for 1965.

f. Percentages for "all classes" include the under $1,000 money income class, which is omitted in this table because income is after subtraction of net losses, and percentages in this class are therefore distorted.

APPENDIX F

Comparison of Payroll Taxes and Income Taxes and Income Tax Benefits of the Aged

This appendix describes the data and the methods used to calculate the distributions of payroll taxes and income taxes and of the loss of revenue that is due to the retirement income credit, the special exemption for the aged, and the exclusion of social security benefits from taxable income under the federal individual income tax (see Chapter VIII). The data were prepared on the basis of a federal individual income tax file for the year 1964.[1]

Estimates of the revenue from a 5 percent or 10 percent tax on wages and salaries up to $7,800, each combined with a 7 percent tax on self-employment income up to $7,800, are given in Table F-1.[2] These taxes are equivalent to a tax of 5 percent each on employers and employees on payrolls up to $7,800, on the assumptions that (a) the employer tax is shifted forward in higher prices and (b) the employer tax is borne by the employee.

Table F-1 also shows the number of returns subject to these earnings taxes with incomes above and below the officially defined "poverty" levels;[3] the number of returns on which these taxes would be higher or

[1] For a description of the file, see Joseph A. Pechman, "A New Tax Model for Revenue Estimating," in Alan T. Peacock and Gerald Hauser (eds.), *Government Finance and Economic Development* (Paris: Organisation for Economic Co-operation and Development, 1965). (Brookings Reprint 102.)

[2] A combined payroll tax of 10 percent for employees and employers and a 7 percent self-employment tax become effective for 1973 and after under the Social Security Act as amended in 1967. When an individual reported wages and salaries below $7,800 and also self-employment income, the 7 percent self-employment tax was applied to the difference between $7,800 and the amount of wages and salaries.

[3] See Mollie Orshansky, "Recounting the Poor—A Five-Year Review," *Social Security Bulletin*, Vol. 29, No. 4 (April 1966), p. 23.

lower than the federal individual income tax at 1965 tax rates; and the effect on the yield of these taxes of providing an exemption of $600 for each person reported as an exemption and a minimum standard deduction of $200 for the taxpayer plus $100 for each exemption (not including the exemptions for age and blindness). In determining the poverty levels, it was assumed that family size was the same as the number of exemptions (other than exemptions for age and blindness) reported on the return. It was also assumed that one-third of all single persons filing returns with incomes below $5,000 were members of families with income above poverty levels.

Table F-2 presents estimates of the effects on federal individual income tax revenues of removing the retirement income credit, the special exemption for the aged, and the exclusion of social security benefits (at 1964 income levels and 1965 income tax rates). The estimates were prepared by adding to the tax liability (after credits) computed for each return in the tax file the amount of the retirement income credit, and then recalculating tax liability on the assumption that the special exemption for the aged and the exclusion of social security benefits are removed in that order.[4]

The effects of the tax changes shown in Table F-2 would be slightly different if the calculations were reversed, but the differences would be small. The estimates are presented separately for nontaxable and taxable returns.

[4] To estimate social security benefits, married and nonmarried aged persons receiving benefits and married and nonmarried nonaged persons receiving benefits were distributed by benefit levels on the basis of official data for 1964. (U.S. Department of Health, Education, and Welfare, Social Security Administration, *Social Security Bulletin, Annual Statistical Supplement, 1964*, Tables 80–83, pp. 76–79.) The proportion of aged receiving zero benefits was based on data presented in the 1963 Survey of the Aged. (Lenore A. Epstein and Janet H. Murray, *The Aged Population of the United States: The 1963 Social Security Survey of the Aged*, Social Security Administration, Office of Research and Statistics, Research Report No. 19 [1967], Table 2.8, p. 282.) For the nonaged, this proportion was calculated by taking the ratio of nonbeneficiaries to the population aged 20–64 for December 1964 (estimated from U.S. Bureau of the Census, "Marital Status and Family Status: March 1964 and 1963" and "Marital Status and Family Status: March 1965," *Current Population Reports*, Series P-20, No. 135 [1965] and No. 144 [1965], respectively).

Table F-1. *Payroll Taxes of 5 Percent and 10 Percent: Distribution above and below Poverty Levels, Comparison with Federal Individual Income Tax, and Effect on Yield of Providing Exemptions and Minimum Standard Deduction, 1964*

(Dollar amounts in billions; numbers in millions)

Item	1964 Federal Individual Income Tax Returns			Amount of Tax on Earnings[a]	
	Number	Amount of ordinary income[b]	Amount of tax at 1965 tax rates[c]	5 percent tax on payrolls[d]	10 percent tax on payrolls[d]
Returns with income below poverty levels[e]	12.7	$ 14.9	$0.2	$0.8	$1.5
Returns with income above poverty levels[e]	52.7	376.1	43.9	14.3	27.2
Total	65.4	391.0	44.1	15.1	28.7
Returns with 5 percent earnings tax higher than 1965 federal income tax	21.5	56.3	1.2	3.0	—
Returns with 5 percent earnings tax lower than 1965 federal income tax	43.9	334.7	42.9	12.2	—
Total	65.4	391.0	44.1	15.1	—
Returns with 10 percent earnings tax higher than 1965 federal income tax	37.2	140.2	7.4	—	13.4
Returns with 10 percent earnings tax lower than 1965 federal income tax	28.2	250.8	36.7	—	15.3
Total	65.4	391.0	44.1	—	28.7
Yield of earnings taxes with exemptions and minimum standard deduction[f] Applicable to all earnings	65.4	391.0	44.1	8.7	16.5
Applicable only to those with incomes less than the value of exemptions and minimum standard deductions	65.4	391.0	44.1	14.4	27.3

Source: Special tabulation based on a sample of approximately 100,000 federal individual income tax returns filed for the year 1964. Figures are rounded and will not necessarily add to totals.

a. Tax of 5 percent or 10 percent applies to wages and salaries; tax of 7 percent is applied to self-employment income. Maximum earnings subject to tax are $7,800.

b. Ordinary income is adjusted gross income exclusive of capital gains and losses, plus excluded sick pay and dividends.

c. 1965 individual income tax rates applied to 1964 taxable income.

d. Combined with a 7 percent tax on self-employment income.

e. Poverty levels based on March 1965 population estimates were obtained from Mollie Orshansky, "Recounting the Poor—A Five-Year Review," *Social Security Bulletin*, Vol. 29, No. 4 (April 1966), p. 23.

f. $600 per capita regular exemption plus minimum standard deduction of $200 for the taxpayer and $100 for each exemption (other than for age and blindness).

Table F-2. *Effects on Tax Revenue of Removal of Retirement Income Credit, Special Exemption for the Aged, and Exclusion of OASDI Benefits under the Federal Individual Income Tax Regulations, by Ordinary Income Class, 1964*

(In millions of dollars)

Ordinary Income Class[a]	Federal Individual Income Tax Liability (at 1965 rates)[b]	Effect of Removing			
		Retirement income credit[c]	Special exemption for the aged[d]	Exclusion of OASDI benefits[e]	All three
		All Returns			
Under $1,000	80.9	1.1	6.5	107.6	115.2
$1,000– 2,000	340.7	4.8	51.1	241.3	297.1
2,000– 3,000	764.3	21.7	86.4	197.4	305.5
3,000– 4,000	1,330.5	27.0	78.2	169.4	274.6
4,000– 5,000	1,879.0	24.6	55.8	135.1	215.5
5,000– 7,000	5,358.8	30.5	87.4	233.7	351.6
7,000–10,000	9,467.1	23.6	74.9	193.0	291.6
10,000–15,000	9,377.1	13.1	52.6	130.6	196.3
15,000–25,000	5,480.8	9.0	38.8	72.7	120.5
25,000 or more	9,990.8	7.7	46.6	74.5	128.8
Total	44,070.0	163.0	578.3	1,555.4	2,296.6
		Taxable Returns			
Under $1,000	80.9	1.1	4.1	13.1	18.3
$1,000– 2,000	340.7	3.9	16.6	83.9	104.5
2,000– 3,000	764.3	17.9	46.5	105.4	169.8
3,000– 4,000	1,330.5	23.7	61.1	136.4	221.2
4,000– 5,000	1,879.0	22.6	52.0	127.3	201.9
5,000– 7,000	5,358.8	30.4	86.2	230.1	346.7
7,000–10,000	9,467.1	23.5	74.6	192.4	290.7
10,000–15,000	9,377.1	13.1	52.5	130.4	196.0
15,000–25,000	5,480.8	9.0	38.8	72.7	120.4
25,000 or more	9,990.8	7.7	46.6	74.5	128.8
Total	44,070.0	152.9	478.9	1,166.4	1,798.3
		Nontaxable Returns			
Under $1,000	0	0.0	2.5	94.4	96.9
$1,000– 2,000	0	0.8	34.5	157.3	192.6
2,000– 3,000	0	3.7	39.9	92.1	135.7
3,000– 4,000	0	3.3	17.1	33.0	53.4
4,000– 5,000	0	2.0	3.9	7.8	13.7
5,000 or more	0	0.2	1.6	4.2	6.0
Total	0	10.0	99.5	388.9	498.3

Source: Special tabulation based on a sample of approximately 100,000 federal individual income tax returns filed for the year 1964. Figures are rounded and will not necessarily add to totals.

a. Ordinary income is adjusted gross income exclusive of capital gains and losses, plus excluded sick pay and dividends.

b. 1965 individual income tax rates applied to 1964 taxable income.

c. Retirement income credit is 15 percent of retirement income other than social security benefits up to $1,524 ($2,286 for married couples).

d. A special exemption of $600 is permitted for persons over 65 years of age.

e. OASDI benefits are not included in income subject to federal income tax.

APPENDIX G

Statistical Tables

Table G-1. *OASDI Benefits, Old-Age Assistance Payments, and Personal Income, 1940, 1945, 1950–67*

(Dollar amounts in millions)

Calendar Year	OASDI Benefits			Old-Age Assistance Payments	Personal Income	Percentage of Personal Income	
	Total	OASI	DI			OASDI benefits	Old-age assistance payments
1940	$ 35	$ 35	—	$ 475	$ 78,285	0.04	0.61
1945	274	274	—	727	171,113	0.16	0.42
1950	961	961	—	1,470	227,619	0.42	0.65
1951	1,885	1,885	—	1,474	255,595	0.74	0.58
1952	2,194	2,194	—	1,533	272,455	0.81	0.56
1953	3,006	3,006	—	1,597	288,163	1.04	0.55
1954	3,670	3,670	—	1,593	290,136	1.26	0.55
1955	4,968	4,968	—	1,608	310,889	1.60	0.52
1956	5,715	5,715	—	1,677	333,006	1.72	0.50
1957	7,404	7,347	$ 57	1,773	351,101	2.11	0.50
1958	8,576[a]	8,327[a]	249[a]	1,830	361,174	2.37	0.51
1959	10,298[b]	9,842[b]	457[b]	1,883	383,528	2.69	0.49
1960	11,245	10,677	568	1,928	400,953	2.80	0.48
1961	12,749	11,862	887	1,890	416,814	3.06	0.45
1962	14,461	13,356	1,105	1,962	442,617	3.27	0.44
1963	15,427	14,217	1,210	2,029	465,487	3.31	0.44
1964	16,223	14,914	1,309	2,045	497,462	3.26	0.41
1965	18,311	16,737	1,573	2,054	537,760	3.41	0.38
1966	20,051	18,267	1,784	1,908	584,005	3.43	0.33
1967	21,418	19,468	1,950	1,859	626,400	3.42	0.30

Sources: U.S. Department of Health, Education, and Welfare, Social Security Administration, *Social Security Bulletin, Annual Statistical Supplement, 1965*, Tables 25 and 108, pp. 28, 103; *The 1968 Annual Report of the Board of Trustees of the Federal Old-Age and Survivors Insurance and Disability Insurance Trust Funds*, H. Doc. 288, 90 Cong. 2 sess. (1968), Tables 14 and 18, pp. 30, 36; U.S. Department of Health, Education, and Welfare, Social and Rehabilitation Service, worksheets; U.S. Department of Commerce, Office of Business Economics, *The National Income and Product Accounts of the United States, 1929–1965, Statistical Tables* (1966), Table 2.1, pp. 32, 33, and *Survey of Current Business*, Vol. 47, No. 7 (July 1967), Table 2.1, p. 20, and Vol. 48, No. 4 (April 1968), Table 10, p. 5.
a. January through November.
b. Includes December 1958.

Table G-2. Income, Expenditures, and Assets of OASI Trust Fund, 1937–67, and DI Trust Fund, 1957–67
(In millions of dollars)

Calendar Year	Income	Contributions					Expenditures				Total Assets
	Total[a]	Total	Employer-employee tax	Self-employment tax	Deposits under state agreements	Interest	Total	Benefit payments	Administrative expense	Transfers with railroad retirement account[b]	
					OASI Trust Fund						
1937	767	765	765	—	—	2	1	1	—	—	766
1938	375	360	360	—	—	15	10	10	—	—	1,132
1939	607	580	580	—	—	27	14	14	—	—	1,724
1940	368	325	325	—	—	43	62	35	26	—	2,031
1941	845	789	789	—	—	56	114	88	26	—	2,762
1942	1,085	1,012	1,012	—	—	72	159	131	28	—	3,688
1943	1,328	1,239	1,239	—	—	88	195	166	29	—	4,820
1944	1,422	1,316	1,316	—	—	107	238	209	29	—	6,005
1945	1,420	1,285	1,285	—	—	134	304	274	30	—	7,121
1946	1,447	1,295	1,295	—	—	152	418	378	40	—	8,150
1947	1,722	1,557	1,557	—	—	164	512	466	46	—	9,360
1948	1,969	1,685	1,685	—	—	281	607	556	51	—	10,722
1949	1,816	1,666	1,666	—	—	146	721	667	54	—	11,816
1950	2,928	2,667	2,667	—	—	257	1,022	961	61	—	13,721
1951	3,784	3,363	3,355	—	9	417	1,966	1,885	81	—	15,540
1952	4,184	3,819	3,632	149	38	365	2,282	2,194	88	—	17,442
1953	4,359	3,945	3,642	236	67	414	3,094	3,006	88	—	18,707
1954	5,631	5,163	4,848	221	95	447	3,741	3,670	92	−21	20,576

Year										|[b]	
1955	6,174	5,713	5,277	319	118	454	5,079	4,968	119	−7	21,663
1956	6,703	6,172	5,390	520	262	526	5,841	5,715	132	−5	22,519
1957	7,383	6,825	6,043	486	297	556	7,507	7,347	162	−2	22,393
1958	8,114	7,566	6,506	512	548	552	8,646	8,327	194	124	21,864
1959	8,577	8,052	6,977	536	539	532	10,308	9,842	184	282	20,141
1960	11,372	10,866	9,497	633	737	516	11,198	10,677	203	318	20,324
1961	11,823	11,285	9,749	753	782	548	12,432	11,862	239	332	19,725
1962	12,574	12,059	10,284	840	934	526	13,973	13,356	256	361	18,337
1963	15,063	14,541	12,570	865	1,106	521	14,920	14,217	281	423	18,480
1964	16,258	15,689	13,549	920	1,220	569	15,613	14,914	296	403	19,125
1965	16,110	16,017	13,758	959	1,300	593	17,501	16,737	328	436	18,235
1966	21,302	20,580	18,103	859	1,617	644	18,967	18,267	256	444	20,570
1967	24,034	23,138	n. a.	n. a.	1,943	818	20,382	19,468	406	508	24,222

DI Trust Fund

Year										|[b]	
1957	709	702	679	—	22	7	59	57	3	—	649
1958	991	966	829	62	74	25	261	249	12	—	1,379
1959	932	891	771	69	51	41	485	457	50	−22	1,825
1960	1,063	1,010	871	68	70	53	600	568	36	−5	2,289
1961	1,104	1,038	899	68	71	66	956	887	64	5	2,437
1962	1,113	1,046	888	76	82	67	1,183	1,105	66	11	2,368
1963	1,165	1,099	940	75	84	66	1,297	1,210	68	20	2,235
1964	1,218	1,154	997	66	90	64	1,407	1,309	79	20	2,047
1965	1,247	1,188	1,019	73	96	59	1,687	1,573	90	24	1,606
1966	2,079	2,006	1,783	67	156	58	1,947	1,784	137	25	1,739
1967	2,380	2,286	n. a.	n. a.	183	78	2,090	1,950	109	31	2,029

Sources: U.S. Department of Health, Education, and Welfare, Social Security Administration, *Social Security Bulletin, Annual Statistical Supplement, 1965*, Tables 28 and 29, pp. 31, 32; *The 1968 Annual Report of the Board of Trustees of the Federal Old-Age and Survivors Insurance and Disability Insurance Trust Funds*, H. Doc. 288, 90 Cong. 2 sess. (1968), Tables 14 and 18, pp. 30, 36; Social Security Administration worksheets. Figures are rounded and will not necessarily add to totals.

n.a. Not available.

a. Totals for the years 1946–51 include relatively small amounts appropriated from general funds to meet costs of benefits with respect to certain veterans; totals for 1966 and 1967 include $78 million (OASI trust fund) and $16 million (DI trust fund), appropriated for the same purpose for each of those years.

b. Payments from the railroad retirement account, indicated by negative figures, increase income and total assets; payments from the trust fund to the account, indicated by positive figures, increase expenditures and reduce total assets.

Table G-3. *Federal Budget Receipts, by Source, 1958–67*[a]

Fiscal Year	Total	Taxes						Premiums for Insurance and Retirement	Other
		Individual income	Corporation income	Excise	Employment[b]	Estate and gift	Customs		
Amount (millions of dollars)									
1958	79,617	34,724	20,074	10,638	10,548	1,393	781	682	777
1959	79,048	36,719	17,309	10,578	10,952	1,333	925	769	463
1960	92,481	40,715	21,494	11,676	13,916	1,606	1,105	768	1,200
1961	94,393	41,338	20,955	11,860	15,583	1,896	982	866	913
1962	99,656	45,571	20,523	12,534	16,172	2,016	1,142	873	825
1963	106,578	47,588	21,579	13,194	18,858	2,167	1,206	944	1,042
1964	112,702	48,697	23,492	13,731	21,004	2,394	1,252	1,006	1,126
1965	116,855	48,792	25,461	14,570	21,177	2,716	1,442	1,079	1,617
1966	130,901	55,446	30,073	13,061	24,439	3,066	1,767	1,126	1,923
1967	149,591	61,526	33,971	13,719	31,475	2,978	1,901	1,853	2,168
Percentage of Total									
1958	100	43.6	25.2	13.4	13.2	1.7	1.0	0.9	1.0
1959	100	46.5	21.9	13.4	13.9	1.7	1.2	1.0	0.6
1960	100	44.0	23.2	12.6	15.0	1.7	1.2	0.8	1.3
1961	100	43.8	22.2	12.6	16.5	2.0	1.0	0.9	1.0
1962	100	45.7	20.6	12.6	16.2	2.0	1.1	0.9	0.8
1963	100	44.7	20.2	12.4	17.7	2.0	1.1	0.9	1.0
1964	100	43.2	20.8	12.2	18.6	2.1	1.1	0.9	1.0
1965	100	41.8	21.8	12.5	18.1	2.3	1.2	0.9	1.4
1966	100	42.4	23.0	10.0	18.7	2.3	1.3	0.9	1.5
1967	100	41.1	22.7	9.2	21.0	2.0	1.3	1.2	1.4

Source: *The Budget of the United States Government, Fiscal Year 1969* (1968), p. 539. Figures are rounded and will not necessarily add to totals.

a. Receipts are net after refunds.

b. Includes old-age, survivor, disability, and health insurance taxes and deposits of taxes allocated to unemployment trust funds.

Table 84. Coverage Status of Wage and Salary Workers and the Self-[...] 1950–67

(In thousands, except for percentages)

Year[a]	Eligible for Coverage						Not Eligible for Coverage				
	Total[b]		Coverage in effect				Total[c]		Agricultural workers	Federal, state, and local government workers	Domestic service workers
			Total								
	Number of persons	Percentage of paid employees	Number of persons	Percentage of paid employees	Wage and salary workers	Self-employed	Number of persons	Percentage of paid employees			
1940	26,800	57.7	26,800	57.7	26,800	—	19,600	42.2	8,000	3,700	2,300
1945	42,000	68.9	42,000	68.9	42,000	—	19,000	31.1	6,400	5,300	1,600
1950	38,700	64.5	38,700	64.5	38,700	—	21,300	35.5	5,000	5,800	2,000
1951	49,700	79.5	49,500	79.2	45,300	4,200	12,800	20.5	5,100	4,800	900
1952	50,700	80.1	50,500	79.8	46,400	4,100	12,500	19.7	4,900	5,000	900
1953	51,300	80.4	51,100	80.1	47,100	4,000	12,500	19.6	4,800	4,800	900
1954	50,100	79.8	49,800	79.3	45,700	4,100	12,700	20.2	4,800	4,900	900
1955	58,700	91.0	55,000	85.3	48,300	6,700	5,800	9.0	900	2,100	800
1956	60,400	91.5	57,200	86.7	50,300	6,900	5,600	8.5	700	2,200	900
1957	60,200	91.2	57,400	87.0	50,600	6,800	5,800	8.8	800	2,300	900
1958	59,400	91.5	56,800	87.5	50,100	6,700	5,500	8.5	600	2,200	900
1959	61,000	91.6	58,500	87.8	51,600	6,900	5,600	8.4	600	2,200	900
1960	62,000	91.9	59,400	88.0	52,600	6,800	5,500	8.1	500	2,200	900
1961	62,300	91.8	59,700	87.9	53,000	6,800	5,600	8.3	500	2,300	1,000
1962	63,600	91.8	61,000	88.0	54,600	6,400	5,600	8.1	500	2,300	1,000
1963	64,600	92.0	61,900	88.2	55,600	6,300	5,700	8.1	500	2,400	900
1964	66,000	92.1	63,300	88.3	57,100	6,200	5,800	8.1	500	2,400	1,000
1965	68,000	92.4	65,600	89.1	59,400	6,200	5,600	7.6	400	2,400	900
1966	70,300	92.5	68,000	89.5	62,000	6,000	5,700	7.5	400	2,600	900
1967	71,500	93.0	68,900	89.6	63,000	6,000	5,400	7.0	400	2,700	700

Sources: U.S. Department of Health, Education, and Welfare, Social Security Administration, *Social Security Bulletin, Annual Statistical Supplement, 1966*, Table 23, p. 30, and Social Security Administration worksheets.
a. Annual figures are averages based on the calendar week in the months of March, June, September, and December for which the U.S. Bureau of the Census Current Population Surveys were taken.
b. Includes persons for whom elective coverage has not been arranged.
c. In addition to agricultural, government, and domestic workers, this figure includes a miscellaneous category consisting chiefly of nonagricultural self-employed persons and employees of nonprofit organizations.

319

Table G-5. *Monthly Cash Benefit Awards to Selected Beneficiary Families under the 1967 Amendments to the Social Security Act*

(In dollars)

Beneficiary-Family	Average Monthly Earnings of Insured Worker										
	$74 or less	$100	$150	$200	$250	$300	$350	$400	$450	$550	$650
	Monthly Benefit Awards										
Retired or disabled worker											
Worker alone											
Aged 65 or over	55.00	71.50	88.40	101.60	115.00	127.10	140.40	153.60	165.00	189.90	218.00
Aged 62	44.00	57.20	70.80	81.30	92.00	101.70	112.40	122.90	132.00	152.00	174.40
Worker aged 65 with spouse											
Aged 65 or over	82.50	107.30	132.60	152.40	172.50	190.70	210.60	230.40	247.50	284.90	323.00
Aged 62	75.70	98.40	121.60	139.70	158.20	174.80	193.10	211.20	226.90	261.20	296.80
Worker aged 62 with spouse											
Aged 65 or over	71.50	93.00	115.00	132.10	149.50	165.30	182.60	199.70	214.50	247.00	279.40
Aged 62	64.70	84.10	104.00	119.40	135.20	149.40	165.10	180.50	193.90	223.30	253.20
Widow											
Aged 62 or over	55.00	59.00	73.00	83.90	94.90	104.90	115.90	126.80	136.20	156.70	179.90
Aged 60	47.70	51.20	63.30	72.80	82.30	91.00	100.50	109.90	118.10	135.90	156.00
1 surviving child	55.00	55.00	66.30	76.20	86.30	95.40	105.30	115.20	123.80	142.50	163.50
Mother[a] and 1 child	82.60	107.40	132.60	152.40	172.60	190.80	210.60	230.40	247.60	285.00	327.00
Mother[a] and 2 children	82.50	107.40	132.60	161.70	202.50	240.00	280.80	322.50	354.60	395.70	434.40
Maximum family benefit	82.50	107.30	132.60	161.60	202.40	240.00	280.80	322.40	354.40	395.60	434.40

Source: U.S. Department of Health, Education, and Welfare, Social Security Administration, *Social Security Bulletin, Annual Statistical Supplement, 1966*, Table 22.
a. Widow under 62.

Table G-6. *Number of Workers under OASDI, by Insured Status, 1940, 1945, 1950–67*

(In millions)

At Beginning of Year	Total Number of Living Workers[a]	Living Workers Insured for Retirement and Survivor Benefits					Living Workers Insured in Event of Disability
		Total insured	Fully insured			Currently insured only	
			Total	Permanently insured	Not permanently insured		
1940	40.7	22.9	22.9	0.6	22.3	b	—
1945	69.6	38.6	31.9	2.8	29.1	6.7	—
1950	80.8	45.7	40.1	14.9	25.2	5.6	—
1951	82.7	59.8	59.8	21.0	38.8	b	—
1952	88.0	62.8	62.8	22.9	39.9	b	—
1953	90.8	68.2	68.2	25.6	42.7	b	—
1954	93.1	71.0	71.0	27.7	43.4	b	—
1955	94.7	70.6	70.2	29.9	40.4	0.4	31.9
1956	98.6	71.4	70.5	32.5	38.0	0.9	35.4
1957	101.4	74.3	74.0	36.1	38.0	0.3	37.2
1958	103.8	77.0	76.1	38.3	37.9	0.9	38.4
1959	105.3	78.9	76.5	40.3	36.2	2.4	43.4
1960	107.4	79.7	76.7	42.2	34.6	3.0	46.4
1961	109.4	85.4	84.4	47.6	36.8	1.0	48.5
1962	111.2	89.1	88.5	53.3	35.3	0.5	50.5
1963	113.3	90.4	89.8	54.9	34.8	0.6	51.5
1964	115.6	92.0	91.3	56.6	34.7	0.8	52.3
1965	118.1	93.7	92.8	58.3	34.5	0.9	53.3
1966	121.3	95.9[c]	94.9[c]	60.3[c]	34.6	0.9	55.0
1967	125.0	98.3[c]	97.2[c]	62.0[c]	35.2	1.0	56.0

Source: U.S. Department of Health, Education, and Welfare, Social Security Administration, *Social Security Bulletin, Annual Statistical Supplement, 1966*, Table 45, p. 52.

a. Estimated number of persons who had covered employment at any time during the period 1937 to year shown.

b. Persons currently insured before July 1940, or currently insured after August 1950 and before July 1954, are also fully insured.

c. Includes transitionally insured persons.

Table G-7. *OASDI Monthly Benefit Awards: Number and Average Monthly Benefit, by Type of Beneficiary, 1940, 1945, 1950-67*

Year	Total	Retired Workers[a]	Disabled Workers[b]	Wives and Husbands[a,e]	Children[d]	Widowed Mothers[e]	Widows and Widowers[a,f]	Parents[a]	Persons with Special Age-72 Benefits[g]
					Number				
1940	254,984	132,335	—	34,555	59,382	23,260	4,600	852	—
1945	462,463	185,174	—	63,068	127,514	55,108	29,844	1,755	—
1950	962,628	567,131	—	162,768	122,641	41,101	66,735	2,252	—
1951	1,336,432	702,984	—	228,887	230,500	78,323	89,591	6,147	—
1952	1,053,303	531,206	—	177,707	183,345	64,875	92,302	3,868	—
1953	1,419,462	771,671	—	246,856	212,178	71,945	112,866	3,946	—
1954	1,401,733	749,911	—	236,704	212,796	70,775	128,026	3,461	—
1955	1,657,773	909,883	—	288,915	238,795	76,018	140,624	3,538	—
1956	1,855,296	934,033	—	384,562	211,783	67,475	253,524	3,919	—
1957	2,832,344	1,424,975	178,802	578,012	313,163	88,174	244,633	4,585	—
1958[h]	2,113,465	1,041,668	131,382	379,473	286,782	81,467	199,320	3,373	—
1959[h]	2,501,802	1,089,740	177,811	444,816	426,935	102,020	252,683	7,797	—
1960	2,336,144	981,717	207,805	394,174	415,719	92,607	239,267	4,855	—
1961	3,046,653	1,361,505	279,758	471,786	579,742	98,449	251,275	4,138	—
1962	3,004,501	1,347,268	250,634	463,069	572,624	99,925	267,051	3,930	—
1963	2,729,559	1,145,602	223,739	412,153	560,698	104,960	278,709	3,698	—
1964	2,552,063	1,041,807	207,592	375,968	533,794	106,249	283,263	3,390	—
1965	3,072,426	1,183,133	253,499	390,198	783,202	100,005	359,431	2,958	—
1966	4,722,483	1,647,524	278,345	478,094	1,056,049	107,135	403,595	3,202	748,539
1967	3,597,152	1,161,393	301,463	407,221	984,354	110,756	355,668	2,659	273,638

Average Monthly Benefit (dollars)

Year								
1940	22.71	—	12.15	12.20	19.60	20.36	13.09	—
1945	25.11	—	13.04	12.65	19.85	20.17	13.10	—
1950 (Jan.–Aug.)	29.03	—	15.02	14.32	22.65	21.65	14.65	—
1950 (Sept.–Dec.)[i]	33.24	—	19.72	22.82	35.42	36.89	37.99	—
1951	37.54	—	20.54	23.09	32.22	34.88	36.02	—
1952 (Jan.–Aug.)	39.65	—	21.57	24.10	33.00	35.07	35.89	—
1952 (Sept.–Dec.)[j]	58.11	—	29.84	30.55	42.20	40.75	43.58	—
1953	56.76	—	29.15	31.70	44.40	41.45	45.55	—
1954 (Jan.–Aug.)	56.98	—	29.21	31.91	44.92	41.62	46.06	—
1954 (Sept.–Dec.)[k]	66.36	—	34.36	35.96	50.33	45.78	53.20	—
1955	69.74	—	35.72	37.35	53.08	49.67	54.73	—
1956	67.36	—	34.52	39.30	55.71	53.70	56.16	—
1957	67.59	81.38	34.23	38.90	56.82	53.91	58.18	—
1958	74.47	84.64	36.46	39.60	57.56	55.53	61.07	—
1959	81.46	91.84	39.41	43.01	65.52	60.92	67.49	—
1960	81.73	91.16	39.58	42.25	65.93	62.10	70.14	—
1961 (Jan.–July)	80.17	90.76	39.04	40.33	61.06	62.15	70.33	—
1961 (Aug.–Dec.)[l]	75.33	91.95	36.74	37.21	60.54	69.20	75.97	—
1962	78.80	92.71	38.34	39.61	61.14	70.49	77.84	—
1963	80.30	94.40	38.82	40.93	61.34	71.59	78.44	—
1964	81.24	94.98	39.01	41.90	61.31	73.06	80.21	—
1965 (Jan.–Aug.)	82.69	93.26	39.31	41.24	61.65	73.80	80.59	—
1965 (Sept.–Dec.)[m]	89.20	101.30	42.59	56.78	68.03	75.36	85.77	—
1966	93.75	101.40	43.29	50.72	67.96	74.16	83.10	34.33
1967	89.74	101.83	41.61	50.37	69.25	77.67	86.15	34.19

Sources: U.S. Department of Health, Education, and Welfare, Social Security Administration, *Social Security Bulletin, Annual Statistical Supplement, 1966*, Table 50, and *Social Security Bulletin*, Vol. 31, No. 4 (April 1968), Tables M-14 and M-16, pp. 56–57. The average monthly benefit figures are official Social Security Administration data.

a. Persons aged 65 and over (and aged 62–64, beginning 1956 or women and 1961 for men).
b. July 1957–October 1960, disabled workers aged 50–64; beginning November 1960, disabled workers under age 65.
c. Includes, beginning 1950, wife beneficiaries under age 65 with entitled children in their care, beginning 1958, benefits payable to wives and husbands of disability beneficiaries, and beginning September 1965, entitled divorced wives.
d. Includes, beginning 1957, disabled persons aged 18 and over whose disability began before age 18, beginning 1958, dependent children of disability beneficiaries, and beginning September 1965, entitled full-time students aged 18–21.
e. Includes, beginning 1950, surviving divorced mothers with entitled children in their care.
f. Includes, beginning September 1965, widows aged 60–61 and entitled surviving divorced wives aged 60 and over.
g. Authorized by 1966 legislation for persons aged 72 and over not insured under the regular or transitional provisions of the Social Security Act.
h. 1958 data are for January through November. 1959 data include December 1958.   i. Incorporates the effects of the 1950 amendments to the Social Security Act.
j. Incorporates the effects of the 1952 amendments to the Social Security Act.   k. Incorporates the effects of the 1954 amendments to the Social Security Act.
l. Incorporates the effects of the 1961 amendments to the Social Security Act.   m. Incorporates the effects of the 1965 amendments to the Social Security Act.

Table G-8. *OASDI Monthly Benefits in Current-Payment Status, by Type of Beneficiary,*[a] *1940, 1945, 1950–67*

At End of Year	Total	Retired Workers	Disabled Workers	Wives and Husbands	Children	Widowed Mothers	Widows and Widowers	Parents	Persons with Special Age-72 Benefits
				Number					
1940	222,488	112,331	—	29,749	54,648	20,499	4,437	824	—
1945	1,288,107	518,234	—	159,168	390,134	120,581	93,781	6,209	—
1950	3,477,243	1,770,984	—	508,350	699,703	169,438	314,189	14,579	—
1951	4,378,985	2,278,470	—	646,890	846,247	203,782	384,265	19,331	—
1952	5,025,549	2,643,932	—	737,859	938,751	228,984	454,563	21,460	—
1953	5,981,420	3,222,348	—	887,845	1,053,195	253,873	540,653	23,506	—
1954	6,886,480	3,775,134	—	1,015,892	1,160,770	271,536	638,091	25,057	—
1955	7,960,616	4,473,971	—	1,191,963	1,276,240	291,916	701,360	25,166	—
1956	9,128,121	5,112,430	—	1,433,507	1,340,995	301,240	913,069	26,880	—
1957	11,128,897	6,197,532	149,850	1,827,048	1,502,077	328,309	1,095,137	28,944	—
1958[b]	12,430,234	6,920,677	237,719	2,031,091	1,624,135	353,964	1,232,583	30,065	—
1959	13,703,918	7,525,628	334,443	2,208,017	1,831,548	376,145	1,393,587	34,550	—
1960	14,844,589	8,061,469	455,371	2,345,983	2,000,451	401,358	1,543,843	36,114	—
1961	16,494,762	8,924,849	618,075	2,510,199	2,279,462	428,138	1,697,308	36,731	—
1962	18,053,395	9,738,500	740,867	2,678,531	2,547,057	451,984	1,859,191	37,265	—
1963	19,035,489	10,263,331	827,014	2,748,809	2,686,959	461,675	2,010,769	36,932	—
1964	19,799,539	10,668,731	894,173	2,783,308	2,787,453	470,597	2,158,912	36,365	—
1965	20,866,767	11,100,584	988,074	2,806,912	3,092,659	471,816	2,371,433	35,289	—
1966	22,767,252	11,658,443	1,097,190	2,860,026	3,392,970	487,755	2,602,015	34,540	634,313
1967	23,707,453	12,019,371	1,193,559	2,879,878	3,586,219	496,462	2,769,833	33,516	728,555
				Amount (thousands of dollars)					
1940	4,070	2,539	—	361	668	402	90	11	—
1945	23,801	12,538	—	2,040	4,858	2,391	1,893	81	—
1950	126,857	77,678	—	11,995	19,366	5,801	11,481	535	—
1951	154,791	96,008	—	14,710	22,739	6,776	13,849	709	—
1952	205,179	130,217	—	19,178	28,141	8,273	18,482	887	—
1953	253,792	164,659	—	24,017	32,517	9,517	22,096	986	—
1954	339,342	223,272	—	32,271	40,996	12,089	29,526	1,189	—
1955	411,613	276,942	—	39,416	46,444	13,403	34,152	1,256	—
1956	482,593	322,537	—	48,326	50,324	14,262	45,780	1,365	—
1957	605,455	400,250	10,904	62,802	57,952	16,102	55,944	1,501	—
1958[b]	697,529	459,201	19,516	71,230	64,130	17,886	63,977	1,588	—
1959	845,144	547,749	29,765	84,254	80,716	21,579	79,047	2,034	—
1960	936,321	596,849	40,668	90,503	93,275	23,795	89,054	2,178	—
1961	1,071,693	675,154	55,374	98,276	104,818	25,425	110,179	2,466	—
1962	1,181,725	741,961	66,673	105,072	116,166	26,838	122,475	2,541	—
1963	1,259,912	789,064	74,922	108,481	123,052	27,438	134,403	2,552	—
1964	1,325,445	827,548	81,473	110,549	128,898	27,954	146,476	2,547	—
1965	1,516,802	931,532	96,599	120,796	159,428	30,882	174,883	2,683	—
1966	1,638,548	983,338	107,627	123,263	175,100	31,983	192,821	2,642	21,777
1967	1,723,556	1,026,046	117,466	125,063	187,092	32,687	207,702	2,588	24,911

Sources: U.S. Department of Health, Education, and Welfare, Social Security Administration, *Social Security Bulletin, Annual Statistical Supplement, 1965*, Table 27, p. 30, and *Social Security Bulletin*, Vol. 31, No. 4 (April 1968), Tables M-9, M-10, M-11, pp. 52, 53. Figures are rounded and will not necessarily add to totals.
a. See footnotes to Table G-7 for persons included in each beneficiary class.
b. November data; December data not available.

Table G-9. *OASDI Average Monthly Benefits in Current-Payment Status, by Family Group, 1940, 1945, 1950–66*

(In dollars)

At End of Year	Retired-Worker Families		Survivor Families				Disabled-Worker Families		
			Aged widow only	Widowed mother and children				Worker, wife under age 65,[b] and children	
	Worker only	Worker and wife aged 62 and over[a]		1 child	2 children	3 or more children	Worker only	1 child	2 or more children
1940	22.10	36.40	20.30	33.90	47.10	51.30	—	—	—
1945	23.50	38.50	20.20	34.10	47.70	50.40	—	—	—
1950	42.20	71.70	36.50	76.90	93.90	92.40	—	—	—
1951	40.30	70.20	36.00	77.30	93.80	92.00	—	—	—
1952	47.10	81.60	40.70	87.50	106.00	101.30	—	—	—
1953	48.80	85.00	40.90	90.10	111.90	109.00	—	—	—
1954	56.50	99.10	46.30	103.90	130.50	126.80	—	—	—
1955	59.10	103.50	48.70	106.80	135.40	133.20	—	—	—
1956	59.90	105.90	50.10	109.90	141.00	138.70	—	—	—
1957	60.90	108.40	51.10	114.30	146.30	144.80	72.80	—	—
1958	62.60	111.20	51.90	117.00	151.70	150.70	81.70	170.10	165.50
1959	68.70	121.60	56.70	129.70	170.70	178.60	87.90	182.80	188.30
1960	69.90	123.90	57.70	131.70	188.00	181.70	87.90	184.70	192.20
1961	71.90	126.60	64.90	135.00	189.30	182.80	87.70	186.50	193.80
1962	72.50	127.90	65.90	137.30	190.70	186.80	88.00	185.80	194.70
1963	73.20	129.40	66.90	139.40	192.50	190.40	88.60	186.70	196.10
1964	73.90	130.70	67.90	141.60	193.40	192.10	89.20	187.70	197.10
1965	80.10[c]	141.50[c]	73.90[c]	153.00	219.80	218.10	95.40	201.00	216.30
1966	80.60[c]	142.50[c]	74.30[c]	154.30	221.90	218.80	95.80	202.00	217.80

Source: U.S. Department of Health, Education, and Welfare, Social Security Administration, *Social Security Bulletin, Annual Statistical Supplement, 1966*, Table 28, p. 34.
a. Excludes wife aged 62–64 with entitled children in her care.
b. With entitled children in her care.
c. Reflects benefits to individuals entitled under the transitional insured-status provisions.

Table G-10. *Public Assistance: Number of Recipients and Total and Average Monthly Payments, by Program, 1940, 1945, 1950–67*

Year	Total[a]	Old-Age Assistance	Medical Assistance for the Aged	Aid to the Blind	Aid to the Permanently and Totally Disabled	Aid to Families with Dependent Children[b]	General Assistance (cases)[c]
Recipients, December (thousands)							
1940	—	2,066	—	73	—	—	1,239
1945	—	2,056	—	71	—	—	257
1950	—	2,789	—	98	69	2,234	413
1951	—	2,708	—	97	127	2,044	323
1952	—	2,646	—	99	164	1,992	280
1953	—	2,591	—	100	195	1,942	270
1954	—	2,565	—	102	224	2,174	351
1955	—	2,553	—	105	244	2,193	314
1956	—	2,514	—	107	269	2,271	305
1957	—	2,487	—	108	291	2,498	345
1958	—	2,455	—	110	328	2,851	434
1959	—	2,394	—	109	350	2,953	399
1960	—	2,332	15	108	374	3,080	431
1961	—	2,269	72	103	396	3,582	411
1962	—	2,226	110	100	437	3,828	354
1963	—	2,194	150	98	479	3,981	352
1964	—	2,159	225	96	527	4,292	346
1965	—	2,127	279	95	575	4,457	310
1966[d]	—	2,073	n.a.	84	588	4,666	663
1967[d]	—	2,073	n.a.	83	646	5,309	782
Total Payments (millions of dollars)							
1940	1,035.0	475.0	—	21.8	—	133.2	405.0
1945	989.7	726.6	—	26.6	—	149.7	86.9
1950	2,395.4	1,469.9	—	52.9	8.1	553.7	295.4
1951	2,394.6	1,474.5	—	55.5	57.9	561.7	195.3
1952	2,464.0	1,532.9	—	61.3	90.9	553.8	171.8
1953	2,547.1	1,596.7	—	65.7	115.4	562.3	151.4
1954	2,653.0	1,592.8	—	67.8	137.1	593.5	198.1
1955	2,756.9	1,608.1	—	71.1	156.5	639.1	214.3
1956	2,861.1	1,676.7	—	77.0	176.7	663.3	197.7
1957	3,099.0	1,773.0	—	83.6	200.8	754.7	213.4
1958	3,433.6	1,829.6	—	87.4	228.2	895.0	307.2
1959	3,680.0	1,883.0	—	90.7	260.0	1,002.7	344.4
1960	3,804.3	1,927.8	5.4	94.2	288.2	1,062.5	322.5
1961	4,115.2	1,890.5	113.0	93.2	317.2	1,236.7	356.0

Table G-10. *(concluded)*

Year	Total[a]	Old-Age Assistance	Medical Assistance for the Aged	Aid to the Blind	Aid to the Permanently and Totally Disabled	Aid to Families with Dependent Children[b]	General Assistance (cases)[c]
		Total Payments, concluded (millions of dollars)					
1962	4,457.1	1,961.5	245.9	93.9	360.9	1,395.5	292.7
1963	4,736.1	2,028.7	300.8	96.3	416.8	1,477.0	279.6
1964	5,096.2	2,044.7	447.6	98.1	474.8	1,648.7	272.7
1965	5,505.4	2,053.6	588.8	100.5	561.2	1,825.0	259.3
1966	6,313.1	1,907.9	295.1	90.3	565.7	1,923.9	336.4
1967	7,804.4	1,858.8	64.2	89.9	611.9	2,279.9	389.2
		Average Monthly Payments (dollars)					
1940	—	20.26	—	25.38	—	9.85	24.28
1945	—	30.88	—	33.52	—	15.15	32.72
1950	—	43.95	—	46.56	45.41	21.13	46.65
1951	—	46.00	—	49.05	49.46	22.36	47.09
1952	—	50.90	—	54.91	53.50	23.98	49.82
1953	—	51.50	—	55.67	53.44	23.77	50.53
1954	—	51.90	—	56.37	54.93	23.96	57.29
1955	—	53.93	—	58.08	56.18	24.35	55.04
1956	—	57.99	—	63.15	58.82	25.79	56.14
1957	—	60.69	—	66.35	60.15	26.90	59.74
1958	—	64.08	—	68.29	62.58	28.29	68.94
1959	—	65.99	—	71.31	64.94	29.03	69.51
1960	—	68.45	195.84	73.17	67.64	30.07	71.62
1961	—	68.78	192.90	74.57	70.38	31.29	67.95
1962	—	75.46	205.18	80.16	73.51	31.02	66.80
1963	—	77.04	201.58	82.03	75.74	31.82	67.95
1964	—	78.89	196.87	85.77	80.60	33.82	68.62
1965	—	79.87	189.73	92.00	87.27	35.53	68.97
1966[d]	—	68.05	n.a.	86.85	74.75	36.25	80.10
1967[d]	—	70.15	n.a.	90.45	80.60	39.50	87.65

Sources: U.S. Department of Health, Education, and Welfare, Social Security Administration, *Social Security Bulletin, Annual Statistical Supplement, 1965*, Tables 108 and 109, pp. 103, 104; *Social Security Bulletin*, Vol. 31, No. 4 (April 1968), Table M-23, p. 63; Social Security Administration worksheets.

n.a. Not available.

a. Beginning October 1950, total exceeds sum of columns because of inclusion of vendor payments for medical care from general assistance funds and from special medical funds; data for such expenditures partly estimated for some states.

b. Between October 1950 and October 1962 includes as recipients the children and one parent or caretaker relative; beginning October 1962, may include both parents or one caretaker relative other than a parent. The average monthly payment shown is per recipient; the average payment per family is considerably larger ($148.09 in 1965).

c. Excludes Idaho beginning September 1957, Nebraska, September 1952–December 1953 and beginning November 1963, and Indiana beginning January 1962; data not available.

d. Represents recipients of money payments only. Not strictly comparable with preceding years.

APPENDIX H

Selected Bibliography

Books and Monographs

Advisory Council on Social Security, 1938. *Final Report, December 10, 1938.* S. Doc. 4. 76 Cong. 1 sess. Washington: Government Printing Office, 1939.

Advisory Council on Social Security, 1948. *Old-Age and Survivors Insurance.* A Report to the Senate Committee on Finance from the Advisory Council on Social Security. S. Doc. 149. 80 Cong. 2 sess. Washington: Government Printing Office, 1948.

Advisory Council on Social Security, 1965. *The Status of the Social Security Program and Recommendations for Its Improvement.* Washington: Government Printing Office, 1965.

Advisory Council on Social Security Financing, 1958. *Financing Old-Age, Survivors, and Disability Insurance.* Washington: Government Printing Office, 1959.

Altmeyer, Arthur J. *The Formative Years of Social Security.* Madison: University of Wisconsin Press, 1966.

American Assembly. *Economic Security for Americans.* New York: Columbia University, Graduate School of Business, 1954.

Ball, Robert M. *Pensions in the United States.* A Study Prepared for the Joint Committee on the Economic Report by the National Planning Association. 82 Cong. 2 sess. Washington: Government Printing Office, 1952.

Bancroft, Gertrude. *The American Labor Force: Its Growth and Changing Composition.* New York: Wiley, 1958.

Barlow, Robin, Harvey E. Brazer, and James N. Morgan. *Economic Behavior of the Affluent.* Washington: Brookings Institution, 1966.

Baumol, William J. *Welfare Economics and the Theory of the State.* 2d ed. Cambridge: Harvard University Press, 1965.

Bayo, Francisco. *United States Population Projections for OASDHI Cost Estimates.* Washington: U.S. Department of Health, Education, and Welfare, Social Security Administration, Office of the Actuary, Actuarial Study No. 62, 1966.

Bernstein, Merton C. *The Future of Private Pensions.* New York: Free Press, 1964.

Beveridge, Sir William. *Social Insurance and Allied Services.* New York: Macmillan, 1942.

Board of Trustees of the Federal Old-Age and Survivors Insurance and Disability Insurance Trust Funds. *The 1967 Annual Report of the Board of Trustees of the Federal Old-Age and Survivors Insurance and Disability Insurance Trust Funds.* H. Doc. 65. 90 Cong. 1 sess. Washington: Government Printing Office, 1967.

————. *The 1968 Annual Report.* H. Doc. 288. 90 Cong. 2 sess. Washington: Government Printing Office, 1968.

Bowen, William G., and others (eds.). *The American System of Social Insurance: Its Philosophy, Impact, and Future Development.* Princeton Symposium. New York: McGraw-Hill, 1968.

Brennan, Michael J., Philip Taft, and Mark B. Schupack. *The Economics of Age.* New York: Norton, 1967.

Bridges, Benjamin, Jr. *Net Worth of the Aged.* Washington: U.S. Department of Health, Education, and Welfare, Social Security Administration, Office of Research and Statistics, Note No. 14, 1967.

Burns, Eveline M. *The American Social Security System.* Boston: Houghton Mifflin, 1949.

————. *Social Security and Public Policy.* New York: McGraw-Hill, 1956.

Cagan, Phillip. *The Effect of Pension Plans on Aggregate Saving: Evidence from a Sample Survey.* National Bureau of Economic Research, Occasional Paper 95. New York: Columbia University Press, 1965.

Carlson, Valdemar. *Economic Security in the United States.* Economics Handbook Series. New York: McGraw-Hill, 1962.

Carroll, John J. *Alternative Methods of Financing Old-Age, Survivors, and Disability Insurance.* Ann Arbor: University of Michigan, Institute of Public Administration, 1960.

Chamber of Commerce of the United States. *Poverty: The Sick, Disabled and Aged.* Washington: Chamber of Commerce, 1965.

Chase, Samuel B., Jr. (ed.). *Problems in Public Expenditure Analysis.* Washington: Brookings Institution, 1968.

Cohen, Wilbur J. *Retirement Policies Under Social Security.* Berkeley: University of California Press, 1957.
Committee on Economic Security. *Report to the President of the Committee on Economic Security.* Washington: Government Printing Office, 1935.
Douglas, Paul H. *Social Security in the United States: An Analysis and Appraisal of the Federal Social Security Act.* 2d ed. New York: McGraw-Hill, 1939.
Epstein, Abraham. *Insecurity—A Challenge to America.* 2d rev. ed. New York: Random House, 1938.
Epstein, Lenore A., and Janet H. Murray. *The Aged Population of the United States: The 1963 Social Security Survey of the Aged.* U.S. Department of Health, Education, and Welfare, Social Security Administration, Office of Research and Statistics, Research Report No. 19. Washington: Government Printing Office, 1967.
Friedman, Milton. *Capitalism and Freedom.* Chicago: University of Chicago Press, 1962.
Gallaway, Lowell E. *The Retirement Decision: An Exploratory Essay.* U.S. Department of Health, Education, and Welfare, Social Security Administration, Division of Research and Statistics, Research Report No. 9. Washington: Government Printing Office, 1965.
Gordon, Margaret S. *The Economics of Welfare Policies.* New York: Columbia University Press, 1963.
——— (ed.). *Poverty in America.* San Francisco: Chandler, 1965.
Green, Christopher. *Negative Taxes and the Poverty Problem.* Washington: Brookings Institution, 1967.
Haber, Lawrence D., and Rena Kling. *OASDHI Beneficiaries Receiving Government Pensions.* Washington: U.S. Department of Health, Education, and Welfare, Social Security Administration, Office of Research and Statistics, Note No. 2, 1968.
Harris, Seymour E. *Economics of Social Security; The Relation of the American Program to Consumption, Savings, Output, and Finance.* New York: McGraw-Hill, 1941.
Holland, Daniel M. *Private Pension Funds: Projected Growth.* National Bureau of Economic Research, Occasional Paper 97. New York: Columbia University Press, 1966.
International Labour Office. *The Cost of Social Security, 1958–1960.* Geneva: La Tribune de Genève, 1964.
Kreps, Juanita M. *Lifetime Allocation of Work and Leisure.* U.S. Department of Health, Education, and Welfare, Social Security Ad-

ministration, Office of Research and Statistics, Research Report No. 22. Washington: Government Printing Office, 1968.

Lampman, Robert J. (ed.). *Social Security Perspectives; Essays.* Madison: University of Wisconsin Press, 1962.

Long, Clarence D. *The Labor Force under Changing Income and Employment.* National Bureau of Economic Research, General Series No. 65. Princeton: Princeton University Press, 1958.

Merriam, Ida C. *Social Security Benefits and Poverty.* Washington: U.S. Department of Health, Education, and Welfare, Social Security Administration, Office of Research and Statistics, Note No. 6, 1967.

———. *Social Security Financing.* Social Security Administration, Federal Security Agency, Division of Research and Statistics, Bureau Report No. 17. Washington: Government Printing Office, 1953.

Morgan, James N., Martin H. David, Wilbur J. Cohen, and Harvey E. Brazer. *Income and Welfare in the United States.* New York: McGraw-Hill, 1962.

Myers, Robert J. *Methodology Involved in Developing Long-Range Cost Estimates for the Old-Age, Survivors, and Disability Insurance System.* Washington: U.S. Department of Health, Education, and Welfare, Social Security Administration, Division of the Actuary, Actuarial Study No. 49, 1959.

———. *Social Insurance and Allied Government Programs.* Homewood, Illinois: R. D. Irwin, 1965.

———, and Francisco Bayo. *Long-Range Cost Estimates for Old-Age, Survivors, and Disability Insurance System, 1966.* Washington: U.S. Department of Health, Education, and Welfare, Social Security Administration, Office of the Actuary, Actuarial Study No. 63, 1967.

Orshansky, Mollie. *Who Was Poor in 1966.* Washington: U.S. Department of Health, Education, and Welfare, Social Security Administration, Office of Research and Statistics, Note No. 23, 1967.

Pechman, Joseph A. *Federal Tax Policy.* (See especially Chapter 7, "Payroll Taxes.") Washington: Brookings Institution, 1966.

President of the United States. *Aid for the Aged.* Message from the President of the United States Transmitting a Review of Measures Taken To Aid the Older Americans and Recommendations for Legislation To Provide Further Aid. H. Doc. 40. 90 Cong. 1 sess. Washington: Government Printing Office, 1967.

———. *Manpower Report of the President Including a Report on Manpower Requirements, Resources, Utilization, and Training by the*

United States Department of Labor. Washington: Government Printing Office, 1968.

――――. *Revision of Our Tax Structure.* Message from the President of the United States Transmitting Recommendations Relative to a Revision of Our Tax Structure. H. Doc. 43. 88 Cong. 1 sess. Washington: Government Printing Office, 1963.

President's Committee on Corporate Pension Funds and Other Private Retirement and Welfare Programs. *Public Policy and Private Pension Programs: A Report to the President on Private Employee Retirement Plans.* Washington: Government Printing Office, 1965.

Richardson, J. Henry. *Economic and Financial Aspects of Social Security.* Toronto: University of Toronto Press, 1960.

Rubinow, Isaac M. *Social Insurance.* New York: Holt, 1916.

Schottland, Charles I. *The Social Security Program in the United States.* New York: Appleton-Century-Crofts, 1963.

Social Security Board. *Social Security in America. The Factual Background of the Social Security Act as Summarized from Staff Reports to the Committee on Economic Security.* Washington: Government Printing Office, 1937.

Somers, Herman M., and Anne R. Somers. *Medicare and the Hospitals: Issues and Prospects.* Washington: Brookings Institution, 1967.

Steiner, Peter O., and Robert Dorfman. *The Economic Status of the Aged.* Berkeley: University of California Press, 1957.

Tax Foundation, Inc. *Economic Aspects of the Social Security Tax.* New York: Tax Foundation, Inc., 1966.

――――. *Issues in Future Financing of Social Security.* New York: Tax Foundation, Inc., 1967.

Turnbull, John G. *The Changing Faces of Economic Insecurity.* Minneapolis: University of Minnesota Press, 1966.

U.S. Congress. House. Committee on Ways and Means. *Actuarial Cost Estimates for the Old-Age, Survivors, Disability, and Health Insurance System as Modified by the Social Security Amendments of 1967.* 90 Cong. 1 sess. Washington: Government Printing Office, 1967.

――――. *Analysis of the Social Security System.* Pt. 6: *The Legal Status of OASI Benefits* and App. II: *Miscellaneous Documents.* Hearings. 83 Cong. 1 sess. Washington: Government Printing Office, 1954.

――――. *Economic Security Act.* Hearings on H. R. 4120. 74 Cong. 1 sess. Washington: Government Printing Office, 1935.

――――. *Issues in Social Security.* A Report by the Committee's Social

Security Technical Staff. 79 Cong. 1 sess. Washington: Government Printing Office, 1946.

———. *President's Proposals for Revision in the Social Security System.* Pts. 1, 2, 3, 4. Hearings on H.R. 5710. 90 Cong. 1 sess. Washington: Government Printing Office, 1967.

U.S. Congress. Joint Economic Committee. *European Social Security Systems, A Comparative Analysis of Programs in England, Sweden, and the Common Market Countries, Together with a Description of the U.S. System.* Materials prepared for the Committee. Economic Policies and Practices, Paper No. 7. 89 Cong. 1 sess. Washington: Government Printing Office, 1965.

———. *Old Age Income Assurance.* Compendium of Papers on Problems and Policy Issues in the Public and Private Pension System. Pt. I: *General Policy Guidelines.* Pt. II: *The Aged Population and Retirement Income Programs.* Pt. III: *Public Programs.* Pt. IV: *Employment Aspects of Pension Plans.* Pt. V: *Financial Aspects of Pension Plans.* Pt. VI: *Abstracts of the Papers.* 90 Cong. 1 sess. Washington: Government Printing Office, 1967 (Pts. II, III, IV, V), 1968 (Pts. I, VI).

———. *Old Age Income Assurance: An Outline of Issues and Alternatives.* Materials prepared by the Committee Staff for the Subcommittee on Fiscal Policy. 89 Cong. 2 sess. Washington: Government Printing Office, 1966.

———. *Productivity, Prices, and Incomes.* Materials prepared by the Committee Staff for the Joint Economic Committee. 89 Cong. 2 sess. Washington: Government Printing Office, 1967.

U.S. Congress. Senate. Committee on Finance. *Economic Security Act.* Hearings on S. 1130. 74 Cong. 1 sess. Washington: Government Printing Office, 1935.

U.S. Department of Health, Education, and Welfare, Office of Assistant Secretary for Program Coordination. *Income and Benefit Programs.* Washington: Government Printing Office, 1966.

U.S. Department of Health, Education, and Welfare, Social Security Administration. *Social Security Handbook on Retirement Insurance, Survivors Insurance, Disability Insurance, Health Insurance for the Aged.* 3d ed. Washington: Government Printing Office, 1966.

U.S. Department of Health, Education, and Welfare, Social Security Administration, Office of Research and Statistics. *The Poor in 1965 and Trends, 1959–65.* Washington: HEW, Office of Research and Statistics, Note No. 5, 1967.

———. *Recent Foreign Social Security Developments.* Washington: HEW, Office of Research and Statistics, Note No. 1, 1968.

———. *Social Security Bulletin, Annual Statistical Supplement, 1966.* Washington: Government Printing Office.

———. *Social Security Programs Throughout the World, 1967.* Washington: Government Printing Office, 1967.

———. *State and Local Government Employment Under Old-Age, Survivors, Disability, and Health Insurance, 1956–1965.* RS: S-11. Washington: HEW, 1966.

Wentworth, Edna C. *Employment After Retirement: A Study of the Postentitlement Work Experience of Men Drawing Benefits Under Social Security.* U.S. Department of Health, Education, and Welfare, Social Security Administration, Office of Research and Statistics, Research Report No. 21. Washington: Government Printing Office, 1968.

Wetzler, Elliot. *Determination of Poverty Lines and Equivalent Welfare.* Arlington, Virginia: Institute for Defense Analyses, Economic and Political Studies Division, Research Paper P-277, 1966.

Witte, Edwin E. *The Development of the Social Security Act.* Madison: University of Wisconsin Press, 1962; second printing, 1963.

Articles

Aaron, Henry J. "Rate Progressivity and the Direct Taxation of Personal Income." *Taxes—The Tax Magazine,* Vol. 44, No. 7 (July 1966), pp. 497–503.

———. "The Social Insurance Paradox," in Joint Economic Committee, *Old Age Income Assurance.* Compendium of Papers on Problems and Policy Issues in the Public and Private Pension System. Pt. V: *Financial Aspects of Pension Plans,* pp. 15–18. 90 Cong. 1 sess. Washington: Government Printing Office, 1967. Reprinted from *Canadian Journal of Economics and Political Science,* Vol. 32, No. 3 (August 1966), pp. 371–74.

———. "Social Security: International Comparisons," and "Benefits Under the American Social Security System," in Otto Eckstein (ed.), *Studies in the Economics of Income Maintenance,* pp. 13–72. Washington: Brookings Institution, 1967.

Antonovsky, Aaron. "Social Class, Life Expectancy and Overall Mortality." *Milbank Memorial Fund Quarterly,* Vol. 45, No. 2, Pt. 1 (April 1967), pp. 31–73.

Ball, Robert M. "Policy Issues in Social Security." *Social Security Bulletin,* Vol. 29, No. 6 (June 1966), pp. 3–9.

———. "Social Insurance and the Right to Assistance." *Social Service Review*, Vol. 21, No. 3 (September 1947), pp. 331–44.

———. "Some Reflections on Selected Issues in Social Security," in Joint Economic Committee, *Old Age Income Assurance*. Compendium of Papers on Problems and Policy Issues in the Public and Private Pension System. Pt. I: *General Policy Guidelines*, pp. 48–57. 90 Cong. 1 sess. Washington: Government Printing Office, 1968.

———. "What Contribution Rate for Old-Age and Survivors Insurance?" *Social Security Bulletin*, Vol. 12, No. 7 (July 1949), pp. 3–9.

Bishop, George A. "Issues in Future Financing of Social Security," in Joint Economic Committee, *Old Age Income Assurance*. Compendium of Papers on Problems and Policy Issues in the Public and Private Pension System. Pt. III: *Public Programs*, pp. 21–71. 90 Cong. 1 sess. Washington: Government Printing Office, 1967.

Bok, Derek C. "Emerging Issues in Social Legislation: Social Security." *Harvard Law Review*, Vol. 80, No. 4 (February 1967), pp. 717–64.

Brittain, John A. "The Real Rate of Interest on Lifetime Contributions Toward Retirement Under Social Security," in Joint Economic Committee, *Old Age Income Assurance*. Compendium of Papers on Problems and Policy Issues in the Public and Private Pension System. Pt. III: *Public Programs*, pp. 109–32. 90 Cong. 1 sess. Washington: Government Printing Office, 1967. Brookings Reprint 143.

Burns, Eveline M. "Private and Social Insurance and the Problem of Social Security," in *Analysis of the Social Security System*. App. II: *Miscellaneous Documents*, pp. 1471–79. Hearings. House Committee on Ways and Means. 83 Cong. 1 sess. Washington: Government Printing Office, 1954.

———. "Social Insurance in Evolution." *American Economic Review*, Vol. 34, No. 1, Supplement, Pt. 2 (March 1944), pp. 199–211.

———. "Social Security in Evolution: Toward What?" *Canadian Tax Journal*, Vol. 14, No. 4 (July-August 1966), pp. 326–36. Reprinted from *Social Service Review* (June 1965).

Campbell, Colin D., and Rosemary G. Campbell. "Cost-Benefit Ratios under the Federal Old-Age Insurance Program," in Joint Economic Committee, *Old Age Income Assurance*. Compendium of Papers on Problems and Policy Issues in the Public and Private Pension System. Pt. III: *Public Programs*, pp. 72–84. 90 Cong. 1 sess. Washington: Government Printing Office, 1967.

Chen, Yung-Ping. "Inflation and Productivity in Tax-Benefit Analysis for Social Security," in Joint Economic Committee, *Old Age In-*

come Assurance. Compendium of Papers on Problems and Policy Issues in the Public and Private Pension System. Pt. III: *Public Programs,* pp. 85–108. 90 Cong. 1 sess. Washington: Government Printing Office, 1967.

Cohen, Wilbur J., and William L. Mitchell. "Social Security Amendments of 1961: Summary and Legislative History." *Social Security Bulletin,* Vol. 24, No. 9 (September 1961), pp. 3 ff.

Committee on Social Insurance Terminology of the American Risk and Insurance Association. "Definitions Approved or Under Discussion by the Operating Committees," in *Bulletin of the Commission on Insurance Terminology of the American Risk and Insurance Association,* Vol. 3, No. 1 (January 1968), pp. 1–5.

Deran, Elizabeth. "Income Redistribution Under the Social Security System." *National Tax Journal,* Vol. 19, No. 3 (September 1966), pp. 276–85.

————. "Some Economic Effects of High Taxes for Social Insurance," in Joint Economic Committee, *Old Age Income Assurance.* Compendium of Papers on Problems and Policy Issues in the Public and Private Pension System. Pt. III: *Public Programs,* pp. 181–201. 90 Cong. 1 sess. Washington: Government Printing Office, 1967.

Diamond, Peter A. "National Debt in a Neoclassical Growth Model." *American Economic Review,* Vol. 55, No. 5 (December 1965), pp. 1126–50.

Eckstein, Otto. "Financing the System of Social Insurance," and Joseph A. Pechman, "Discussion of the Paper by Otto Eckstein," in William G. Bowen and others (eds.), *The American System of Social Insurance: Its Philosophy, Impact, and Future Development.* New York: McGraw-Hill, 1968.

————. "A Survey of the Theory of Public Expenditure Criteria," Jack Hirshleifer, "Comments," and "Reply by Mr. Eckstein," in *Public Finances: Needs, Sources, and Utilization,* pp. 453–63, 495–501, 503–04. National Bureau of Economic Research, Special Conference Series No. 12. Princeton: Princeton University Press, 1961.

————, and Thomas A. Wilson. "The Determination of Money Wages in American Industry." *Quarterly Journal of Economics,* Vol. 76, No. 3 (August 1962), pp. 379–414.

Epstein, Lenore A. "Early Retirement and Work-Life Experience." *Social Security Bulletin,* Vol. 29, No. 3 (March 1966), pp. 3–10.

————. "Workers Entitled to Minimum Retirement Benefits Under OASDHI." *Social Security Bulletin,* Vol. 30, No. 3 (March 1967), pp. 3–13.

"Estimating Equivalent Incomes or Budget Costs by Family Type."
   Monthly Labor Review, Vol. 83, No. 11 (November 1960), pp.
   1197–1200.
Gallaway, Lowell E. "The Aged and the Extent of Poverty in the
   United States." *Southern Economic Journal,* Vol. 33, No. 2 (Octo-
   ber 1966), pp. 212–22.
————. "Negative Income Tax Rates and the Elimination of Poverty."
   National Tax Journal, Vol. 19, No. 3 (September 1966), pp. 298–
   307.
Gerig, Daniel S., and Robert J. Myers. "Canada Pension Plan of 1965."
   Social Security Bulletin, Vol 28, No. 11 (November 1965), pp. 3–
   17.
Gordon, Margaret S. "National Retirement Policies and the Displaced
   Older Worker," in P. From Hansen (ed.), *Age With A Future,*
   pp. 591–601. Copenhagen: Munksgaard, 1964. Distributed by F. A.
   Davis, Philadelphia. University of California, Berkeley, Institute
   of Industrial Relations, Reprint 250.
Harberger, Arnold C. "Taxation, Resource Allocation, and Welfare,"
   in John F. Due (ed.), *The Role of Direct and Indirect Taxes in
   the Federal Revenue System,* pp. 25–80. A Conference Report of
   the National Bureau of Economic Research and the Brookings
   Institution. Princeton: Princeton University Press, 1964.
Hart, Marice C. "Old-Age, Survivors, and Disability Insurance: Early-
   Retirement Provisions." *Social Security Bulletin,* Vol. 24, No. 10
   (October 1961), pp. 4–13.
Harvey, Ernest C. "Social Security Taxes—Regressive or Progressive?"
   Reed R. Hansen, "A Comment." *National Tax Journal,* Vol. 18,
   No. 4 (December 1965), pp. 408–14, and Vol. 19, No. 2 (June 1966),
   pp. 204–06.
Hasenberg, Werner. "Income-Tax Treatment of Old-Age Pensions and
   Contributions Here and Abroad." *Social Security Bulletin,* Vol.
   29, No. 8 (August 1966), pp. 10–18.
Killingsworth, Charles C., and Gertrude Schroeder. "Long-Range Cost
   Estimates for Old-Age Insurance," and "Reply." *Quarterly Journal
   of Economics,* Vol. 65, No. 2 (May 1951), pp. 199–213, and Vol. 66,
   No. 2 (May 1952), pp. 293–96.
Lerner, Abba P. "Consumption-Loan Interest and Money," and "Re-
   joinder." *Journal of Political Economy,* Vol. 67, No. 5 (October
   1959), pp. 512–18, 523–25.
Macauley, Hugh. "Tax Measures Providing Income Assistance to Older
   Persons," in Joint Economic Committee, *Old Age Income Assur-*

ance. Compendium of Papers on Problems and Policy Issues in the Public and Private Pension System. Pt. III: *Public Programs,* pp. 169–80. 90 Cong. 1 sess. Washington: Government Printing Office, 1967.

Maidenberg, H. J. "Personal Finance: Annuities at Age 65." *New York Times,* June 22, 1967, p. 51.

Mincer, Jacob. "Labor-Force Participation and Unemployment: A Review of Recent Evidence," in Robert A. Gordon and Margaret S. Gordon (eds.), *Prosperity and Unemployment.* New York: Wiley, 1966, pp. 73–112.

———. "The Short-Run Elasticity of Labor Supply," in Gerald G. Somers (ed.), Industrial Relations Research Association, *Proceedings of the Nineteenth Annual Winter Meeting, San Francisco, California, December 28–29, 1966,* pp. 219–29. Madison, Wisconsin: Industrial Relations Research Association, 1967.

Murray, Roger F. "Economic Aspects of Pensions: A Summary Report," in Joint Economic Committee, *Old Age Income Assurance.* Compendium of Papers on Problems and Policy Issues in the Public and Private Pension System. Pt. V: *Financial Aspects of Pension Plans,* pp. 36–114. 90 Cong. 1 sess. Washington: Government Printing Office, 1967. Reprinted from National Bureau of Economic Research, No. 85, General Series.

Musgrave, Richard A. "The Role of Social Insurance in an Overall Program for Social Welfare," in William G. Bowen and others (eds.), *The American System of Social Insurance: Its Philosophy, Impact, and Future Development.* New York: McGraw-Hill, 1968.

Myers, Robert J. "Analysis of Whether the Young Worker Receives His Money's Worth Under Social Security," Memorandum in *President's Proposals for Revision in the Social Security System,* Pt. I, pp. 331–41. House Committee on Ways and Means, Hearings on H.R. 5710. 90 Cong. 1 sess. Washington: Government Printing Office, 1967.

———. "Long-Range Cost Estimates for Old-Age Insurance: Comment." *Quarterly Journal of Economics,* Vol. 66, No. 2 (May 1952), pp. 286–93.

———. "A Method of Automatically Adjusting the Maximum Earnings Base Under OASDI." *Journal of Risk and Insurance,* Vol. 31, No. 3 (September 1964), pp. 329–40.

———. "Old-Age, Survivors, Disability, and Health Insurance Provisions: Legislative History, 1935–65." U.S. Department of Health, Education, and Welfare, Social Security Administration. Leaflet. Washington: HEW, July 1965.

————. "The Value of Social Security Protection in Relation to the Value of Social Security Contribution," Memorandum in *President's Proposals for Revision in the Social Security System*, Pt. I, pp. 330–31. House Committee on Ways and Means, Hearings on H.R. 5710. 90 Cong. 1 sess. Washington: Government Printing Office, 1967.

Orshansky, Mollie. "Counting the Poor: Before and After Federal Income-Support Programs," in Joint Economic Committee, *Old Age Income Assurance*. Compendium of Papers on Problems and Policy Issues in the Public and Private Pension System. Pt. II: *The Aged Population and Retirement Income Programs*, pp. 177–231. 90 Cong. 1 sess. Washington: Government Printing Office, 1967.

————. "Recounting the Poor—A Five-Year Review." *Social Security Bulletin*, Vol. 29, No. 4 (April 1966), pp. 20–37.

————. "More About the Poor in 1964." *Social Security Bulletin*, Vol. 29, No. 5 (May 1966), pp. 3–38.

————. "The Poor in City and Suburb, 1964." *Social Security Bulletin*, Vol. 29, No. 12 (December 1966), pp. 22–37.

Palmore, Erdman. "Work Experience and Earnings of the Aged in 1962: Findings of the 1963 Survey of the Aged." *Social Security Bulletin*, Vol. 27, No. 6 (June 1964), pp. 3–14, 44.

Pechman, Joseph A. "Individual Income Tax Provisions of the Revenue Act of 1964." *Journal of Finance*, Vol. 20, No. 2 (May 1965), pp. 247–72. Brookings Reprint 96.

————. "A New Tax Model for Revenue Estimating," in Alan T. Peacock and Gerald Hauser (eds.), *Government Finance and Economic Development*, pp. 231–44. Paris: Organisation for Economic Cooperation and Development, 1965. Brookings Reprint 102.

————, Henry J. Aaron, and Michael Taussig. "The Objectives of Social Security," in Joint Economic Committee, *Old Age Income Assurance*. Compendium of Papers on Problems and Policy Issues in the Public and Private Pension System. Pt. III: *Public Programs*, pp. 5–20. 90 Cong. 1 sess. Washington: Government Printing Office, 1967. Brookings Reprint 144.

Peterson, Ray M. "The Coming Din of Inequity." *Journal of the American Medical Association*, Vol. 176, No. 1 (April 8, 1961), pp. 34–40.

————. "The Future of Private Pension Plans." *Journal of Risk and Insurance*, Vol. 33, No. 4 (December 1966), pp. 603–20.

————. "Misconceptions and Missing Perceptions of Our Social Security System (Actuarial Anesthesia)." *Transactions of the Society of Actuaries*, Vol. 11, Meeting No. 31 (November 1959), pp. 812–919.

————. "Old-Age Income Assurance by Lifetime Income Spreading with

Deferred Taxation as the Natural Treatment," in Joint Economic Committee, *Old Age Income Assurance.* Compendium of Papers on Problems and Policy Issues in the Public and Private Pension System. Pt. III: *Public Programs,* pp. 209–39. 90 Cong. 1 sess. Washington: Government Printing Office, 1967.

Resnick, Michael. "Annual Earnings and the Taxable Maximum for OASDHI." *Social Security Bulletin,* Vol. 29, No. 11 (November 1966), pp. 38 ff.

Samuelson, Paul A. "An Exact Consumption-Loan Model of Interest With or Without the Social Contrivance of Money," and "Reply." *Journal of Political Economy,* Vol. 66, No. 6 (December 1958), pp. 467–82, and Vol. 67, No. 5 (October 1959), pp. 518–22.

———. "Social Security." *Newsweek,* February 13, 1967, p. 88.

Saville, Lloyd. "Flexible Retirement," in Juanita M. Kreps (ed.), *Employment, Income, and Retirement Problems of the Aged.* Durham, North Carolina: Duke University Press, 1963, pp. 140–77.

Seidman, Bert. "The Case for Higher Social Security Benefits." *AFL-CIO American Federationist,* Vol. 74, No. 1 (January 1967), pp. 1–8.

Shulman, Harry. "Reduced Benefit Awards to Retired Workers: Measuring Extent of Early Retirement." *Social Security Bulletin,* Vol. 29, No. 10 (October 1966), pp. 27–29.

Taussig, Michael K. "Negative Income Tax Rates and the Elimination of Poverty: Comment." *National Tax Journal,* Vol. 20, No. 3 (September 1967), pp. 328–37.

Thompson, Earl A. "Debt Instruments in Both Macroeconomic Theory and Capital Theory." *American Economic Review,* Vol. 57, No. 5 (December 1967), pp. 1196–1210.

Tobin, James, Joseph A. Pechman, and Peter M. Mieszkowski. "Is a Negative Income Tax Practical?" *Yale Law Journal,* Vol. 77, No. 1 (November 1967), pp. 1–27. Brookings Reprint 142.

Waldman, Saul. "Old-Age Benefits for Workers Retiring Before Age 65." *Social Security Bulletin,* Vol. 29, No. 2 (February 1966), pp. 38–43.

———. "OASDI Benefits, Prices, and Wages: A Comparison." *Social Security Bulletin,* Vol. 29, No. 8 (August 1966), pp. 19–23, 30.

———. "OASDI Benefits, Prices, and Wages: 1966 Experience." *Social Security Bulletin,* Vol. 30, No. 6 (June 1967), pp. 9–12, 36.

Wootton, Barbara. "The Impact of Income Security upon Individual Freedom," in James E. Russell (ed.), *National Policies for Education, Health and Social Services,* pp. 381–98. Garden City, New York: Doubleday, 1955.

Index

Index

Aaron, Henry J., 49n, 72n, 159n, 240n, 294, 296

Actuarial balance in OASDI system, 68–69, 95, 240; congressional concern with, 139, 151, 160, 171; defined, 153; delayed retirement credits, 145–46; need to de-emphasize, 156, 221; relationship with cost estimates, 151–53, 159–60, 162, 166–67, 172

Administrative costs, 38–39, 59, 87, 145, 205–06, 236

Age requirements for benefits, 40–41, 280, 286–87

Age-72 benefits, 3, 41–43, 104, 107–08, 163, 196n, 205, 262

Aged: defined, 133; economic status, 4, 6–26, 28–31, 54, 106, 108, 116, 179; health, 136–38, 143; health insurance, 1, 3, 141, 174n, 182, 202n, 254, 261; ineligible for benefits, 105–06; investment income, 61; in labor force, 7–13, 25, 124–28, 132–33, 144–48, 296–97, 304; living arrangements, 20–21; negative income tax, 199–201, 216; old-age assistance, 21–22, 31–32, 46–48, 53–54, 93–94, 106–09, 114–18; retirement benefits (*see* Old-age benefits); retirement test (*see also* Earnings test), 122; social security objectives re, 55–56, 58, 64–66, 118, 215–18; survey of (*1963*), 105, 132n, 133; tax exemptions, 145, 201–04, 213, 225, 308–11; unemployment, 7–12, 136–37, 140–42; work incentives, 120–30, 148, 185–88, 226–27, 296–97

Agricultural workers. *See* Farm workers

Altmeyer, Arthur J., 31n

AME. *See* Average monthly earnings

Antonovsky, Aaron, 21n

Armed forces, social security benefits, 37–38, 110, 205–06, 262

Assets, of aged, 6, 13–18, 26

Assistance, public. *See* Public assistance

Automatic adjustment of benefits, 99–103

Average monthly earnings (AME), 79, 81, 241, 247, 257

Ball, Robert M., 59n, 65n, 67n, 98n, 196n

Bancroft, Gertrude, 125n

Barlow, Robin, 187n

Baumol, William J., 62n

Bayo, Francisco, 105n, 153n, 154n, 155n, 158n, 235n, 240n

Beneficiaries: number and type, 41–45; relation to working population, 134–36, 153

343